Dialects at School

Like its predecessor, *Dialects in Schools and Communities*, this book illuminates major language-related issues that educational practitioners confront, such as responding to dialect-related features in students' speech and writing, teaching Standard English, teaching students about dialects, and distinguishing dialect difference from language disorders. It approaches these issues from a practical perspective rooted in sociolinguistic research, with a focus on the research base for accommodating dialect differences in schools. Expanded coverage includes research on teaching and learning and attention to English language learners.

All chapters include essential information about language variation, language attitudes, and principles of handling dialect differences in schools; classroom-based samples illustrating the application of these principles; and an annotated resources list for further reading. The text is supported by a companion website (www.routledge.com/cw/Reaser) providing additional resources including activities, discussion questions, and audio/visual enhancements that illustrate important information and/or pedagogical approaches.

Comprehensive and authoritative, *Dialects at School* reflects both the relevant research bases in linguistics and education and educational practices concerning language variation. The problems and examples included are authentic, coming from the authors' own research, observations and interactions in public school classrooms, and feedback in workshops. Highlights include chapters on oral language and on reading and writing in dialectally diverse classrooms, as well as a chapter on language awareness for students, offering a clear and compelling overview of how teachers can inspire students to learn more about language variation, including their own community language patterns. An inventory of dialect features in the Appendix organizes and expands on the structural descriptions presented in the chapters.

Jeffrey Reaser is an Associate Professor, North Carolina State University, USA.

Carolyn Temple Adger is a Senior Fellow, Center for Applied Linguistics, USA.

Walt Wolfram is William C. Friday Distinguished University Professor, North Carolina State University, USA.

Donna Christian is a Senior Fellow and former President and Chief Executive Officer, Center for Applied Linguistics, USA.

Dialects at School
Educating Linguistically Diverse Students

Jeffrey Reaser
Carolyn Temple Adger
Walt Wolfram
Donna Christian

Routledge
Taylor & Francis Group

NEW YORK AND LONDON

First published 2017
by Routledge
711 Third Avenue, New York, NY 10017

and by Routledge
2 Park Square, Milton Park, Abingdon, Oxon, OX14 4RN

Routledge is an imprint of the Taylor & Francis Group, an informa business

Library of Congress Cataloguing in Publication Data
A catalog record for this book has been requested

ISBN: 978-1-138-77744-6 (hbk)
ISBN: 978-1-138-77745-3 (pbk)
ISBN: 978-1-315-77262-2 (ebk)

Typeset in Times New Roman
by Keystroke, Neville Lodge, Tettenhall, Wolverhampton

Visit the companion website at www.routledge.com/cw/Reaser

Printed and bound in Great Britain by
TJ International Ltd, Padstow, Cornwall

Brief Contents

Keyword lexical set for English vowels based on Wells (1982)   xiii

Preface   xv

1 An Introduction to Language Variation in America   1

2 Exploring Dialects   31

3 Variation in Dialect Systems   51

4 Languages in Contact   82

5 Establishing Language Norms   107

6 Dialects and Language Assessment   127

7 Dialect Policy and Oral Language Program Development   150

8 Dialects and Writing   177

9 Language Variation and Reading   201

10 Dialect Awareness for Students   232

Appendix   268

Index   293

Contents

Keyword lexical set for English vowels based on Wells (1982)   xiii

Preface   xv

1 An Introduction to Language Variation in America   1
   Scenario 1
   Deficit Versus Difference 1
      Cultural Differences 6
   Issues and Definitions 7
      Popular Meanings of Dialect 8
      Accent and Dialect 9
   Sources of Dialect Differences: Region and Social Class 10
   Language Variation and Judgments about Correctness 13
      Language, Logic, and Language Complexity 15
      Standard English 17
   Dialects and Understanding 19
   Multiple Dialects in Schools 21
   Language Attitudes in Society 22
   Discussion Questions 27
   Links of Interest 28
   Further Reading 28
   References 29

2 Exploring Dialects   31
   Scenario 31
   Dialect Change in the United States 32
   Language Study 34
   Analyzing Linguistic Differences 36
      Levels of Language Differences 36
      Linguistic Factors Contributing to Language Variation 38
      *Social and Historical Factors Contributing to Language
         Variation 41*
   Examining Dialect Patterns 43
   Discussion Questions 47

Links of Interest 48
Further Reading 48
References 49

3 Variation in Dialect Systems   51
Scenario 51
Vocabulary Differences 52
Pronunciation Differences 55
  Pronunciation Differences in Which Consonants are Added 55
  Pronunciation Differences in Which Vowels are Added 56
  Pronunciation Differences in Which Consonants are Lost 56
  Pronunciation Differences in Which Vowels are Lost 58
  Pronunciation Differences in Which Consonants are
    Changed 58
  Pronunciation Differences in Which Vowels are Changed 59
  Pronunciation Differences in Which Vowels are Merged 61
  Pronunciation Differences in Which Vowel Systems
    are Shifted 62
  Beyond Consonants and Vowels in Pronunciation 63
Grammatical Differences 65
  Grammatical Differences Related to Verbs and Verb Phrases 65
    Differences Involving the Verb *To Be* 65
    Differences Involving Other Verbs 66
    Negation 69
  Grammatical Differences Related to Nouns and Noun Phrases 69
    Pronouns 70
  Grammatical Differences Related to Adjectives and Adverbs 71
Illustrative Dialect Samples 72
  Appalachian Ghost Story 73
  Wild Life 74
  Notes on Transcripts 76
    Pronunciation 76
    Grammatical Differences 77
Discussion Questions 78
Links of Interest 79
Further Reading 79
References 80

4 Languages in Contact   82
Scenario 82
African American English 83
  The Origins of African American English 86
  The Changing State of African American English 88
  Some Cultural Differences and Their Linguistic Significance 89

Latino English 90
   The Origins of Latino English 91
   The Status of Latino English 93
   Latino English at School 94
Asian American English 95
   Is There an Asian American Dialect? 97
Language Contact and Cultural Norms 99
Living with Language Behavior Difference 101
Discussion Questions 102
Links of Interest 103
Further Reading 103
References 104

5 Establishing Language Norms   107
Scenario 107
Perceptions of Language Decline 109
   Declining Standards of Usage? 109
   Consequences of Deficit Thinking 112
   Language Prescription 114
Technology, Literacy, and the Health of Modern English 118
   Norms and Texting 120
The Specialized Language of Schools 121
Discussion Questions 123
Links of Interest 124
Further Reading 124
References 125

6 Dialects and Language Assessment   127
Scenario 127
Assessing Students' Literacy Skills 129
Diversity and Standardized Testing 131
   Test Norming 132
   Question Design 133
   Test Design 134
   What is Being Measured? 136
   Difference versus Disorder 139
Oral Language Assessment 140
Discussion Questions 146
Links of Interest 146
Further Reading 147
References 147

7 Dialect Policy and Oral Language Program Development   150
Scenario 150
Standard English and Social Reality 151

Group Reference and Dialect Learning 154
Professional Organizations' Positions on Dialects and Dialect
    Education 158
Language Policy and Curriculum Development 161
    Recommendations for Policy Development 161
    Recommendations for Curriculum Development 164
Methods of Teaching Spoken Standard English 168
Learning the Language of School 171
Discussion Questions 172
Links of Interest 173
Further Reading 173
References 174

8 Dialects and Writing   177
Scenario 177
Oral and Written Language 178
    Differences between Oral and Written Language 178
Vernacular Dialect and Writing 180
    Vernacular Influence in Writing 181
    Difference and Error in Written Language 184
Teaching Writing 186
Editing 188
    Approaches to Editing 189
    Peer Editing 190
Evaluation of Students' Writing 190
    Classroom-Based Assessment 192
    Marking 193
Writing in the Vernacular Dialect 194
    Writing to Extend Thinking 194
    Choosing the Vernacular in Writing 194
    Dialogue Journals 195
Discussion Questions 197
Links of Interest 197
Further Reading 198
References 198

9 Language Variation and Reading   201
Scenario 201
Written Language and Spoken Language 203
What Do Teachers Need to Know about Dialects to Teach
    Reading? 204
    The Nature of Language Diversity 205
    The Role of Physiology 205
    Some Effects of Misunderstanding Reading Miscues 207
    Language and Culture 208

Teaching Children to Relate Sound to Print 210
  Effects of Dialect Differences on Reading Aloud 211
  Comprehension Strategies 212
  Dialects and Meaning-Based Reading Instruction 213
Teaching Children to Comprehend Text 213
  Vocabulary 214
  Background Knowledge and Comprehension 215
Reading Materials and Dialect Differences 216
  Matching Materials and Dialects 217
  Dialect Readers 217
  Language Experience 219
  Vernacular Dialect for Rhetorical Purpose 219
Reading and the Acquisition of Standard English 220
Accommodating Social and Cultural Identity in Teaching
  Reading 221
Reading Tests and Dialect Differences 222
  Pronunciation, Grammar, and Vocabulary Differences 222
  Background Knowledge 224
  Other Fairness Factors 225
Discussion Questions 227
Links of Interest 228
Further Reading 228
References 228

10 Dialect Awareness for Students   232
Scenario 232
Investigating Dialects 235
Components of Dialect Awareness Programs 237
  Introduction to Language Diversity 238
  Language Attitudes 238
  Levels of Dialect 241
  Dialect Patterning 245
  Language Change 254
Implementing Dialect Awareness Curricula 256
  Dialect Awareness Beyond K–12 256
The Importance of Dialect Awareness for All Students 261
Discussion Questions 263
Links of Interest 264
Further Reading 264
References 265

Appendix   268
Index   293

Keyword lexical set for English vowels based on Wells (1982)

Table 0.1 Keyword lexical set for English vowels based on Wells (1982).

Keyword	International Phonetic Alphabet	Examples
FLEECE	[i]	*beet, heed, leap*
KIT	[ɪ]	*bit, hid, sip*
FACE	[e]	*bait, hate, great*
DRESS	[ɛ]	*bet, head, step*
TRAP	[æ]	*bat, had, lap*
COMMA	[ə]	*about, soda, caramel*
STRUT	[ʌ]	*but, hut, rub*
GOOSE	[u]	*boot, hoot, few*
FOOT	[ʊ]	*book, hood, could*
GOAT	[o]	*boat, hoed, dome*
THOUGHT	[ɔ]	*bought, hawed, caught*
LOT	[ɑ]	*bod, hot, lock*
PRICE	[ai]	*bide, hide, aisle*
MOUTH	[au]	*bout, how, noun*
CHOICE	[ɔi]	*boy, ahoy, void*

Preface

Curiosity about language variation and the role that dialects play in society is natural: Everyone has a story to tell about an encounter with language variation. In education, concern with this topic has always been high, rising cyclically to extraordinary levels. Pedagogies stemming from critical race and gender theory universally affirm that American students' diversity represents a rich array of linguistic and cultural resources, but many questions remain about how teachers go about—and should go about—educating linguistically diverse students in ways that affirm rather than punish linguistic variation. Many of these issues remain unresolved. In *Dialects at School: Educating Linguistically Diverse Students*, we address this natural interest and educational concern about dialects by considering some of the major issues that confront educational practitioners. This work is rooted in questions that have arisen in workshops, surveys, classes, discussion groups, and conversations with practitioners and teacher educators. Thus, the volume is intended to address important needs in a range of educational and related service fields. No background in linguistics or sociolinguistics is assumed on the part of the reader.

Although the discussion in this volume has an empirical research base, we do not give detailed documentation in the text. Instead, we synthesize current understandings and provide key references to our own work and that of others. In a sense, this is a kind of translation and interpretation work in which we attempt to bring together the practical concerns of educators and the vantage point of sociolinguistics.

Dialects at School: Educating Linguistically Diverse Students grows out of the second edition of *Dialects in Schools and Communities* (Adger, Wolfram, & Christian, 2007). The first edition of that book was inspired by the response to an earlier work, *Dialects and Education: Issues and Answers*, by Walt Wolfram and Donna Christian, published by Prentice-Hall, Inc. (1989). In this new book, Jeffrey Reaser has taken the lead in reconsidering and expanding the discussion of many of the issues addressed in those earlier works, taking into account recent research on dialects and on English as an additional language, and publications for audiences beyond linguistics. While parts of *Dialects in Schools and Communities* (2nd Ed.) are preserved in this text, many sections are entirely new. We have also organized the information differently.

Three key updates in this volume are: 1. Integration of current perspectives on educational standards and assessments into the discussion of implications of language variation; 2. Attention to an expanded range of dialects, including but not limited to Latino English, which is growing in prominence; and 3. Inclusion of information about English language learners and the linguistic diversity they bring to modern classrooms.

In Chapter 1, "An Introduction to Language Variation in America," we note popular concerns with the nature of language variation, and in Chapter 2, "Exploring Dialects," we consider more specific, technical issues about the characteristic structures of different dialects. In Chapter 3, "Variation in Dialect Systems," we examine in some detail language variation in the dialects of social and regional groups. Chapter 4, "Languages in Contact," looks at three case studies of languages in contact: African American English, Latino English, and East Asian immigrant English. In that chapter, we highlight how cultural differences with respect to language norms affect students' interactions in school contexts. Chapter 5, "Establishing Language Norms," examines perceptions of declining standards for language and education and some of the ways in which language differences are construed as problems. It also looks at different ways in which language norms emerge, including in electronic forms of communication. Chapter 6, "Dialects and Language Assessment," considers how different language assessments and standardized tests can disproportionately and negatively affect vernacular dialect speakers. The school impacts of dialect differences in speaking, writing, and reading are examined in chapters 7 through 9. Chapter 7, "Dialect Policy and Oral Language Program Development," takes up questions about teaching Standard English—whether to do it and how it might be done more effectively. Chapter 8 moves on to "Dialects and Writing," and Chapter 9 addresses issues of "Language Variation and Reading." The final chapter, "Dialect Awareness for Students," points to the value of dialect education in schools so that students will come to understand dialects as natural and normal language phenomena. This chapter describes concrete strategies for addressing misunderstandings about dialects that contribute to inequity at school and elsewhere in the society. Each chapter opens with a scenario that asks readers to think through some questions related to the focus of the chapter. Each chapter concludes with discussion questions, web links of interest, suggestions for further reading, and references. The volume ends with a catalog of vernacular structures described in more technical terms. It is not a complete inventory of any dialect or all vernacular features, but it organizes and expands on the structural descriptions discussed in the chapters. It also presents other important dialect features. Though we intend this book as a unified and cohesive volume, we recognize that some readers will only read the chapters that are most aligned with their interests. To support these readers, we have tried to make each chapter fundamentally independent. Some repetition across chapters is required to support those who read the chapters selectively.

This volume is intended for use by teacher interns and practicing teachers in elementary and secondary schools; early childhood specialists; specialists in reading and writing; speech/language pathologists; special education teachers; teachers of English as a second language (ESL) and English language learners; and educators in various language specialties. These fields now consider information about language variation to be an important part of professional preparation. Teachers in all content areas will benefit from learning about language variation and the issues that surround it in view of the increasing emphasis on oral and written language in learning. The treatment of social and cultural dimensions of language use is particularly relevant to teaching social studies.

Obviously, this re-examination of dialects in schools cannot answer all of the questions that practitioners raise about language variation and education. We have attempted to respond to practitioners' concerns as far as possible and to admit where the research findings are limited or ambiguous. We offer the book as an updated, still-interim report on the state of language variation and education in the United States. We hope that we have represented faithfully the kinds of concerns that practitioners have brought to us in the past few decades, and we dedicate this work to those who have raised them. In the process of examining the issues concerning dialects at school, we have learned that there are few easy answers to the questions about language variation raised by practitioners.

Many colleagues, students, and friends have offered help in one form or another. We thank each one heartily: John Baugh, Phillip Carter, Danica Cullinan, Stephany Dunstan, Amanda Godley, Katie Hennenlotter, Gretchen McCulloch, Caroline Myrick, Jennifer Nolan, Joy Kreeft Peyton, Paul Reed, and Joel Schneier. Additionally, we are grateful for the financial support of the William C. Friday endowment at NC State. We deeply appreciate the gifts of those who have helped in these and other ways. Two students have contributed to this book in extensive ways. Arianna Janoff efficiently assumed many tasks related to preparing the final manuscript, including taking the lead on formatting and obtaining copyright permissions. Indexing was completed by Frankie Pennington and KellyNoel Waldorf. Many of the online activities supporting this volume were pioneered by Nicolette Filson; her creative pedagogy continues to make language awareness accessible and exciting to all.

—Jeffrey Reaser
Raleigh, North Carolina

—Carolyn Temple Adger
Washington, DC

—Walt Wolfram
Raleigh, North Carolina

—Donna Christian
Washington, DC

An Introduction to Language
Variation in America

Scenario

Students in your first grade class have been practicing telling and writing narratives in chronological order. One day during the second month of class, you read a story about two brothers who both wanted a toy train. You ask for volunteers to retell the story's order of events. Darius, a 6-year-old African American student, enthusiastically raises his hand and you call on him. He says:

> Once upon a time, a little boy wanted to play with the train. And he tryna get the train, but his mean brother holdin' it up high. So the big boy put it under his bed. When the big brother in the kitchen eatin' his sandwich, the little boy take he train and he put it in his toy box. Then the big boy came back and he thinkin' of the train. And he look under the bed but he don't find nothin'.

from Seymour, 2004, p. 4

What's your first impression of Darius' response? What strengths do you see in Darius' response? What concerns do you have about Darius' response? If you were Darius' teacher, how would you respond to his retelling of this story?

Deficit Versus Difference

Darius' narrative highlights a common challenge for teachers all over the United States: Evaluating language use can be a difficult task that requires knowledge of child development, language acquisition, and cultural diversity. Adding to the challenge is the fact that these evaluations can have a dramatic impact on students' educational pathways—at every educational level—where misinformed or inappropriate evaluations and invalid interpretations can severely limit students' chances of attaining high levels of academic achievement. Darius' narrative employs, for his age, above average narrative markers (e.g., "when" and "then") as well as knowledge of the language of thought (e.g., "He thinkin' of"). In many ways, the narrative is exceptional for a 6-year-old; however, as it is easy to be distracted by Darius' use of nonstandard language, teachers might overlook the fact that the narrative reflects developmentally advanced linguistic features. In fact, it would not at all be unusual for poorly informed teachers to recommend that Darius be evaluated for a speech disorder. And while diagnoses have become far less biased over the past half century, African American students are still about two to three times as likely as white students to be diagnosed with speech or language impairments and mental retardation (Aud, Fox, & Kewal-Ramani, 2010, p. 40).

This discrepancy in rates of diagnosis is a remnant of deficit positions with respect to language that were the norm until the 1960s and still common until the 1980s. According to the deficit position, speakers of dialects with vernacular forms have a handicap—socially and cognitively—because the dialects are illogical, sloppy, or just a "collection of errors." Intelligence test scores and results of standardized language measures may be cited as evidence for this position (Herrnstein & Murray, 1994), but issues of test bias are typically overlooked. Consider, for example, one shocking statement of deficit thinking by Florence Goodenough, a pioneer in the field of developmental psychology and standardized and IQ testing, who published findings in which bilingual school children scored lower on IQ tests than monolingual Americans. She offered two possible explanations for the discrepancy: either "The use of a foreign language in the home is one of the chief factors in producing mental retardation" or . . . "A more likely explanation is that these nationality groups whose intellectual ability is inferior do not readily learn the new language" (Goodenough, 1926, p. 393). It is unimaginable today that an educated person would make such a statement about one national group being mentally inferior to another, but such thinking was pervasive not too long ago. We now know the real reason for Goodenough's findings: The tests she was employing were culturally and linguistically biased, and they assessed differences as deficits or deficiencies.

Deficit positions still characterize personal thinking and permeate institutional policy, notwithstanding efforts to confront them, so it is essential that teachers, administrators, and other education practitioners are able to recognize potential deficit thinking and policies that reproduce this position. Perhaps nowhere has the deficit view been as strongly reinforced as in "language gap" studies such as Betty Hart and Todd Risley's (1995) influential book, *Meaningful Differences in the Everyday Experience of Young American Children*, which claims to document a 30-million word gap for poor children—in terms of the number of words a child is exposed to—by age 3. In framing the rationale for their study, the researchers note:

> Undertaking to remediate, improve, or add to present skill levels assumes the existence of some "difference," "delay," or "deficit" relative to a norm. But when we listened to the [children of poverty] talk during free play, *they seemed fully competent to us, well able to explain and elaborate the topics typical in preschool interactions.* We became increasingly uncertain about which language skills we should be undertaking to improve.

> We decided we needed to know, not from our textbooks, but from advantaged children, what skilled spontaneous speech at age 4 is in terms of grammar and content.
>
> *Hart & Risley, 1995, p. 8 [italics added]*

Even while the researchers deemed the children to be "fully competent" and as "well able" to use language as other preschoolers, they knew these children must have a deficit. They asked, "What's wrong with these kids' language?" rather than "What's different about these kids' language?" Deficit-oriented, "language gap" research continues to this day (see, e.g., Fernald, Marchman, & Weisleder, 2013) despite serious critique of Hart and Risley's research methods and conclusions (e.g., Baugh, 2016) and decades of research documenting the differences in language and literacy practices among varied societal groups (e.g., Heath, 1983, 2012; Zentella, 1997).

The deficit position is gradually being replaced by the difference position, which seeks to understand sociocultural difference—including language difference—without the need for evaluating the alternatives. Such approaches might ask how one group uses language and literacy in different ways from another group, without judging one way to be superior (see Heath, 1983, for one such study). As applied to language, the difference approach might ask how the dialect patterns (such as pronunciation or word choice) of one group, say, rural Southerners, differ from another, say, urban Southerners, or how women use discourse strategies differently from men.

Pursuing the issue of difference versus deficit, we arrive at a core tenet of sociolinguistics: No variety of a language is inherently better than another in terms of its logic, its systematic structure, or its ability to express creative and complex thought. Extending this idea leads to the conclusion that no speakers have a diminished ability inherently to function cognitively and expressively as a result of the variety of the language that they acquire. This principle means that judgments about students' academic abilities based on their dialect are always inappropriate. Notwithstanding this linguistic truth, the realities of social attitudes about language cannot be denied, and these attitudes strongly influence how language variation is interpreted in a variety of academic and non-academic situations. For example, we know that students speaking non-mainstream dialects lag behind Standard English speakers in achievement on standardized assessments, a fact that has attracted a deficit interpretation (Herrnstein & Murray, 1994). This apparent lag can be explained in a number of ways. Two interpretations are outlined here. First, it is possible that a vernacular-speaking student has had teachers who, because of deficit thinking, held low expectations of the student, perhaps interpreting vernacular forms as indicative of a social or cognitive handicap, based on a belief that the forms are illogical, sloppy, or just bad grammar. Such thinking results in a self-fulfilling prophecy of under-achievement (Rosenthal & Jacobson, 1968).

A second interpretation is that the lag in achievement is likely to be an artifact of cultural or linguistic bias in the standardized assessment. The issue of test bias is critical, as discussed in the opening section of this chapter, as it can lead to negative educational outcomes, including recommendations for remedial language and other educational services (to remedy a deficit indicated by the test outcomes). To a large extent, the concept of compensatory programs evolved from test bias. Educational programs were designed to fill in the gaps in language and other skills caused by what was called *linguistic and environmental disadvantage*. Members of more powerful social groups—roughly, the middle class—often believe that members of stigmatized groups must change in order to be accepted. And members of these stigmatized groups often adopt positions passed on to them by language and school authorities. Success in school for children from these disenfranchised groups, for example, may depend on changing aspects of their language and language use, and adapting to school norms, which are generally more like the norms of the powerful groups than those of the stigmatized groups. For members of a mainstream, powerful group, no change or adaptation is necessary. As a result, children from some groups become more at risk for school failure even though they are not intrinsically disadvantaged. To put it succinctly: The educational system expects students from nonmainstream backgrounds to accommodate to the social and linguistic norms of mainstream students without much, if any, instruction on how to do so. Schools, effectively, require more of the students who arrive at school less prepared to meet the expectations of the mainstream educational context than those who have been born into privileged classes.

The contrasting perspective, and the one advocated here, is the difference position that views groups of speakers simply in terms of the differences among their language systems. Because no one linguistic system can be shown to be inherently better, there is no reason to assume that using a particular dialect is associated with an inherent deficit or advantage. The difference position calls into question the evidence from test scores and school performance that is used to prescribe remediation. If educators assume that a particular dialect is best, if they formally accept and encourage only that dialect, and if they test ability and achievement only through the medium of that dialect, then it should not be surprising that students who enter school already speaking it fare better than those who use a different dialect. An understanding of the social attitudes and values concerning dialects and their speakers is thus essential for dealing with language differences.

From time to time, these contrasting positions, which have been discussed for decades now, produce acrimonious debate in the public arena. For example, in 1996, the Board of Education of the Oakland (CA) Unified School District adopted a resolution that recognized Ebonics, or African American English, as a language system to be taken into account in teaching schoolchildren Standard English. Taking the view that Ebonics, the language spoken by many of their

African American students, is a legitimate linguistic system (albeit different from Standard English), the Oakland school district proposed to use the students' knowledge of Ebonics in teaching Standard English. In this way, the schools would respect and take advantage of students' linguistic competence as a resource for language development rather than viewing it as a deficit. Their intention was neither to eradicate Ebonics nor to teach it, as some thought, but to help students add another language system.

The resolution provoked wide comment, much of it scathing denunciation of vernacular dialect (and its speakers) and the school system's acceptance of what was viewed as deficient language. Everyone had something to say— prominent persons in government, civil rights, entertainment, and education; ordinary citizens; national organizations concerned with linguistic research and language teaching; and many, many reporters and editorial writers. In fact, the debate even extended to a U.S. Senate subcommittee hearing on the topic in which academic linguists defended the program while others on the panel, including a journalist and a preacher, attacked it. At the heart of the Ebonics controversy was the long-standing conflict between the deficit and the difference positions. It further illustrated that anyone who uses the language can be seen as an expert, even if he or she has never studied the language scientifically. Claiming authority is a key component to maintaining language subordination (Lippi-Green, 2012).

The principle of linguistic subordination is straightforward: The speech of dominant groups will be viewed as superior to the speech of socially subordinate groups. But the effects of linguistic subordination can be subtle and insidious. Linguistic subordination is perpetuated through seemingly common sense notions and propositions. This process is described by Lippi-Green (2012, p. 70). When non-experts claim language authority—as seen in the Ebonics case—misinformation about language and language norms can be spread. For example, a set of prescriptions may take on authority through means such as historical usage and arguments about logic or aesthetics. The corollary process is that all other usages are deemed inappropriate or dis-preferred. Language varieties that employ these other usages are then deemed inappropriate or dis-preferred, or they are trivialized in some way. These steps create a language-based system of value in society by which success and failure can be judged (Bourdieu, 1977; Foucault, 1971). This system is upheld through examples and counter-examples. Lippi-Green notes that "conformers" are often cited as evidence to support the system, framed as "See what you can accomplish if you only try," while "non-conformers" are vilified or marginalized through such frames as "See how willfully stupid, arrogant, unknowing, uninformed and/or deviant these speakers are" (2012, p. 70). Promises and threats concretize the system: "Employers will/will not take you seriously" or "Doors will open/ shut." Aside from the fact that these promises arise from a merit system that has no actual linguistic basis, they are fundamentally false promises that serve to ratify and reinforce the current social hierarchy. For example, as Lippi-Green notes, "Black children who learn [Standard English] will not be given automatic access to the rewards and possibilities of the Anglo middle-class world" (2012, p. 193). Other cultural differences complicate the social dynamics that govern groups' and individuals' acceptance in society.

Cultural Differences

Linguistic differences between social groups are just one element of a larger set of cultural differences. Groups are identified by their own members and by others according to the set of linguistic and cultural characteristics that they share. *Culture* is used here in just this sense: patterns of behavior, including language behavior, shared by members of a group. Not only ways of speaking, but also values, attitudes toward education, conceptualizations of politeness, and virtually all socially determined constructs can vary from one group to the next. Mainstream groups—roughly corresponding to the middle and upper middle class—are generally considered to exhibit acceptable behavior, both linguistically and culturally. These norms can seem like common sense to those raised within these cultures, but they may feel unusual to those raised in other cultures. For example, mainstream Americans see eye contact during a conversation as a sign of politeness or engagement, but such action can be seen as offensive or inappropriate in many American Indian cultures. The key to understanding such differences is that an appropriate action in one culture may be deemed inappropriate in another, and yet each group's preferred cultural norm is seen as "common sense" within that group. Cultural norms—including those governing language practices—tend to be acquired without formal instruction, which makes them appear to be either common sense or universal human qualities rather than culturally specific norms.

The classroom consequences of cultural differences are similar to those caused by linguistic differences; in fact, there is considerable overlap, because cultural norms constrain how language is appropriately used. Cultural norms guide the interactions of students with teachers and fellow students. Research reports have noted numerous instances in which behaviors have been misinterpreted because of a cultural difference between teacher and student. For example, studies show that American Indian children in the Southwest have been labeled as passive or nonverbal and have had their level of intelligence misjudged because they seem unresponsive in the classroom to Anglo teachers (Erickson & Mohatt, 1982; Philips, 1993). In response to such reports, the California State Department of Education created a resource guide to help teachers better understand such cultural differences. For example, the guide notes that because cooperation is highly valued, "When a fellow Indian student does not answer a question in class, some Indian students may state that they too do not know the answer, even though they might" (Prescott, 1991, p. 35). In such a case, the teacher may assume the whole class is suffering from a deficit. The guide cites cultural reasons why Indian students might resist praise, resist being pushed ahead of their peers, resist help from a teacher or resist answering promptly, and for a number of other behaviors. Given the value mainstream educational systems place on compliance, it is clear why non-Indian teachers might misconstrue the intent of such actions.

Researchers also report culture clash and misunderstanding in ethnically mixed classrooms. African American children sometimes get reprimanded for calling out an answer before being nominated by the teacher or for humming and making other sounds while working independently (Delpit, 1995). Although these actions may reflect cultural patterns that are expected and valued in the children's community, a teacher from a different cultural background may see the actions as disrespectful and the children as disobedient.

Shirley Brice Heath has looked carefully at the language and culture patterns that children bring to school from their home communities. In a classic study of three communities—working-class white, working-class African American, and middle-class townspeople—Heath (1983) traced difficulties faced by both sets of working-class children in the middle-class-oriented schools. The ultimate explanation, she found, was due to differences between the school and home communities. Although structural dialect patterns were involved, the differences extended to discourse. For example, the conception of what story and storytelling mean, a crucial notion in language arts instruction, turned out to vary from one community to another. For one group, the term was used in a narrow and negative sense of an untrue account intended to deceive; in the other group, a story could include departures from fact, but with no intention to mislead the audience. Heath's study demonstrates that broad patterns of language and cultural beliefs and behavior are relevant to children's success in the educational context.

All too often, people in education and in the public generally have avoided discussing differences between home and institutional expectations openly because these matters are considered too political or sensitive. However, being knowledgeable about differences is important: Ignoring the practical consequences of these differences, or pretending they do not exist, certainly is not in the best interests of children or education.

Issues and Definitions

People who share important cultural, social, and regional characteristics typically speak similarly, and people who differ in such characteristics usually differ in language or dialect as well. The term *dialect* is generally used to refer to a variety of a language associated with a regionally or socially defined group of people. This definition of *dialect* is not a rigorous one, but it carries an important implication: Linguistically, no dialect is more valuable, interesting, logical, or worthy of study than another. The term *dialect* used this way is neutral—no evaluation is implied, either positive or negative.

Consider this example of a dialect difference: The patterns or *rules* of some dialects require that *anymore* be used only in negative sentences (those with *not* or some other negative), such as "I don't go there anymore," or in questions such as "Do you go there anymore?" In other dialects, *anymore* can occur in affirmative sentences as well as negative, such as "Houses in this neighborhood are expensive anymore" or "Anymore, houses in this neighborhood are expensive." This dialect difference usually corresponds to region: All speakers of English use *anymore* in negative contexts; those who also use it in affirmative sentences (a structure called *positive anymore*) are generally located in midland areas of the United States, running through Pennsylvania, Ohio, and westward. The important point is that neither pattern of *anymore* usage is linguistically right or wrong; they are merely different. Furthermore, both variations are part of a dialect.

Everyone is part of some group that can be distinguished from other groups in part by how group members talk. In fact, a person cannot speak a language without speaking a dialect of that language. If a person speaks the English language, that person necessarily speaks some dialect of the English language. Research shows that dialects are complete linguistic systems and thus have structural integrity, but social evaluation attributes higher status to some dialects than to others. That is, views of the relative merit of a language variety or dialect are based on social, not linguistic, grounds.

Popular Meanings of Dialect

In common usage, the term *dialect* often carries a negative connotation, contrasting with the neutral technical meaning just presented. *Dialect* is sometimes used to refer to a social or geographical variety of English that is not the preferred—or standard—one. For example, many Americans refer to the speech of African Americans or European Americans from rural Appalachia as "dialect" to signal a negative evaluation of the variety. Such use of the term *dialect* incorrectly assumes that only certain groups of people speak a dialect; but as noted above, everyone speaks some variety—or dialect—of their language. Because of how common this usage of the term is, language specialists may avoid the term *dialect;* instead, they use the terms *language variety, language difference, language variation*, and *linguistic diversity* to avoid the negative connotations sometimes associated with *dialect*.

The question of terminology becomes especially difficult when people want to refer to the speech of people who do not speak a standard variety. The most common labels have been *nonstandard dialect, nonmainstream dialect*, and *vernacular dialect*. Although these terms can be used synonymously and all are in common use, we use them to denote different types of language. We use the term *vernacular* to describe dialects and dialect features that have a substantial social stigma. The term *nonstandard* is used to describe dialect features that contrast with those found in Standard English. We do not describe dialects as *nonstandard* because the label implies an evaluation, which is inappropriate. We use the term *nonmainstream* to describe dialects and dialect features that contrast with the norms of Standard English but lack the strong social stigma attached to vernacular dialects and forms.

Accent and Dialect

When it comes to terms for language differences, the term *accent* is popularly used to refer to how people pronounce words. So, if a person pronounces *car* without the final *r*, as in "cah," or *pin* and *pen* both as "pin," these pronunciations might be considered characteristic of a particular accent. References to accent may include differences other than pronunciation, but the focus is usually on pronunciation.

Examples of situations in which someone might use the term *accent* can provide a basis for comparing what is commonly meant by *accent* with what may be meant by *dialect*.

1. Someone watching an interview with a Russian tennis player at the U.S. Open might remark, "She has a very heavy accent."
2. Someone who grew up in northeastern New England moves to Chicago. A native Chicagoan might observe, "You can tell where she's from the minute she opens her mouth—she really has a strong New England accent."
3. Someone originally from Chicago goes to a university in northeastern New England. A New Englander might remark, "That person must be from Chicago. She says some words with a real accent."

The tennis situation involves someone who most likely learned English as an additional language and whose speech still shows influence from the native language. This is the classic foreign accent that might be more specifically labeled as a Russian accent, a Swedish accent, and so forth. The other two situations contain references to variation within a single language. Here the meaning of *accent* is closer to the technical meaning of *dialect*. Of course, *accent* is more restricted because it refers primarily to pronunciation, and there are differences other than pronunciation among dialects.

The term *accent* may carry negative connotations similar to those for the popular use of *dialect*, although they are typically less severe. Despite the fact that each variety of English has its own pronunciation patterns, it is often assumed by non-vernacular-speaking people that only other people have accents. Thus, the native Chicagoan meeting someone from New England may think that it is only the New Englander who speaks with an accent, whereas the native New Englander may think that only the Chicagoan speaks with an accent. Of course, both of them have an accent, just as everyone speaks a dialect. Some accents (and dialects) receive more attention than others, including, for example, what people call a Southern accent, a Boston accent, a New York accent, and a British accent, all of which have stereotyped features that others recognize quite readily (and may assign a label to, such as Southern "drawl," or "Brooklynese"). Although negative connotations are sometimes associated with having an accent, there can be positive evaluations as well. For instance, many North Americans hold a British accent in high esteem. Pronunciation, the main basis for accent, is one level at which dialects differ from each other. There are other levels, including vocabulary, grammar, and social conventions for language use, as will be explored in the following chapters.

Sources of Dialect Differences: Region and Social Class

Language differences have diverse origins, but they all derive from the basic principle that when groups of people are physically or socially separated in some way, their language patterns diverge because the groups follow different paths of language change. Many of the regional differences in U.S. English can be traced to combinations of history and physical factors in the country's geography. Some patterns can be explained by looking at settlement history. The language patterns of the early immigrants remain influential in the areas they settled as well as in the areas into which they migrated. Characteristics of physical geography affected these migration patterns and helped shape today's language variation in the country. Natural barriers such as mountains and rivers may have isolated some groups from others, allowing language to evolve differently even in spatially proximate locations with shared settlement histories.

There have been a number of attempts to delineate regional dialects of English in the United States (e.g., Carver, 1987; Kurath, 1949; Labov, Ash, & Boberg, 2006). Using vocabulary or pronunciation differences, linguistic geographers generally recognize several major dialect areas and a number of subareas within them. Many cautions are warranted, including the impossibility of identifying discrete boundaries and the relative importance of different lines, but the map of dialects shown in Figure 1.1 represents a fairly common agreement among dialectologists (i.e., linguists who study dialects) on how dialect boundaries can be roughly delineated. This map, from Carver (1987), gives only a regional distribution, however, and it is based on vocabulary differences alone. In Figure 1.2, a map based on pronunciation from Labov, et al. (2006) is superimposed on the map based on vocabulary in Figure 1.1. Despite the difference in the level of language (pronunciation vs. vocabulary) and a time lapse of a half century in terms of data collection for the maps, there is an amazing parallel in the regional dialect configuration. Within and across areas, social, cultural, age, and gender considerations complicate the picture immensely.

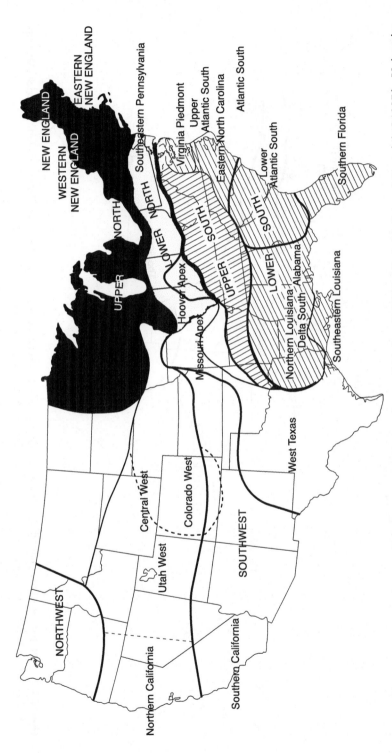

FIGURE 1.1   Dialect map of the United States. (From *American Regional Dialects* [1987] by Craig M. Carver.) Copyright©1987 by University of Michigan Press. Reprinted with permission.

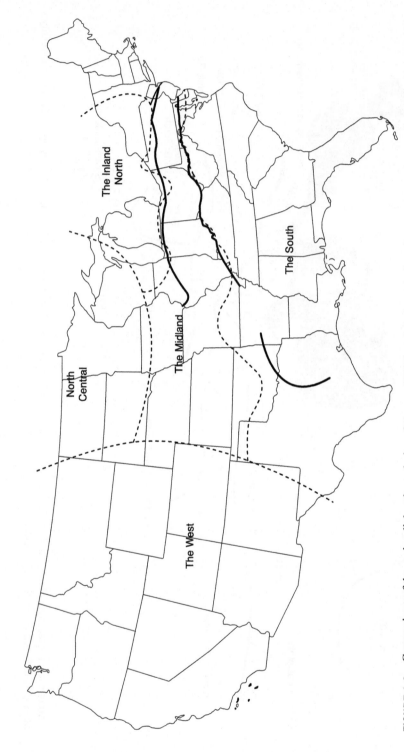

FIGURE 1.2 Comparison of the major dialect boundaries of Carver (1987) and the boundaries of an overall view of North American Dialects from the *Atlas of North American English* (Labov, et al., 2006). Used with permission.

Social and cultural factors are also responsible for diversity in ways of speaking. Social status and ethnic distinctions in our society are often reflected in language differences, along with age and gender distinctions. Typically, the greater the social distance between groups, the greater the language differences. This principle does not always work exactly, but it is a reasonably accurate predictor of how language differences reflect group behavior differences.

Social status and regional differences interact, and there can sometimes be as much variation within a regional dialect as between regional dialects. Thus, it can be expected that a white lawyer from the South will speak differently from a white farmer, banker, or salesman from the same region. Further, Southern African Americans in these professions may speak differently from their white counterparts and from African Americans in other regions of the country. And of course, even within each professional category, there is variation: Not all Southern White politicians sound like Kevin Spacey's character in *House of Cards*. Many factors, including geographical, social, and cultural, are important in distinguishing groups of individuals from each other in American society, so it should not be surprising that they are also important in understanding language differences.

Language Variation and Judgments about Correctness

People sometimes ask how many dialects of English there are. Somewhat surprisingly, there is no simple or agreed-on answer to this question. Every speaker of a dialect has subtle differences from other speakers of the same dialect, and of course, each of us can use different forms or styles of the dialect. There is no clear criterion for determining where one dialect ends and another begins, so counting how many dialects there are is ultimately an imprecise activity. Dialects do not come in neat packages, and many factors must be considered in distinguishing them.

It is safe to say, however, that the English language is made up of numerous dialects, an estimate that grows quickly if we include variation in England, Australia, Jamaica, and other countries where English is the dominant language! And while there is no one correct way to speak English, certain language patterns are preferred over others, according to social norms (which may vary as well) and power relations among groups. Patterns used by mainstream groups in a region are often referred to as the "correct" use of English, but that notion of correctness is based on social acceptability, not linguistic value. Judgments of correctness in other situations are typically based on some objective facts. For example, the result of an addition problem, such as 7 plus 3, has one correct solution (10), and all others are incorrect (11, 9, etc.). To make comparable judgments of correctness for language, we must look for a set of facts against which we might judge whether something in language is correct or incorrect.

Finding the relevant set of facts for judging correctness in language is not as straightforward as it is for arithmetic. One principle that might be used is the judgments of proficient English speakers to decide what can and cannot count as English. For example, a sentence like "They will arrive tomorrow" would be judged to be a good example of the English language by proficient speakers and therefore would be correct. However, both "Arrive will tomorrow they" and "Ils arriveront demain" would be judged incorrect as English sentences, although the latter would qualify as correct for another language. Similarly, *pencil* would be considered to be a correct form in English, but *tloshg* would not be accepted. In each case, judgments are made by identifying what speakers of English might say, as opposed to what they would not say, based on their knowledge of the language. In other words, the determination is made based on the answer to the question, "Is it English or isn't it?"

This criterion becomes less clear, and more controversial, however, when it is applied to examples of vernacular English. Since speakers of different dialects form sentences differently in some ways, some proficient speakers might deem certain sentences well-formed while others would not. Consider two English sentences that may be used by proficient native speakers of English: "He done it wrong" and "I can't see nothing." When someone utters these sentences, it would be disingenuous to claim that he or she is not speaking English; many people might deem them bad, improper, or incorrect English, but no one would claim they are not English. In this case, correctness is determined by social rather than linguistic acceptability. There is no single basis, in terms of objective facts, for determining whether "He did it wrong" or "He done it wrong" is a better way to convey information. The conclusion from this demonstration is that many correctness standards rely on judgments of social acceptability, rather than technical assessments of linguistic patterning. The socially unacceptable forms, like "He done it," are often termed *nonstandard*, to contrast them with *standard* forms, but they are nonstandard only because they are socially disfavored, not because they are linguistically invalid, illogical, or corrupt.

The evaluation of certain ways of saying something is closely associated with the social status of the people who speak that way. This valuing is not just an individual's decision about the utterance: It is also the society's evaluation of different groups, including their ways of speaking. As children are socialized, they learn these attitudes—sometimes unconsciously, sometimes through expressed regulations and rules—just as they learn eating behavior. They learn to eat peas with a fork instead of with a spoon or their fingers. The nutritional content of peas is the same regardless of how they eat them, and all three ways succeed in getting the peas into their mouths; but society socializes us into viewing one way as proper or correct and the other ways as unacceptable. In a similar way, the communicative effectiveness of *I done it* or *I did it* is identical, but we have been socialized into considering only one alternative as correct or proper and the other as incorrect or bad.

As noted previously, figuring out linguistic standards is straightforward; per the principle of linguistic subordination, speakers from socially disfavored groups have dialects that are not regarded as highly as those of people from more socially favored groups (Lippi-Green, 2012). Given that beliefs about language correctness are widely shared by members of a society, most people never question the validity of these judgments. This lack of scrutiny is essential to the persistence of deficit views of language described in the opening of this chapter, which creates social and academic disadvantage for members of nonmainstream groups.

Language, Logic, and Language Complexity

Like the notion of correct language, the idea that some dialects are more logical than others results from the broader social attitudes that surround language, not from features of the language itself. Believing that standard forms of English are inherently better than other forms, some people maintain that certain linguistic structures are more logical than others, more systematic, and even more advantageous for cognitive development. There is no evidence, however, to support the contention that any language variety will interfere with the development of reasoning ability or the ability to express logical concepts.

The use of so-called double negatives—two negative forms in a single sentence—is often cited as evidence that a particular language variety of English is illogical. According to this argument, two negatives in a sentence such as "They can't go nowhere" should cancel each other so that the meaning becomes positive ("They can go somewhere"). Because sentences like the former one are intended to have a negative interpretation, the claim is made that the structure is illogical. (Notice, though, that according to this position, "Nobody can't go nowhere," with three negatives, would have to be accepted as a negative sentence.) However, no natural language is based on the logic of formal mathematics. Natural logic allows both "They can't go anywhere" and "They can't go nowhere" to have a negative interpretation, depending on the language use conventions of the particular dialect community. In fact, the pattern with two negatives is the norm in many of the world's languages. In French, the use of two negative words [*ne . . . rien*] is the current standard for making a negative utterance, as in "Je ne sais rien," which would be translated literally as "I don't know nothing." Similarly, in Spanish the standard for negative utterances uses both *no* and *nada*, as in "No hace nada," which is (literally) "She or he isn't doing nothing." In English, both sentences express the exact same sentiment, but the singly negated form is socially acceptable, whereas the doubly negated form is not.

It is interesting to note that multiple negation was an acceptable structure for English in the past. During the Old English (approximately 500–1100 AD) and Middle English (approximately 1100–1500 AD) periods, the only way certain negative sentences could be formed was through the use of double negatives (e.g., "There was no man nowhere so virtuous" [from Chaucer's description of the Friar in *The Canterbury Tales*, cited in Pyles & Algeo, 1982]). In these periods, no mathematicians decried such formations as illogical. Favoring the use of a single negative in sentences like "They can't do anything" is a relatively recent development in English.

Another misperception of vernacular features is that they reflect a learner's incomplete learning of the standard dialect. Common descriptions of certain language features reveal and reinforce this notion, such as *leaving off the endings of words* or *not using complete sentences*. In some cases, the English speakers who are said to leave off the endings of words are really applying a pronunciation pattern that all English speakers use to a limited degree. For example, in casual speech, all speakers of English sometimes pronounce a word like *fast* as "fas'," leaving off the final *t* sound, as in "fas' break." If you listen carefully to the speech of those around you, you will probably be able to observe this process in use. It is one of the pronunciation patterns of English that applies more often in casual speech.

But this pronunciation rule applies differently in some dialects, and those occurrences are often noticed by speakers of other dialects. In certain dialects, the pattern is simply more common, and this higher frequency makes it noticeable. The pronunciation also varies in where it occurs. While all dialects leave off the *t* sound in "fas' break," it is less common to omit the final *t* sound in phrases like "fas' or slow" or "fas' absorbing." Because the absence of the *t* sound before a word that starts with a vowel is less common than before a word that starts with a consonant, speakers of other dialects are more likely to notice it when it occurs in the speech of those who produce the *fas' or slow* pattern. In fact, not pronouncing certain sounds at the end of words is really a case of an English language rule of pronunciation that is used with minor, but noticeable, differences by different groups.

While differences like this pronunciation feature involve simple changes in forms that are found in many dialects of a language, other variations involve unique language forms that mark subtle but important distinctions in meaning. Verb forms in sentences such as "I liketa died," "I done took out the garbage," and "I be doing my homework" encode meanings that would have to be worded differently in standard varieties of English. For example, to capture the exact meaning of "I be doing my homework" in Standard English, one would have to include an extra adverb, as in "I do my homework everyday"; to capture the specific meaning of "I done took out the garbage," one would have to say something like "I have already finished taking out the garbage." These examples are just a few of many that exist between dialects of English, but they demonstrate that the relationship between standard and vernacular forms in English cannot be dismissed as a matter of faulty logic, incomplete learning, or language simplification.

Standard English

Although native speakers of English have no difficulty making decisions about what is standard and nonstandard English, defining what exactly constitutes the standard variety is actually a difficult if not impossible task (Niedzielski & Preston, 2000), somewhat like the task Supreme Court Justice Potter Stewart faced when trying to define pornography, which he eventually abandoned by noting merely, "I know it when I see it." While there is really no single dialect of English that corresponds to a Standard English, speakers of English know it when they hear it. The speech of a certain social group of people does define what is considered standard in English; however, the norms for Standard English are not identical in all communities. Furthermore, there are multiple sets of norms in any community related to the formality of a situation.

The norms of language usage that members of a society consider to be acceptable constitute their informal language standard. These norms are fairly flexible and regionalized so that there is an informal Standard American English for the South, an informal Standard American English for the Northeast, and so forth. These norms are also subjective: Different people may evaluate standards somewhat differently based on their backgrounds.

The term *Formal Standard English*, also called *school English, academic English,* and *standardized English,* often refers to the English prescribed in grammar books and privileged in academic contexts. This term contrasts importantly with *Standard English* in that *Formal Standard English* most often refers to the norms reflected in written language. To specify this distinction, it is sometimes referred to as *edited English* or *standard written English.* For example, the formal standard dictates that distinctions should be made in the use of *lay* and *lie* or *who* and *whom,* that one should avoid ending a sentence with a preposition, and so on. However, acceptable spoken language usage does not necessarily conform to these norms. Informal Standard English would allow sentences such as "They're the ones you should depend on" with no stigma attached, despite the final preposition. In fact, an utterance like "They are the ones on whom you should depend" is probably less acceptable in everyday social interaction because of its formality. Using "whom" in speech, even correctly, can carry a social penalty as it is generally seen as stuffy. All students, even those who speak mainstream varieties of English, will need to learn the Formal Standard English patterns of written language in their English language arts classes, if they do not already know them.

Considering the definitions posed above, it should be clear that no one speaks the standard language consistently. Americans tend to prefer relatability over properness (consider the political litmus test, "Which candidate would you rather have a drink with?"), so using Standard English in casual contexts can carry a steep social cost. Formal Standard English is generally limited to the written language of educated people, and it is heard only in the most formal speaking style of highly educated members of society. Using that variety in everyday life would likely create an unfavorable impression. Given the widespread agreement on what constitutes Standard English and the importance the language variety plays in society, it is worth spending more time examining what it is and how the standard came to be defined.

First, one observation needs to be made about the importance of informal language usage by otherwise standard speakers. Because all speakers use a range of styles, depending on the situation of speaking, someone who is considered a speaker of Standard English may at times use certain language patterns that are clearly not standard. For example, in an appropriate context, a speaker of a standard variety might use double negatives or *ain't*. In fact, a number of U.S. presidents have used nonstandard forms in various addresses, including President Obama, who once said "You ain't seen nothin' yet" at a gathering of elite Hollywood donors (Youngman, 2009). This usage did not indicate that the president had suddenly become a speaker of a vernacular dialect; instead, nonstandard forms are quite useful for evoking a sense of toughness, comradery, or resiliency.

A number of different varieties qualify as informal Standard English. For example, a Standard English speaker from Maine and a Standard English speaker from Tennessee would have quite different pronunciation patterns and probably certain other differences as well in their informal styles of speech. They would both be accepted as Standard English speakers in their own communities, however, and in most others as well, despite the fact that their accents might be noticed outside their home region. In both communities, the standards derive from the dialects typical of local, middle-class speakers, who are also the people who are often in gatekeeping roles in the society, including teachers and employers.

Standard American English, then, is a composite of the real spoken language of these groups who are generally professionals, the educated middle class. Because members of these groups in Chicago might sound quite different from their counterparts in Atlanta or Boston, it is important to recognize the existence of a number of dialects of Standard American English. For the most part, there is more in the grammar of Standard English speakers that is shared across communities than in pronunciation, but there are still some regional grammar differences, many of which will be examined in subsequent chapters, that provide evidence that no single set of standard grammatical features exists.

To consider regional varieties of English fully, we must also recognize a range of World Englishes, the varieties of English spoken in other countries. Just as in the United States, there are standard and vernacular English language varieties in countries that were colonized by English speakers, where English has become the mother tongue of most people (e.g., New Zealand) or where it functions as a second language spoken by nearly everyone for certain purposes, such as business and higher education (e.g., Nigeria). English is used for special purposes in many other countries as well, and local standards for the language have developed. When these English speakers move to other English-speaking countries, including the United States, they may find that speech considered standard in their own country is found difficult to understand, odd, even nonstandard, according to the standards of the host country. Here again, Standard English is relative to the particular norms of the speech community. Standard Singapore English is very different from any version of Standard American English. Thus, it is more accurate to speak of Standard Englishes than of just one Standard English. This distinction is important whether one refers to the standard varieties within a country or to the varieties of English around the world.

We use the term *Standard English* as a proper noun with a capital *s* on *Standard*, but we intend it as a collective noun. We also contrast Standard English (spoken) with Formal Standard English (written) as appropriate. The term *Mainstream American English* denotes language varieties that would be considered unremarkable in most educational settings. We use *Mainstream American English* only when it is important to allow for more local variation than might be assumed by the term *Standard English*. In sum, Standard English is a collection of the socially preferred dialects from various parts of the United States and other English-speaking countries. Mainstream American English or mainstream English is a collection of socially appropriate or allowable dialects in schools and other similar social contexts.

Dialects and Understanding

Given differences among English dialects, it stands to reason that communication misunderstandings may occasionally occur among speakers of different dialects. Although problems in comprehension and interpretation can arise, their precise sources are not always clear.

Certainly, there are mainstream English speakers who claim not to understand vernacular speakers. To put this in perspective, however, it is useful to note that the same claim may come from a person traveling through another region, such as a Northerner in the South or a person from the mainland visiting a historically isolated island area in the Chesapeake Bay or the Outer Banks off the coast of North Carolina. In most cases, such reports are exaggerated ("I couldn't understand a word he was saying!") and are based on a few items that may legitimately prove troublesome for an outsider to comprehend. Someone visiting Appalachia for the first time may have difficulty comprehending certain *ire* words such as *fire* (pronounced much like "far") or *buyer* (pronounced much like "bar"), or a vocabulary item such as "garret" for *attic* or "vittles" for *food*, unless there is sufficient context to interpret these items. Such isolated problems would not usually result in a breakdown in a conversation. However, it is worth noting that simply expecting to not understand a speaker can result in a self-fulfilling prophecy in which a listener actually struggles to comprehend the speech more than if they did not have such negative expectations (see, e.g., Rubin, 2001).

Such attitudes may affect understanding in a variety of contexts. If speakers of a dominant dialect feel that a vernacular version of the language is inferior, then they may attribute their comprehension problems primarily to the vernacular speakers' inability to make themselves understood, even though the standard speaker's preconceived attitudes may really be to blame. In a test of this claim, students were divided into two groups to listen to a recorded lecture. One group was told that the professor was a native English speaker and the other group was told that the professor spoke English as a second language. As predicted, students in the second group claimed to have more difficulty understanding the lecture, and they did worse on a test evaluating how much they learned from the lecture (Rubin, 2001). The relative status of groups can play a prominent role in the comprehension of language varieties as well (Fasold, 1984; Lippi-Green, 2012). Typically, the higher status group claims comprehension difficulties with the lower status group, not the converse. Speakers of the mainstream variety seem unwilling to make the kinds of language adjustments that enhance comprehension across dialects; instead, they shift the burden of communication entirely onto the vernacular speaker. The difference in expectations of understanding between groups is especially important in educational settings: Schools simply expect and assume that vernacular-speaking students will comprehend standard varieties, whereas the converse does not hold. This expectation forms one of the obstacles faced by students who arrive at school speaking vernacular varieties that mainstream speaking students do not encounter.

Comprehension of Standard English cannot be assumed to be equivalent for all speakers of English regardless of their dialect background, however. In fact, people of different dialect and cultural backgrounds may comprehend particular constructions differently. For instance, there may be differences in literal or nonliteral interpretations of sentences: "Get out of here!" may be interpreted as a command or as an expression of disbelief. "Are you going to try to get to the grocery store?" may be interpreted as a literal question about managing to accomplish an activity or as a polite request. Different inferences may be drawn from particular sentence constructions or word choices: Instructions in a testing situation to "repeat what I say" may be interpreted by students from some backgrounds as a request to paraphrase the test-giver's words and by those from other backgrounds as a request to repeat the utterance verbatim. Studies have found cultural differences in understanding some words in certain contexts, such as *summarize* when it is used as part of a writing prompt (Minami & McCabe, 1995). For example, when asked to summarize, students of East Asian heritage may describe a moral from a text instead of retelling events in sequence.

Subtle types of miscomprehension of standard language conventions by vernacular speakers can have an effect just as significant as more transparent cases of vocabulary confusion. For example, standardized educational tests assume that all students understand the Standard English directions for a task in exactly the same way. If this is not the case, then the scoring of responses given by different groups of students as correct or incorrect may be called into question. These cases are extremely important in understanding the full range of potential miscomprehension across dialects. Only painstaking, detailed analysis of extended sequences of interaction can uncover meaning loss.

Multiple Dialects in Schools

Once a teacher has accepted the scientific basis for dialect variation, there are three basic alternatives for dealing with multiple dialects in schools:

- Accommodate all dialects.
- Require that a dialect of Standard English be learned and used.
- Identify a position somewhere between these two.

These three positions are explored in more detail in Chapter 7, but it is useful now to begin thinking about how each may play out in classrooms. The first alternative, accommodating all dialects, derives from the fact that all dialects are inherently equal and the assumption that no one should be penalized because of his or her dialect. This alternative could mean making a conscious effort to allow full use of a student's native dialect of English as the base on which learning will build.

The other extreme position is to formally establish that a dialect of Standard English must be acquired to replace the vernacular dialect. Support for this position comes from the belief that a standard variety is needed for success in education and access to society. While such approaches may flow from administrative decisions (see, for example, one such program advocated in Lemov, 2010), more commonly this approach emerges silently when teachers are not providing opportunities for students to explore and use nonstandard dialects in oral and written forms. Teachers who never accept nonstandard forms are tacitly subscribing to a policy of eradicating vernacular dialects in favor of Standard English.

The third alternative falls between these two extremes. It is undoubtedly the direction most often followed, usually implicitly, in schools. The native dialect is accepted for certain uses, and a dialect of Standard English is encouraged or demanded for other uses. In terms of mastering certain skills, a plan like the following might be formulated. In recognition of the fact that most written language uses a standard variety, a student would be expected to develop the capability to read and write a Standard English dialect, but would not be required to eliminate the native dialect in classroom talk. Teachers would help students work toward competence with the standard written forms of the language, both in reading and in writing. The student would thus be using two (or more) dialects of English for different purposes, much as people naturally use different styles of speaking for different situations. An advantage to such an arrangement is that the oral dialect in which children are expert when they come to school can be overtly valued rather than merely tolerated. A more centralized implementation of this approach might involve intentionally teaching code-switching, where students' use of formal and vernacular varieties is dependent on the context rather than the medium; students would be expected to be able to switch between vernacular structures in their writing and in their speech (Wheeler & Swords, 2006, 2010). A number of factors should be considered when deciding how to address the reality of dialect diversity in the classroom; these will be discussed throughout this book.

Language Attitudes in Society

The issues arising over language variation in education are just one reflection of dialect issues in the broader social context, where language remains one of the last bastions of discrimination. Unsurprisingly, research demonstrates that speakers of vernacular dialects are generally held in low esteem (Lippi-Green, 2012; Preston, 1996; Shuy & Fasold, 1973). This view typically extends well beyond their language to other personal attributes, including their morality, integrity, and competence. Attitudes about language can trigger a whole set of stereotypes and prejudices based on underlying social and ethnic differences. In research on discriminatory practices in housing, John Baugh discovered that when callers to rental agents sounded Anglo, they were more likely to be shown a house or apartment than were callers who sounded African American or Chicano. Baugh (2003) calls this practice *linguistic profiling* after the practice of racial profiling in other realms of social conduct, such as identifying motor vehicle violations, felons, or terrorists. Since language can serve as the vehicle for discriminatory practice, Rosina Lippi-Green calls it "the last back door to discrimination" and notes that the "door stands wide open" (2012, p. 74).

An interesting aspect of language attitude studies is the evidence about the young age at which such attitudes may be acquired. In fact, one study showed that children as young as 3 to 5 years of age were quite accurate in recognizing differences in language and made associations with other types of behavior on the basis of language differences (Rosenthal, 1977). Another study found that negative associations with vernacular dialects and foreign accented English were reinforced through kids' cartoons and Disney movies (Lippi-Green, 2012). These films also reinforce the societal bias toward linguistic contributions from men, which are considered more valuable than those from women (Fought & Eisenhauer, 2016; Guo, 2016). Kinzler and DeJesus (2012) found that children in the "North" (Illinois) and the "South" (Tennessee) express stereotypes similar to those of adults by the age of 10. Northern-accented individuals are deemed "smarter" and "in charge" while Southern-accented speakers are described as sounding "nicer" (Kinzler & DeJesus, 2012). Such findings, combined with research about the socialization of prejudice, indicate linguistic prejudice begins early in life and manifests itself in many different details of behavior (e.g., Aboud, 2005).

Of course, some dialect differences are observed without prejudice in American society. Many regional vocabulary differences are considered matters of curiosity alone, such as the different words for a paper container (*bag, sack,* and *poke*) or words for a carbonated beverage (*soda, pop, soda pop, sodi-water, coke, co'cola, dope,* etc.). Americans typically would not think that someone is uneducable, incompetent, or immoral simply because the person called a submarine sandwich a *sub, grinder, torpedo,* or *hoagie.* At the same time, as discussed above, the dialects of particular classes and ethnic groups are often viewed stereotypically as signaling deficits in intellectual capability and/or morality.

There are two possible ways of addressing these inequities regarding the social dialects of English. One would be to eliminate the differences between dialects; the other would be to change the negative attitudes toward some dialects that are the source of the inequities.

Complete elimination of dialect differences is not a practical solution because variation is an inherent characteristic of every language. The other possibility, eliminating the misconceptions about the significance of dialect differences, involves changing people's language attitudes. The set of attitudes about what is good and what is bad in language usage that children acquire with their native language develops into a set of opinions used to judge people by the way they speak. Language attitudes are generally shared by the members of a speech community, leading to a common evaluation of certain language patterns and the people who use them. Box 1.1 illustrates the different attitudes people can have toward dialects that are different from Standard English. The difference in responses to the two dialects indicates clearly that the commenters are projecting their attitudes toward the social groups onto the language.

BOX 1.1: SPEAKING OF PREJUDICE

The Language and Life Project at NC State University produces language documentaries of local and national interest. They offer vignettes of these videos on their YouTube channel. User comments about the vignettes often reveal how the users feel about the dialect and can vary dramatically depending on which dialect is being documented. The comments follow the principle of linguistic subordination, whereby the dialects of groups that are more socially subordinate are considered to be worse than those of other groups. Compare the following comments on vignettes from two distinctive dialects. The first dialect is the Outer Banks Brogue of North Carolina. It is the only dialect of American English commonly mistaken as non-American. This fact highlights how different it is from Standard English. The second dialect is Lumbee English. It is a distinctive dialect that is mostly Southern but has some distinctive patterns of grammar and pronunciation. Interestingly, some of these patterns are shared with the Outer Banks Brogue, including a special use of *weren't* and the pronunciation of the vowel in *side* as something more like "soid." Lumbee English is spoken by the Lumbee Indians who live in Southeastern North Carolina. Despite having both state recognition (since 1885) and federal recognition (since 1956), the Lumbee receive no federal entitlements from the Bureau of Indian Affairs. Their status as "real Indians" also remains the subject of much suspicion by many people. This skepticism has contributed to the group's maligned social status. All comments are reproduced with original spelling and punctuation.

User comments about the Outer Banks Brogue

(www.youtube.com/watch?v=jXs9cf2YWwg&list=PL8csRAB3UNkyFJH 2alPKGui-35JHaNHQC&index=5)

4th dimension:	"I'm from Raleigh. I love hearing coastal folk. I like the variation in our state"
Edith Smith:	"Love this. . . I'm from East End if Long Island and we sound a lot like you"
Wyatt Collins:	"those fishermen at 3:04 – pure awesomeness"
Lex5576:	"I hope the folks out on the barrier islands keep on talking like they've proudly done for eons. I think the coastal brogue accent is awesome, just one more thing that makes North Carolina unique. A bunch of people I've met in other states that have travelled our coast don't make fun of brogue speaking people. If anything, they're fascinated that English influence has lasted all these years. But again, the Carolina coast was one of the very first areas colonized by England, so there's good reason for the accent"
Sew Sallysew:	"when i hear this beautiful dialect spoken it is music to my ears. I love it down east, i love it with all my heart. . . there is no other dialect of English that is more music then this. . . I love these people. I can trace my ancestry on my father side since before the Revolutionary war.. I pray and home that this dialect never dies out."

Notice how commenters connect the dialect to the history and culture of the region. They frame it positively as something to be proud of and to preserve. Contrast these responses with those responding to a vignette on Lumbee English, a dialect that shares some linguistic features, but is spoken by a group that remains socially stigmatized. Notice also that all commenters assume expert status in their evaluation of the dialect and culture.

User comments about Lumbee English

(www.youtube.com/watch?v=4BLzH8UGZrE)

Sein "Yvena Oreofe Merritt" Maestro:	"chile this aint nuttin but ebonics. we the same lol wel.. we been put the the same ish too."
Gustavo otero:	"You don't even know your own language your traditions are stolen your tribe is been made up quit telling your self your native cause your not"
AzSureno:	"there not federally recognized because other tribes like actual natives disaprove. of them they know there fake"
Bj Beasley:	"This has got to be the biggest crock of shit I've ever seen. Trying to rationalize the lumbee ignorant way of talking. That's what this video "be's" doing. And all of the lumbees commenting all have one thing in common, they're willing to show you their true ignorance. Look at all of the comments by them. They will not accept anyone's opinion. They're quick to say how they will fight you if you say that to their face. What a bunch of wasted people. No other group in this nation is more ignorant and dumb, than the lumbees."

Language prejudices seem more resistant to change than many other kinds of prejudice. This persistence is tied to several factors, including the fact that language is acquired without instruction (cf. mathematics, which requires formal instruction), which leads people to develop *implicit attitudes* about language from their parents and peers. Implicit attitudes exist in humans' subconscious minds and individuals have no recollection of their forming; yet they influence every interaction with other people (Greenwald & Banaji, 1995). When systems like language or cultural norms are developed in this way, people tend to have very little awareness of their actual patterns and workings: "Language, like gravity, is one of those things with which everyone is familiar but few can adequately describe and explain. This is a surprising fact considering the intimate part it plays in our lives, but people have less privileged access to many of their own mental processes than they often imagine" (Graddol & Swann, 1989, p. 4). Such attitudes only change through experiential discovery, not through direct instruction, meaning that teachers must create experiences for students to discover truths about language variation. This is a tall order, perhaps, but far more possible than eliminating language variation.

The fact that people do not have access to their own mental processing of language differences makes it easy for otherwise fair-minded people to discriminate against others based on their dialect. For example, in contemporary American society, the rejection of an applicant for a job based on gender or ethnicity could result in litigation. But rarely is rejection on the basis of speech being challenged; and when it is, the challenge may be deemed frivolous. Clearly the stakes are high, which is why linguists have without exaggeration made claims like, "In the lives of individuals and of society, language is a factor of greater importance than any other" (de Saussure, 1916/1983, p. 7), or "Language should be as much an object of public scrutiny as any of the other things that keenly affect our lives—as much as pollution, energy, crime, busing, and next week's grocery bill" (Bolinger, 1979, p. 407).

Dominant culture members are not the only ones who show language prejudice against vernacular dialects. Vernacular dialect speakers themselves may hold vernacular dialects in low esteem, at least with respect to occupational and social competence in mainstream society. It is not unusual to find a spokesperson for a minority group decrying prejudice in other spheres of behavior but exhibiting the same kind of prejudice against the vernacular dialect as mainstream authorities do. This attitude may make dialect prejudice seem more acceptable, but it is not more acceptable than any other prejudice. The high level of dialect prejudice found toward vernacular dialects by both mainstream and vernacular speakers is a fact that must be confronted honestly and openly by those involved in education about language and dialects.

The key to attitudinal changes lies in developing a genuine respect for the integrity of the diverse varieties of English. Knowledge about dialects can reduce misconceptions about language in general and the accompanying negative attitudes about some dialects. Informal attitude surveys given before and after the presentation of information about dialects demonstrate that such attitudinal change does occur (Henderson, 2016; Reaser, 2006). Because the educational implications of language attitudes are so great, developing a knowledge base about dialects in schools is especially important.

One strategy for stimulating attitudinal change is through examining language myths. Collecting comments about dialects expressed in casual conversation or in the media can make clear just how judgmental people can be about other people's talk (as demonstrated earlier in Box 1.1). A close look at this evidence may reveal the nature of underlying attitudes not only about language, but also about other attributes of individuals who use certain language varieties.

Over time, studying systematic rules of language variation can help students replace unexamined beliefs with research-supported understandings.

Another productive approach to combating unwarranted language beliefs is teaching students to study language variation in their own communities. Chapter 10 includes sample lessons from units on language variation that have been taught in English language arts and social studies classes. When interacting with materials like these, students in both elementary and secondary classrooms find dialect study fascinating partly because they can contribute their own knowledge to it. These lessons provide a model for developing further units on language variation, as well as interdisciplinary units on human variation. Before that, however, Chapters 2 and 3 examine how linguists study language and document some of their findings about variation in different dialects. Chapter 4 examines the language situations that gave rise to African American English and Latino English. It also examines the context in which current immigrants from East Asia are learning English. Chapter 5 examines how language norms develop and how changes are interpreted. Chapters 6 through 9 then discuss the importance of those findings for standardized language assessment, educational policy, classroom instruction, writing, and reading.

Discussion Questions

1. What is your reaction to the deficit position regarding some children's language, as discussed in this chapter? Do you think the deficit position is common in schools today?
2. How does the deficit position contrast with the difference position?
3. This book addresses variation in English according to social groups and geographic location. Do you have examples of how social group norms and geographic group norms interact, such as some pronunciation differences between Standard English in the South and Standard English in the Northeast?
4. Do you have evidence that other languages vary too? Can you give some examples? Are the social consequences similar to those discussed in this chapter?
5. Throughout the book, the term *rules* is used to refer to regular patterns in language and language use. Distinguish this meaning of the term from its other meanings.
6. The term *dialect* also has several senses. What is the technical meaning of the term and how does it contrast with other meanings?
7. This first chapter introduces topics pertinent to dialects and schools that are pursued more fully in subsequent chapters. Which topics are most familiar to you, and which are fairly new? How are they relevant to your professional life?
8. The chapter suggests three alternatives for dealing with multiple dialects in schools. Which alternative does your school use? What is the evidence of this?

Links of Interest

1. Read a linguist's take on the authenticity of Kevin Spacey's Southern Dialect in *House of Cards:* www.vox.com/2015/2/27/8119829/house-of-cards-spacey-southern-accent
2. Watch two vignettes of linguist John Baugh talking about linguistic profiling: [shorter] www.youtube.com/watch?v=HJ778_tsqjs OR [longer] www.youtube.com/watch?v=q_NpwCkDpCs
3. Watch an advertisement from the U.S. Department of Housing and Urban Development (HUD) designed to raise awareness of linguistic profiling: www.youtube.com/watch?v=zup2qlFuCDc
4. Read an article about different forms of language profiling: www.pbs.org/speak/seatosea/americanvarieties/DARE/profiling/
5. Take a quiz that can pinpoint where you are from based on your speech: www.nytimes.com/interactive/2013/12/20/sunday-review/dialect-quiz-map.html
6. Read what linguists have discovered about how much male and female characters speak in animated Disney films: www.washingtonpost.com/news/wonk/wp/2016/01/25/researchers-have-discovered-a-major-problem-with-the-little-mermaid-and-other-disney-movies/
7. Watch videos about dialects at the YouTube channel of the Language and Life Project at NC State University: www.youtube.com/user/NCLLP
8. Sort through a collection of blogs that explore issues related to the so-called "language gap" and mascot names of sports teams: http://linguisticanthropology.org/socialjustice/initiatives/
9. Read the Linguistic Society of America's "Linguistics in everyday life" page, with links to a number of short articles about a variety of language topics from the origins of language to communicating with someone who has had a stroke: www.linguisticsociety.org/content/linguistics-everyday-life#Domain

Further Reading

Denham, K., & Lobeck, A. (2010). *Linguistics at school: Language awareness in primary and secondary education.* Cambridge, UK: Cambridge University Press.
    The contributors to this volume include both researchers and classroom teachers. Relevant sections include the role of classroom teachers in implementing language awareness programs and the stories of teachers who have implemented these programs.

Lippi-Green, R. (2012). *English with an accent: Language, ideology and discrimination in the United States* (2nd ed.). London/New York: Routledge.
    This engaging volume examines how social attitudes toward accents are institutionalized in numerous settings and perpetuated in the media, at work, and via cultural transmission so that people whose accents are not considered prestigious may suffer discrimination or job loss.

McKay, S. L., & Hornberger, N. H. (Eds.). (1996). *Sociolinguistics and language teaching.* Cambridge, UK: Cambridge University Press.
    Teachers in culturally diverse schools will find important background information in this collection of chapters on Language and Society, Language and Variation, Language and Interaction, and Language and Culture.

Napoli, D. J. (2003). *Language matters: A guide to everyday thinking about language*. New York, NY: Oxford University Press.

> This small volume gives straightforward answers to a range of frequently asked questions about language: How do we acquire language? Why is it hard to learn a second language? Does language equal thought? The section on language in society addresses dialects and creoles, gender differences in language use, spelling reform, and the status of English in the United States.

Rickford, J. R., & Rickford, R. J. (2000). *Spoken soul: The story of Black English*. New York, NY: John Wiley & Sons.

> A rich and engaging examination of the current and historical discussions surrounding African American English, this volume illuminates the social importance of language in powerful ways.

References

Aboud F. E. (2005). The development of prejudice in childhood and adolescence. In J. F. Dovidio, P. Glick, & L. A. Rudman (Eds.), *On the nature of prejudice: Fifty years after Allport* (pp. 310–326). New York, NY: Blackwell.

Aud, S., Fox, M. A., & Kewal-Ramani, A. (2010). *Status and trends in the education of racial and ethnic groups*. NCES 2010–015. Washington, DC: National Center for Education Statistics. Available online at http://nces.ed.gov/pubs2010/2010015.pdf

Baugh, J. (2003). Linguistic profiling. In S. Makoni, G. Smitherman, A. Ball, & A. K. Spears (Eds.), *Black linguistics: Language, society, and politics in Africa and the Americas* (pp. 155–168). New York, NY: Routledge.

Baugh, J. (2016). Meaning-less differences: Exposing fallacies and flaws in "the word gap" hypothesis that conceal a dangerous "language trap" for low-income American families and their children. *International Multilingual Research Journal, 11*(1), 39–51.

Bolinger, D. (1979). The socially-minded linguist. *The Modern Language Journal, 63*(8), 404–407.

Bourdieu, P. (1977). The economics of linguistic exchanges. *Social science information, 16*(6), 645–668.

Carver, C. M. (1987). *American regional dialects: A word geography*. Ann Arbor, MI: University of Michigan Press.

Delpit, L. (1995). *Other people's children: Cultural conflict in the classroom*. New York, NY: The New Press.

Erickson, F., & Mohatt, G. (1982). Cultural organization of participation structures in two classrooms of Indian students. In G. Spindler (Ed.), *Doing the ethnography of schooling: Educational anthropology in action* (pp. 132–174). New York, NY: Holt, Rinehart, and Winston.

Fasold, R. (1984). *The sociolinguistics of society*. Oxford, UK: Basil Blackwell.

Fernald, A., Marchman, V. A., & Weisleder, A. (2013). SES differences in language processing skill and vocabulary are evident at 18 months. *Developmental Science, 16*(2), 234–248.

Foucault, M. (1971). Orders of discourse. *Social Science Information, 10*(2), 7–30.

Fought, C., & Eisenhauer, K. (2016, January). A quantitative analysis of gendered compliments in Disney princess films. Paper presented at the 90th Annual Meeting of the Linguistic Society of America. Washington, DC.

Goodenough, F. L. (1926). Racial differences in the intelligence of school children. *Journal of Experimental Psychology, 9*(5), 388–397.

Graddol, D., & Swann, J. (1989). *Gender voices*. Malden, MA: Blackwell Publishing.

Greenwald, A. G., & Banaji, M. R. (1995). Implicit social cognition: Attitudes, self-esteem, and stereotypes. *Psychological Review, 102*(1), 4–27.

Guo, J. (2016, January 25). Researchers have found a major problem with *The Little Mermaid* and other Disney Movies. *Washington Post*. Retrieved from www.washingtonpost.com/news/wonk/wp/2016/01/25/researchers-have-discovered-a-major-problem-with-the-little-mermaid-and-other-disney-movies/

Hart, B., & Risley, T. R. (1995). *Meaningful differences in the everyday experience of young American children*. Baltimore, MD: Paul H. Brookes Publishing.

Heath, S. B. (1983). *Ways with words: Language, life and work in communities and classrooms*. Cambridge, UK: Cambridge University Press.

Heath, S. B. (2012). *Words at work and play*. Cambridge, UK: Cambridge University Press.

Henderson, M. H. (2016). *Sociolinguistics for kids: A curriculum for bilingual students.* Unpublished doctoral dissertation, University of New Mexico.

Herrnstein, R. J., & Murray, C. (1994). *The bell curve: The reshaping of American life by differences in intelligence.* New York, NY: The Free Press.

Kinzler, K. D., & DeJesus, J. M. (2012). Northern = smart and Southern = nice: The development of accent attitudes in the United States. *The Quarterly Journal of Experimental Psychology, 66*(6), 1146–1158.

Kurath, H. (1949). *Handbook of the linguistic geography of New England.* Ann Arbor, MI: University of Michigan Press.

Labov, W., Ash, S., & Boberg, C. (2006). *Atlas of North American English: Phonology and phonetics.* Berlin, Germany: Mouton de Gruyter.

Lemov, D. (2010). *Teach like a champion: 49 techniques that put students on the path to college (K–12).* San Francisco, CA: Jossey-Bass.

Lippi-Green, R. (2012). *English with an accent: Language, ideology, and discrimination in the United States* (2nd ed.). New York, NY: Routledge.

Minami, M., & McCabe, A. (1995). Rice balls and bear hunts: Japanese and North American family narrative patterns. *Journal of Child Language, 22*(2), 423–445.

Niedzielski, N. A., & Preston, D. R. (2000). *Folk linguistics.* New York, NY: Walter de Gruyter.

Philips, S. U. (1993). *The invisible culture: Communication in classroom and community on the Warm Springs Indian Reservation* (2nd ed.). Prospect Heights, IL: Waveland.

Prescott, S. (Ed.). (1991). *The American Indian: Yesterday, today, and tomorrow. A handbook for educators.* Sacramento, CA: California State Department of Education.

Preston, D. R. (1996). Whaddayaknow? The modes of folk linguistic awareness. *Language Awareness, 5*(1), 40–77.

Pyles, T., & Algeo, J. (1982). *The origins and development of the English language* (3rd ed.). New York, NY: Harcourt Brace Jovanovich.

Reaser, J. (2006). *The effect of dialect awareness on adolescent knowledge and attitudes.* Unpublished doctoral dissertation, Duke University.

Rosenthal, M. S. (1977). *The magic boxes and Black English.* Washington, DC: ERIC Clearinghouse.

Rosenthal, R., & Jacobson, L. (1968). *Pygmalion in the classroom: Teacher expectation and pupils' intellectual development.* New York, NY: Holt, Rinehart & Winston.

Rubin, D. L. (2001). Help! My professor (or doctor or boss) doesn't talk English! In J. Martin, T. Nakayama, & L. Flores (Eds.), *Readings in intercultural communication: Experiences and contexts* (pp. 127–137). Boston, MA: McGraw-Hill.

de Saussure, F. (1983). *Course in general linguistics.* (R. Harris, Trans.) Peru, IL: Open Court. (Original work published 1916).

Seymour, H. N. (2004). The challenge of language assessment for African American English-speaking children: A historical perspective. *Seminars in Speech and Language, 25*(1), 3–12.

Shuy, R. W., & Fasold, R. (1973). *Language attitudes: Current trends and prospects.* Washington, DC: Georgetown University Press.

Wheeler, R. S., & Swords, R. (2006). *Code-switching: Teaching Standard English in urban classrooms.* Urbana, IL: National Council of Teachers.

Wheeler, R. S., & Swords, R. (2010). *Code-switching lessons: Grammar strategies for linguistically diverse writers, grades 3–6.* Portsmouth, NH: Firsthand Heinemann.

Youngman, S. (2009, May 27). Obama in L.A., 'You ain't seen nothing yet.' *The Hill.* Retrieved from http://thehill.com/homenews/news/19845-obama-in-la-you-aint-seen-nothing-yet

Zentella, A. C. (1997). *Growing up bilingual: Puerto Rican children in New York.* Malden, MA: Blackwell.

2

Exploring Dialects

Scenario

Deriving meaning from language is a remarkable feat. Doing this well requires a staggering amount of knowledge, most of which exists in our brain below the level of consciousness. Consider a sentence like, "The cow jumped over the moon." In English, we rely on word order to make sense of things. So while we might recognize the literal impossibility of a cow jumping over the moon, we respond differently to a sentence that is equally impossible: "The moon jumped over the cow." Despite equal odds of each sentence being true, we understand that an animate noun (cow) has more ability to jump than an inanimate noun (moon) and accept the first ordering while rejecting the second, again, despite the literal impossibility of either event coming true. Consider now the following sentences:

1. The farmer drove the cows into the barn.
2. The farmer drove the truck into the barn.
3. The farmer drove the barn into the cows.
4. The farmer drove the cows crazy.

Which sentence has the greatest probability of occurring? Which has the least? How do you know? How does the verb *drove* change meaning among the different usages? How might you go about defining the term *drive*? When you read sentence 1 by itself, you probably imagine the farmer on foot or horseback working a herd of cows into the barn. Can you also picture cows in the back of a truck being driven by a farmer? Why is that version less likely? If sentences 1 and 2 are presented in reversed order, chances are you would visualize cows in the back of a truck when reading sentence 1. Why do you think this is? What does it mean with regard to language processing? Try to describe what most people do not like about sentence 3. Can you create a literal picture of it happening? Why is it so improbable?

This exercise is silly, but it illustrates some important concepts for this chapter and beyond. First, many people assume that outside of relatively ambiguous sentences (e.g., "We need more intelligent administrators"), most sentences have straightforward interpretations. The result of this assumption is that we believe that communication happens more simply than it does in reality. Interpretation is always affected by context. The priming effect that happens when switching the order of the first two sentences demonstrates that what we understand depends on context: in this case, what came first. Priming effects can be achieved verbally or nonverbally and are remarkably influential in biasing interpretations. What does all of this mean for dialect variation? It means that language, something that is all around us and so important to our daily lives, is not nearly as concrete as we assume it to be.

Most of us are oblivious to the inner workings of speech production and processing. We know what a verb is, but we may struggle to explain different uses of "the same" verb. We know that both *moon* and *cow* are nouns, but we might not expect to draw on our knowledge of jumping ability in describing the difference between them. Yet because that knowledge exists in our heads, we can draw on it in interpreting and discussing the sentences in the scenario. In this chapter, we begin to examine questions like "What does it mean to explore language variation?" and "How do teachers and students investigate dialect difference?" Coming to understand more about the vast language knowledge in our brains is one of the joys of language exploration. Accessing our own language knowledge is essential to examining critically the assumptions we make about language in general and to developing the vocabulary and taxonomies that are useful in teaching others about language.

Language plays such a central role in teaching and learning that educators tend to have a natural interest in the language patterns of the communities represented by their students. While there are some resources about different varieties for those who are not professional linguists, they do not apply to every community. However, teachers and practitioners do have direct access to dialect data from their students and their communities. They can learn about the local dialect norms by looking at the actual speech of their students in the classroom, in the hallways, and on the playground. Studying language variation helps bring into consciousness some knowledge about the patterns of a language.

Given the array of social factors that affect language variation described in Chapter 1 and the fact that language is constantly changing in every community, it is clear that documenting linguistic varieties has to be an ongoing endeavor. For that reason, it is essential that teachers and other practitioners learn about how and why language varies. This chapter will help you to start understanding the methods that are used to explore language patterns in different communities.

Dialect Change in the United States

All dialects are constantly changing, but not always in the ways that are assumed. For example, people have often assumed that dialects are converging because we are being influenced by what we hear in the media. While the precise effect of the mass media on dialect differences is difficult to determine (though many linguists have investigated that question [e.g., Chambers, 1998; Stuart-Smith, 2007]), a couple of points need to be made to counter the common assumption. People may recognize media language as sounding different from their own speech, and even as representing a prestige variety, but they are unlikely to view it as a model to emulate. Most studies find that outside of vocabulary items, which speakers can easily assimilate into their dialects, the effect of mass media on language in the United States is actually quite limited (Stuart-Smith, 2007). This minor influence by the media is partly due to the fact that people are not in direct social contact with the people on television and radio. Generally, people talk like those they identify with and whose approval they seek (Bell, 2001), and the truth is, few of us seek out the approval of members of the media: There is little point in adjusting your speech to match that of television newscasters if they will never know you did it. You might talk to your television, but your television does not talk back to you, which is what is required for the types of evaluations that ultimately shape our speech. This lack of direct social contact makes the mass media much less influential than peer group members and common-interest groups with whom a speaker interacts frequently.

Instead of promoting convergence of dialects, media language reveals the usefulness of dialect differences and may even reinforce them. Some media personalities project a regional and/or ethnic dialect, or conversational style, using it as a positive attribute. In local programming, the use of regional and ethnic dialects may be intentional as a way to symbolize affinity with the local population. For example, advertisements for local car dealerships often feature speakers of the local dialect in an attempt to appear more trustworthy. Even national companies create region-specific ads and slogans, such as a McDonald's campaign in the South with the slogan, "Breakfast with a Southern accent." Examining the variation within and across television markets can form the basis of classroom investigations into linguistic and social variation. The accessibility of and increased searchability of mass media makes television content an attractive option for teachers looking to integrate dialect information into their classes. In leading these discussions, it is important for teachers to frame discussions as investigating language change and to avoid unfounded assumptions that media is leveling variation (ironing out differences) or corrupting the language. The section below models this approach.

Though dialects are ever-changing, there are some cases where dialects are moving away from historical local forms towards more supra-regional norms (see, e.g., Weldon, 2006; Wolfram, 2006). This is particularly true for smaller, historically isolated or remote communities that possessed highly localized dialects. Older speakers of various social, regional, and ethnic varieties tend to differ more in their speech than members of the younger generation in that same variety. Increased education, increased accessibility to formerly isolated geographical areas, and expanded occupational opportunities have all likely played some role, but a combination of factors, rather than one primary reason, accounts for this change.

The fact that some dialect differences have lessened, however, hardly foreshadows the extinction of English dialects in the United States. There is every reason to believe that different dialects will continue to be maintained and even enhanced in some instances. For example, recent studies of language variation in the Western United States show advancing dialects in northern regions of California (Eckert & Mendoza-Denton, 2006); Utah (Bowie & Morkel, 2006); Portland, Oregon (Conn, 2006); and Seattle, Washington (Fridland, Kendall, Evans, & Wassink, 2016). Likewise, important differences in vowel pronunciations are moving the dialects of the large Northern cities in the Great Lakes region (Chicago, Detroit, Cleveland, etc.) away from neighboring dialects (Labov, Ash, & Boberg, 2006). In fact, the patterns of change in American dialects simultaneously reveal both convergence and divergence. In general, smaller, traditionally isolated dialects tend to lose their distinctiveness as their isolation decreases. Broader regional and social dialects, however, rarely converge; instead, they tend to differentiate more over time. Thus, the dialects of the large Northern cities are becoming more, not less, different from traditional Southern speech. In the long run, these differences are a tribute to the dynamic traditions and heritages that combine to make up the regional and social fabric of American life.

Language Study

Investigating students' language patterns has not been a common activity for teachers, and it is not easy. A study of English language arts teachers and their classroom practices revealed that teachers felt ill-prepared to teach about language (Applebee, 1989, p. 8), which resulted in teachers spending only about 3% of their instructional time on language, compared to 80% on teaching literature (Applebee, 1989, p. 13). At the same time, literacy scholars and professional organizations have called for increased attention to language and language diversity in the English language arts curriculum (see, e.g., CCCC/NCTE, 1974; Delpit, 1988). Yet, surveys have pointed to educators continuing to hold views like the dialect myths discussed in Chapter 1, including the idea that vernacular dialects are grammatically deviant from Standard English and that vernacular-speaking students are less intelligent than their standard-speaking peers (Blake & Cutler, 2003; Cross, DeVaney, & Jones, 2001; Dyson & Smitherman, 2009; Godley, Carpenter, & Werner, 2007).

Teaching about language takes time and specialized knowledge, and it is clear that this specialized knowledge has not been stressed in many teacher education programs. But as the demographics of the teaching profession homogenize and the demographics of the student population continue to diversify (see, e.g., Goldring, Gray, & Bitterman, 2013), it is more important than ever for teachers to be exposed to linguistic perspectives on language so that they will be better equipped to meet the language and literacy needs of their diverse students (Godley, Sweetland, Wheeler, Minnici, & Carpenter, 2006). One apparent challenge to increasing attention to language for students is the already full language arts curriculum. This challenge can be overcome by including language study as part of—rather than distinct from—the study of literature and writing. In fact, research has demonstrated that this integrated approach is far more effective than examining these domains independently (Sweetland, 2006; Weaver, 1996). However, this approach requires that teachers have knowledge of linguistic research and methods.

Dialect study can be integrated into education in a variety of ways. Teachers can involve their students in scientific inquiry into language variation in their communities, as suggested in the dialect awareness lessons outlined in Chapter 10. They can use literature as a means of discussing issues of dialect (Dean, 2008) or incorporate it into writing instruction (Brown, 2009). At the school district level, the curriculum and instruction department might integrate dialect description projects into multidisciplinary curricula for students, ongoing professional development for teachers, and speech/language assessment updating. Dialect description projects also fit well into standards implementation and curriculum revision efforts because various U.S. national and state standards (typically language arts and social studies) specify that students should understand dialect variation. In fact, "Language" is one of the major strands of the Common Core State Standards (CCSS), a set of academic standards in mathematics and English language arts/literacy for grades K to 12 that have been adopted in many states (CCSS, 2010).

Anyone can begin to explore dialects simply by listening more closely to speech in everyday life. In fact, most people are already good observers of language in a selective way. They readily notice features different from their own in the speech of others. But what they notice and how they interpret their observations are often filtered through their attitudes, assumptions, and stereotypes. For this reason, it is important for teachers to be familiar with some basic methodologies used in systematic language study so that they can design effective educational experiences and help students make sense of the rich speech data they collect.

Linguistic analysis that provides data to inform instruction is not beyond the reach of practitioners who want to improve their practice. We worked with a team of speech/language pathologists in Baltimore City Public Schools who conducted field work to describe the local vernacular dialects. Using an inventory of vernacular features drawn from research, team members checked to see which features occurred in their students' speech. They also identified some previously undescribed vernacular features. As a result of their work, Baltimore's speech/language assessment specialists devised a program that would take into account local language norms so that vernacular dialect speakers would not be inappropriately labeled *language disordered* based on features of language variation (Wolfram & Adger, 1993; see also Adger & Schilling-Estes, 2003).

To understand the precise nature of language patterning, it is essential to document both linguistic and social factors. In this chapter, we explore dialect patterns and how to describe them. We start by examining some of the ways speech data can be organized linguistically and then turn our attention to the social correlates of that variation.

Analyzing Linguistic Differences

Levels of Language Differences

In order to help sort through complex language data, linguists often categorize variation into what are called *levels*: systems of vocabulary, pronunciation, grammar, and pragmatics. In fact, each of these levels of language can tell us very different things about a language variety, or dialect.

Perhaps the most obvious and accessible level of language is vocabulary: Dialects may use different words for the same thing or they may use the same word with different meanings. For example, in some regions of New England, *tonic* refers to what in other regions of the United States is called *pop*, *soda pop*, or simply *soda* (and those other dialects have a different, more specific meaning for *tonic*). At the same time, *soda* may be used for a carbonated drink in one region and a carbonated drink with ice cream in it in another region. The retention of the term *icebox* by members of older generations where younger speakers say *refrigerator* also reflects this level of difference, as do the British forms *jumper*, *chemist*, and *boot* for American *sweater*, *drugstore*, and (car) *trunk*, respectively. Differences in vocabulary shed light on, among other things, the economic ecology of the speech community. For example, dialects found on islands might have numerous dialect-specific words for water conditions (e.g., *slick cam* to describe flat water) whereas dialects found in farming communities might have specialized words for weather (e.g., *mizzle* for light rain). Dialect vocabulary reveals a good bit about the topography, economics, ecology, and values of a speech community. Words can also often index group membership and age within a community.

The second level of language is pronunciation, which can be further divided into pronunciations related to vowels or consonants, and features related to pitch, timing, and intonation. Pronunciation differences can be thought of as different ways of saying the same word. For example, consonant-based pronunciation differences include saying *greasy* with a *z* sound instead of an *s* sound or not pronouncing an *r* after a vowel, as in "cah" for *car*. An example of a vowel-based pronunciation difference is pronouncing the word *time* as something like "tahm," as found in a number of Southern-based varieties of English.

Dialects also contrast with each other in terms of the way that words are constructed and combined in sentences—the grammatical patterns of the language system. For example, in some rural areas of the South (reflecting an affinity with dialects of the British Isles), the plural -*s* may be left off nouns of measurement when a quantifying word precedes the noun, as in "four mile down the road" or "sixteen pound of fish." Speakers of other dialects would use the plural -*s* in these phrases. With respect to the combinations of words in sentences, an indirect question may be expressed as "He asked me could he go to the movies" or as "He asked me if he could go to the movies," and negative patterns may be expressed as "He didn't do anything" or "He didn't do nothing." In some dialects, both of these alternatives are used; in others, only one alternative is used. Similarly, a grammatical difference between British and American English reveals itself in responses to the question "Have you read that book?" A British speaker might say, "No, but I should have done," and an American speaker might say, "No, but I should have." Grammar changes more slowly than the other levels of language, so the level of grammatical differences often reveals the history of a dialect.

Though people may think of the Southern use of *y'all* as a simple vocabulary difference, it actually fulfills a grammatical function in denoting second-person plural pronouns so that they align with other pronouns in distinguishing between singular and plural (e.g., *I/we, you/y'all, he-she-it/they*). Note, for example, how different regional dialects may distinguish between singular and plural second-person forms: In the Southern highlands extending to Pittsburgh, folks may say *y'uns* or *yinz,* while in Northern cities people may refer to *youse* or *you guys* to indicate the plural of singular *you.* We thus see that different dialect forms may fulfill a similar grammatical function.

Beyond differences in levels of vocabulary, pronunciation, and grammatical structure, there is also variation in how members of groups use particular language forms and conversational strategies to accomplish their communicative goals in social interaction. A Northerner and a Southerner may both use the terms of respect *sir* and *ma'am,* but in contrasting ways that reflect different sociocultural conventions governing respect and familiarity. One social group may feel that it is appropriate to ask people what they do for a living, whereas another group may consider that question rude or invasive. Some communities consider interruptions rude while others interpret them as a sign of engagement (Tannen, 2005). Some of these implicit rules are explicitly discussed in socializing children, but many are part of the unconscious knowledge of members of a speech community about how to get along in the world through talking. Patterned differences in language use related to social and cultural group membership can be hard to pinpoint, but they may readily lead to cross-cultural communication conflict because they often represent highly sensitive dimensions of interaction. Speakers' knowledge of these conventions, like the knowledge highlighted in the opening scenario to this chapter, tends to exist below the level of consciousness, which can make them some of the most elusive aspects of language mastery for English language learners. Teachers can be more effective if they acquaint themselves with the interactive practices of their students, but few resources are currently available. One exception is a guide produced by the California State Department of Education for teachers working with American Indian students (Prescott, 1991).

Groups of people who share basic expectations about language use—speech communities (Hymes, 1974)—also differ in the ways that they carry on conversations. For example, in some speech communities, speakers overlap each other's talk enthusiastically in a good, satisfying conversation, whereas in other communities, a speaker is likely to stop talking when another one starts. Even what makes for a good conversational contribution can vary from group to group (Tannen, 2005). In his radio show *A Prairie Home Companion*, Garrison Keillor often referred humorously to what a good Minnesotan or a good Lutheran would say. One of his stories includes a conversation in which a new boat owner responds to compliments by talking about the expense and time involved in maintaining the boat—as a good Minnesotan should, says Keillor—rather than saying how much fun it is (National Public Radio broadcast, July 1986). Speakers of English from other backgrounds might find such a response to a compliment to be inappropriate and even insulting.

Linguistic Factors Contributing to Language Variation

The previous section offered one method of categorizing dialect differences—according to language level. But why does language constantly change to begin with? As it turns out, there are both linguistic and social reasons for its dynamic nature. This section describes some of the pressures from inside the language that cause it to vary as it does. Although not all linguistic variation can be explained by these forces, internal linguistic pressures work to reduce the number of irregular forms in a language, reduce redundancy, and increase clarity.

Languages can tolerate irregularity (or exceptions) in their grammatical patterns, but over time, many irregular patterns become more regular. English maintains a number of irregular patterns, including irregular plurals (*sheep, feet, children,* etc.), past-tense verb forms (*was, did, cut, sang, bought, broke,* etc.), and past-participle verb forms (*been, done, cut, sung,* etc.). These irregular forms can be explained by examining the history of English, which had classes of verbs and nouns, each with its own set of conjugations (much like Classical Latin or modern Russian, Polish, etc.). Over time, certain patterns spread by analogy from one class to another, so that now most English plurals take an *-s* and most past-tense forms take an *-ed*. These endings have become the "regular" patterns for noun plurals and past tense. The shift to a fully regular pattern has slowed somewhat in Standard English since the 1800s for social reasons, such as the rise of dictionaries and grammar books, which tend to reinforce current, slightly obsolete standard usage (Curzan, 2014; Millward, 2012). Yet because internal linguistic pressure continues to push to regularize the remaining irregular forms, various dialects have forms like these: "I growed the pumpkins" and "Three deers eat the food I leaved out for the gooses." Because the variation shown here makes an irregular form conform to the regular pattern, linguists call these features *past tense regularization* and *plural regularization*. Regularization of past-participle verb forms continues to progress more rapidly across English dialects than regularization of past-tense forms. Within the past half century, forms such as *sawn, mown,* and *proven* have become rarer in usage, replaced by regularized *-ed* endings, as in "I have proved him wrong" or "I had mowed the lawn before the rain."

Another manifestation of reducing irregularity in language is what linguists call *leveling*, which occurs when irregular verb forms are made regular across the verb paradigm (that is, across all grammatical subjects). Consider the present-tense forms of the irregular verb *to be*. While Standard English alternates between *am, is,* and *are* based on grammatical subject, some dialects use *is* for all grammatical subjects (*I is, we is, they is,* etc.). The same thing happens in the past tense, with dialects tending to level to the form *was* for all subjects. All English verbs are irregular with third-person singular subjects (*she/he/it*), requiring that an *-s* be added to the verb in Standard English (cf. *I/we/you/they run* vs. *she runs*). As might be expected, some dialects level out this irregularity, resulting in sentences like "She run." It should be noted that in all cases of leveling, no grammatical information is lost, as these verb endings convey the same grammatical information about number as does the subject, so these differences, while noticeable and stigmatized socially, never cause comprehension problems.

All languages have some degree of redundancy. Consider the sentence "He is a man." The grammatical concept of singular person is reflected in all four words, masculinity is contained in both "he" and "man," and "he" and "is" both convey a third-person subject (neither the speaker nor the addressee). Given the amount of redundancy in English, it is not surprising that some dialects reduce that redundancy. For example, some dialects may omit the plural *-s* from nouns of measurement that co-occur with a quantifier, as in "four mile down the road" or "sixteen pound of fish." These sentences still convey all the grammatical information of their standard counterparts because in these cases the *-s* is redundant with the quantifier (number), which alerts the listener to the plural state of the noun. Notice that **mile down the road* and **pound of flounder* do not adequately convey the pluralness of the noun (the asterisk is used to mark sentences that are not well formed in a dialect or a language).

The final major linguistic pressure for language change is the push to promote clarity. Perhaps the best example comes from examining the patterns of past-tense *be* leveling found in vernacular dialects. As noted above, when dialects level past-tense *be*, the typical manifestation is that *was* is used for all subjects (*I was, they was, we was,* etc.). However, in many of these dialects, a second leveling process happens when negative sentences are produced. Instead of using *wasn't*, these dialects often level to *weren't* or *won't*, so that a speaker might say *I, you, (s)he, we, you, they was* and *I, you, (s)he, we, you, they weren't* or *won't*. In this alignment, *was* is used for positive sentences (e.g., "I was there"; "They was there") and *were(n't)* and *won't* are used only in negative sentences. This configuration is fascinating because on the surface, it is so unexpected. When both forms of leveling happen in the same dialect, it reduces the possibilities of mishearing a positive sentence as negative or vice versa; *was* and *weren't* sound more different from each other than *was* and *wasn't*.

With these language tendencies in mind, as teachers engage their students in conversations about language variation, they can ask them to consider how the constructs of irregularity, redundancy, and clarity might help explain the observed patterns. For example, consider how regularity might apply to words for newer objects, such as the plural of *mouse,* the device for controlling a computer, or the plural of *Pokemon.*

There are other linguistic pressures that cause dialect variation (see Wolfram & Schilling, 2016, for more on linguistic processes), but many of these are difficult to understand without diving more deeply into linguistic theory than would be appropriate here. One concept that needs to be mentioned, though, is *naturalness,* which is used in evaluating contrasts between language features, such as particular sounds in discussions of pronunciation. Naturalness is roughly equivalent to the relative commonness or rarity of a feature in the world's languages. For example, the *t* sound is one of the most common consonant sounds around the world, whereas the sounds represented by the spelling "th" (e.g., *this* or *with*) are much less common. The less common the form, the more likely it is to vary in dialects. This helps explain why so many English dialects use other sounds in these instances, such as in "dese" for *these,* "smoove" for *smooth,* or "birfday" for *birthday.* Another feature of Standard English not found in many other languages is the strings of consonants before and/or after vowels (e.g., *strength*). Such clusters of consonants may be particularly difficult for some English learners, who may leave off a consonant (e.g., "tas'" for *task*), following the patterns of their first languages that do not include clusters of consonants. English learners may also insert a vowel in order to break up consonant clusters (e.g., "es-top" for *stop*). Because specialized linguistic knowledge is needed to analyze cases such as these, it may be beyond the reach of classroom teachers in discussing language variation with their students. But such information might be useful to speech/language pathologists and teachers of English language learners as it can allow them to understand and even predict what aspects of English are likely to challenge their students most. Perhaps the most important conclusion here is that language varies according to principles, not in idiosyncratic ways.

Social and Historical Factors Contributing to Language Variation

The colonial history of the United States contributed greatly to current regional variation. Put simply, the settlers arriving in different parts of the (eventual) United States brought with them different dialects of English and, of course, other languages that left an imprint. And while the dialects spoken today are not identical to the dialects of each region's original settlers, there are a number of features that reflect what linguists call the *founder effect*, which is the enduring influence of the first language variety of English spoken in the region. It is important to note that at no point was English in the United States ever homogeneous. Instead, the regional variation that was established via the diverse settlements of the Eastern seaboard has been preserved and, in some ways, amplified through time. As settlers migrated westward, they took their dialects with them, which helps explain why specific dialect regions (northern, midland, and southern) extend westward to the Mississippi in roughly parallel bands. Just west of the Mississippi, with fewer topographic barriers, dialects mixed more freely than in the East, giving rise to a new dialect of American English. And while regional variation is perhaps the most noticeable linguistic variation in the United States, what is most important for teachers to be aware of is that much dialect variation exists within these broad regions (see Wolfram & Ward, 2006, for a collection of essays highlighting some of this inter- and intra-regional variation).

Studies of differences in language forms have found significant variation among groups defined by age, socioeconomic status (SES), gender, and ethnicity, in addition to geographical region (Wolfram & Schilling, 2016). On the surface, none of this should seem surprising. Certainly everyone has perceptions about how the speech of teenagers is different from those a generation or two older, or that within a community, those with greater wealth tend to speak differently than the poor. What is important is not merely the fact that the variation exists, but also the social meanings of these variations. Examining a few of these features reveals some interesting observations about how important language is to understanding group and individual contrasts.

Differences between age groups often stem from language patterns that individuals acquired early and have maintained more or less throughout life. In studies of certain parts of the South, for example, members of the older age group were found to pronounce words like *water* and *war* without an *r* sound at the end of the word. Younger speakers, in contrast, consistently used an *r* after a vowel (Feagin, 1990). These differences are subject to evaluation.

Whether generational changes are viewed as language deterioration or innovation probably relates to which generational group the commenter belongs to. The finding that older groups largely maintain the speech patterns they acquired as children allows linguists to get a glimpse into the language of the past. For example, by interviewing a speaker born in 1920, linguists can get a sense of the language patterns from the 1930s to the 1940s, when the speaker was in the formative years of development. For this reason, interviews with elderly community members have been an important part of many linguistic survey projects. This finding also means that characteristics of children's language in a community should not be inferred from examining the speech of the adults.

Generational differences can signal language change over time, but sometimes the difference can be due to the fact that not all linguistic patterns are stable throughout the lifespan. In such cases, what appears at first to be generational shift might actually be *age grading*, which involves predictable shifts in language patterns over the course of the lifetime. For example, studies find that individuals use more slang and profanity in their teen and young adult years and taper off as they age. Studies have found other intriguing evidence of linguistic age grading (see Wagner, 2012). In a longitudinal study of 70 African American children over the first 20 years of their lives (Van Hofwegen, 2015), a roller coaster pattern of vernacular use was found for the participants' formative years. The trajectory of vernacular dialect use from 4 years of age, before the children entered school, through age 20, when they had completed their K–12 education, is shown in Figure 2.1 (adapted from Van Hofwegen & Wolfram, forthcoming). The relative incidence of vernacular features per sentence is shown for seven different age points during the early lifespan.

Figure 2.1 shows that children entering school were relatively vernacular in their speech, then reduced their use of vernacular features during the first few years of schooling. However, as middle-school students (grades 6–8), their incidence of vernacular features peaked, but then reduced again in secondary and post-secondary school. One of the conclusions from this study is that the linguistic model children target shifts over the early lifespan from parents, to teachers, to peers. These diverse inputs can help explain why no two people use language in exactly the same way. Thus, dialects are not static; individuals change their dialect patterns as they age and are exposed to different influences.

Other social factors—SES, gender, ethnicity—can operate in similar ways within a community. As with age, these social differences often correlate with linguistic differences. And like age, the social meanings of these factors are more complex than they might appear at first. For example, gender and ethnicity are fluid categories that cannot be separated and analyzed independently of each other. Further, since all language users have different styles in their repertoires, the discourse context further complicates analysis and understanding of these social factors. Speakers make unconscious choices from their linguistic repertoires depending on such factors as how formal they feel the situation is,

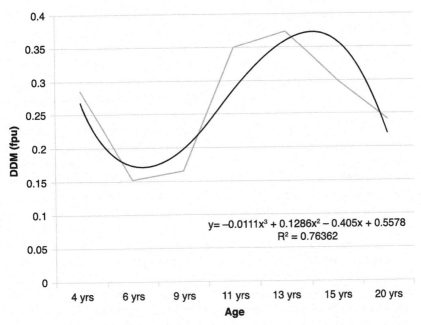

FIGURE 2.1 African Americans' vernacular feature usage across sixteen years

their relationship with others in the situation, and what others have just said. With a close friend, someone might say something like "Watcha feel like doin'?" in a conversation about going out; and with a casual acquaintance it might be "What d'ya wanna do?" In a more formal context, it might be more like "What would you like to do?" Although these are approximate renditions of how the sentences would sound, they demonstrate that pronunciation, word choice, and grammar can all change according to the circumstances of speaking.

So, in observing language patterns, it is important to keep in mind the social factors that link with differences in language forms. Although it is instructive to sample a range of styles if that is possible, the natural language patterns of a community are generally most transparent in the more casual styles. In a casual setting, people tend to use their language rules in the most natural way, avoiding overcorrection or erratic fluctuation of language items.

Examining Dialect Patterns

The most reasonable approach to investigating the features that make up a dialect is a systematic, organized study of particular language structures. As a rule, it is most effective to single out one or two features at a time for scrutiny because it is difficult to keep track of multiple structures. The levels of language outlined above are useful in deciding what type of feature to select for various kinds of inquiry. For example, grammar features might be most useful for learning about the effect of early settlers of the community, whereas vocabulary features might reveal more about the local economic ecology. It is also important to consider which social groupings and social occasions of language use are of interest. For example, it may be appropriate to examine a linguistic feature in casual, unmonitored speech for one project but to look at the same feature in formal contexts—say, in conjunction with speech disorder assessments—in another.

The first steps in studying different language items are quite simple. Although linguists have had specialized training for investigating language structures and writing precise formulas to describe them, anyone can make significant observations about language patterns by following principles of careful observation. The procedure begins with noticing an item in someone's speech (including our own). For example, in an urban school setting, we may hear some children using forms like "He home today" or "You out." We know that other speakers might say "He's home today" or "You're out" in these same contexts, and so we decide to investigate this structure further. We start listening to other children as they talk at lunch time in order to get the casual style of speech. Basically, we can listen for interesting structures anywhere that language is used in the community in an unselfconscious way as we naturally overhear conversations at the park or on a bus. If the forms that originally drew our attention are heard in the informally gathered data, it would suggest that they are not just a slip of the tongue because they occur in the speech of other community members. In other words, these observations indicate a language pattern that deserves a closer look. We start by compiling examples (e.g., writing them down on 3 x 5 cards or on a smartphone) of the natural use of language in a community or language use in a specific context, like on television or the radio. It is particularly important to record examples rather than rely on memory so that we can look back at the data to get some ideas concerning the organization of specific patterns. Ideally, we would also catalog as much social information as possible about the speaker and the discourse context of the usage; however, it may be impractical to gather this information during an exploratory study.

When we collect examples from real language use, we are likely to make two general observations. First, different people use the structure in different ways. Second, the same speaker may use the structure at some times, but not at others. These observations are basic to analyses of language variation. Investigation of language variation asks (a) what alternative forms occur in different language varieties? and (b) when and where does the form under study occur? With this in mind, we return to our examples, "He home today" and "You out." With reference to other dialects, we observe that the dialect in question does not use a verb form where Standard English uses *is* or *are*:

Vernacular English	Standard English
He home today	He's home today
You out	You're out

For this structure, our first study question is answered fairly simply: The difference between dialects lies in the presence of certain forms of the verb *be*, as opposed to their absence. (In other cases, the alternatives may not be presence or absence but different forms, as would be the case for leveling for the past tense of *be*, where the alternatives might be *was* and *were*.)

The second study question is a little more difficult because it requires examining the linguistic environment surrounding this form. The question about the context for this dialect structure is this: In what type of phrases can a speaker omit the verb *be*? As a starting point, we assume that the patterns of the language under study govern where a structure is permissible and where it is not. In this case, we are seeking a pattern for where the *be* verb can be absent and where it must be present. Turning to the collected examples, and following the scientific method, we can make hypotheses about how a pattern works that can then be checked against the data. This analytic process can be illustrated by looking at some data.

Absence of *be*

He in the Army now	He at school
They messing around	They not here
We in trouble today	She taking medicine
She not home now	Y'all messing around now
You nice today	We in school—don't mess around
We playing around now	He gonna do it—I know he is

Our first impression from listening to the speaker(s) might have been that the verb *be* can be absent in their dialect wherever it is present in Standard English. However, when we start looking at the examples more closely, we find that the pattern appears less extensive than that. The first thing we notice is that we have no examples where past-tense forms of *be* are absent; for example, we do not have examples such as "We down there yesterday." At first, we are not sure if this is because those forms are not deleted or because we just didn't hear any past-tense usages. Since we are prone to only take note of things that differ from Standard English, we decide to gather more data, listening closely for past-tense forms. Indeed, when the data are examined, *be* in the past tense is never omitted: It is always present. We also note that in our data there are no first-person singular subjects (i.e., *I*), and like past-tense *be*, when we listen again, we note that these speakers never omit *am*.

In setting up data collection tasks, it is important to consider all the possible variations of a form and collect data for each of them. In this case, both presence and absence of a feature have to be collected. Taking into account all of the different forms that *be* can take, we may initially notice that absence occurs only where *be* would take a conjugated form in Standard English (as in all of the examples listed above). That is, the examples include no cases where *be* is absent in a sentence like "He wants to be home" (i.e., no examples such as *"He wants to home") or "He should be here now" (i.e., no examples like *"He should here now"); and there are many cases where *be* is present as in nonfinite forms like *to be, should be,* and so forth. From looking at the examples, we conclude that the pattern is limited to certain constructions: two conjugated forms of *be* (i.e., *is* and *are*). That conclusion provides a working hypothesis that we will target in more data collection and analysis until we are reasonably satisfied that the pattern holds.

We could continue the investigation to find some more details of conjugated *be* absence. But the point here is simply to demonstrate the iterative data analysis process. We proceeded systematically, making a hypothesis and checking it with the data. One by one, we varied grammatical features in the linguistic context—conjugated versus bare form of the verb, tense, pronoun person, and number. The rule emerged from actual data—dialect items as used in a natural conversation—rather than from our first impression. Invariably in dialect study, questions come up that were not anticipated in the original observations. For that reason, linguists often record speech. When we have extensive recordings, we can simply go back and check certain things we had not looked at previously. In our example with *be*, we needed to go back and look for cases of past tense as well as examples with the pronoun *I* to see if any absence of *was, were,* or *am* occurred. An overview of this process is outlined in Box 2.1.

BOX 2.1: STEPS IN DESCRIBING DIALECT FEATURES

1. Identify a possible dialect feature for study.
2. Collect data.

   - Listen to casual talk in the speech community to determine that the structure is widely used.
   - Write down or record actual examples from casual talk.
   - Identify corresponding form(s) in other dialects.

3. Analyze data.

   - Develop hypotheses about the linguistic context in which the form occurs. Hunt for patterns in the data, considering linguistic forms preceding and following the feature, various forms the feature can assume, etc.
   - Check the hypotheses against more data.
   - Accept, reject, or refine hypotheses.
   - Repeat the two previous steps, looking for both differences and similarities with other dialects and testing stereotyped explanations.
   - Stop when no new information appears.

It can be difficult to observe all the grammatical contexts required to test a hypothesis sufficiently. In such cases, word games can be created to elicit the forms in question. For example, if we wanted to see what happens to *be* verbs when the subject is *I*, we might set up a simple task of changing a stimulus sentence with a non-first-person subject to a response sentence with a first-person subject. Speakers from the community can be oriented to the task with sample items unrelated to the forms of interest (e.g., "Here are some sentences that I want you to change: I will give a sentence like *He went to the store* and you say, *I went to the store, too*"). After they have learned the pattern, the respondents are given stimulus sentences with the form being studied (e.g., Stimulus: *They going to the game*; Response: *I'm going to the game, too*). Such games are not difficult to construct, and they can give access to some valuable data. However, it is important to use this kind of information only as supplemental data, because word games do not always give the same results as ordinary speech. In combination with other data, however, this direct elicitation of structures can make an important contribution to understanding particular features.

While most language practitioners may not do extensive analysis of the type described in this section, it is important to understand the procedures that linguists go through in describing a language pattern, and it may prove to be helpful when forms are uncovered that linguists have not yet described. As language changes, there are always emerging patterns that need to be described and patterns that have not yet been described by linguists. Opportunity for language exploration abounds. Local communities always show language variation. Schools themselves can be rich grounds for exploring language variation. If social groups prove difficult to survey, age-based differences may be more appropriate for community-based studies. Finally, the internet and other media offer tremendous potential for analysis. Television and movie scripts are increasingly available online—although in such scripts the language is constructed, not natural. Social media user comments and blogs offer access to (often) unstylized written language produced in the sort of social contexts that can reveal a lot about language users. Though students may need guidance in conducting such research, the language analysis tools provided in this chapter along with the techniques in the following chapters should allow students and teachers to explore dialects scientifically.

Discussion Questions

1. The chapter argues that the effects of the media on people's speech are minimal and limited to words and phrases. Are you aware of any influence the media may have had on your speech? Why do you think this happened (or didn't happen)?
2. The chapter asserts that dialect differences are part of the country's traditions and heritage. Explore that idea. Do you agree?

3. Do you believe that your own education about dialect diversity has been adequate? How do you explain it?

4. Are you aware of language change in progress? Think about regularization of irregular verbs. What variation regarding regularization have you noticed (think about the past tense of *wake up*). Think about changes in the pronoun system where *they* is being used for third-person singular (as in "If a young child goes near the pool, they could fall in" or "Everyone should bring their coat"). Which forms do you think will win out? Why?

5. The text says that "Individuals change their dialect patterns as they age and are exposed to different influences." Do you think your dialect has changed? If so, how and why?

6. How might teachers and other education practitioners use the technical descriptions of dialect features provided in this book?

7. Research into dialect differences is ongoing. Are there features you have noticed that you would like to have described precisely? Who might carry out this research?

8. Does the chapter mention dialect features that you have never heard? How can you explain that?

Links of Interest

1. Explore the Center for Applied Linguistics Collection at the Library of Congress's American English Dialect Recordings: www.loc.gov/collections/american-english-dialect-recordings-from-the-center-for-applied-linguistics/

2. Read an article about what people in the Pacific Northwest think about their dialect: www.seattlepi.com/local/article/A-Northwest-dialect-That-s-Goofy-some-say-1174476.php

3. Read blog posts from a linguist who examines the role of language in Appalachian Mountain communities: http://mountainmanlinguistics.blogspot.com/

4. Discover the regional distribution of over 100 dialect features at the Harvard Dialect Survey project: www4.uwm.edu/FLL/linguistics/dialect/maps.html

5. Examine 100 sample entries from the *Dictionary of American Regional English*: http://dare.wisc.edu/words/100-entries

6. Explore heatmaps of numerous American English dialect features: www4.ncsu.edu/~jakatz2/project-dialect.html

Further Reading

Hazen, K. (2015). *An introduction to language*. Malden, MA: John Wiley & Sons.
This introductory tour of language and language variation touches on methodologies that students and teachers can employ in their own language studies. The volume also contains many visual resources and activities.

Perry, T. & Delpit, L. (Eds.). (1998). *The real Ebonics debate: Power, language, and the education of African American children*. Boston, MA: Beacon Press.
This collection contains academic papers, interviews, and personal essays stemming from the Oakland Ebonics controversy. The perspectives combine to offer a nuanced understanding of issues of race, language, and education in the United States.

Wolfram, W., & Ward, B. (Eds.). (2006). *American voices: How dialects differ from coast to coast*. Malden, MA: Blackwell.
This collection presents short, readable essays by well-known linguists about both familiar and little-known dialects thriving in North America and beyond. The sections are divided into the South, the North, the Midwest, the West, Islands, and Sociocultural Dialects. It is the most complete discussion of particular dialects currently available.

Wolfram, W., & Schilling, N. (2016). *American English: Dialects and variation* (3rd ed.). Malden, MA: John Wiley & Sons.
This description surveys the social and linguistic factors that account for dialects and the functions that dialects serve. It introduces students and a general audience to the principles underlying language variation. The discussion attempts to limit technical terminology but provides an extensive glossary and appendix of dialect structures to assist readers.

References

Adger, C. T., & Schilling-Estes, N. (2003). *African American English: Structure and clinical implications*. Rockville, MD: American Speech-Language-Hearing Association.
Applebee, A. N. (1989). *The teaching of literature in programs with reputations for excellence in English*. Albany, NY: University of New York-Albany Center for the Learning and Teaching of Literature, Report 1.1. Retrieved from http://files.eric.ed.gov/fulltext/ED315753.pdf
Bell, A. (2001). Back in style: Reworking audience design. In P. Eckert & J. Rickford (Eds.), *Style and sociolinguistic variation* (pp. 139–169). Cambridge, UK: Cambridge University Press.
Blake, R., & Cutler, C. (2003). AAE and variation in teachers' attitudes: A question of school philosophy? *Linguistics and Education, 14*(2), 163–194.
Bowie, D., & Morkel, W. (2006). Desert dialect (Utah). In W. Wolfram & B. Ward (Eds.), *American voices: How dialects differ from coast to coast* (pp. 144–148). Malden, MA: Blackwell.
Brown, D. W. (2009). *In other words: Lessons on grammar, code-switching, and academic writing*. Portsmouth, NH: Heinemann.
Chambers, J. (1998). TV makes people sound the same. In L. Bauer & P. Trudgill (Eds.), *Language myths* (pp. 123–131). New York, NY: Penguin.
Common Core State Standards (CCSS). (2010). *Common Core State Standards for English language arts & literacy in history/social studies, science, and technical subjects*. Washington, DC: National Governors Association Center for Best Practices & Council of Chief State School Officers. Available online at: www.corestandards.org/
Conference on College Composition and Communication (CCCC)/National Council of Teachers of English (NCTE). (1974). *Resolution on students' right to their own language*. www.ncte.org/positions/statements/righttoownlanguage
Conn, J. (2006). Dialects in the mist (Portland, OR). In W. Wolfram & B. Ward (Eds.), *American voices: How dialects differ from coast to coast* (pp. 149–155). Malden, MA: Blackwell.
Cross, J. B., DeVaney, T., & Jones, G. (2001). Pre-service teacher attitudes toward differing dialects. *Linguistics and Education, 12*(2), 211–227.
Curzan, A. (2014). *Fixing English: Prescriptivism and language history*. Cambridge, UK: Cambridge University Press.
Dean, D. (2008). *Bringing grammar to life*. Newark, DE: International Reading Association.
Delpit, L. D. (1988). The silenced dialogue: Power and pedagogy in educating other people's children. *Harvard Educational Review, 58*(3), 280–299.
Dyson, A. H., & Smitherman, G. (2009). The right (write) start: African American language and the discourse of sounding right. *The Teachers College Record, 111*(4), 973–998.
Eckert, P., & Mendoza-Denton, N. (2006). Getting real in the Golden State (California). In W. Wolfram & B. Ward (Eds.), *American voices: How dialects differ from coast to coast* (pp. 139–143). Malden, MA: Blackwell.

Feagin, C. (1990). The dynamics of a sound change in Southern States English: From R-less to R-ful in three generations. In J. A. Edmondson, C. Feagin, & P. Mülhäusler (Eds.), *Development and diversity: Linguistic variation across time and space* (pp. 129–146). Dallas, TX: Summer Institute of Linguistics.

Fridland, V., Kendall, T., Evans, B. E., & Wassink, A. B. (Eds.). (2016). *Speech in the western states, Vol. 1: The coastal states.* Durham, NC: Duke University Press.

Godley, A. J., Carpenter, B. D., & Werner, C. A. (2007). "I'll speak in proper slang": Language ideologies in a daily editing activity. *Reading Research Quarterly, 42*(1), 100–131.

Godley, A. J., Sweetland, J., Wheeler, R. S., Minnici, A., & Carpenter, B. D. (2006). Preparing teachers for dialectally diverse classrooms. *Educational Researcher, 35*(8), 30–37.

Goldring, R., Gray, L., & Bitterman, A. (2013). Characteristics of public and private elementary and secondary school teachers in the United States: Results from the 2011–12 schools and staffing survey. First look. Washington, DC: National Center for Education Statistics. Available online at: http://nces.ed.gov/pubs2013/2013314.pdf

Hymes, D. (1974). *Foundations in sociolinguistics: An ethnographic approach.* Philadelphia, PA: University of Pennsylvania Press.

Labov, W., Ash, S., & Boberg, C. (2006). *Atlas of North American English: Phonology and phonetics.* Berlin, Germany: Mouton de Gruyter.

Millward, C. M. (2012). *A Biography of the English language* (3rd ed.). Boston, MA: Wadsworth.

Prescott, S. (Ed.). (1991). *The American Indian: Yesterday, today, and tomorrow. A handbook for educators.* Sacramento, CA: California State Department of Education.

Stuart-Smith, J. (2007). The influence of the media. In C. Llamas, L. Mullany, & P. Stockwell (Eds.), *The Routledge companion to sociolinguistics* (pp. 140–148). London, UK: Routledge.

Sweetland, J. (2006). *Teaching writing in the African American classroom: A sociolinguistic approach.* Unpublished doctoral dissertation, Stanford University.

Tannen, D. (2005). *Conversational style: Analyzing talk among friends.* Oxford, UK: Oxford University Press.

Van Hofwegen, J. (2015). The development of African American English through childhood and adolescence. In S. Lanehart (Ed.), *Oxford handbook of African American English* (pp. 454–474). Oxford, UK: Oxford University Press.

Van Hofwegen, J., & Wolfram, W. (forthcoming). On the utility of composite indices in longitudinal language study. In S. E. Wagner & I. Buchstaller (Eds.), *Using panel data in the sociolinguistic study of variation and change.* London, UK: Routledge.

Wagner, S. E. (2012). Age grading in sociolinguistic theory. *Language and Linguistics Compass 6*(6), 371–382.

Weaver, C. (1996). *Teaching grammar in context.* Portsmouth, NH: Heinemann.

Weldon, T. (2006). Gullah Gullah islands (Sea Island, SC, GA). In W. Wolfram & B. Ward (Eds.), *American voices: How dialects differ from coast to coast* (pp. 178–182). Malden, MA: Blackwell.

Wolfram, W. (2006). Dialects in danger (Outer Banks, NC). In W. Wolfram & B. Ward (Eds.), *American voices: How dialects differ from coast to coast* (pp. 189–195). Malden, MA: Blackwell.

Wolfram, W., & Adger, C. T. (1993). *Handbook on dialects and speech and language assessment.* Washington, DC: Center for Applied Linguistics.

Wolfram, W., & Schilling, N. (2016). *American English: Dialects and variation* (3rd ed.). Malden MA: John Wiley & Sons.

Wolfram, W., & Ward, B. (Eds.). (2006). *American voices: How dialects differ from coast to coast.* Malden, MA: Blackwell.

Variation in Dialect Systems

Scenario

Examine the words in each line below. For each line, circle any words that are pronounced identically.

1. here, hear, hair
2. effect, affect
3. pin, pen, pan
4. for, four, fore
5. caught, cot
6. steel, still
7. pool, pull, pole
8. hock, hawk
9. sale, sell
10. Mary, marry, merry, Murray
11. herd, heard
12. chair, cheer
13. celery, salary
14. hoarse, horse
15. there, their, they're

What do you make of the words that are spelled differently but that you pronounce the same? Do you think of them simply as homophones that you have learned to distinguish in writing? Is it at all surprising to learn that which words you circle depends in part on your age and the dialect you speak? For example, if you thought *sale* and *sell* sounded the same, you are likely from the South. If you circled *chair* and *cheer*, you are most likely from New York City. If you did not circle *hoarse* and *horse*, you are probably from the Boston area or you are an older Southerner. If you did not circle *Mary, marry,* and *merry* as being pronounced the same, you are likely from certain areas in the Northeastern United States or you learned English outside of the United States.

Many of these merged vowel pronunciations go unnoticed in the speech of Americans. Because people seldom comment on them, people with the merged pronunciations may live their whole lives without realizing that there are other people out there who make distinctions in those words. For example, Jeffrey Reaser, one of the authors of this book, discovered his *caught/cot* merger at the age of 20, when in his first linguistics class he was frustrated by a homework assignment that assumed students pronounced the words differently. Subtle language variations can be quite revealing of a speaker's background. While many dialect features are obvious cues to speakers' backgrounds, such as the use of uninflected *be* ("Sometimes my ears be itching") or a unique dialect word (*bunko steerer* for *swindler*), in other cases, identifying the dialect to which a feature belongs and interpreting differences can be challenging. This chapter offers some guidance in the identification and interpretation of both subtle and obvious dialect features.

The previous chapter outlined the processes linguists use to investigate language differences, which can be followed by non-linguists. It also highlighted the social and internal linguistic pressures that shape language variation and change. This chapter summarizes some of the findings about variation in dialects of English in the United States. This chapter should not be seen as a comprehensive description; instead it provides an overview of the kinds of language differences that characterize dialects and the linguistic processes involved. It identifies many of the features teachers are likely to encounter and provides information about how and why such features exist and what they reveal about a dialect or an individual. Descriptions of these features and information about what dialect they are typically associated with are found in the Appendix to this book. The chapter is organized according to the levels of language, as described in the previous chapter.

Vocabulary Differences

Differences in vocabulary are some of the most obvious features of dialects. To understand the basis for vocabulary differences, certain questions can be useful. For example, is the word used by a whole community or only by a subgroup within the community? Does the word reveal anything about the group's identity or stance with respect to the broader community? Does the word reveal something about the economic ecology or social situation of the area? The topography? The values of the community? Is the word used differently—or not at all—by different generations? Does the word seem to come from other words that exist independently in English? If so, is it a compounding of two words (e.g., *chick-flick*) or a blending of parts from two words, as in the Standard English word *brunch*, from *breakfast* and *lunch*, or the nonmainstream dialect word *touron*, a blend of *tourist* and *moron*? Is the word being used as a different part of speech than is typical (e.g., *tree* as a verb, as in "The dogs treed the cat")? Is the word a shortened version of a Standard English word (e.g., *za* for *pizza*)? Linguists give names to each of these processes; some of the more common ones are listed in Box 3.1. If there is no explanation for the word based on the local community or other words in Standard English, it may be a preservation of an older form. For example, the use of *bald* to refer to a treeless area on a mountain is an older form that is becoming increasingly rare. Likewise, the term *mommuck*, used by Shakespeare to mean "to tear," is still preserved in some isolated dialects where it can mean "to harass" or "to put in disarray." When teachers or students uncover unfamiliar words, resources such as the *Oxford English Dictionary, the Medieval English Dictionary*, or the *Dictionary of American Regional English* may help explain the term's origin, development, and distribution. New word innovations in the language can often be described by one of the processes outlined in Box 3.1.

BOX 3.1: COMMON WORD FORMATION PROCESSES

Process	Description	Examples
Acronym/ Alphabetism	New word is created by combining initial sounds or letters of other words	*Sonar* (sound navigation and ranging); *PC* (personal computer; political correctness)
Blending	Parts of two words or part of one and all of another word are combined to form a new word (cf. *compounding*)	*Infomercial* (information + commercial); *lupper* (lunch + supper); *manny* (man + nanny)
Borrowing	Word is borrowed from another language (may be altered slightly)	*Okra* (Igbo); *keg* (Old Norse); *depot* (French); *canyon* (Spanish); *admiral* (Arabic)
Clipping	One or more syllables is removed from a word to form a new word with identical meaning	*Za* (pizza); *taxi* or *cab* (taxicab); *frat* (fraternity); *fridge* (refrigerator)
Coining	Entirely new, previously nonexistent word is invented. Often in the process of creating commercial products (cf. *proper names*)	(at least initially) *Lolita*; *Catch-22*; *Aspirin*; *Kleenex*; *Xerox*; *Frisbee*; *YouTube*; *Google*

Process	Description	Examples
Compounding	Two whole words are combined (cf. *blending*).	*Chick-flick*; *go-to*; *to-do*; *upscale*
Conversion	Existing word is used as a new part of speech without changing its form (cf. *derivation*)	*To ghost*; *to adult*; *to tree* (a cat); (take a) *walk* (as a noun)
Proper names	A brand name, personal name, or other proper noun is generalized to refer to a class of things as opposed to a specific thing (cf. *coining*)	*Aspirin*; *trampoline*; *butterscotch*; *zipper*; *yo-yo*; *google* (to mean any internet search); *uber* (to mean any ridesharing service)

The word formation processes at work in a given dialect are no different from those affecting the inventory of words in English over time. But dialects do develop their own distinctive vocabularies through the processes described in Box 3.1. Some vocabulary distinctiveness occurs when dialects use existing terms with new connotations or denotations, just as happens with languages. Some of these vocabulary changes may be due to *figurative extension* (also called *metaphorical extension*) when a new meaning is assigned due to a feature that is shared between the original and the new referent. For example, *ice* can be used to refer to *diamonds* since they share the property of clearness. The use of the term *sub* or *torpedo* to describe a long sandwich is an example of how figurative extensions can lead to regional dialect variation. Many such vocabulary innovations are highly localized, as in the use of the term *camel-back* to describe humps on the beaches throughout the Outer Banks of North Carolina.

Existing vocabulary items can take on narrower or broader reference in a dialect or a language. Historical examples nicely illustrate these processes. The word *dog* originally referred to a specific breed, but has since broadened in its usage. The converse is true of the term *hound*, which has narrowed over time. Narrowings are common in the history of English, including the following: *meat* (any food), *corn* (any grain), *apple* (any fruit), etc. Over time, words generally take on more specific meanings.

Linguists also describe two shifts in connotation. Occasionally words become associated with more elevated or baser connotations. For example, the gendered pairs *governor* and *governess* and *mister* and *mistress* once indexed the same social level for the male and female referent. Over time, the connotation of the female term has lowered, so that *governess* is now used to refer to someone who provides childcare as opposed to someone from a politically dominant class. *Mistress* has taken on more negative connotations. The opposite process can also occur, as when Michael Jackson elevated the connotation of the term *bad*. All of these semantic shifts are possible in dialects. Investigating the vocabulary of a dialect means investigating not only the unique words that are used, but also the common words that are used in unique ways. Students' familiarity with dialect vocabulary, especially generational slang, makes it perhaps the level of language most accessible to their inquiry and analysis. Students' understanding of the subtle nuances of word usage can lead to important discussions about language variation and change, as well as informing traditional educational topics like word choice, diction, and style.

Pronunciation Differences

Contrasting pronunciation patterns also differentiate dialects. Typically, vowel pronunciation differences distinguish regional dialects, whereas consonant pronunciation differences tend to distinguish the social dialects. Dialect differences in pronunciation are widely recognized, but they are not always viewed in terms of pronunciation rules—regular patterns that apply to similar items. Instead, people may use impressionistic labels such as *drawl*, *twang*, or *accent*, or descriptors such as *nasal* and *flat* in referring to regional pronunciation patterns. Researchers have found that the term *nasal* is applied by non-linguists equally to voices that are highly nasal and to voices that are highly de-nasalized (Niedzielski & Preston, 2000), suggesting that such descriptions are seldom deployed in linguistically accurate and precise ways. In this section, we will briefly mention some groups of pronunciation differences across dialects, all of which are described more precisely in the Appendix.

To understand a dialect difference involving pronunciation, it is useful to ask two questions: 1. Is the difference a matter of something missing, added, or changed? 2. Is the difference related to vowels, consonants, or both? We organize this section according to the different combinations of answers to these two questions. We also recognize that some pronunciation differences may arise due to other factors, such as syllable stress.

Pronunciation Differences in Which Consonants are Added

Sometimes there appears to be something extra in a dialect pronunciation when compared to a standard variety pronunciation. Some vernacular dialects have preserved older pronunciation patterns where Standard English has subsequently lost sounds. In such cases, it might sound like dialects are adding in a nonstandard sound. For example, the pronoun it used to be *hit*, and in isolated regions of Appalachia and islands along the Southeastern United States, *initial h-retention* can still be heard (along with *hain't,* which was also previously standard) (Montgomery & Hall, 2004).

In other cases, a consonant intrudes where there was not one previously. Historically, consonant intrusions have changed a host of words, including turning *brammel* into *bramble, thunner* into *thunder,* and *thimmle* into *thimble* (Millward, 2012). One of the most common consonant intrusions in American English is *intrusive t,* which occurs in a small set of words ending in an *s* or *f* sound, as in *oncet, twicet, clifft,* and *acrosst.* See the Appendix for more information about other instances of *intrusive t.*

Another common consonant addition is *intrusive r,* which can appear in words like *wash/warsh.* This pronunciation is common in the Midwestern United States and is generally limited to specific words. Other dialects—specifically, those that have *r* dropping—may insert *r* into a variety of words based on an extension of a linguistic pattern. *R*-dropping dialects drop the *r* when it comes after a vowel but not before another vowel. Thus, they would drop the *r* in *ca'by the garage* but not in **ca' in the garage.* So, when speakers of this dialect encounter a situation where a word that ends with a vowel is followed by a word that starts with a vowel, they may insert an *r* sound between the words, as in "vanillar ice cream" or "That's the idear of it." (This pattern is explained in more detail in the Appendix.)

Pronunciation Differences in Which Vowels are Added

Vowels can also be added to words, resulting in an additional syllable. Some English language learners make heavy use of this feature to break up strings of consonants, as in *es-tar* for *star.* In doing so, they are adhering to the underlying patterns of their native languages that do not use two consonants together. The added vowel breaks the two consonants into separate syllables. An unstressed vowel can sometimes also occur in somewhat idiosyncratic ways, as in the common pronunciation of *athlete* as "a-thuh-lete."

Pronunciation Differences in Which Consonants are Lost

Losses of consonants and vowels are more common than intrusions, and are particularly socially meaningful. The *r-dropping* mentioned above, in which an *r* sound is dropped after a vowel but not if another vowel follows it, is stereotypical of Boston, but it occurs throughout parts of the Northeast including New York City, where it is now associated with the speech of those of lower socioeconomic classes. Until about World War II, *r*-lessness was associated with upper class speech in the Northeast, and it can be heard in the recorded speech of many prominent Americans of that time, such as Franklin Delano Roosevelt (Labov, 2010). Southern vernaculars have also been historically *r*-less, but fewer and fewer Southern speakers have maintained this feature.

You can listen to a Northern and Southern *r*-less speaker on this book's companion website. Like *r*, *l* may sometimes be reduced or lost in words like *yolk, almond, wolf,* and *palm*. This pattern is common in New England and in the South.

A second environment where consonant losses are common is in certain types of sequences or clusters of consonants at the end of words. Specifically, these clusters of consonants must end with a *t, d, p, b, g,* or *k* sound, as in "fas' break," and the second consonant of the cluster may be omitted (the *-t* in *fast*). Consonant clusters are not common in the world's languages, suggesting they are relatively unnatural linguistic features, and as such, are subject to much variation. While all speakers have *consonant cluster reduction* (CCR) occasionally in their speech, some dialects have it more extensively or have it patterned in different ways. For example, while all speakers of English are likely to have CCR when the cluster is followed by another consonant, as in *mist* ("mis' my plants"), African American English speakers are more likely than others to also have it before vowels ("mis' on the water") (Wolfram, 1986). CCR is one of the most important features for teachers and speech pathologists to be aware of because this common pronunciation feature can manifest in ways that make it appear as though a speaker or writer lacks grammatical understanding. The pronunciations of *mist* and *missed* are identical, despite the spelling difference. After CCR, *missed* sounds like the past tense has been left off ("miss' the bus" or "miss' opportunity"). In a tremendous number of regular verbs, the *-ed* that signals past tense in writing is pronounced with a single consonant sound, either a *t* sound or a *d* sound, depending on the sound that precedes it: *guessed, fished, wrecked, lapped,* and *puffed* all end with a *t* sound while *raised, garaged, charged, smoothed, loved, trained, framed,* and *grilled* all end with a *d* sound. (Interestingly, this CCR process explains why today we see spelling and pronunciation variation of *ice(d) tea*. It also explains how the term *skim milk* replaced *skimmed milk*.) Many English language learners and speakers of Englishes resulting from historical language contact (e.g., Latino English, Vietnamese English, Hawaiian English) manifest higher rates of CCR than speakers of other dialects (Wolfram, 1986). It is not uncommon for speakers of these dialects to utter phrases such as "Yesterday, he pass' me a Coke and I drank it," where the irregular verb (*drank*) is conjugated in a standard way for the past tense and the regular verb (*passed*) appears to lack the standard conjugation. Such sentences provide evidence that the speaker is using a pronunciation pattern rather than a grammatical pattern.

W sounds are also subject to being deleted when they occur at the start of words. This process underlies the contractions of *was, would,* and *will,* in sentences like "She's here last week," "He'd be there if he could," and "They'll be gone later." While all dialects use the latter two forms to some extent, the contraction of *was,* as in the first sentence, is common mostly in Southern vernaculars. *Initial w-reduction* gives rise to another Southern form, the use of *young'uns,* which is derived from *young ones* (in this example it is critical to note that despite its spelling, *ones* starts with a *w* sound).

Pronunciation Differences in Which Vowels are Lost

There are times when a vowel or a whole syllable is absent from a word. Any unstressed vowel or syllable is apt to be deleted sometimes, resulting in pronunciations such as *'cause, 'round, 'member, kar-mel,* and *fam-ly.* A class of words that end with "ire" or "our" pronunciations can also undergo the loss of a syllable alongside a change in vowel quality. In areas with a heavy Scots–Irish influence, including the Appalachian Mountains, two-syllable words like *fire, briar,* and *flour/flower* are pronounced as a single syllable, like *far, brar,* and *fla'r.* This feature is different than the word formation process *clipping* described in Box 3.1. While this specific type of vowel deletion happens only with unstressed syllables (it is pronunciation, not spelling, that signals which words are likely to undergo this process), clipping can result in stressed syllables or multiple syllables being dropped, as in *phone* from *telephone.*

Pronunciation Differences in Which Consonants are Changed

Most often, instead of sounds being added or deleted, they undergo some sort of change. One of the most common consonant changes, often erroneously called *g*-dropping, might at first appear to be a consonant deletion. Words that end in *-ing* are often said as though they end in *-in'.* Although the *-g* appears in spelling, it is not pronounced as a *g* sound (no one says "running-ga"). When it appears at the end of a word, the spelling convention *-ng* is used for a single nasal sound that is produced toward the back of the mouth (technically the *velum*). This sound can be experienced by focusing on the tongue as it pronounces pairs of words like *kin* and *king,* or *sin* and *sing.* In each case, there is no *g* sound; the only difference is that in the first words of the pairs, the nasal sound is made directly behind the teeth (at the alveolar ridge), while the nasal sound for the second word in each pair is produced further back. So, when dialects pronounce *running* as "runnin'," they are not phonetically dropping a consonant; they are shifting where in the mouth the consonant is produced, which is why linguists prefer to call this feature *nasal fronting* rather than *g-dropping.*

Another common consonant shift involves the various pronunciations of sounds that are typically spelled with the letters "th." In English, there are actually two different sounds that are spelled this way; the contrast can be heard in the word pairs *thy* and *thigh* or *bathe* and *bath.* In both sets of words, the first *th* sound is voiced while the second is unvoiced. This difference is the same as between *v* (voiced) and *f* (voiceless). And despite being spelled with two letters, the *th* sounds are each single sounds and not a combination of two sounds as the spelling might suggest. Linguists and other language practitioners use the symbols /ð/ and /θ/ to differentiate between the sounds represented by the "th" in *bathe* and *bath,* respectively. These sounds are not found in many other languages, suggesting they are not nearly as natural as other English consonant sounds. As noted in the previous chapter, less natural sounds are more likely to show dialect variations. Like consonant cluster reduction, these variations are most prominent in dialects that have grown out of language contact situations. Although the pronunciations of *these, them,* and *those* as "dese," "dem," and "dose" are stereotypical for several vernacular dialects, speakers may substitute a sound for *th* in other linguistic contexts, as in *da* for *the* or *tree* for *three.* Middle-class groups may use the *d* for *th* pronunciation to some extent in casual speech, such as in "Who's der?" for "Who's there?", whereas working-class groups simply use it more often.

There is a tremendous number of other consonant shifts in English dialects. Following is a small sample of the types of variation that exist in the United States. In some African American English dialects, word initial *str-* sequences may be pronounced as *skr-*, as in "skreet" (*street*). Sometimes when words contain two adjacent sounds that are very similar, one sound will change to make the pronunciation more efficient. For example, some rural Southern speakers will say "chimbly" for *chimney*, since the *m* and *n* sounds are so similar. Finally, sometimes the order of consonants will reverse in a word. Although the most common example of this process, "*aks*" for *ask*, is highly stigmatized, this process has produced the modern pronunciations and spellings of words like *bird* (formerly *brid*) and *wasp* (formerly *waps*) (Millward, 2012). Other examples in American English dialects include the pronunciations "per-fess-or" for *pro-fess-or* and "per-tect" for *pro-tect.*

Pronunciation Differences in Which Vowels are Changed

Eclipsing all other pronunciation differences in American English in frequency of occurrence are vowel production differences. Vowel differences are among the most diagnostic features of regional dialects but not as prominent in marking stigmatized vernacular speech. Three types of variation in the vowel system are examined below: vowel changes, vowel mergers, and vowel shifts.

Although it is not a technical term, we use *vowel changes* to describe patterned changes that are limited to single vowels. For this discussion, we use the keyword lexical set of Wells (1982) to denote which vowel is being changed in the dialect. The lexical set of vowel classes can be found following the table of contents in the front of this volume. This convention is useful because it allows us to discuss vowel variation without using more specialized notation systems like the International Phonetic Alphabet. The keyword system works as follows. For each vowel class, an exemplar word containing that vowel is selected. Following the convention established by Wells (1982), we note these keywords in SMALL CAPS.

In rural Southern varieties, word-final unstressed COMMA vowels (in phonetic terminology, the "schwa," the last sound in the word *comma*) are pronounced higher in the mouth, so *soda, extra,* and *Florida* sound like "sodi," "extry," and "Floridi." Another Southern vowel change—more prominent in the Appalachian Mountain region—involves words that end with an unstressed GOAT vowel, like *yellow* and *mosquito*, in which the final sound gets pronounced as "er," as in "yeller" and "mosquiter" (or, combining with a vowel absence, "'skeeter"). Because this change only occurs where the final GOAT vowel is unstressed, words like *though* and *bestow* do not participate in the variation. Perhaps the most important and stereotyped vowel change of the U.S. South involves the PRICE vowel. In most dialects, the tongue glides upward in the mouth throughout the duration of the vowel. In the U.S. South, the tongue stays relatively stationary toward the bottom of the mouth, changing what is typically a diphthong (a combination of two vowels) into a single vowel sound or monophthong. Throughout the South, words like *time* are pronounced as "tahm." Some Southern varieties lose the glide before both voiced (e.g., *tide*) and voiceless (e.g., *tight*) consonants while others have a glide before voiceless consonants (Thomas, 2001). Voiced consonants can be distinguished from voiceless consonants by resting the hand lightly on the throat while making a sound. The vibrations felt during a *z* sound or *b* sound indicate voicing, while the lack of vibration felt during an *s* sound or a *p* sound indicates a lack of voicing.

The PRICE vowel has other regional variations. In the Tidewater area of Virginia and other Eastern communities, the vowel is raised slightly so that it starts more toward the middle of the mouth than the bottom. This difference can be difficult to perceive, but a word like *price* might sound more like "prayce." Because this pronunciation is strongly associated with Canadian English, it is often called *Canadian Raising,* but there are regions in Tidewater Virginia, for example, where this trait occurs quite independently. In these dialects, the MOUTH vowel is also similarly raised, though not typically as far as is reflected in the stereotypical "oot and aboot" rendition. Listen to these pronunciations in the links at the end of this chapter. Finally, on the Outer Banks of North Carolina, the PRICE vowel is raised and backed, so that it sounds more like the typical American pronunciation of the CHOICE vowel. This distinctive pronunciation is what has led to residents being referred to as *Hoi Toiders*, from the local pronunciation of *high tide* as something more like "hoi toid." And while these speakers are often singled out for their unique dialect, this particular pronunciation used to be widespread in the Chesapeake Bay region and in New York City, where it can still occasionally be heard (Thomas, 2001). Often co-occurring with this pronunciation, the other central diphthong, the MOUTH vowel, is pronounced with a glide that goes forward, more like most Americans would say the PRICE vowel. Thus, a word like *brown* sounds more like "brine" or "brain."

Just as Southerners pronounce the PRICE vowel as a monophthong (as in "tahm" for *time*), Pittsburghers pronounce the MOUTH vowel without tongue movement, giving rise to the locally significant pronunciation of *downtown* as "dahntahn" (Eberhardt, 2009). The same monophthongization process also gives Minnesotans (and those in surrounding states) their distinctive pronunciation of the GOAT vowel (Allen, 1976).

Another vowel change involves the TRAP vowel, which can be raised (pronounced with the tongue higher in the mouth) in certain cases in some dialects. Most white varieties of English raise the vowel when it is followed by a nasal sound, as in *pan*, which typically is pronounced higher in the mouth than *pat* (Thomas, 2001). However, some dialects in the Northeastern and Midwestern United States raise all instances of this vowel, such that *bag* sounds more like "beg."

Pronunciation Differences in Which Vowels are Merged

As was seen in the opening scenario to this chapter, all dialects are subject to vowel mergers, which occur when one vowel encroaches on the space in the mouth where another vowel is pronounced. Often these mergers go completely unnoticed by those who participate in them. For example, the vast majority of Americans outside of a few pockets of the South and New England merge the vowel in word pairs like *hoarse/horse* and *four/for* so that the words sound the same. Another common merger involves the three-vowel merger (or various configurations where two of the three sound the same) of the words *Mary, merry,* and *marry*, which is now found in most areas outside the Northeast (Labov, Ash, & Boberg, 2006). Both of these examples of vowel merger occur only before the *r* sound, and for good reason. Because the properties of the *r* sound are similar to those of vowels, this sound, as well as the *l* sound and nasal sounds, affects vowels more than other consonants do. This process is evident in words like *pull, pole,* and *pool.* In the South, as well as throughout the Appalachian region (including Pittsburgh), the vowels in *still* and *steal* can be merged, which explains why Pittsburgh locals call their beloved football team "the Stillers" (Thomas, 2001). Another merger typical of the South is the loss of the distinction between words like *fail* and *fill.* In these areas, it is not uncommon to see ads that read, "For sell. . .," which reflects not a traditional malapropism but instead the influence of the dialect's vowel system where *sale* and *sell* can sound the same.

Perhaps the most commented upon merger in English in the United States is the so-called *pin/pen* merger that is common throughout the South and in other restricted areas, even parts of California (Thomas, 2001). Historical data reveal that the merger spread rapidly after the Civil War so that by the mid-twentieth century, 90% of Southern speakers had it (see McDavid & O'Cain, 1980; Pederson, McDaniel, & Adams, 1986–1993). (Listen to a Southerner with this merger on the companion website.) This merger is found in almost the same regional distribution as the ungliding of the PRICE vowel discussed just above, in which *time* is pronounced "tahm" (and, although unrelated, the areas where kudzu can grow). Although the merger involves the KIT and DRESS vowels, Southerners would differentiate between these vowels in words like *bit/bet, pig/peg,* and *pick/peck* but not in pairs like *tin/ten, kin/Ken,* and *sinned/ send* (listen to a Southerner pronounce these pairs on the companion website). Examining the data reveals that the merger only takes place before nasal consonants. Given the limited environment and types of words in which the merger can operate, it rarely leads to communicative difficulty, but most Southerners now instinctively ask for an "ink pen" or "straight pin" instead of risking being misunderstood. Yet as a feature of Southern English, it is highly stigmatized and many Southerners are ashamed to admit it is part of their speech patterns. Furthermore, some Southerners actually attempt to change their speech pattern to eradicate the merger.

Contrasting with the stigma of the Southern *pin/pen* merger is a merger that spans from Pennsylvania west to the Mississippi River, at which point it spreads out through vast swaths of the West. In this merger, the vowels in the LOT and THOUGHT classes are merged in all environments, leading word pairs like *cot/caught, bot/bought, don/dawn* to be pronounced the same. How is it that this merger, which covers an area of comparable size to the Southern *pin/pen* merger, goes unnoticed by its speakers, whereas Southerners are keenly aware of their merger? It has to do with social marking and regionalism, since the South as a dialect area is more heavily stigmatized than the Midwest and West. This contrast in the evaluation of these two mergers is revealing. Clearly, judgments about the goodness of language are not based on the language itself or the extent to which a feature actually causes communicative difficulty; instead, the judgment reflects a social assessment about the value of the particular group that uses the feature. Language is merely a target for the stereotypes and prejudices we all carry.

Pronunciation Differences in Which Vowel Systems are Shifted

The Northern Cities Vowel Shift is a still-progressing change that has spread among the cities throughout the Great Lakes region, reaching now as far west as Minneapolis, MN. The shift actually involves a chain of shifts: As one vowel moves and encroaches on another (in terms of where the vowels are formed in the mouth), the vowels may merge or the second vowel may move out of the way, often near another vowel, continuing the chain reaction (Labov, 1994). In this case, the THOUGHT vowel moves toward the LOT vowel, which then moves forward to the TRAP spot, which raises into the area where DRESS is located. DRESS moves backward in the mouth along with KIT and STRUT. Thus, *caught* sounds more like *cot,* which then sounds more like *cat.* In the front of the mouth, *mad* sounds more like *med*, which in turn sounds more like *mud*. The vowels that move in this shift are diagrammed in Figure 3.1. The left side of this diagram is the front of the mouth and the right side is the back. All of these shifts seem like they could cause tremendous communicative difficulty, and in fact, identifying words in isolation can be quite difficult for those who do not speak the dialect. For example, in a series of experiments conducted by William Labov (2010), the vast majority of people heard a word like *block* as "black" when they were exposed to the word in isolation. However, when participants heard the word in context (e.g., "living on one block"), they all interpreted it correctly. It is important to recognize that communication involves using many cues, and so these pronunciation variations, while dramatic, rarely cause much difficulty in actual conversation.

The Southern Vowel Shift distinguishes a major American regional dialect (Labov, 1991). Unlike the Northern Cities Shift, this vowel shift is becoming less common, although it can still be heard in rural areas of the South and prominently in a few urban areas such as Memphis, TN (Fridland, 2001). Historically this shift was found alongside the PRICE ungliding and *pin/pen* merger described above. In this shift, the front lax (KIT and DRESS) and tense (FLEECE and FACE) vowels trade places, giving pronunciations like *feesh* for *fish* and *bait* for *bet*. Meanwhile, the back vowels in the GOOSE and GOAT classes move forward (Thomas, 2001). The vowels affected in this shift are diagrammed in Figure 3.2. The TRAP and LOT vowels are included to aid comparisons to the Northern Cities Shift.

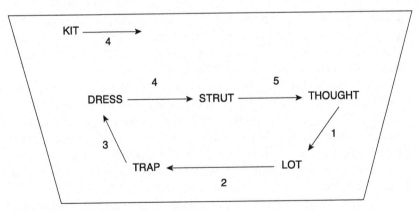

FIGURE 3.1 Northern Cities Vowel Shift

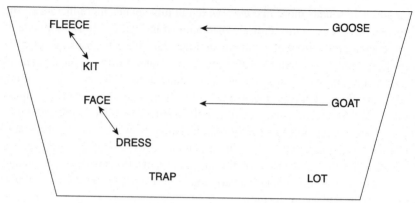

Figure 3.2 Southern Vowel Shift

Beyond Consonants and Vowels in Pronunciation

In addition to contrasting consonant and vowel patterns, there are other prominent pronunciation differences among dialects. Popular discussions of social and ethnic differences in English dialects may include impressions of characteristics such as voice quality (for example, voice raspiness), high and low pitch ranges, nasality, and general resonance. To a large extent, these qualities are idiosyncratic; however, some features such as voice raspiness may also be molded by community norms. For example, a stylized use of raspiness among teenaged and young adult African American males has been observed. Recently, a voice quality called *vocal fry* or *creakiness* associated with women's speech has been discussed in academics and the media (Khazan, 2014; Yuasa, 2010) with quite different interpretations. While linguists simply describe it and correlate its use with social groups and activities, the media has tended to interpret it in terms of social norms of appropriateness.

Several studies have suggested that the range between high and low pitch used by African American speakers when compared to white speakers (e.g., Loman, 1975; Tarone, 1973; Thomas, 2007) is a function of culturally acquired language differences. Studies also suggest that women in American society typically have a greater pitch range than men do (Ochs, 1992). Pitch distribution over a sentence is what is commonly referred to in popular parlance as *inflection*; the technical term used by linguists is *intonation*.

The rhythm or beats of syllables in a sentence can vary too. English typically gives extra prominence to the stressed words in a phrase and tends to run together the other syllables. So, in the phrase "He 'went to the 'store," *went* and *store* usually get greater prominence than the other parts of the sentence (the marks preceding *went* and *store* indicate heavier stress). Other languages, including Cantonese, Cherokee, Italian, Spanish, and Turkish, may give an equal beat to each of the syllables in the sentence, as in "'He 'went 'to 'the 'store" (Roach, 1982). This gives an impression of choppiness to those who have learned the conventional English timing system. Speakers of English whose pronunciation is influenced by a language with this even stress on syllables may have stress patterns that contrast noticeably with those of other dialects. In Latino English, a variety spoken by millions of people of Hispanic descent in the United States, stress patterns contrast notably with those of other dialects (Santa Ana, 1991). Speakers of this dialect are likely to stress words that receive little stress in most other English dialects, as in the word *go* in a sentence like "Do you want to go to the store?" It can also result in words like *because* being pronounced with full stress on the first syllable, as in "BEE-cause." These differences in rhythm can be heard in the English of Latinos whose families have long since abandoned Spanish (Thomas & Carter, 2006), suggesting that it is an important linguistic marker of Latino identity beyond bilingualism.

Grammatical Differences

Dialects also contrast in aspects of grammatical usage. For example, the addition of -*s* to a verb form to mark agreement with certain types of subjects (*she walks* compared with *they walk*) is a grammatical process, as is the contrast in word arrangement that signals the difference between a statement and a question ("You are going" vs. "Are you going?"). Because grammatical differences have been so extensively studied in English dialects, we forgo citing individual studies except when necessary. For overviews of this research, see Finegan and Rickford (2004), Fought (2003), Green (2002), Montgomery and Hall (2004), Rickford (1999), and Wolfram and Schilling (2016), among many others.

Grammatical differences between dialects are generally more subject to social evaluation than those in pronunciation, which tend to carry a stronger regional association. These evaluations of language forms reflect the general patterns of social evaluation in which social class differences are less tolerated than regional differences. The following sections provide brief overviews of typical grammatical variations found in vernacular dialects of American English, and encountered in classrooms, organized by the canonical parts of speech.

Grammatical Differences Related to Verbs and Verb Phrases

Differences Involving the Verb To Be

A few grammatical structures were mentioned in Chapter 2. The scenario in which a teacher collects data about missing forms of the verb *to be* is the start of an investigation into *be absence*. In Southern English, forms of *are* may be omitted in places where the verb can be contracted ("They goin'" but not in "I know they are"), and in African American English, both *are* and *is* forms can be absent ("They goin'" and "He playin'"). Although *am* and past-tense forms of *be* may be omitted in Caribbean Englishes, no American English dialects have significant absence of those verb forms. Other constraints govern *be* absence. For example, it is more likely that the form of *be* will be omitted when it is acting as a helping verb (or *auxiliary*), as in "She gonna go" or "We gettin' a treat" and less likely that it will be absent when it is used as a main verb, as in "He at school" or "They hungry."

Leveling, as discussed in the previous chapter, is a linguistic process that can affect the forms of *be* especially, because of that verb's highly irregular conjugations. In many working-class dialects, the agreement pattern is simplified so that the forms *is* and *was* are used with all subjects ("The dogs is barking"; "They was barking").

Another use of the verb form *be* has been noted in working-class African American communities, signifying a meaning distinction not found in other dialects. In sentences like "Sometimes they be acting silly," the verb indicates an activity that takes place habitually (it happens at various intervals over a period of time), which is why it is often referred to as *habitual be.* This habitual *be* form must be distinguished from constructions that look similar but do not carry the meaning of habitual occurrence. Constructions that seem comparable, such as "They be here tomorrow" and "They be here if they could" actually result from the absence of the auxiliary forms *will* and *would*, respectively, and they are different from the habitual use of *be*. For the most part, the habitual use of *be* is limited to the speech of working-class African American English speakers.

Differences Involving Other Verbs

Two other patterns related to verbs have already been mentioned. The first is the regularization of past-tense forms in which irregular verbs (such as *swim/ swam*) are made past tense through the addition of an -*ed* suffix (e.g., *swimmed*). This pattern can be found in all vernacular dialects. The second pattern, the omission of -*s* on present-tense verbs following third-person singular subjects (e.g., *he/she/it swim*), results from the process of leveling and is found almost exclusively in working-class dialects used in some African American communities. The -*s* verbal suffix for the present tense has another interesting variable use. In some Appalachian and Southern communities, the -*s* suffix is heard on verbs occurring with plural subjects as well as with singular subjects, especially if the subject involves a collective noun: "People goes" or "A lot of them goes." The -*s* suffix also occurs frequently in these Southern dialects if the subject is a coordinate noun phrase as in "James and Willis goes a lot." However, the -*s* tends not to be used in these dialects if the plural subject is a pronoun (*they*).

The -*ed* suffix, which is used to mark past tense on regular verbs (e.g., "They walked" and "They have walked"), may be absent due to consonant cluster reduction, described in the section on pronunciation (where the *kt* sounds at the end of *walked* may reduce to *k* in an utterance like "They walk' five miles yesterday"). The suffix can also be absent in verbs whose past-tense form does not involve a consonant cluster, such as *mended* and *knitted*. This pattern may also be applied to irregular verbs so that their present-tense form is used in a past tense context, as in "Yesterday, he bring me two apples." The regular -*ed* suffix can also be used by analogy in irregular verbs, resulting in past tense regularization, such as *cutted, gived,* or *throwed.* A similar process can move regular verbs to an irregular pattern or irregular verbs to a different irregular verb pattern. This process is behind recent innovative forms in Standard English like *dove* (formerly *dived,* patterned on *drive/drove*) and *snuck* (formerly *sneaked,* patterned on *stick/stuck*). It also explains why some dialects change the irregular verb *bring/brought/brought* to *bring/brang/brung,* by analogy to verbs like *sing* and *ring.*

Another variation found with verb forms is the use of past-tense forms where Standard English requires a past-participle form and vice versa. Standard English speakers can differentiate past-tense and past-participle forms by contrasting two simple sentences: "Yesterday I __VERB__" for past tense and "I have __VERB__" for past participle. So, the past tense for *write* is *wrote* and the past participle is *written.* But many English verbs have identical past-tense and past-participle forms, and Standard English is continuing to increase the number of verbs for which these forms are identical. Over the past century, irregular past-participle forms like *mown, abode,* and *clad* have been nearly universally replaced by *mowed, abided,* and *clothed* (Millward, 2012).

All vernacular dialects have some variation of past-tense and past-participle forms. For example, a dialect might use a past-participle form where Standard English would take a past-tense form, as in "They seen something" or "We done our work." Alternatively, it may use a past-tense form where Standard English would use a past-participle form, as in "I had went to the store" or "She has took the pear." Finally, some vernacular dialects, especially those in the South, may simply use a *different irregular verb form,* such as "I hearn [heard] it last night" or "It just riz [rose] up from the swamp."

Auxiliary or "helping" verbs in English convey information about the manner and time that an event took place, or convey information about the speaker's relationship to what is being said. Compare the following sentences in which the auxiliaries have been underlined:

> They <u>had</u> walked to the store.
> They <u>were</u> walking to the store.
> They <u>had been</u> walking to the store.
> They <u>should have been</u> walking to the store.

The sentences provide a sample of how English can use auxiliaries to differentiate an action that has been completed versus one that is ongoing versus one that was going on when something else happened. In the final sentence, the auxiliary *should* conveys that the speaker is offering an opinion about what would have been appropriate. Vernacular dialects of English employ a number of additional auxiliary forms. Most of the time these special auxiliary uses are based on words that already exist in the language, but they are recoded with special grammatical information. Because the forms already exist in Standard English, their use in vernacular dialects can be camouflaged or misinterpreted.

The *habitual be* feature described above is one such example of a special auxiliary form. It describes a state of being or action that is periodic as opposed to punctual or continuous. Another example, *completive done,* which is found in both Southern and African American vernaculars, uses *done* to emphasize a completed action. Thus, "She done wrote her paper" conveys that the action took place well in the past and has been completed for some time. In this structure, the verb following *done* occurs in the past tense (in other words, *"He done send the pictures" and *"She done written the check" would not be acceptable).

Remote time been is another special auxiliary form for capturing information about an event in the past. In this instance, when *been* is stressed, it conveys grammatical information suggesting that an action took place long ago but is still relevant. For example, "I been married" would mean that the speaker was married a long time ago and remains married. This form, found in African American Vernacular English, is sometimes misinterpreted as missing *have,* but in fact the construction with *have* carries a contrasting grammatical meaning. For mainstream American English speakers, the stressed been in "I been married" may be interpreted as "They were once married but are no longer married," a drastically different meaning from being married a long time.

In some dialects, modal forms (*should, can, may, might,* etc.), can be paired in the auxiliary, as in "I might could come to your party" or "You might should clean your room." These combinations, called *double modals* or *multiple modals,* have a long history in English, and are still standard in some languages related to English. They are found chiefly in the South where they tend to not carry much social stigma. The meaning of these combinations is more than a simple addition of the two standard modals. The first combination in the examples above, *might could,* conveys a meaning such as "I have the ability to do what is being requested, but there is very little chance of my actually doing it, but since I've phrased it this way, you really can't be mad at me when the request is not fulfilled." Put more succinctly, it's one of the most polite ways of saying "Probably not." The second example, *might should,* can be used as a polite way of issuing a command, softening the directive "Take out the garbage" with "You might should take out the garbage."

The Appendix catalogs a number of additional special auxiliary forms found in American dialects, but one final example will be mentioned here. One of the most robust linguistic changes that English has ever witnessed has been occurring over the past few decades and has spread so quickly that it can now be heard in English all over the globe. This exciting change involves new ways of introducing reported or imagined speech, which was traditionally done with *say,* as in "She said, 'I really love calculus!'" Now, the verbs *go* and *like* have all but taken over this function for younger speakers. Once associated with Valley Girl talk in California, now English speakers everywhere are unfazed by sentences like "So I was like, 'Do you really like cats?' and he goes, 'Well, I mean, I like dogs better.'" But, language never stands still, and these new forms are already giving way to yet another new way of introducing reported speech (or even nonverbal communication), by using *all* as a verb, as in "I was all, [eye roll] 'Sorry, but I can't love a dog person.'" These forms, which are called *quotative say, like, go,* and *all* because of their function, are structures that students have strong intuitions about in terms of who uses them and how they are used. That level of engagement, along with the fact that they are quite common, makes these forms interesting topics for student inquiry projects.

Negation

Negation is another grammatical structure where significant variation is found in English dialects. Sentences with more than one negative form are quite noticeable. Most studies of dialects in working-class communities note the negative patterns in sentences like "We didn't go nowhere," "They couldn't find no food," and "It don't never run good." These patterns have been compared to the standard pattern that allows only one negative to occur. In *multiple negation,* or *negative concord,* a negative form is attached to both the verb and the indefinites (*nowhere, no*) or adverbs (*never*) following the verb. Thus, the forms that can carry negation are made to agree with each other. In addition, inversion of subject and auxiliary in negation has been observed in some Southern communities, along with the more widespread pattern in which the negative indefinite word follows the verb: "Couldn't nobody see it" (a statement meaning "Nobody could see it," not a question) and "Ain't nobody gonna do it!"

Another common but highly stigmatized feature of negation in vernacular dialects is the use of *ain't.* This form is used to correspond to the Standard English negative version of *is, are, am, has,* and *have,* in cases like "They ain't here" and "I ain't found it." In working-class African American speech, it can also be used for *didn't,* as in "She ain't go yesterday." Despite the highly negative attitude often expressed toward *ain't,* it persists in widespread use in many speech communities.

Grammatical Differences Related to Nouns and Noun Phrases

Although the systems of verb endings show more extensive differences between dialects, noun forms vary too. In working-class African American communities, absence of the plural -*s* suffix has been observed in phrases like "two card" or "all them book." In some rural Southern or Appalachian dialects, the plural suffix may be absent only with nouns that signify weights and measures, particularly when a numeral is used, as in "three pound" or "twenty mile." Another pattern affects irregular plurals in English (nouns that form the plural in ways other than adding -*s*, such as *foot/feet*). Some members of working-class Southern and African American communities apply the regular pluralization pattern to these singular nouns so that they may say "two foots," "many sheeps," or "the firemans," for example.

Another noun suffix that shows dialect difference is the possessive -*s* ending. Some speakers from working-class African American communities may omit the possessive -*s* ending, using "my friend jacket" as a correspondence to the standard *my friend's jacket*. A characteristic observed in some rural Appalachian communities and in isolated Southeastern island communities is the use of the forms *your'n* and *our'n* in places where the standard form is *yours* and *ours* (*his'n* and *her'n* occur as well), as in "This jacket is your'n."

Pronouns

There exists a tremendous amount of variation among pronouns in American English dialects, much of which involves regularization through analogy and rule extension. Perhaps the most common rule extension involves using the object form instead of the subject form in subjects with two or more people, as in the examples, "Me and Adeline are going swimming" or "Owen and them will be home soon." In part because such forms are so commonly corrected in the speech of young children, hypercorrection of these forms can also occur when these coordinate subjects are used in object position, as in "The book belongs to Steve and I." Such constructions occur commonly in speech, but they are considered incorrect according to Formal Standard English conventions.

Another extension of pronoun from one grammatical function to another is the use of an object form, especially *them*, in place of a demonstrative pronoun (i.e., *this, that, these, those*). Examples include "Them cars are fancy" and "She ate them tomatoes." These extended uses of pronouns can be found in vernacular dialects across the United States.

A more regionalized pronoun variant involves special second-person plural pronoun forms to fill out the subject pronoun paradigm. Historically, English contrasted second-person singular *thou* with second-person plural *you*. By the eighteenth century, however, this distinction had been lost (Millward, 2012). Dialects occasionally reintroduce this contrast through innovative forms, including *youse* (near New York City, Philadelphia), *y'all* (the South), *yinz* (Pittsburgh), *you'uns* (Appalachia), and *un* (Gullah).

The South maintains an additional distinction of the object pronoun, using it in a *personal dative* construction. Dative constructions indicate the process of giving, as in "Jenny gave Sarah some water" or "He gave her some water." In the South, it is possible to adapt this construction to situations where the giver and the receiver are the same subject, as in "I got me a new truck" or "We got us a problem," indicating a more personal, special relationship to the object.

Regularization is also a process that affects pronoun usage in American dialects. Standard English maintains an irregular reflexive pronoun system. In the chart below, it can be seen that the pronouns for first- and second-person all use possessive forms (*my, our, your*).

First singular	*myself*	First plural	*ourselves*
Second singular	*yourself*	Second plural	*yourselves*
Third singular	*himself/herself*	Third plural	*themselves*

For third-person singular masculine subject and third-person plural subjects, the root of the word is the object form of the pronoun (*him, them*). Regularizing this paradigm so that the base of each pronoun is the possessive pronoun, on analogy with the other reflexive pronouns, results in the forms *hisself* and *theirselves,* which are both found in vernacular dialects across the United States.

Grammatical Differences Related to Adjectives and Adverbs

For adjectives and adverbs, the suffixes that have nonstandard alternative usages are the comparative (*-er*) and the superlative (*-est*) markers. In the standard pattern, these endings are used typically with words of one or two syllables (*stronger, friendliest*). For some words with two syllables, and all words with three or more syllables, the standard pattern uses *more* and *most* preceding the word rather than the suffix (*more efficient, more foolish*). However, this pattern differs across dialects. In some varieties, the suffixes may be added to words that go with *more/most* in standard patterns, resulting in forms like *beautifuler* and *awfulest*. Also, some forms that are irregular in the standard pattern may be treated differently (e.g., *bad/worse/worst*). Forms based on analogy with the regular form—such as *baddest, gooder, worser*— have also been observed. Comparatives and superlatives like the ones mentioned here have been documented in a wide range of dialects and are not restricted to any particular group. It is worth noting that Standard English is currently undergoing a shift in which two-syllable adjectives take *more/most* (Kyto & Romaine, 2000). Perhaps as a means of improving clarity, more and more adjectives are starting to take *more/most* including adjectives such as *handsome, common,* and *gentle* (i.e., *more gentle* is overtaking *gentler*). The commonness of these structures makes this change in progress one that students can investigate either by doing web searches (they can search for competing forms *handsomer* and *more handsome* and compare the results) or by listening to mass media.

Another change in progress involves the increased use of adverbs without their *-ly* suffix, as in "They answered wrong" instead of "They answered wrongly" or "Drive slow" instead of "Drive slowly." Such constructions are particularly common with comparatives, as in "Drive slower" instead of "Drive more slowly" or "You should answer quicker" instead of "You should answer more quickly." Most good dictionaries have kept up with this change, and now include unmarked adverbial uses under the same entry as their adjective forms. For example, dictionary.com includes as a definition for the word *slow* "adverb, in a slow manner; slowly: 'drive slow'." Most of the time these usages go unnoticed, but in some vernacular dialects in the Appalachian and Ozark Mountains, this pattern extends to adverbs that most other dialects still mark with an *-ly*; for example, a sentence like "They're from Texas original" is found in the vernacular dialect, but it is a stigmatized form.

There are a number of other interesting dialect variations in adverb usage. All dialects of English can use *anymore* with negative sentences, such as "We don't watch DVDs anymore," but in the Midlands region (and spreading to other regions), it is also possible to use it in positive sentences, "We stream movies anymore." Finally, one of the domains in which English is constantly changing relates to the adverbs used to intensify a feeling or emotion. Perhaps the need for new intensifiers is caused by overuse, but in recent history, American dialects have used, among other adverbs, *right, plumb, wicked, quite, really, pretty, absolutely, very, hella, ridiculously,* and *so*. Some certainly seem more familiar than others, but all function in roughly the same way, as in "That was very/so/hella good."

These limited examples presented in this chapter are just the tip of the dialect iceberg, but they do demonstrate a number of points about the nature of language. First, they highlight the systematic nature of linguistic patterns. Second, many of them illustrate the consistency with which linguistic forces shape the language. Third, they demonstrate that some dialects' features are more noticeable than others. Some differences are quite stigmatized while others are matters of quaintness and curiosity, reminding us that when people make judgments about a language structure or a dialect, they may really be making a judgment about the group associated with that dialect and not about the linguistic properties of the form itself.

Illustrative Dialect Samples

In doing dialect study, it is important to remember that not all speakers use all of the features of a dialect. Our discussions refer to a composite picture of some dialects, rather than the dialect of any one person. To illustrate the actual use of some variable structures in speech, we present two annotated passages taken from live speech samples. The first example, "Appalachian Ghost Story," comes from an interview with an elderly white woman who lived her entire life in the southern part of West Virginia. The second passage is from a conversation with an 11-year-old African American boy from Baltimore, MD. For these samples of vernacular speech, dialect features are noted and described following the samples. Odd-numbered superscripts refer to pronunciation differences, and even-numbered superscripts refer to grammatical differences. We have chosen to use regular spelling for the most part so that the majority of the pronunciation differences are not indicated in the spelling. The punctuation roughly reflects the pausing and intonation patterns in the flow of speech, rather than written language conventions. For frequently occurring features such as *d* for *th* and *n* for *ng*, we only mark the first five instances of the feature in the typescript. Original audio recordings of these passages can be accessed on this book's companion website.

Appalachian Ghost Story

I was always kindy[1] afraid to stay by myself, just me, you know, it was gettin'[3] about time for me to get in, so Ingo, he'd[2] went[4] over to this man's house where we carried our water from, and to get some water, and, ooh, the moon was so pretty and bright, and I thinks[6], heck, hit's[5] dark, I hear him a-talkin',[3,8] a-settin'[3,8] over there in the field where the spring is, I'll just walk down the road and meet him, you know, ooh, it was so pretty and light. I got down there and I hearn[10] something shut the churchhouse door, but I didn't see a thing, and the moon, oh the moon was as pretty as daylight, and I didn't see nothin.'[3,12] And he come[14] on the walk, pitty-pat, pitty-pat, and I just looked with all my eyes, and I couldn't see a thing, come out that gate, iron[7], slammed it and hit[5] just cracked, just like a[9] iron[7] gate, it will just slam it there. And all at once, something riz up[10] right in front of me. Looked like it had a white sheet around it, and no head. I liketa[16] died. That was just a little while before Florence was born. I turned around and I went back to the house just as fast as I could go, and about that time, Ingo come[14] along and he says[6], "I set the water up," and he said, "I'm going down the churchhouse," he said, "I hearn[10] somebody go in," he said, "They went through that gate." And he walked across there and he opened the door and he went in the churchhouse. And they had him a-lookin'[3,8] after the church, you know, if anybody went in, he went down there. He seen[18] something was the matter with me, I couldn't hardly[20] talk. I told him, I said, "Well, something or other, I hearn[10] it, I seen[18] it, whenever I started over to meet you, and I couldn't get no[12] further." So he went down there and he took his lantern, of course, we didn't have flashlights then, took his lantern, had an old ladder, just spokes, just to go up beside of the house, he looked all behind the organ, all behind every bench, he went upstairs and looked in the garret, not a thing in the world he could find. Not a thing. Well, it went on for a right smart little[32] while and one day Miss Allen was down there. Her girls come down there very often and sweep the church and clean it. So one evenin'[3], they come[14] up the house, you know, and I's[11] tellin' them. They said, "Honey, don't feel bad about that," she said, "Long as you live here, you'll see something like that," said "they[34] was, in time of the war, they[34] was a woman, that somebody'd cut her head off and they'd buried her in the grave down there." And they said there'd been so many people[24] live in the house we live in, would see her, and said "That's what it was," said, "it just had a white sheet wrapped around it." And we didn't live there very long cause I wouldn't stay. He worked away and aw heck—I's[11] just scared to death but still Miss Allen told me, she said, "Don't be afraid because hain't[5,26] a thing that'll hurt you."

Wild Life

Child:	And then I went home. And then I was watchin',[3] um, Wild Life, about animals.
Interviewer:	And which animal did you see?
Child:	And a[9] elephant and a rhino was[22] fightin'.[3] The elephant kicked[17] the rhino down. And then it start[30] grabbin'[3] its whole body with[21] its, with[21] its.
Interviewer:	Tusk, trunk.
Child:	Yeah, thr[13]ow him but he couldn't get him up but it ran. And then it was this little dancin'[3] chickens, that do like this, like Indians, so they were jumpin'[3] up and down doin'[3] a dance.
Interviewer:	Why?
Child:	I don't know.
Interviewer:	Were they mad at each other?
Child:	No, they was[22] dancin'.
Interviewer:	They were happy. Did they have music (makes sound of music)?
Child:	Yeah, with[21] they[36] mouth,[21] they go uh uh uh uh and stuff. It[34] was a whole lot of them doin' it. And then the Indians'll come out and do it with[21] them.
Interviewer:	And then the Indians would dance with the chickens? Wow!
Child:	And then we saw a movie with, uh, lions, uh uh cheetah, and um gorillas on it, and they said a, a dog[15] bit the baby and it died.
Interviewer:	Bit a real baby?
Child:	(Nods yes)
Interviewer:	Oh.
Child:	And then that man had anoth[21]er tiger, a po[19]lice came to the house and shot that one and they got anoth[21]er one.

Interviewer:	This is all on Wild Life?
Child:	(Nods)
Interviewer:	With the elephant and the rhinoceros? All this happened on Wild Life?
Child:	(Nods)
Interviewer:	Wow.
Child:	And then another one came on about the, uh, white lions and stuff. Don't you know them[38] white ones?
Interviewer:	White lions?
Child:	Tigers I mean.
Interviewer:	White tigers. Tigers are orange with black stripes, thank you.
Child:	No, they[40] white too. Uh huh. They got white—they got white, then they got white, I mean, black stri[23]pes goin' down.
Interviewer:	That's a zebra.
Child:	Um uhm, it's[34] another one, that's a snow tiger.
Interviewer:	Oh, the snow tigers, oh, okay.
Child:	And then that man had one. Then, we went to a black, a black panther. It wasn't[25] no[12] black panth[21]er, it was something, black what you call em, I don't know.
Interviewer:	Uh-huh.
Child:	And then, it[34] was a um, we was[22] lookin' at monkeys jumpin' up and down, had—
Interviewer:	Monkeys are funny, huh?
Child:	And they were hittin' each other—and then it[34] was one that went to the doctor's and he was uh (makes noises). Cause—
Interviewer:	A monkey went to the doctor?
Child:	[27]Cause he ain't[26] want to get his shot. Went in his leg. And he said (noises) and he got a needle shot in his leg and he say[6] (noises). And then the man gave him a peppermint so he could suck on it. And then he was bitin' his glasses. Then he put them on and was lookin' at the camera. And then when he got home he said that lady said he don't[28] like to say no so he had bang[30,42] on the table and all that. And then that lady gave him a sucker and he was suckin' on it.
Interviewer:	Just like a little kid, huh?
Child:	And then he had diapers on, had a little jumper.
Interviewer:	(laughs) She kept him in her house? Oh, so it was like her pet monkey? Or was it a monkey out in the jungle? Oh.
Child:	And then they'd take him places with[21]em, like a diner and all.
Interviewer:	Don't you think the monkey will run away?
Child:	He won't run away.
Interviewer:	Did they have him on a leash? Like they do a dog?

Child:	No. And then when they got him home, they were jumpin' on a big trampoline.
Interviewer:	All three of them?
Child:	No, just one.
Interviewer:	Oh, just the monkey?
Child:	Yeah.
Interviewer:	The lady wasn't jumpin' on the trampoline too?
Child:	No, she was watchin' them [27]cause they was[22] jumpin' up and down, walkin' around.

Notes on Transcripts

Pronunciation

1. In an unstressed, final syllable of a word, the COMM<u>A</u> vowel or the schwa sound [ə] can be changed to the high vowel *ee* of *beet*, as in "sofy" for *sofa* or "kindy" for *kinda*.

3. The *-ing* form in a final unstressed syllable may be changed from an *ng* sound to an *n* sound.

5. Before the items *it* and *ain't* an older English *h* may be retained, resulting in items like "hit" for *it* or "hain't" for *ain't*.

7. The sequence *ire* in items like *tire, fire,* or *iron* may be collapsed to a single syllable, resulting in pronunciations such as "arn" for *iron*, "tar" for *tire*, "far" for *fire*, and so forth.

9. The form *a* may be generalized to occur before items that begin with a vowel (e.g., *a apple, a iron*) as well as those that begin with a consonant (e.g., *a pear*).

11. Initial *w* sounds may be deleted in an unstressed syllable, resulting in forms like "young'uns" for *young ones* or "we's" for *we was*.

13. Following a consonant, *r* may be deleted before GOAT and GOOSE vowels, so that *throw* becomes "th'ow" and *through* becomes "th'u."

15. The THOUGHT vowel is centralized to schwa (like the final sound in COMM<u>A</u>) so that *dog* and *Doug* sound the same.

17. When a stop consonant like *t* or *d* follows another consonant, thus creating a consonant blend or cluster, the final consonant may not be pronounced—so that *happened* may be pronounced as "happen."

19. Stress may shift on syllables of certain words. *Police* is stressed on the first syllable, and the vowel of the stressed syllable becomes like the vowel in GOAT instead of the vowel in COMM<u>A</u> (PO-lease vs. pah-LEASE).

21. When it occurs in a medial or final position of a word, the voiceless *th* sound may be pronounced as *f*, as in "deaf" for *death*; and the voiced *th* sound may be pronounced as *v*, as in "muh-ver" for *mother*.

23. The consonant cluster *str* is pronounced as *skr*. *Street* becomes "skreet" or *stream* becomes "skream."

25. Before nasal sounds (*m*, *n*, and the sound spelled *ng*), certain consonants can be altered. Voiceless *th* may become *t* (*nothing* becomes "not'n"), *z* may become *d* (*wasn't* may become "wadn't"), and *v* may become *b* (*seven* may become "sebm").

27. Unstressed syllables may be deleted. *Because* may be rendered as "'cause," *remember* as "'member."

Grammatical Differences

2. A pronoun form may be used after a subject noun, as in "My mother she . . ." or "The man in the middle, he . . ."

4. The past form of an irregular verb may be generalized as the past-participle form, as in "He had went" or "She had did."

6. Present-tense forms may be used in animated narratives of past time events, including an -*s* on non-third-person forms, as in "I says" or "We goes."

8. An *a*- prefix may attach to verbs or adverbs ending in -*ing* as in "He was a-hunting" or "He makes money a-building houses."

10. Different irregular verb forms may be used in past-tense forms, as in "brang" (for *brought*), "hearn" (*heard*), or "tuck" (*took*).

12. Multiple negatives may include a negative marker in the verb phrase and a negative indefinite form following the verb, as in "I didn't see nothin'" or "She ain't goin' nowhere."

14. A present-tense root of an irregular verb may be used in past-tense forms as well, as in "She come late yesterday" or "Last year he run in the race."

16. The special modal form *liketa* is used to mark a significant event that was averted. It may be used in figurative and literal senses.

18. The past-participle form of an irregular verb may be generalized to a simple past-tense form, as in "He seen it" or "She done it."

20. Multiple negation may involve negative marking in the verb phrase and an adverb following the verb, as in "They don't hardly eat" or "She shouldn't never go."

22. The conjugated forms of *be* may be regularized to *is* in the present tense, as in "We is here now," or *was* in the past tense, as in "They was there."

24. Relative pronoun forms can be absent if they are the subject of a relative clause, as in "That's the dog bit me." In standard dialects, these relative pronouns can only be absent when they are the object of the relative clause, as in "That's the house he was building."

26. The form *ain't* can be used for be + not, have + not, and did + not, as in "He ain't here," "She ain't done it," or "He ain't go."

28. The third-person singular present tense form -*s* may be absent from the verb, so that forms such as "She go" or "He don't" may occur.

30. The past-tense marker -*ed* may be deleted, as in "After the movie, we want to go to that restaurant, but it wasn't open."

32. The adverbs *right, right smart,* and *right smart little* are used to intensify attributes, such as "She's right tall" or "He took a right smart little while."
34. For the expletive use of *there* in Standard English (e.g., "There's a new boy in my class"), vernacular dialects may use *it* (e.g., "It's a new boy in my class") or *they* (e.g., "They's a new boy in my class").
36. The subject form of the third-person plural pronoun *they* can serve the possessive function, as in "Let's go to they house."
38. The demonstrative pronoun *those* may be replaced by *them* to get "Them dogs was barking all night long."
40. The copula may be omitted, as in "She crazy."
42. The past participle may occur in place of the simple past, as in "They went to the game and they had yelled at the umpire."

Discussion Questions

1. There are a number of other word formation processes beyond those listed in Box 3.1. Two of the more socially fascinating are *backronyms* and *retronyms*. The former involves creating a phrase based on an existing word or name, as in "Fix or repair daily" for *Ford,* or the brand of women's apparel, *GRITS,* which stands for "Girls raised in the South." *Retronyms* involve renaming an item due to some advance in technology. For example, prior to the electric guitar, all *acoustic guitars* were simply *guitars.* The advent of the widespread cellphone usage created the need for the term *landline.* What do backronyms and retronyms reveal about society? What purposes do these forms serve?
2. Unlike some of the examples cited in this chapter, some words take on new meanings without people objecting much. Technology is a locus of new word and meaning creation. For example, the following words have all taken on new meanings due to technology: *cloud, troll, tag, poke, tweet,* and *a feed.* Why is it that many of these new definitions are readily accepted? Can you think of other technology related words that fit this pattern? Can you think of other domains where word and meaning creation is commonly accepted? Can you think of other domains where word and meaning creation is often reviled?
3. How might teachers and other education practitioners use the technical descriptions of dialect features that this chapter provides?
4. Research into dialect differences is ongoing. Are there features you have noticed that you would like to have described precisely? Who might carry out this research?
5. Does the chapter mention dialect features that you have never heard? How can you explain that?

Links of Interest

1. Look for information about etymology and language history in the online version of the *Oxford English Dictionary* (subscription is required for full access, but lots of interesting information is available for free): www.oed.com/
2. Explore English in the time period between Chaucer and Shakespeare at the online *Middle English Dictionary*: http://quod.lib.umich.edu/m/med/
3. Discover the regional distribution of over 100 dialect features at the Harvard Dialect Survey project: www4.uwm.edu/FLL/linguistics/dialect/maps.html
4. Listen to the difference between a Northern *R*-less dialect and a Southern *R*-less dialect: www.talkintarheel.com/chapter/4/audio4–1.php and www.talkintarheel.com/chapter/4/audio4–2.php
5. Read an article about the Northern Cities Vowel Shift: www.slate.com/articles/life/the_good_word/2012/08/northern_cities_vowel_shift_how_americans_in_the_great_lakes_region_are_revolutionizing_english_.html
6. Watch a video of William Labov explaining the Northern Cities Shift and his "gating experiments" that examined how well people understood speakers of this dialect: www.youtube.com/watch?v=7Xppob-ilgA
7. Listen to a speaker with the *pin/pen* merger: www.talkintarheel.com/chapter/3/audio3–9.php
8. Check out lists of English word borrowings organized by language: https://en.wikipedia.org/wiki/Lists_of_English_words_by_country_or_language_of_origin
9. Listen to examples of so-called Canadian Raising: www.yorku.ca/twainweb/troberts/raising.html
10. Read an article about the social meanings of "vocal fry": http://languagelog.ldc.upenn.edu/nll/?p=20797

Further Reading

Schneider, E. W., Kortmann, B., Burridge, K., Mesthrie, R., & Upton, C. (Eds.). (2004). *A handbook of varieties of English, vol. 1: Phonology*. Berlin, Germany: Mouton de Gruyter.
Kortmann, B., Schneider, E. W., Burridge, K., Mesthrie, R., & Upton, C. (Eds.). (2004). *A handbook of varieties of English, vol. 2: Morphology and syntax*. Berlin, Germany: Mouton de Gruyter.
These two volumes are intended for language scholars, but they may be useful to others who want to examine the sounds and grammars of different dialects. The volumes are organized by language variety and offer descriptions of distinctive language features.

Tannen, D. (2011). *That's not what I meant!: How conversational style makes or breaks relationships* (paperback ed.). New York, NY: William Morrow.
Using scenes from everyday life, Tannen explores the communication ups and downs that everyone experiences and traces them to desires for both closeness and distance and different groups' ways of maintaining relationships. Although she does not specifically treat language in school, her insights hold for communication there as well.

Wolfram, W., & Reaser, J. (2014). *Talkin' Tar Heel: How our voices tell the story of North Carolina*. Chapel Hill, NC: University of North Carolina Press.
> Written for a general audience, this book examines the rich linguistic traditions of the U.S. South with special attention to the distinctive dialects of North Carolina.

Wolfram, W., & Schilling, N. (2016). *American English: Dialects and variation* (3rd ed.). Malden, MA: John Wiley & Sons.
> This description surveys the social and linguistic factors that account for dialects and the functions that dialects serve. It introduces students and a general audience to the principles underlying language variation. The discussion attempts to limit technical terminology but provides an extensive glossary and appendix of dialect structures to assist readers.

References

Allen, H. B. (1976). *The linguistic atlas of the Upper Midwest: Volume 3, pronunciation*. Minneapolis, MN: University of Minnesota Press.

Eberhardt, M. (2009). African American and white vowel systems in Pittsburgh. In M. Yaeger-Dror & E. R. Thomas (Eds.), *African American English speakers and their participation in local sound changes: A comparative study* (pp. 129–157). Durham, NC: Duke University Press.

Finegan, E., & Rickford, J. R. (Eds.). (2004). *Language in the USA: Themes for the twenty-first century*. Cambridge, UK: Cambridge University Press.

Fought, C. (2003). *Chicano English in context*. New York, NY: Palgrave.

Fridland, V. (2001). The social dimension of the Southern vowel shift: Gender, age and class. *Journal of Sociolinguistics, 5*(2), 233–253.

Green, L. J. (2002). *African American English: A linguistic introduction*. Cambridge, UK: Cambridge University Press.

Khazan, O. (2014, May 29). Vocal fry may hurt women's job prospects. *The Atlantic*. Retrieved from www.theatlantic.com/business/archive/2014/05/employers-look-down-on-women-with-vocal-fry/371811/

Kyto, M., & Romaine, S. (2000). Adjective comparison and standardization processes in American and British English from 1620 to the present. In L. Wright (Ed.), *The development of Standard English, 1300–1800: Theories, descriptions, conflicts* (pp. 171–194). Cambridge, UK: Cambridge University Press.

Labov, W. (1991). Three dialects of English. In P. Eckert (Ed.), *New ways of analyzing variation in English* (pp. 1–45). New York, NY: Academic.

Labov, W. (1994). *Principles of linguistic change: Internal factors*. Malden, MA: Blackwell.

Labov, W. (2010). *Principles of linguistic change: Cognitive and cultural factors*. Malden, MA: Wiley-Blackwell.

Labov, W., Ash, S., & Boberg, C. (2006). *Atlas of North American English: Phonology and phonetics*. Berlin, Germany: Mouton de Gruyter.

Loman, B. (1975). Prosodic patterns in a Negro American dialect. In H. Ringbom, A. Ingberg, R. Norrman, K. Nyholm, R. Westman, and K. Wikberg (Eds.), *Style and text: studies presented to Nils Erik Enkvist* (pp. 219–242). Stockholm, Sweden: Sprakforlaget Skriptor.

McDavid Jr, R. I., & O'Cain, R. K. (Eds.). (1980). *Linguistic atlas of the middle and south Atlantic states*. Chicago, IL: University of Chicago Press.

Millward, C. M. (2012). *A Biography of the English language* (3rd ed.). Boston, MA: Wadsworth.

Montgomery, M., & Hall, J. S. (2004). *Dictionary of Smoky Mountain English*. Knoxville, TN: University of Tennessee Press.

Niedzielski, N. A., & Preston, D. R. (2000). *Folk linguistics*. New York, NY: Walter de Gruyter.

Ochs, E. (1992). Indexing gender. In A. Duranti & C. Goodwin (Eds.), *Rethinking context: Language as an interactive phenomenon* (pp. 335–358). Cambridge, UK: Cambridge University Press.

Pederson, L., McDaniel, S. L., & Adams, C. M. (Eds.). (1986–1993). *Linguistic atlas of the Gulf States* (7 vols.). Athens, GA: University of Georgia Press.

Rickford, J. R. (1999). *African American Vernacular English: Features, evolution, educational implications*. Malden, MA: Blackwell.

Roach, P. (1982). On the distinction between "stress-timed" and "syllable-timed" languages. In D. Crystal (Ed.), *Linguistic controversies: Essays in linguistic theory and practice in honour of F. R. Palmer* (pp. 73–79). London, UK: Hodder Arnold.

Santa Ana, A. (1991). *Phonetic simplification processes in the English of the Barrio: A cross-generational sociolinguistic study of the Chicanos of Los Angeles.* Unpublished doctoral dissertation, University of Pennsylvania.

Tarone, E. E. (1973). Aspects of intonation in Black English. *American Speech, 48*(1/2), 29–36.

Thomas, E. R. (2001). *An acoustic analysis of vowel variation in New World English.* Durham, NC: Duke University Press.

Thomas, E. R. (2007). Phonological and phonetic characteristics of African American vernacular English. *Language and Linguistics Compass, 1*(5), 450–475.

Thomas, E. R., & Carter, P. M. (2006). Prosodic rhythm and African American English. *English World-Wide, 27*(3), 331–355.

Wells, J. C. (1982). *Accents of English, 3 vols.* Cambridge, UK: Cambridge University Press.

Wolfram, W. (1986). Language variation in the United States. In O. L. Taylor (Ed.), *Nature of communication disorders in culturally and linguistically diverse populations* (pp. 73–115). San Diego, CA: College Hill Press.

Wolfram, W., & Schilling, N. (2016). *American English: Dialects and variation* (3rd ed.). Malden, MA: Wiley Blackwell.

Yuasa, I. P. (2010). Creaky voice: A new feminine voice quality for young urban-oriented upwardly mobile American women? *American Speech, 85*(3), 315–337.

4

Languages in Contact

Scenario

Assume for a moment that you have traveled to France and have just made a new acquaintance. Further, assume that this person speaks only French while you speak English but have taken a class or two of French in high school. You know some words but not enough to be proficient in the grammar. Imagine how this conversation might unfold. Perhaps your new friend will convey important time indicators by using words like "demain" (*tomorrow*) in addition to future tense verb conjugations. Perhaps your friend will leave off tricky verb, noun, and adjective endings altogether in order to ensure that you are hearing the correct root words. When you speak, you likely use few or no auxiliary verbs or anything more than rudimentary verb endings. You might suggest that tomorrow you two meet by the red house by translating that phrase using your English grammar as "rouge maison," as opposed to the standard French grammar in which adjectives follow the nouns they modify, as in "maison rouge." Furthermore, you struggle with French pronunciations when they involve conventions different from what you are used to in English, like the way French speakers nasalize certain vowels, or how they pronounce the "r" in a word like *Paris* (with a trill way at the back of the mouth).

Describe how you might feel trying to communicate in such a situation. What aspects of communication would you feel highly confident of? What aspects would you not feel confident of? Who has the greater burden to ensure communication happens in a situation like this, the monolingual speaker or the (semi-)bilingual speaker? Does the same apply to speakers with competence in multiple dialects? How much focus will you give to pronunciation as opposed to meaning?

Certainly, communication is possible even with your minimal language competency, but it is likely that you and your acquaintance will suffer some misunderstandings. The longer you speak with this person, the better your competency will get, but no one would ever mistake you for a native speaker. There will always be aspects of your native language that will mark you as a language learner in French—or any other language learned later in life. Many of the difficulties are predictable, based on the grammar and sound system differences between your native language and the language you are learning.

The situation presented here does not reflect the social dynamics of most language contact situations; however, some of the same linguistic forces do apply to such situations.

This chapter examines briefly three language contact situations in the United States and the language varieties that arose from them. African American English, which grew out of the historical slave trade is explored first. Then, Latino English is examined both historically and currently. Finally, the information from these two portraits is used to illuminate the contact situations faced by immigrants from East and Southeast Asia. These three situations are selected because they are relevant in many areas of the country. A number of more local language contact situations have contributed to English language variation in many regions, including Cajun English, Puerto Rican English, English of the Pennsylvania Dutch, and the diverse dialects of English spoken by American Indian groups across the United States. Because the previous chapters and the Appendix describe many of the linguistic features of these language varieties, the primary focus in this chapter is on the social dynamics of three contact situations and how they have shaped the resulting language varieties. Often these dynamics result in different social values and cultural norms among the cultural groups that are reflected in the conventions of social interaction and language use. Such perspectives are critical for teachers who increasingly do not look like or share the language backgrounds of their students (Boser, 2014).

African American English

The variety of English that has received most attention by far over the last several decades is *African American English* (AAE). In this section, we provide an overview of this dialect, some information about how it is currently developing, its status in educational contexts, and some of the cultural norms that result in particular linguistic behaviors in the classroom. Before diving in, however, a few introductory caveats are important. First, genetics plays no part in the language variety a person speaks. AAE is transmitted in the same way as other cultural norms. Thus, being classified as "black" does not imply any competency in AAE and being white does not preclude someone from fluency in AAE. Second, like American English in general, there is tremendous regional and class-based variation in AAE. For example, it is not spoken in the same way in rural Mississippi and in New York City, nor is it spoken the same way in all economic classes within a community.

Third, like all language varieties, the dialect is systematically patterned, and linguists have studied the rules that govern these patterns. These patterns exist for the same reasons that they exist in all varieties of language. AAE has been shaped by linguistic and social forces that have shaped English varieties around the world and within the United States. Because of this overlapping history, there are many overlapping linguistic features between AAE and regional U.S. dialects. Sometimes the differences between AAE and these other dialects are obvious (e.g., habitual *be* "She be late for school"), and sometimes they involve subtle nuances (e.g., the sentence "She been married" is likely to be interpreted differently by AAE speakers than by speakers of other varieties). Other times the differences between varieties are not in the feature used but in the frequency of usage (e.g., while both Southern Vernacular English and AAE have absence of *are* in some sentences, as in "We hungry," it is more frequent in AAE).

Fourth, like all dialects of American English, AAE is evolving. Just as the major regional varieties in the United States described in the previous chapter are diverging from each other, so too is AAE diverging from regional white varieties. Fifth, AAE is subject to the same types of stylistic variation that characterize all language varieties, and many AAE speakers can deploy multiple styles of AAE. Versions of the variety that are most dissimilar from Standard English are often termed "vernacular." More recently, linguists have started to recognize and describe a Standard AAE dialect, in parallel to the usage of Standard English as described in Chapter 1 (Britt & Weldon, 2015). Finally, the status of the variety as either a separate language or as a dialect of American English remains a controversial question in political and educational contexts. In part because of this controversy, but also because labels for groups are often controversial, naming the variety has been and remains contentious.

During the Ebonics debate of 1997, the question was raised as to whether African American English is a dialect of English or a language on its own (Wolfram, 1998). This matter has never been entirely resolved. Although the criteria used to distinguish a dialect from a language are sometimes debated by linguists, the kinds of differences that distinguish African American English and Standard English are those that typically characterize dialects rather than separate languages. When the linguistic characteristics of African American English and Standard English are placed side-by-side, we find many more shared language features than distinctive ones. The level of intelligibility between speakers of Standard English and AAE also suggests a dialect rather than a language difference. For the most part, vernacular speakers understand what Standard English speakers are saying, and speakers of Standard English who have some exposure to vernacular dialects comprehend what vernacular speakers are saying. This generalization does not rule out some problems in understanding each other, but any difficulty in comprehension does not match that found between speakers of different languages. This conclusion in no way trivializes the challenge these language differences can create in educational settings. In fact, subtle differences may pose even greater challenges in educational contexts, as they may be more likely to go unnoticed or be misinterpreted. It is impossible for a school to not notice, for example, monolingual Mandarin-speaking children. These children can generally expect to receive appropriate educational accommodations. Dialect differences may not rise to this level of consciousness, and inappropriate conclusions may be drawn about vernacular speakers because of their language.

A comparison of French and English, Spanish and English, or even Spanish and Italian would make the differences between African American English and Standard English seem trivial. Compare the degree of difference, for example, in Standard English "They're talking," AAE "They talkin'," French "Ils parlent," Spanish "Ellos están hablando," Portuguese "Eles estão a falar," and Italian "Stanno parlando." Clearly AAE and Standard English are more similar to each other than to any of the forms in the related but separate Romance languages. Most linguists, then, conclude that the kinds of language differences found between vernacular and standard varieties of English distinguish dialects of the same language, rather than separate languages. Nonetheless, numerous scholars and educators prefer to use the term *African American Language* as a means of highlighting the important differences between it and Standard English. Fundamentally, the choice of label is based more on ideological stance or purpose than linguistic criteria. We use *African American English* following Green (2002) for the rationale she lays out in her excellent linguistic introduction to the variety.

AAE is one of the most prominent vernacular dialects of U.S. English, due in part to its difference from Standard English and due in part to the politics of race in American society. This variety of English has combined a number of vernacular English forms in a unique way. Its uniqueness lies not so much in distinct language forms that are found only in that dialect, although there are a few, but in the particular combination of forms that make up the dialect. AAE is not alone in its distinctiveness. Other U.S. dialects also contrast remarkably with Standard English. For example, some isolated dialects on the Southern seaboard—such as those of Tangier Island and Smith Island in Virginia and Maryland, and Ocracoke and Harkers Island on the Outer Banks of North Carolina—are probably more difficult to comprehend in natural conversation for speakers of other varieties than AAE. However, AAE is certainly the most prevalent native English vernacular dialect in the United States in terms of numbers of speakers, and probably the most important in terms of sociopolitical and education ramifications. For these reasons it is one of the most important language varieties for teachers and language practitioners to be familiar with.

AAE has often been misrepresented. This dialect has received considerable attention in the media, which has focused on everything from teenage rapping to hip hop to Ebonics and Standard English instruction, but media stories often characterize it very inaccurately and judgmentally. Remarkably, while it is now nearly universally considered unacceptable to describe a cultural group as substandard, it is common to hear people refer to AAE as substandard, broken English, or even gibberish. The internet is rife with so-called "Ebonics translators" and memes that employ inaccurate and often disparaging depictions of the variety. Despite the fact that AAE is often exceptionalized and criticized, linguists are unified in their view regarding the validity of the variety: "Linguists argue contentiously about the details of language structure, including dialect differences, but there is remarkable consensus about the fundamental nature of African American speech—or any dialect for that matter" (Wolfram & Reaser, 2014, p. 155). At the core of this "fundamental nature" is an understanding of the language variety's history, its grammatical patterning, and its cultural importance.

The Origins of African American English

The history of African American English is somewhat different from that of other British-derived dialects of English, and this history, combined with the social conditions in which African Americans have participated in American society, accounts for the uniqueness of the dialect. However, the origin or origins of AAE remains an open linguistic question, and one that is still in dispute.

There are two prevailing views about the origins of AAE. One holds that slaves simply learned over a couple of generations the English of vernacular-speaking indentured servants and those who managed the plantations. The other theory holds that AAE developed out of a language contact situation called *creolization*, in which the words of the new language (English) are mapped onto the grammatical structures of a kind of modified universal grammar that may show traits of the native (West African) languages of the slaves. It is important to note that these theories are not mutually exclusive. Both situations may have occurred in different social contexts. These two processes of origin are described below.

A creole language is a hybrid that can develop in language contact situations where there is no shared language. The language that contributes the words to the creole is sometimes called the lexifier or base language; typically, this language has more social prestige or economic importance. A number of creoles exist throughout the world, including English-based creoles (e.g., *Jamaican, Krio*), French-based (e.g., *Haitian Creole, Louisiana Creole*), Dutch-based (e.g., *Negerhollands, Berbice*), and Portuguese-based (e.g., *Papiamento, Saramaccan*). According to some linguists, AAE is a product of this language contact process, and in its earliest form, may have sounded similar to *Gullah*, an English-based creole still spoken in the Sea Islands of South Carolina and Georgia (Mufwene, 1996; Rickford, 1997; Singler, 1998).

This type of language contact process is probably what happened on the West Coast of Africa as Europeans from various countries, including the British Isles, developed trade routes. Over time, an initial and intermediary language (a *pidgin*) became an established means of communication as children acquired it as a native language (a creole). It must be remembered that imprisoned

Africans were separated from others who spoke their language as a means of quelling any uprising. In many cases, members of different African groups that had been fierce rivals found themselves in a situation where working together was to their advantage. In order to do this, the slaves needed to create a *medium of interethnic communication*, which can be thought of as a *pidgin*. Over time, this language that was created out of necessity became a language of power. It could be used to resist or undermine oppression, and thus it bound the speakers together socially in a critical way. This new *medium of ethnic solidarity*, created out of significant cultural and linguistic diversity, helped forge a new ethnicity (African American) and a linguistic marker of that new culture—African American English (Roberge, 2012). From the beginning, it seems, AAE may have been powerful because it was similar, but not identical, to English. The early language served as a symbol of solidarity, but it also allowed the slaves to communicate subversive messages that overseers would not have understood. (The language today may still show signs of subversiveness, which helps explain why so much slang originates from AAE [Smitherman, 2000]. One aspect of slang is that it is meant to be exclusive to a group.) This early interlanguage was then brought to the Americas with the importation of slaves. In the American South, it mixed further with Southern White Vernacular varieties of English.

In this language-mixing process, some of the same principles that governed the opening scenario in this chapter shape language in powerful ways. For example, the initial variety that is created when languages are in contact relies heavily on content words as opposed to function words and grammatical suffixes. The lack of items like conjunctions and linking verbs does not obscure meaning in sentences like "Tomorrow, red house." Grammatical suffixes like markers for plurals, possessives, past tense, and participle forms are typically dropped altogether. Distinctions between pronoun classes can also be eliminated (*he/his/him* may all become "he" or "him"). As the hybrid language develops, these grammatical concepts are likely to be reintroduced, but not in ways that conform exactly to either of the languages in contact. For example, in Jamaican, the past tense is noted not with an *-ed* ending, but with a preverbal marker derived from the English word *been*. Thus, Standard English "I loved her" would be said as "Mi ben love she" in Jamaican (Patrick, 1999). When linguists examine modern vernacular AAE, the lack of features like possessive *-s*, the expanded copula absence, and the expanded domain of plural *-s* absence can certainly seem like holdovers from an earlier creole language. But the change from that creole was neither instantaneous nor complete. African American English today is not a creole like the Caribbean creoles, but it still has some traces of its creole past combined with many features of Southern English. The historical origin, the addition of Southern features, and the fact that the dialect developed in a largely segregated society have resulted in a unique dialect of English.

In contrast to the creolization view, some linguists believe that AAE's origin was entirely or mostly shaped through contact with vernacular-speaking white indentured servants (e.g., Bailey, Maynor, & Cukor-Avila, 1991; Poplack, 1999; Wolfram & Thomas, 2002), along with the retention of some traits from the original contact situation. Within this position there are significantly different views of the particulars, but the general view is that older AAE was more regionalized. Though the preponderance of evidence is from post-abolitionist times, the earliest data available suggest that older African Americans living in isolated communities sound a good bit like the whites in the region, be it rural Texas, the Outer Banks, or the Appalachian Mountains. However, there are subtle differences in the speech of these older African Americans and their white counterparts, suggesting the possibility of remnants of language contact shaping the dialect. One study of isolated African American communities in Hyde County, NC, finds that the local African American dialect began to diverge rapidly from the local white dialect following integration of the schools (Wolfram & Thomas, 2002). In describing this research, Wolfram and Reaser (2014) write, "The trajectory of divergence suggests that speech became much more marked for ethnicity during [integration] and that black youth did not want to 'sound white'" (p. 177). The youngest African American speakers from this isolated community have now assimilated many of the AAE features that were previously restricted to urban areas. The sorts of AAE features described in the previous two chapters and the Appendix may now appear in most dialects of AAE, suggesting that the language variety is a powerful symbol of African American culture and identity.

The Changing State of African American English

The divergence of AAE from white dialects may seem surprising given increased mobility among African Americans and an educational system that systematically reinforces norms associated with middle class, often white, language varieties. A tremendous amount of evidence, however, supports the conclusion that these language varieties are indeed diverging. One of the earliest studies to note this was Labov (1987). His explanation for the linguistic divergence was the increasing pattern of de facto segregation among urban African Americans, which might promote divergence among dialects because social or physical segregation tends to promote divergence. This conclusion seems at odds with the conclusion of Wolfram and Thomas (2002) noted above, which appeals to the identity factor in explaining divergence. But being segregated should, over time, lead to linguistic divergence, which is what happened to the Romance languages (French, Spanish, etc.). Additionally, being socially separate but in proximity also appears to bolster linguistic difference. In the first case (segregation), we expect linguistic processes to govern the divergence. In the latter case (social distance), personal and cultural identity is more influential.

The current trajectory of AAE is of utmost importance to educators. Effectively, with each year that passes, the educational system is receiving children who speak a variety more dissimilar from Standard English than the students did the prior year. And given demographic shifts among student and teacher populations (Boser, 2014), it appears that the language backgrounds of students and teachers are growing further apart. Of course, variation within AAE means that individuals or students from some areas may not reflect this trend. But the degree of difference between AAE and Standard English has even prompted some researchers and school systems to look to bilingual instructional programs for pedagogies that might help African American students add Standard English to their linguistic repertoires (Baugh, 1999).

Some Cultural Differences and Their Linguistic Significance

Dialect differences have sometimes been interpreted as a lack of interest in educational achievement. It is common to hear words like "lazy" and "uneducated" to describe both AAE and its speakers. Sometimes these evaluations are based on a misunderstanding of the important but subtle pragmatic and/or discourse differences in how groups use language. Given that AAE grew out of resistance to and subversion of an imposed cultural norm, it should not be surprising that members of this cultural group may use AAE to highlight solidarity and resist assimilation. In fact, anthropologist Signithia Fordham (1998) found that in the high school in Washington, DC, where she did field work, African American students used AAE as one way of refusing to comply with culturally alien aspects of schooling.

Lisa Delpit (1988), an educational anthropologist, reports an anecdote involving some white teachers who felt that an African American teacher in their school was very authoritarian. Speaking loudly and using direct commands rather than indirect suggestions (e.g., "Talk louder, Paula" is direct; "I don't think people can hear you, Paula" is indirect), this teacher struck her colleagues as displaying her power, rather than striving to create the democratic environment they favored. Delpit points out that the African American teacher was following a different set of interactional norms than the white teachers expected. In that teacher's community, authority is not assumed by virtue of status; it is created in the give and take of institutional life. In the school context, teachers from this cultural group act out their authority status in concert with their students, says Delpit, creating and maintaining a social structure that they lead and that casts children as students. These teachers are authoritative leaders, not authoritarian dictators. Judging from their own cultural perspective on appropriate teacher talk, the white teachers had misconstrued the social identities that the African American teacher was assembling with her students, the purpose of her talk, aspects of her oral language, the tone being created, and perhaps even the genre of talk. Students who use such discourse strategies may be interpreted by white teachers in similar negative ways.

Numerous other differences in African Americans' language use have been noted by other linguists, educational researchers, and anthropologists. Some of these findings involve differences that stem from ethnicity, while others suggest that the nature of "teacher talk" and "school language" can also contribute (Foster, 1995). Teachers should not leave unexamined the conventions and discourse routines that students are expected to use in schools. Teachers' own acculturation to these norms may blunt their understanding of how profoundly they may impact students who have different patterns and norms. In fact, James Gee suggests that social and linguistic conventions are tied together in what he calls a "primary Discourse," which "integrate[s] words, acts, values, beliefs, attitudes, and social identities as well as gestures, glances, body position, and clothes" (1989, p. 6). According to this view, acceptable social interaction is complex because it involves verbal and nonverbal communication along with speakers' ongoing evaluation of context, all of which is influenced by social identities that vary by group and individual. In Gee's view of literacy instruction, teachers must examine powerful discourses so they can enable students to be successful in the types of "saying-writing-doing-being-valuing-believing combinations" (1989, p. 6) that schools value. Approaches and programs such as those described in Alim (2005) and Harris-Wright (1999) aim to assist teachers in expanding African American students' understandings of diverse communication styles across many social settings. Harris-Wright (1999), in particular, examines social interaction closely.

The pronunciation, vocabulary, and grammar differences between AAE and Standard English are critically important in educational contexts, and knowledge of these differences can help teachers better meet the literacy and other educational needs of AAE-speaking students. Just as important, however, are the cultural differences that result in different ways of using language. These differences are less likely to be attributed to dialect difference and thus more unlikely to be addressed appropriately.

Latino English

The term *Latino English* is used by linguists to designate an ethnic variety of English spoken by some people of Hispanic descent. The dialect formed out of the collision of two languages (English and Spanish), though under very different circumstances than the crucible of the transatlantic slave trade for AAE. This section examines the history and status of the dialect, dispelling some common misconceptions along the way. As with AAE, naming the variety is contentious. We employ *Latino English* as, arguably, the least problematic term among such options as Chicano English, Hispanicized English, Spanglish, Latin@ English, and Latinx English (see Wolfram & Reaser, 2014, for more on these labels).

The Origins of Latino English

Linguists know more about the origins of Latino English than they do about the origins of AAE, due in part to the fact that more recent contact allows for better records and data. However, it is not correct to speak of a single origin for Latino English, but instead of multiple, separate origins in different places. It must be remembered that the Spanish controlled large swaths of what is now the United States. In fact, the founding of the mission at Santa Fe, NM, predates the founding of Jamestown, VA, by two years (1605 and 1607, respectively). Of course, the first permanent European settlement in the United States occurred with the Spanish-established St. Augustine, FL, in 1565. Beginning in the sixteenth century, Spanish was the most common European language spoken throughout much of what is now Florida, Texas, New Mexico, Arizona, California, Colorado, and Utah. This Spanish monopoly held for nearly three centuries before politics, war, and gold brought English speakers into contact with Spanish speakers.

The area of the United States previously occupied by Mexico, including Texas, Arizona, New Mexico, and California, is where one version of Latino English grew up. In these areas, English and Spanish often would come to exist side-by-side and bilingualism was the norm. It is sometimes surprising to Americans to discover that in this area of the country, there are still towns and areas where English is seldom heard (see, e.g., Kolker, 1999). Throughout much of this region, however, bilingualism remained the norm, though more recently, Spanish has increasingly lost ground to English. South Florida is another location where Spanish and English have coexisted for some time, though the local Latino English dialect in Miami is distinct from Latino English in the Southwest (Carter & Lynch, 2015, forthcoming).

In other areas of the United States, contact between English and Spanish has happened more recently. From 1980 to 2000, the United States received a wave of immigrants from Spanish-speaking countries. In some cases, these new arrivals came to places that had previously had few people of Hispanic heritage, including the Southeastern United States other than Florida (Pew Research Center, 2013). In such places, a variety of Latino English developed as the immigrants learned English (see, e.g., Carter, 2013).

The classic model of language shift for immigrant families has suggested that it typically takes three generations to switch languages. Generally, the first generation arriving in a new place maintains the heritage language. The second generation is bilingual in the heritage language and the local language. The third generation tends to be monolingual in only the local language (see Grosjean, 1982, for a detailed account of this process). Of course there are individual exceptions, but this process has been observed with numerous U.S. immigrant groups arriving in the nineteenth and early twentieth centuries, including

Germans, Poles, Swedes, and Italians. In the case of Spanish in the United States, the shift would look like this:

Generation 1 – immigrant: Spanish only
Generation 2 – native born: Bilingual Spanish and English
Generation 3 – native born: English only

Because the migration of Spanish speakers to the Southeast has happened so recently, linguists have been able to study the formation of a Latino English variety in real time. One of the surprising findings is that in many cases, the three-generational shift was compressed into two generations. Very few Hispanic immigrants did not learn English, and very quickly it became a challenge for the children born in the United States (the second generation) to maintain much Spanish at all, although these children did have distinctive ways of speaking English.

By comparing phonetic and grammatical systems of the languages in contact, it is possible to anticipate features of a new variety by predicting which sounds and structures may give language learners difficulty. When comparing, for example, the consonant systems of English and Spanish, we see that the languages have substantial overlap in their sound inventories. Spanish speakers learning English would be likely to have little or no trouble pronouncing sounds like *p, b, f, s,* and *n,* because these sounds occur in Spanish as well as in English. In some cases, small differences will be apparent, such as the Spanish *r* being used in place of a traditional English *r,* or the consonants *p, t,* and *k* lacking the small puff of air that accompanies English pronunciations of these sounds at the beginnings of words. While these differences contribute to what is perceived as a Spanish accent, they seldom cause any communicative difficulty.

English has a few sounds that Spanish does not, such as a *v, z, sh, j* (as in *judge*), and one of the sounds represented by the English spelling "th" (Spanish has the initial sound of *thigh* but not that of *thy*). When learning English, it is common for Spanish speakers to substitute the closest sound from their language in place of the English sound that their language lacks. They may substitute, for example, an *s* for a *z,* making the pronunciations of *face* and *phase* sound the same. Spanish speakers may also pronounce *v* sounds more like a *b,* making words like *van* and *ban* sound the same (Swan & Smith, 2001). Some of these difficulties in learning English that result from linguistic contrasts can lead to features that are passed down between generations, especially when a large number of people of shared ancestry live in proximity. Other features will fade in subsequent generations. By the first generation of Spanish speakers born in an English-speaking context, most consonant substitutions will likely move toward more native English-like distinctions between, for example, *b* and *v.* Even though the Latino English dialect is not the same as the speech of Spanish speakers in the process of learning English (for example, Spanish speakers learning English may confuse sounds spelled "ch" and "sh" in English, whereas Latino English speakers do not), speakers of other dialects often have trouble distinguishing monolingual Latino English speakers from Spanish speakers who are learning English as a second language. This difficulty is a testament to the enduring effect language contact situations can have on ethnic dialects. It can also feed language prejudice. Since Americans have difficulty differentiating Latino English and learner English, they may judge the English dialect speakers as non-proficient (Fought, 2003). Also people often maintain an unfair stereotype that "associates Spanish with the poor and uneducated" (Fought, 2006, p. 77).

Because of the nature of the language contact, many of the features of Latino English in the Southeast and Southwest are similar, including the sorts of grammatical, pronunciation, and prosodic differences noted in the previous two chapters. Because of this, at first listen, lay observers may conclude that these dialects are the same. In fact, there is important regional variation in Latino English. Some of this difference may be explained by the fact that the Spanish that shaped the Southwest variety was primarily that spoken in Mexico, while the varieties of Spanish that have shaped Latino English in the Southeast come from a much broader geographical area, including Central America and the Caribbean. Further, Spanish in the Southeast can take on a Southern flavor. Some speakers might incorporate *y'all* and other grammatical features and adopt Southern-sounding vowels, as in the *pin/pen* merger (Wolfram, Kohn, & Callahan-Price, 2011). As is the case with the New York City Puerto Rican community, some speakers may incorporate more African American or local white features into their English dialect, depending on how they identify personally (Zentella, 1997). By contrast, in Miami, Cuban Americans tend to resist local English norms in their speech (Carter & Lynch, forthcoming). As the language variety now in development becomes an important marker of cultural identity, it is likely that it will be preserved from one generation to the next.

The Status of Latino English

Latino English is now the native English dialect of millions of Americans and growing. By some estimates, those of Hispanic heritage are expected to make up 25% of the U.S. population by 2050 (Pew Research Center, 2013). In areas where Latinos have been present for a long time, like the Southwest and California, and where the dialect is quite stable, it can index intra-community social class differences as well as express individual identity. In a study of American-born, young Latino English speakers in Los Angeles, CA, Carmen Fought found the following groupings—some of which overlap—relevant to dialect differences: Gang-affiliated, known gang members, non-gang, taggers, wanna-bes, nerds, moms, boys, girls, "white affiliated kids," and "black affiliated kids" (2003, pp. 55–59). The role of community and personal identity shapes language development in important ways. In more recently established communities, social divisions underlying linguistic differences may also be based on other factors, such as country of origin (Wolfram, Kohn, & Callahan-Price, 2011). Clearly the dialect is marked by tremendous variation.

Latino English at School

Compared to work on AAE-speaking students, there are few studies on Latino English speakers in educational contexts: "Few books have focused on the richness of the cultural, linguistic, and experiential resources that Latino students bring to school, and on what teachers need to know and do to tap into these resources" (Nieto, 2001, p. ix). Of the studies that do exist, research on Latinos in classroom settings has found that cultural patterns regarding appropriate discourse participation can lead to a self-silencing effect. One study of university students on academic probation found that Latino students experienced classes that required participation as "a form of punishment, one that was disproportionately unfair to them as minorities" (White, 2011, p. 256). Students felt "picked on" because they felt ill-prepared for the academic frames expected in classroom discussions. The students reported that when "using his or her own native voice/discursive style, he or she would be judged in a negative manner" (White, 2011, p. 256). All of the Latino students in this study went on to explain that they could use the desired discourse conventions if they had to, but that doing so involved "selling out"; one student, Alex, described this as meaning "talking like White people, acting like White people" (White, 2011, p. 259). More research on the culture of Latino communities is needed before researchers can understand how discourse differences impact the school experience.

Other issues have been discussed for Spanish-English bilingual (Santa Ana, 2002) and Latino English speakers in U.S. schools. Carter (2014) documents the roots of some issues in a lack of understanding that Latino English speakers often do not speak Spanish. He notes that monolingual Latino English students are often subject to the same "Spanish as Threat" discourse that Spanish-speaking immigrants face. Thus, these students may be met with distrust or disdain. He also notes that many "native speakers of English are nevertheless assigned to ESL on the basis of surnames or presumed home language" (2014, p. 219). He notes that these students' English dialect often prevents them from "testing out" of ESL classes because "ESL placement tests that focus on literacy skills effectively keep Latino students with strong oral language skills tracked in ESL" (2014, p. 219). This designation means Latino English speakers become disproportionately exposed to remedial instruction as well as to other difficulties associated with ESL tracking, such as separation from the rest of the school population, scheduling conflicts with core curricular classes, and over-enrollment in vocational education classes. One of the paradoxical by-products of the school Carter observed was that these improperly tracked students were tracked into a fundamentally monolingual experience at school, presumably based on an assumption regarding the value of speaking English, while mainstream English-speaking students took Spanish as a foreign language, presumably based on an assumption about the value of being bilingual. Carter calls this "the double figuration of Spanish class, in which Spanish is promoted for non-Latinos and prohibited for Latinos" (2014, p. 218).

Few studies have examined the reading and writing development of Latino English speakers. Despite its prevalence, Latino English in K–12 classroom settings has been less researched than African American English or native Spanish-speaking English language learners (see, e.g., Valdés, 2001). One of those few studies examined reading errors of struggling readers and concluded that Latino English speakers produced more types of reading errors than AAE speakers of a similar reading level (Labov & Baker, 2010), suggesting that Latino English speakers may need more support than AAE speakers. This finding may undergird why Latino English speakers are disproportionately diagnosed with language disorders, which will be examined in Chapter 6. It also led to the state of Texas issuing a report with recommendations for teaching these students, including having teachers complete professional development that examines the "features of the English varieties in Texas from the perspective of their contrast with the parallel features in standard English" (Wilkerson, et al., 2011, p. 24).

Asian American English

Since the 1980s, much more research has been conducted on immigrants in the broad "Asian American" category. Traditionally, the all-encompassing label "Asian" has been used to describe widely diverse populations, from Japan to Cambodia to Pakistan. Almost 20 million North Americans fit the designation of "Asian," and this population showed the highest percentage growth (46%) of any ethnic category in the United States between 2000 and 2010. The largest ethnic groups are Chinese, Filipino, Indian, Vietnamese, Korean, and Japanese, but there are also other sizeable groups such as Pakistani, Cambodian, Hmong, Thai, and Laotian. Much of the language research has focused on language learning via ESL instruction in the United States and abroad, but more recent research has involved documenting emerging dialects of American English among different Asian groups (Wolfram & Schilling, 2016).

One of the fascinating issues in this research and cultural studies in general involves the fit of these immigrants into the available racial and ethnic categories. Bucholtz (2004) notes that these immigrants are classified as non-white in the United States, but they also tend to be excluded from categorizations such as people or students "of color." This is true in some statistical reporting, too, in which schools report "percent minority" as an accounting of African American and Hispanic students. Yet, a common label for this group, "model minority," clearly designates minority status for Asians. This description merges two contrasting characteristics: "forever foreigner" and "honorary white" (Tuan, 1998). The "forever foreigner" status promotes the notion that Asian Americans are presumed to be primary speakers of their heritage language rather than English, no matter what their actual native language is, while the "honorary white" status presumes English competence and assimilation to white mainstream sociolinguistic norms. The latter also limits the range of linguistic characteristics Asians have available in crafting their social identities.

Asian Americans are subject to other stereotypes that can affect how people perceive them and their use of language, for example, the notion that they are all intelligent but socially inept—hardworking, mild-mannered, nerdy, and high-achieving with special aptitude in math and science. And while such stereotypes portray the group in a positive way, they level the substantial diversity among Asians. Researchers believe that the "model minority" categorization is damaging to the many Asian Americans who do not fit it (Wu, 2001; Reyes, 2011). Lee (1994), for example, investigates the marginalization of Asian American youth who fail to achieve high academic accomplishments despite embracing the stereotypical work ethic. Lee notes that the model minority stereotype offers "smart but uncool" as the only available social category, and students who fail to demonstrate high intelligence have no other positive identity options. Teachers must be sensitive to the cultural, linguistic, and individual variation among a group that is often viewed as more homogenous than it is.

This section examines broadly the diverse experiences that groups of Asian Americans face as their languages come into contact with English in the American educational system. In their guide to learner English, Swan and Smith (2001) offer chapters comparing English phonetics and grammar to each of the following: Malay, Chinese, Japanese, Korean, and Thai. Though the book is intended as a resource and not a definitive description, these chapters combine a tremendous amount of cultural and linguistic variation in problematic ways. For example, the chapter on "Chinese speakers" lumps together speakers of Mandarin, Shanghainese, Taiwanese, and Cantonese, all of which differ substantially from each other and have very different phonologies. The way in which relevant details are obscured by the generalized label "Chinese" reflects the process that most Asian Americans face as they assimilate into American culture. Perhaps there is no firmer reminder of this erasure of difference than the very label "Asian American," since in the mind of many Americans, the term *Asia* excludes the Middle East, a number of former Soviet republics, and even India. More specific designations, such as "East Asian" (China, Japan, Korea, etc.), "Southeast Asian" (Thailand, Laos, Cambodia, Myanmar, Vietnam, the Philippines, Indonesia, etc.), and "South Asian" (India, Pakistan, Afghanistan,

Sri Lanka, etc.), do offer more geographical precision, but each still obscures tremendous ethnic and linguistic diversity.

Is There an Asian American Dialect?

Given the vast ethnic and linguistic variation found in Asia, it may seem somewhat strange to ask whether linguists can identify an Asian American dialect. Unlike the African American and Latino groups discussed above, there does not appear to be any common core of structures that can be identified as Asian American English, although there are, of course, a number of linguistic stereotypes that feed linguistic parodies in popular culture and in comedic routines (Chun, 2004, 2009). For example, parodies of East Asian speakers may focus on the lack of distinction between *r* and *l* generically. In fact, the patterning of *l* and *r* is not the same across the languages of East Asia. Japanese has no contrast between *r* and *l* but includes a single sound that lies phonetically between those sounds in English. Cantonese has *l*, but no equal to the English *r*. Korean has both sounds but the difference is determined by phonetic contexts. A parallel example from English can be discovered by holding your hand in front of your mouth as you say the words *pit* and *spit*. With the former, you feel a puff of air accompanying the *p* sound. There is no puff of air in *spit*. Thus English has two versions of the *p* sound but alternation between them never causes a difference in word meaning in English. In Korean, the difference in pronunciation between *r* and *l* never changes a word's meaning. Finally, some southern dialects of Vietnamese have both consonants whereas other Vietnamese dialects only have *l*. Thus, Asian American students may have quite different productions and perceptions of the English *r* and *l* distinction that come into play when learning the English distinction. These differences in native language cause differences in the English spoken by each immigrant group. This variation is often not perceived by native English speakers who may assume more homogeneity among Asian Englishes than is appropriate.

Broad generalizations about a single *Asian American English* are inappropriate given the linguistic and cultural diversity subsumed under that label. However, a few generalizations are applicable to a number of groups of East and Southeast Asian origin. Studies of the language of Asian immigrants have mostly focused on interlanguage and transfer traits relevant for English language learners, but they may persist as features of a dialect for native English speakers in subsequent generations. For example, many Asian languages do not have grammatical systems that mark past tense by adding morphemes to root verbs. This can make the tense and aspect system of English difficult to learn—and quite vulnerable to transfer from the native language or general principles of second language learning. Other kinds of inflectional suffixes, such as -*s* plural, possessive, and third-person singular, are also quite vulnerable to modification in the process of acquiring English, though these features are seldom maintained in subsequent generations. As in Latino English, some phonetic differences may persist in the English dialects spoken by those of Asian heritage. For example, few Asian languages have the complex sequences of consonants that can occur in English at the beginning (*street, split*) or end (*attempts, twelfths*) of words, making them vulnerable to adaptation for English language learners and the English dialects of subsequent generations (Hall-Lew & Starr, 2010). Vowel variations resulting from language contact may also be preserved in the English dialects of monolingual Asian Americans (Wong & Hall-Lew, 2014).

Though there exists a good bit of research on the English of Asian Americans, most of the linguistic research on these groups focuses on the English language learning of speakers of specific languages. Fewer studies examine the half-, first-, and second-generation speakers as they adapt to American English norms and develop a variety of English in the community. However, when such studies are conducted, they also tend to focus on speakers from a specific region and/or a particular cultural and linguistic heritage rather than a generic group of "Asians." For example, in one study in New York City, Newman and Wu (2011, p. 171) concluded that "Asian Americans—at least Korean and Chinese Americans—are indeed distinct pieces of the U.S. racial dialectal mosaic" although "the cues to racial identity are fewer and subtler than, say, for African Americans and Latinos in New York City." A wide range of social factors may correlate with ethnolinguistic distinctiveness and accommodation, including generational status in the immigrant family, orientation toward ethnic heritage or North American lifestyles, religion, and residency area. However, it must be recognized that all of these influences intersect, and factors such as ethnic orientation are not separable from others such as age, generation, and gender.

Researchers have also examined the incorporation of features from non-mainstream vernacular varieties by Asian Americans in conversational interaction, including the use of slang (Chun, 2001; Reyes, 2011). For example, Angela Reyes (2005, 2011) examined conversations among a group of Philadelphia teenagers whose families came from Cambodia, Laos, and Vietnam to illustrate how they appropriated African American slang expressions such as *aite* ("alright") and *na mean* ("You know what I mean") in a way that differentiated the youth from adults and from each other. For example, Southeast Asian teens with ties to the local African American community used African American slang terms differently from those in the "out-group" with respect to African American contact, establishing their local authority through their use of slang in social interaction. Examining language use, including the way in which slang is appropriated in interaction and discourse is organized, may be as essential as studying particular pronunciation and grammar traits to understanding how language is used to situate speakers from different groups, including groups of students in the classroom.

The vast cultural differences among groups from East and Southeast Asia make for great variety in language use patterns that might impact students in

American classrooms. One study found substantial differences in narrative structure between Japanese American students and American students (Minami & McCabe, 1995). Other work has found differences in interactional preferences, expectations about turn-taking, views of authority, expectations related to gender, and other differences among students of Asian heritage. For example, research suggests that Japanese students do not respond well to being put on the spot, and therefore might not feel comfortable in more spontaneous classroom environments; Korean students, by contrast, adapt more quickly to such environments, though they are likely to pause intentionally—a sign of thoughtfulness—before responding (Swan & Smith, 2001). The linguistic and cultural diversity of these and other immigrant groups means that teachers must invest in coming to understand more about the cultures and language patterns their students bring to class. So often the burden of communication or assimilation is placed entirely on the student who does not speak mainstream American English. Effective teachers should access available resources to help bridge these cultural and linguistic differences.

Language Contact and Cultural Norms

When languages come into contact, it is somewhat straightforward—through comparative linguistics—to predict potential pronunciation and grammar contrasts that might lead to features of a new dialect. However, it is more difficult to predict how differences in cultural norms in the form of discourse and pragmatic conventions will affect the communication patterns of these speakers in educational settings. One of the consistent findings of the three language contact situations described in this chapter is that cultural norms can have profound effects on student and teacher attitudes and expectations. They also suggest that teachers need more information about how classroom norms and expectations might affect their students' participation and achievement.

One of the key understandings for teachers is that we make a tremendous number of assumptions when we communicate. These include assumptions about shared knowledge, pragmatic conventions, and discourse strategies. These all exist well beyond understandings of words and sentences in isolation. It is common for fluent speakers of different cultural backgrounds to have misunderstandings when they communicate because of differences in these assumptions. When the power differential between student and teacher is introduced, these misunderstandings can have profound implications.

Consider some of the assumptions that underlie metaphor. Everyone uses figurative language, and most conventional figures of speech (e.g., *at the end of the day*) are understood automatically by other speakers of the same language. But figurative language is rooted in culture. Even basic metaphors of time and space are culturally based. For much of the world, the past is behind you and the future lies in front of you. Phrases such as "I'm looking forward to meeting you" or "Put that behind you and move on" rely on this basic metaphor.

But in Tuva, spoken in part of Siberia (Rymer, 2012), and in Aymara, spoken in Bolivia (Hirshon, 2006), the past is in front of you and the future behind you. This convention arises from the cultural view that you can see your past but not your future. Thus, the things that you can see (i.e., the past) exist in front of you. In a similar way, graphical representations such as graphs and timelines are structured in English with the past to the left, an orientation that has to do with how the language is read (in English, left to right). Hebrew and Arabic are read right to left, and so they reverse their depictions of time (Hammond, 2012). Dialects of a language also have specific metaphors and idioms. Among social dialects of English, for example, hip hop relies heavily on metaphoric language to create slang items, including, for example, *ice* for *diamonds*. African American English uses the metaphoric term *ashy* to describe dry or discolored skin. Regional dialects also have their specific metaphors, which are often considered to be "quaint" instead of "slangy." As you travel throughout the Southeast to Texas, you might hear numerous variations of the same metaphor. For example, in various places throughout this region, you might hear a heavy rain referred to as a *frog/toad drowner, frog/toad strangler, frog/toad choker,* or *frog/toad floater*. Virtually all communication makes use of some metaphoric language or conventions, so understanding these conventions is important for educators who might otherwise assume all students share their understanding of common metaphors.

Beyond metaphor and figurative language, different groups may have contrasting expectations for engaging in social interaction. Speakers naturally calibrate their talk to aspects of the context and to what others have said, based on their culture's norms for interaction. Certain contexts assume highly predictable language forms and behaviors. For example, everyday occurrences such as greetings are ritualized. That explains why it can be somewhat difficult to respond when a doctor asks "How are you?" as part of a greeting sequence (when it might be a genuine information question). Even sick patients may respond with "Fine" in deference to the ritualistic response. Greeting rituals are governed by cultural norms. In the South, for example, greeting is generally more elaborate than elsewhere in the country and more highly prized. Learning these rituals, an important part of language socialization into a dialect community, can be challenging in language contact situations.

A language ritual in certain African American communities, called *sounding, signifying, joning, woofing, playing the dozens*, and other local terms, involves ritualistic insults among groups of young males and builds on verbal one-upmanship from a fairly low-key exchange at the start to a point of considerable verbal creativity. The insults traded usually include slurs on the opponent and the opponent's family, focusing primarily on the mother.

Schools observe rituals too, of course, such as the events that mark the beginning or end of each day or class period (e.g., "circle time" in elementary schools, "exit slip" routines in higher grades). Rituals such as sitting "criss-cross applesauce" and asking permission to use the bathroom are remarkably important in many classroom contexts, but have little place outside of formal education. All of these routines are likely to include some highly predictable interactional patterns and even recurring phrases and specific terms, although details may well differ from classroom to classroom. Students come to know the special meanings connected with these rituals and how to participate in them. Consider the phrase "Spelling counts." The literal interpretation of the phrase is absurd, but those socialized in American schools will recognize that it informs the students in the class of a parameter of evaluation. Further, when a teacher says, "I want you to be responsible for the material on page 243," or a student says, "Do we have to know the perfect numbers?" special meanings are being conveyed concerning what may appear on a test. Successful participation in the classroom requires understanding these meanings.

Living with Language Behavior Difference

In the face of diverse communicative styles such as those mentioned in this chapter, schools may try to identify some basic guidelines for classroom interaction that all students need to follow. Box 4.1 reproduces rules guiding

BOX 4.1: HOW CLASSROOM RULES REINFORCE
CULTURALLY SPECIFIC NORMS

We will:

1. Enter the room quickly and quietly and take our seats.
2. Look and listen for instructions.
3. Begin work on time.
4. Work carefully and quietly.
5. Respect others.
6. Raise our hands and wait if we have a question or contribution.

These formal guidelines are different from the unconscious interactional rules of culture. For one thing, they are prescriptive rather than descriptive of the patterns that actually underlie social interaction in most classrooms. They are intended to restrict student talk rather than to facilitate interaction. They specify that students will talk only when the teacher calls on them. Actually, in successful, exciting, teacher-led lessons, teachers are likely to reward spontaneous student contributions. Certainly, there are some basic interactional guidelines for school behavior that all students have to follow, but if guidelines that repress talk were actually enforced, they would restrict the communication that is central to learning. Many educators say or show through their interactions with students that a more effective way to diminish communication difficulties due to cultural differences is to foster trust and respect.

classroom interaction that were posted in an elementary classroom along with some commentary on the guidelines.

Culturally-based interactional style differences may get in the way of understanding, but it is also true that not every difference is disruptive. In one multicultural first grade classroom, it became clear that two friends—an African American and a Vietnamese American—had quite different argument participation strategies, but their styles seemed not to conflict (Adger, 1986). The African American boy protested forcefully when other students offended him and continued protesting vigorously to win the argument, whereas the Vietnamese American boy used language to defuse a confrontation. The fact that the boys seemed to have different conversational goals may have made it possible for each to find satisfaction in their arguments with each other. The African American boy could always get the last word because the Vietnamese American boy did not want it, and the Vietnamese American boy could defuse the argument by not seeking to win it. There was also evidence that the children gradually accommodated to the contrasts in each other's interactional style.

This chapter has shown something of the complexity associated with varieties of language that arise out of contact situations and come to be associated with a social group. Features range from the details of vowel differences to the broader patterns of interaction. The goal of the discussion is not to be comprehensive in details, but to raise awareness so that those in various education institutional roles will be sensitive to the pervasive, intricate operation of language differences in our lives. This chapter also demonstrates that in school settings, the burden of linguistic adaptation falls disproportionately on speakers whose English is most dissimilar from mainstream American English, be it the English of a language learner or a vernacular dialect speaker. We aim to open up new perspectives and increase knowledge about the practical role of language variation in everyday lives, especially at school, so that teachers and other language professionals can better assume some of the linguistic burden of these students. Language contact and cultural diversity can result in subtle differences in language use that can produce big differences in educational opportunity and attainment.

Discussion Questions

1. Investigate the notion of Standard African American English. How is it different from vernacular African American English, as described in this chapter? What different social functions does it serve?

2. When authors include vernacular dialect-speaking characters in books, they sometimes make egregious errors in representing their speech. How do you explain this? Is it important that writers represent dialects accurately?

3. Use evidence from this chapter to argue that vernacular dialects are not simply sloppy English.

4. Explain why AAE and Latino English are useful in maintaining social identity for their speakers.
5. Why is there not one unitary version of Latino English?
6. Why is there not one unitary version of Asian American English?
7. Is there a unitary version of AAE?
8. What contrasting discourse styles have you experienced? What contrasting cultural norms do you think account for the contrast?

Links of Interest

1. Compare the *Dictionary of American Regional English* entries for "frog-strangler" and "toad-strangler": www.daredictionary.com/view/dare/ID_00022303 & http://dare.wisc.edu/words/100-entries/toad-strangler
2. Study an article that introduces African American English for speech-language pathologists: http://slp4teachers.wmwikis.net/file/view/African+American+English+-An+Overview.pdf
3. Read an overview of African American English on the *Do You Speak American?* website: www.pbs.org/speak/seatosea/americanvarieties/AAVE/
4. Think about common myths about Spanish in the United States: www.pbs.org/speak/seatosea/americanvarieties/spanglish/usa/
5. Watch a video on Latino English in Texas: www.youtube.com/watch?v=LHteyOWdeqg
6. Learn about some differences between English and Spanish: http://esl.fis.edu/grammar/langdiff/spanish.htm
7. Learn about some differences between English and Japanese: http://esl.fis.edu/grammar/langdiff/japanese.htm
8. Read a guide to teaching English to Vietnamese students: www.sandiego.edu/esl/cultures/vietnamese/teachingvietnamese.htm

Further Reading

Alim, S. H., & Smitherman, G. (2012). *Articulate while black: Barack Obama, language, and race in the U.S.* Oxford, UK: Oxford University Press.
    Written for a general audience, this volume examines the interplay of language, politics, and race through an investigation of Barack Obama's linguistic dexterity. It further examines the coded language that permeates discussions of race and power and perpetuates inequality.

Crystal, D. (1997). *English as a global language.* Cambridge, UK: Cambridge University Press.
    This short volume examines the historical, cultural, media, and economic forces that have helped English spread across the planet. It also examines the different varieties and roles of English in diverse settings.

Green, L. J. (2002). *African American English: A linguistic introduction.* Cambridge, UK: Cambridge University Press.
    An accessible introduction to the phonological, grammatical, and discourse patterns of African American English. The book concludes with sections on African American English in literature, the media, and education.

Fought, C. (2003). *Chicano English in context*. New York, NY: Palgrave.
Written for language scholars, this volume offers a linguistic description of the English spoken by people of Hispanic ancestry. It examines different cohorts of young Chicano English speakers in school settings, which may be useful to some teachers.

Fought, C. (2006). *Language and ethnicity*. Cambridge, UK: Cambridge University Press.
This textbook introduction to the intersection of language and ethnicity is written in a highly engaging style. Grounded in sociological theory, the book examines a number of contexts in the United States and around the world in order to offer a complete picture of the symbiotic relationship between language and ethnicity.

Nero, S. J. (Ed.). (2005). *Dialects, Englishes, creoles, and education*. Mahwah, NJ: Lawrence Erlbaum Associates.
Contributors to this volume focus on a number of varieties of English resulting from language contact, including Caribbean Creole English, Hawaii Creole English, Hispanicized English, West African English and creoles, Indian English, and Philippine English. They explore issues of language attitudes, language policy, and educational programming for speakers of these varieties.

Swan, M., & Smith, B. (Eds.). (2001). *Learner English. A teacher's guide to interference and other problems*. Cambridge, UK: Cambridge University Press.
Written for teachers of English language learners, this volume offers chapters that compare the phonologies and grammars of English and other languages, highlighting differences that are likely to be important in learning English. Many chapters also include information about cultural differences that may affect teacher/student interactions.

References

Adger, C. T. (1986). When difference does not conflict: Successful arguments between Black and Vietnamese classmates. *Text, 6*, 223–237.

Alim, H. S. (2005). Critical language awareness in the United States: Revisiting issues and revising pedagogies in a resegregated society. *Educational Researcher, 34*(7), 24–31.

Bailey, G., Maynor, N., & Cukor-Avila, P. (Eds.). (1991). *The emergence of Black English: Text and commentary*. Philadelphia, PA: John Benjamins.

Baugh, J. (1999). *Out of the mouths of slaves: African American language and educational malpractice*. Austin, TX: University of Texas Press.

Boser, U. (2014). *Teacher diversity revisited*. Washington, DC: Center for American Progress.

Britt, E., & Weldon, T. L. (2015). African American English in the middle class. In S. Lanehart (Ed.), *The Oxford handbook of African American language* (pp. 800–816). Oxford, UK: Oxford University Press.

Bucholtz, M. (2004). Styles and stereotypes: The linguistic negotiation of identity among Laotian American youth. *Pragmatics, 14*(2/3), 127–148.

Carter, P. M. (2013). Shared spaces, shared structures: Latino social formation and African American English in the U.S. South. *Journal of Sociolinguistics, 17*(1), 66–92.

Carter, P. M. (2014). National narratives, institutional ideologies, and local talk: The discursive production of Spanish in a "new" U.S. Latino community. *Language in Society, 43*(2), 209–240.

Carter, P. M., & Lynch, A. (2015). Multilingual Miami: Current trends in sociolinguistic research. *Language and Linguistics Compass, 9*(9), 369–385.

Carter, P. M., & Lynch, A. (forthcoming). On the status of Miami as a southern city: Defining language and region through demography and social history. In J. Reaser, E. Wilbanks, K. Wojcik, & W. Wolfram (Eds.), *Language variety in the New South: Change and variation*. Manuscript under review by University of North Carolina Press.

Chun, E. W. (2001). The construction of white, black, and Korean American identities through African American Vernacular English. *Journal of Linguistic Anthropology, 11*(1), 52–64.

Chun, E. W. (2004). Ideologies of legitimate mockery: Margaret Cho's revoicings of mock Asian. *Pragmatics, 14*(2/3), 263–290.

Chun, E. W. (2009). Speaking like Asian immigrants: Intersections of accommodation and mocking at a U.S. high school. *Pragmatics, 19*(1), 17–38.

Delpit, L. (1988). The silenced dialogue: Power and pedagogy in educating other people's children. *Harvard Educational Review, 58,* 280–298.

Fordham, S. (1998). Speaking standard English from nine to three: Language as guerrilla warfare at Capital High. In S. Hoyle & C. T. Adger (Eds.), *Kids talk: Strategic language use in later childhood* (pp. 205–216). New York, NY: Oxford University Press.

Foster, M. (1995). Talking that talk: The language of control, curriculum, and critique. *Linguistics and Education, 7*(2), 129–150.

Fought, C. (2003). *Chicano English in context.* New York, NY: Palgrave.

Fought, C. (2006). *Language and ethnicity.* Cambridge, UK: Cambridge University Press.

Gee, J. P. (1989). Literacy, discourse, and linguistics: Introduction. *The Journal of Education, 171*(1), 5–176.

Green, L. J. (2002). *African American English: A linguistic introduction.* Cambridge, UK: Cambridge University Press.

Grosjean, F. (1982). *Life with two languages: An introduction to bilingualism.* Cambridge, MA: Harvard University Press.

Hall-Lew, L., & R. L. Starr. (2010). Beyond 2nd generation: English use among Chinese Americans in the San Francisco Bay area. *English Today, 26*(3), 12–19.

Hammond, C. (2012). *Time warped: Unlocking the mysteries of time perception.* Edinburgh: Canongate Books.

Harris-Wright, K. (1999). Enhancing bidialectalism in urban African-American students. In C. T. Adger, D. Christian, & O. Taylor (Eds.), *Making the connection: Language and academic achievement among African-American students* (pp. 53–60). McHenry, IL: Delta Systems and Center for Applied Linguistics.

Hirshon, B. (2006, Aug. 4). Backs to the future. *ScienceNetLinks.* Retrieved from http://sciencenetlinks.com/science-news/science-updates/backs-to-the-future/

Kolker, C. (1999, Aug. 13). Town speaks the language of its people. *Los Angeles Times.* Retrieved from http://articles.latimes.com/1999/aug/13/news/mn-65233

Labov, W. (1987). Are Black and White vernaculars diverging? Papers from the NWAVE XIV panel discussion. *American Speech, 62,* 5–12.

Labov, W., & Baker, B. (2010). What is a reading error? *Applied Psycholinguistics, 31*(4), 735–757.

Lee, Stacey J. (1994). Behind the model-minority stereotype: Voices of high-achieving and low-achieving Asian American students. *Anthropology and Education Quarterly, 25*(4), 413–429.

Minami, M., & McCabe, A. (1995). Rice balls and bear hunts: Japanese and North American family narrative patterns. *Journal of Child Language, 22*(2), 423–445.

Mufwene, S. S. (1996). The development of American Englishes: Some questions from a creole genesis hypothesis. In E. W. Schneider (Ed.), *Focus on the USA* (pp. 231–264). Philadelphia, PA: John Benjamins.

Newman, M., & Wu, A. (2011). "Do you sound Asian when you speak English?" Racial identification and voice in Chinese and Korean Americans' English. *American Speech, 86*(2), 152–178.

Nieto, S. (2001). Foreword. In M. de la Luz Reyes & J. Halcón (Eds.), *The best for our children: Critical perspectives on literacy for Latino students* (pp. ix–xi). New York, NY: Teachers College Press.

Patrick, P. L. (1999). *Urban Jamaican creole: Variation in the mesolect.* Philadelphia, PA: John Benjamins.

Pew Research Center. (2013). Mapping the Latino population, by state, county, and city. Retrieved from www.pewhispanic.org/2013/08/29/ii-ranking-latino-populations-in-the-states/

Poplack, S. (Ed.). (1999). *The English history of African American English.* Malden, MA: Blackwell.

Reyes, A. (2005). Appropriation of African American slang by Asian American youth. *Journal of Sociolinguistics, 9*(4), 509–532.

Reyes, A. (2011). *Language, identity, and stereotype among Southeast Asian American youth: The other Asian.* New York, NY: Routledge.

Rickford, J. R. (1997). Prior creolization of African-American vernacular English? Sociohistorical and textual evidence from the 17th and 18th centuries. *Journal of Sociolinguistics, 1*(3), 315–336.

Roberge. P. T. (2012). Pidgins, creoles, and the creation of language. In M. Tallerman & K. R. Gibson (Eds.), *The Oxford handbook of language evolution* (pp. 537–544). Oxford, UK: Oxford University Press.

Rymer, R. (2012, July). Vanishing voices. *National Geographic*. Retrieved from http://ngm. nationalgeographic.com/2012/07/vanishing-languages/rymer-text

Santa Ana, O. (2002). *Brown tide rising: Metaphors of Latinos in contemporary American public discourse*. Austin, TX: University of Texas Press.

Singler, J. V. (1998). What's not new in AAVE. *American Speech, 73*(3), 227–256.

Smitherman, G. (2000). *Black talk: Words and phrases from the hood to the amen corner* (Revised ed.). New York, NY: Houghton Mifflin.

Swan, M., & Smith, B. (Eds.). (2001). *Learner English. A teacher's guide to interference and other problems*. Cambridge, UK: Cambridge University Press.

Tuan, M. (1998). *Forever foreigners or honorary Whites: The Asian-American experience today*. New Brunswick, NJ: Rutgers University Press.

Valdés, G. (2001). *Learning and not learning English: Latino students in American schools*. New York, NY: Teachers College Press.

White, J. W. (2011). Resistance to classroom participation: Minority students, academic discourse, cultural conflicts, and issues of representation in whole class discussions. *Journal of Language, Identity & Education, 10*(4), 250–265.

Wilkerson, C., Miciak, J., Alexander, C., Reyes, P., Brown, J., & Giani, M. (2011). *Recommended educational practices for Standard English learners*. Austin, TX: Education Research Center, University of Texas at Austin.

Wolfram, W. (1998). Language ideology and dialect: Understanding the Oakland Ebonics controversy. *Journal of English Linguistics, 26*(2), 108–121.

Wolfram, W., Kohn, M., & Callahan-Price, E. (2011). Southern-bred Hispanic English: An emerging socioethnic variety. In J. Michnowicz & R. Dodsworth (Eds.), *Selected proceedings of the 5th workshop on Spanish sociolinguistics* (pp. 1–13). Somerville, MA: Cascadilla.

Wolfram, W., & Reaser, J. (2014). *Talkin' Tar Heel: How our voices tell the story of North Carolina*. Chapel Hill, NC: University of North Carolina Press.

Wolfram, W., & Schilling, N. (2016). *American English: Dialects and variation* (3rd ed.). Malden MA: John Wiley & Sons.

Wolfram, W., & Thomas, E. R. (2002). *The development of African American English*. Malden, MA: Blackwell.

Wong, A. W., & Hall-Lew, L. (2014). Regional variability and ethnic identity: Chinese Americans in New York City and San Francisco. *English Language and Linguistics, 17*(2), 359–390.

Wu, F. (2001). *Yellow: Race beyond black and white*. New York, NY: Basic Books.

Zentella, A. C. (1997). *Growing up bilingual: Puerto Rican children in New York*. Malden, MA: Blackwell.

Establishing Language Norms

Scenario

Imagine you are supposed to get together with a newish friend and you are running late. You text/message your friend, "Hey. Running late. B there in 15." Imagine how you might interpret the following responses:

1. K
2. K.
3. Ok
4. Ok.
5. NP
6. NP.
7. :-)
8. Lol
9. Lol.
10. Typical
11. Typical ;-)
12. Typical.
13. No problem.
14. Looking forward to seeing you
15. Looking forward to whenever you get here
16. whenever
17. [indication that friend is typing, followed by no response]

What sorts of emotions are potentially conveyed through each of the responses? Can you group them in meaningful ways? Can you rank them from seemingly least annoyed to most annoyed? What patterns do you notice in your groupings and rankings? What sorts of norms govern texting? How are these norms formed? How do you learn them? Can you think about times when you had a miscommunication while texting? What caused it? How do features like auto-correct, autocapitalize, and predictive language parsing (in which your phone offers suggestions for what word is likely to come next) affect your texting habits? How do these features affect texting norms?

These response options are brief but meaningful to those who share under-lying expectations—norms—for text communication. Text-users draw on these implicit rules in order to understand the different shades of meaning in the responses. These kinds of language norms are generally acquired informally rather than being explicitly taught: You know the norms for texting as a result of your own experience, and you know how they differ from the norms for other genres of written language. The context and medium of communication trigger particular expectations for language use. For example, brief responses and use of emojis in texting are not only allowed, they are expected.

It turns out that there are several kinds of language norms, and the differ-ences among them are important to an understanding of language variation and its social consequences. The *descriptive* approach to language seeks to uncover the underlying linguistic rules that govern features and patterns, as was illus-trated in the example given in Chapter 2 on the pattern for the absence of the verb *to be* in some sentences. Descriptivism is a rigorous, scientifically based methodology, involving comprehensive analysis of data. Its goal is to discover the norms that the community uses, not to make any judgment about them. In contrast, *prescriptivism* sets out to prescribe explicit language rules that speakers should follow, based largely on opinion and tradition. Linguists are often dismissive of prescriptivism even though this perspective is influential socially. However, it is important for teachers and language practitioners to understand both the scientific perspective on language and other perspectives, like prescriptivism, that may permeate educational contexts through colleagues, students, parents, administrators, or assessments. Because prescriptive rules often play a role in the social critique of vernacular dialects, we explore these kinds of language norms in this chapter.

How people perceive the differences between dialects depends to some extent on how they feel about language norms. If they subscribe to a single set of explicit norms, they may interpret language use that is different from those norms as evidence of the speaker's linguistic or cognitive deficit. Further, they may view changes in the language that depart from traditional norms as evidence of language decay. The view that variation and change are problems—a pervasive, established perspective—is based on a belief that a unitary English language exists, that there is one logical, correct form of English, and that all other varieties are imperfect approximations of it. This prescriptive view generally claims that there are correct and incorrect ways of using a language rooted in etymology, logic, or tradition.

This chapter discusses the process by which certain language forms and patterns become codified as acceptable according to prescriptive norms, while others are rejected as unacceptable or nonstandard. It examines how these language norms evolve and change over time, and the effects they can have when they are used to judge language performance. We then turn to a discussion about the role of new modalities such as social media on language norms.

We conclude by focusing in on the specialized language norms found in school contexts and suggesting again that educators take an active role in understanding the effects of these norms on their students.

Perceptions of Language Decline

Declining Standards of Usage?

There are widespread feelings that the English language is changing for the worse, that it is under siege, and that it needs to be protected from abuse (that is, the rules of Standard English are not being enforced). Many people see vernacular dialects not as a natural part of the variation within any living language, but as evidence that the language as a whole is in serious trouble. One recent guardian of the language was John Simon, who served as theater critic at *New York* magazine for many years and frequently commented on people's use of English. In the PBS program, *Do You Speak American?* (MacNeil/Lehrer Productions, 2005), Simon tells host Robert MacNeil that the state of American English today is "unhealthy, poor, sad, depressing, and probably fairly hopeless." People who share Simon's perspective, *prescriptivists*, generally resist language change and advocate usage norms for everyone to follow. To support their views and approach, they may provide evidence of perceived language decay, including new slang words, lack of distinction between forms (e.g., *less* vs. *fewer*), or new usages of existing words (using *literally* to mean *figuratively* ["It's so hot today that I'm literally melting"]). A linguist's perspective is that language changes are part of the natural life of any living language.

It is easy to find people who object to the linguistic position and see change as an increase in sloppy, lazy usage. Those who hold this view might justify it by citing what they see as a deterioration of standards with respect to a wide variety of practices, including an increase in the usage of dangling modifiers, sentence-ending prepositions, lack of parallelism, and passive voice. In other cases, prescriptivists may cite new words (sometimes called "slang") or a new way of using an existing word as evidence of decline. Because reactions to current language changes in progress can be harsh, we examine parallel changes from the history of the language as a means of illustrating that such evolutions are natural and not a sign of decay.

Consider one example from the early twentieth century. The word *contact* existed only as a noun in English from at least the early 1600s. By the early 1800s, the term was beginning to be used as a verb meaning to bring into physical contact. This conversion from noun to verb seems to have happened without controversy. However, in the early twentieth century, a new usage appeared that was met by the same kind of ire that meets the changing usage of *impact* today. The metaphorical meaning of *contact* to mean "to be in communication with" (e.g., "She contacted me for additional information") is first documented in Theodore Dreiser's 1925 novel, *An American Tragedy*. A 1927 review of the work in *The Spectator* took umbrage at Dreiser's neologism: "Dreiser should not be allowed to corrupt his language" (www.oed.com). Printed evidence cited by the *Oxford English Dictionary* makes it clear that this new usage was adopted quickly by Americans, but the social stigma persisted. Among those who objected to the new use was E. B. White, who wrote in the 1959 edition of *Elements of Style* that "As a transitive verb, the word is vague and self-important. Do not *contact* people; get in touch with them, look them up, phone them, find them, or meet them" (Strunk & White, p. 68). However, this usage is now so commonplace that few would bristle at it. The history of this term in expanding its domain from noun to verb, and along with that its meaning, reveals a few of the forces of change constantly at work within the language.

It is a fundamental tenet of linguistics, based on a considerable body of research, that every living language (a language acquired as a first language) is changing. The only static languages are dead languages (an extinct language or one with no native speakers), such as Classical Latin, Biblical Hebrew, or Sanskrit. Since ongoing language change is an inevitable aspect of language, interpreting that change as decay is simply a matter of social evaluation, not linguistic fact.

The notion that English is on its deathbed is not confined to modern times. A generation or so before John Simon, the theater critic mentioned earlier, Viennese critic Hans Weigel wrote, "Every age claims that its language is more endangered and threatened by decay than ever before. In our time, however, language really is endangered and threatened by decay as never before" (1974, p. 7). A generation before him, George Orwell claimed, "Most people who bother with the matter at all would admit that the English language is in a bad way" (1946, p. 252). This history of lament extends unbroken into the past. A few centuries earlier, in the preface to his 1755 dictionary, British lexicographer and poet Samuel Johnson asserted that "Tongues, like governments, have a natural tendency to degeneration" (Johnson, 2005, p. 27). Even earlier, literary luminary Jonathan Swift wrote (un-satirically, we note), "I do here, in the Name of all the Learned and Polite Persons of the Nation, complain that our language is extremely imperfect; that its daily Improvements are by no means in proportion to its daily Corruptions" (1712, p. 8). Such handwringing over declining language norms is by no means restricted to English. Jacob Grimm claimed that "One hundred years ago, every common peasant knew—that is to say practiced daily—perfections and niceties of the German language of which the best language-teachers nowadays can no longer even dream" (1819, p. x). And of course, the French Académie française has long attempted to guard against what is regarded as the decay of French (www.academie-francaise.fr/). Gaston Paris, a French language enthusiast, lamented in 1862:

[French people] gradually lost the proper and instinctive sense of the laws of the language that they spoke, and let it be corrupted in their mouths, following the vagaries of the time, new needs, whims, and errors. . . . [The language now is] inferior in beauty and logic to the language which preceded it.

pp. 3–4

The language Paris is referring to is Classical Latin, which was thought to have reached its peak during the Golden Age of Virgil and Cicero. It turns out that Cicero did not think the Latin of his age was the peak of purity; he too complained about "kids today." In his history of orators, *Brutus* (46 BC), he notes, "People [in the previous century] in general. . . spoke the Roman language with purity. Time, however, as well at Rome as in Greece, soon altered matters for the worse" (quoted in Watson, 1871, p. 479). Given the consistency of the laments about linguistic deterioration throughout time, it seems remarkable that human language has not been reduced to a series of grunts. Yet throughout all this language variation and change, the expressive capabilities and functionality (i.e., what can be said about the world) of the language remain essentially the same. More important, we see that concern for the deterioration of language is not unique to this generation; in fact, it seems as old as language itself. While the linguistic reality is that all languages vary at every point in time and that they change across time, the interpretation of this language variation and change as decay has been persistent.

Linguists have often dismissed such complaints as scientifically invalid and therefore frivolous; after all, aerospace engineers are generally not concerned with non-expert perceptions of the physics of flight. But judgments of language as in decline have social implications. As noted in Chapter 1, language is acquired and not learned: people use it and evaluate it without much conscious thought. Because people in positions of authority are likely to use a mainstream variety, their dialects are often assumed to be correct—a model for speakers of other dialects. people who grew up speaking a mainstream English dialect may assume that vernacular speakers have failed somehow in their language learning—perhaps due to a lack of effort or intelligence. The fact that the people most likely to hold prescriptivist views of language are in positions that can shape educational language policy means that educational and societal systems typically reinforce ideas about language norms to the benefit of mainstream speakers and the detriment of vernacular speakers. It is not necessary to be versed in the science of language to have sway over language norms. Outside of educational contexts, journalists, writers, and critics like John Simon are all self-appointed language experts; their opinions, while not scientifically based, do affect the way society at large conceptualizes language variation.

Consequences of Deficit Thinking

Language gatekeepers in educational settings—parents, teachers, administrators, language practitioners, test developers, and even other students—need to understand the linguistic facts related to the language-decay thinking described above, as well as its consequences: Such thinking can lead to the sort of deficit views described in the opening pages of this book. We do not suggest that language norms have no place in education; instead, we argue that the norms and policies embraced by schools should be linguistically informed. In order to illustrate the importance of this perspective, we examine in some detail research and educational interventions based on deficit understandings of language differences.

Previous chapters have demonstrated that language is governed by rules at all levels—in other words, it is patterned—and that different groups of people may have contrasting language patterns. This means that there is a danger of analysts misinterpreting a group-based pattern that differs from their own. An especially egregious example comes from an early study of class-based differences in language use. In evaluating participants' retellings of stories about a tornado in Arkansas, researchers concluded that the participants, who were from lower socioeconomic classes, "literally cannot tell a straight story or describe a simple incident coherently" (Schatzman & Strauss, 1955, p. 336). Essentially, this highly evaluative statement is a result of these interviewees (correctly) assuming that the interviewers already knew the context of the tornado, and, thus, they made little attempt to fill in background details. The middle-class interviewees in the study, on the other hand, understood that the retelling task called for them to set the scene for the interviewers. Both positions are reasonable. In typical interactions, normal conversation involves implicitly filling in background information; explicitly stating shared knowledge makes a conversation tedious. It might be said that the interviewees from the lower socioeconomic classes contextualized the task as a conversation while the middle-class interviewees engaged the task as an oral history narrative (and perhaps even recognized it as a testing situation). Viewed this way, it is clear that both groups can indeed "tell a straight story" and "describe a simple incident coherently" (Schatzman & Strauss, 1955, p. 336); it is just that one group meets the expectations of the researchers and the other follows a different set of expectations. The parallel for schools and teachers should be obvious. The evaluation of student work may ignore fundamental differences between students' and teachers' expectations—norms—for language performance. This kind of difference is often interpreted as evidence of deficiency, but it may be evidence of social class or other group membership difference.

Narratives, the language function examined in the early study just mentioned, play a key role in schooling, in both instruction and assessment (think of the number of times each day a student may be asked to recount an experience or describe an event). Class-based differences in narrative structure have been a topic of much interest in education and sociology. In the 1960s, a number of researchers documented what they called the "linguistic deprivation" of speakers from lower socioeconomic classes, which included reduced vocabulary, limited syntax, and more concrete modes of expression. It was argued that middle-class children's language use demonstrated that they understood "the possibilities within a complex conceptual hierarchy for the organization of experience" (Bernstein, 1960, p. 276); that is, they understood complexities and nuances of the world. Children from a lower socioeconomic background, Bernstein claimed, lacked necessary exposure, which "progressively limits the type of stimuli to which the child learns to respond" (Bernstein, 1960, p. 276). The alleged inferior linguistic abilities of the students from lower socioeconomic groups were attributable to the fact that "the normal linguistic environment of the working-class is one of relative deprivation" (Bernstein, 1960, p. 276).

From the work of Bernstein and others, linguistic determinism—the notion that a people's language determines their ability to comprehend, perceive, and categorize things—was embraced in schools. The programs resulting from this belief seem shocking today. One of the best known, called *Teaching Disadvantaged Children in the Preschool* or, more commonly, the "Bereiter-Engelmann program," echoed Bernstein's findings, claiming that poor children lacked "the most rudimentary forms of constructive dialogue" (Bereiter & Engelmann, 1966, p. 39). The authors claim that poor children render the sentence "I ain't got no juice" as "Uni-ga-na-ju," reflecting no understanding that the phrase is not a single word (Bereiter & Engelmann, 1966, p. 34). And finally, they claim that "Language is apparently dispensable enough in the life of the lower-class child for an occasional child to get along without it altogether" (Bereiter & Engelmann, 1966, p. 31); in fact, they use the oral linguistic competence of deaf children as a comparison group for working-class students. The program was implemented and studied over a period of years until a 1978 study on its effectiveness and theoretical assumptions concluded that

> If we are to realistically assess the language of children from different ethnic backgrounds and develop programs that will support their transition into a cultural environment rather different from that of their homes, we must either use naturalistic observation or structure the test situation to conform with the rules governing the child's communicative behavior. Unsubstantiated claims, such as those made by the proponents of a verbal-deprivation hypothesis, will only harm the population of children they are intended to help.
>
> *Steffensen, 1978, p. 16*

Linguistic determinism is discussed here to illustrate the dangers of deficit thinking in schools. While the conclusion that language is dispensable for some seems outrageous today, the deficit–difference debate still persists in other ways and has sometimes been fostered in psychology, sociology, child development, and education. A recent perspective by popular sociologist Annette Lareau, for example, observes that

> In most settings, the children [i.e., of working-class black parents] are free to speak, but they are not usually specifically urged to do so. The overall effect is that language serves as a conduit of daily life, not as a tool for cultivating reasoning skills or a resource to plumb for ways to express feelings or ideas.
>
> *Lareau, 2011, p. 146*

To a linguist, it is simply unimaginable that there are children for whom language is not a tool for reasoning or expressing emotions, yet such thinking remains dangerously pervasive.

While deficit-model programs have been rejected by linguists, deficit thinking persists in classrooms, and such thinking can have damaging effects on students who do not natively speak a standard dialect. Recent studies of classroom teachers have found that many classroom teachers enact policies or pedagogies that reflect deficit views of vernacular speakers (e.g., Dyson and Smitherman, 2009; Godley, Carpenter, & Werner, 2007). Surveys of teachers also find widespread deficit views (e.g., Blake & Cutler, 2003; Cross, DeVaney, & Jones, 2001). These and other recent studies have confirmed that these views are detrimental to students' learning and literacy (e.g., Dyson and Smitherman, 2009; Fairbanks, 1998; Godley, et al., 2007). When deficit views of language persist in school settings, they harm students who, given society's current language norms, are most in need of linguistically sensitive pedagogies.

Language Prescription

The approach to language use that often underlies the views described above is *prescriptivism*, the approach described earlier in which someone viewed as a language authority prescribes the forms that are acceptable. Most commonly, prescriptive approaches are categorical in their assessments; that is, forms are either correct or incorrect, often without regard to context. Prescriptive rules include such well-known examples as "Don't split an infinitive" or "Use *less* with mass nouns and *fewer* with count nouns." They may also include stylistic judgments such as "Avoid the passive voice."

Hazen (2015) offers a useful way of thinking about prescriptivism as well as an alternative viewpoint:

> The *Prescriptively Correct Perspective* assumes that one certain form of the language always works better at all times. It also assumes that this unitary correct form must be protected from variation, which is seen as

corruption or decay. The *Rhetorically Correct Perspective* judges language as good or bad based on how well that language works for that speaker in that context.

p. 11

Many teachers naturally embrace the rhetorically correct perspective in reviewing student writing, allowing students to use more informal language on certain assignments, such as journals or creative writing, though they may still enforce their prescriptive pet peeves. However, when it comes to the oral language students use in the classroom, teachers may be less accepting of certain variants, enforcing prescriptive norms even during moments of informal communication. In elementary schools, it is not uncommon to hear a teacher respond to a child who has asked, "Can I go to the bathroom?" with "I don't know, *can* you?" Such a response ignores the fact that the student's language was rhetorically appropriate even if it was prescriptively incorrect.

Anne Curzan's (2014) analysis of prescriptivism is the most complete treatment of that approach by a linguist. She uses a metaphor of language as a river in order to capture more nuanced ways that prescriptivism affects language development. She suggests that linguists often frame prescriptivism as "the attempt to construct a dam that will stop the river in its tracks" (p. 4). Linguists argue that since the dam (prescriptivism) cannot fully stop the flow of the river (language change), the dam (prescriptivism) must be ineffective. She suggests that it is better to evaluate prescriptivism according to what it does to the flow of the river: "It becomes easier to see how prescriptivism may be able to affect how the language changes . . . the sheer presence of the dam affects the flow of the river" (Curzan, 2014, p. 4). Though prescriptive forces—including teachers and other educational personnel and institutions—lack the ability to stop language change, they are influential in shaping the current of changes to the language.

In order to separate out the various goals, actors, and effects of prescriptivism, Curzan divides it into four non-discrete strands, offering a useful framework for thinking about language standards. The first strand, *standardizing prescriptivism*, is like traffic laws: It attempts to codify rules to ensure easy communication among speakers of a language. The most successful example of standardizing prescriptivism for English is in spelling standardization, which had been completed (more or less) by the end of the eighteenth century. Less successful examples of standardizing prescriptivism result in language stigmas, such as that associated with the word *ain't* and with certain dialect pronunciations, such as *aks* for *ask*. In both cases, use of these forms persists despite attempts to "standardize" them out of the language.

The second of Curzan's strands is *stylistic prescriptivism*, which, instead of setting rules, attempts to detail etiquette-like guidelines. If standardizing prescriptivism is driving laws, then stylizing prescriptivism is driving etiquette.

This category would include suggestions like "use active voice," or "omit needless words" (Strunk, 2009, pp. 21 & 25). Instead of language choices being evaluated as simply correct or incorrect, these choices might be seen as more or less appropriate. For example, Strunk qualifies his position on the passive: "This rule [of avoiding passive voice] does not, of course, mean that the writer should entirely discard the passive voice, which is frequently convenient and sometimes necessary" (2009, p. 18). Such advice is fundamentally about guidelines as opposed to strict prohibitions.

Restorative prescriptivism reflects the view that the language is decaying, as it seeks to restore forms to a past usage that is viewed as more correct or logical. People making arguments for restorative prescriptivism often fall prey to an etymological fallacy, such as insisting that *decimate* be used only when referring to tenths of things. Their rationale is that the root *deci-* is the same as in *decimal* and *decimeter*, and that *decimate* was originally used to mean "to take a tithe [literally a tenth]" or to indicate a form of military discipline in which every tenth person was punished. These same people might scoff at celebrating a "six-month anniversary" (maintaining that since *annus* denotes a year, it is illogical to use it for shorter time periods). Restorative prescriptivists do not intend to send the language back to the time of *Beowulf*; they are selective in their targets. They certainly do not aim to restore pronunciations such as *hit* for *it* or *hain't* for *ain't,* which were common throughout English dialects until the start of the nineteenth century and are still found in dialects such as Appalachian English. Perhaps even more shocking would be a prescriptivist attempting to restore *ask* to its original pronunciation, the root of which was *aks* (Old English *acsion*) (www.oed.com), given the modern-day stigma attached to that pronunciation.

Restorative prescriptivism has at times attempted (and sometimes succeeded) to "restore" usages that never existed. For example, the prohibitions against ending a sentence with a preposition and splitting infinitives both originate from attempts to "restore" English, a Germanic language, to a Latin basis that it never had. John Comly appears to be the first to be bothered by split infinitives, writing in *English Grammar; Made Easy to the Teacher and Pupil,* "An adverb should not be placed between a verb of the infinitive mood and the preposition *to* which governs it" (1803, p. 122). Comly is not the only grammarian who created his rules without linguistic or historical basis. The prohibition against sentence-ending prepositions is older but no less absurd. Joshua Poole is the first known grammarian to record this rule in 1646 in his book *The English Accidence,* which looked to Latin as the ideal. The grammar of Latin makes it impossible to end sentences with prepositions (reported in Yáñez-Bouza, 2008). One final example: When it comes to distance, *further* and *farther* have been used interchangeably throughout the history of the language. The *Oxford English Dictionary* suggests that in Middle English, *farther* (written then as *ferþer*) "is in origin a mere variant of *further*...

The primary sense of *further, farther* is 'more forward, more onward'; but this sense is practically coincident with that of the comparative of *far*. . . Hence *further, farther* came to be used as the comparative of *far*" (www.oed.com)— that is, at least, until 1906, when lexicographer Frank Vizetelly decided that a difference in meaning between the terms must have existed in the past and, therefore, should exist now. Flawed etymological research led him to the conclusion that "*Farther* should be used to designate longitudinal distance; *further* to signify quantity or degree" (Vizetelly, 1906, p. 81). Given the various fallacies associated with restorative prescriptivism, linguists are quick to dismiss it; however, it is clear that these rules do work their way into grammar and style books, from which they can become the basis for evaluation of language use.

Curzan's (2014) final strand is *politically responsive prescriptivism*. This is the kind of prescriptivism that many linguists champion. Words can shape how we view things. As an example, Republican strategist Frank Luntz famously changed the public's opinion of estate taxes by rebranding them "death taxes" as part of the 1994 *Contract with America* (see Luntz, 2007, pp. 164–166). Over the past 50 years, there have been many attempts to adopt non-gendered job names; for example, *waitress* and *waiter* are giving way to *server*. *Firefighter, police officer, letter carrier,* and *flight attendant* are just a few of the other forms that are becoming increasingly the norm. A very recent example of politically responsive prescriptivism involves using *they/their/them/theirs* as a gender-neutral, third-person singular pronoun for reference to humans (e.g., "Every student should open their book"). Using *they/them/their/theirs* to replace *he/him/his/his* has a long and distinguished history. It can be found in the work of writers held in the highest esteem, including Shakespeare and Jane Austen. Though many prescriptive guides maintain that "Every student should bring their book to class" is wrong and that *his* should replace *their* in that sentence, newspaper style guides are increasingly embracing the usage, including the *Washington Post* (Walsh, 2015).

Politically responsive prescriptivism has also influenced the terms we use to refer to social groups. The now universal condemnation of using the *n*-word in a derogatory fashion is a result of this type of prescriptivism. Similar trends are happening with labels for other groups, such as *fag*, which has quickly taken on a large social tax. The debate on the team name of the National Football League's Washington Redskins is largely about how this form of pre-scriptivism should affect the language. Most of the time, politically responsive prescriptivism calls for minority groups being afforded the right to choose the term for referring to them, but, in a few cases, politically responsive prescrip-tivism has resulted in usage norms that are contrary to a group's preference. Two examples are the terms *Native American* and *Hispanic*. In both cases, the labels are rejected by many in the community in part because they are government-created names. The former group generally prefers the term *American Indian* while the latter group prefers terms such as *Latino* or *Chicano* depending on location (Wolfram & Reaser, 2014).

Although prescriptive norms exist, there is really no single set of principles that governs what is considered acceptable and what is not for all speakers of English. Furthermore, each person evaluates the importance of adhering to various norms differently. Thus, everyone in a gatekeeping role has the power to enforce norms that differ from those of students, clients, and subordinates. These differences become especially important for students who are speakers of nonmainstream dialects. Hairston (1981) gathered responses by laymen to 65 sentences each containing one "error" in usage. She found that people judged more harshly the items that contained a vernacular dialect feature than they did the so-called usage errors not associated with specific dialects, even when the non-vernacular sentence used a similar construction. The most harshly judged sentences included vernacular verb forms such as "He brung his secretary" and subject–verb agreement issues, such as "When we was in the planning stages" (Hairston, 1981, p. 796). Non-vernacular forms, including such subject–verb agreement errors as "Enclosed in his personnel file is his discharge papers and job references," were judged far less harshly (Hairston, 1981, p. 805). That similar linguistic patterns might be evaluated so differently demonstrates that teachers and other language practitioners must think critically about the norms they choose to enforce and how they go about doing so.

Technology, Literacy, and the Health of Modern English

Even if people accept that language is only changing, not decaying, many still assume that modern media such as email, online chatting, and texting are reducing the quality of language use in the modern world. A common framing of this argument is that the English of the past has produced writers like Chaucer, Milton, and Shakespeare, while the English of the present has produced Twitter. These objections are based on two kinds of cognitive biases: the sampling bias, in which a non-random sample is compared with a random sample or the general population, and the regressive bias, in which low probability events are estimated to occur more frequently than they really do. These biases combine to form two specious comparisons. First, it is inappropriate to use the writing of selected published authors as indicative of general reading and writing skills at the time. Second, it is nonsensical to compare a few exceptional authors spread over three centuries to the best authors currently living. The first comparison is dispatched easily: While historical literacy rates are imprecise, estimates suggest that less than 10% of British people during Chaucer's time were literate, roughly 15% were literate while Shakespeare was writing, and maybe 50% could read *Paradise Lost* when it was published in 1667 (Buringh & Van Zanden, 2009). Literacy rates decreased slightly throughout the industrial revolution until they started a dramatic climb, crossing the 90% barrier in the early twentieth century for the United States and slightly later in England (National Center for Education Statistics, n.d.). Put simply, rates of literacy—the ability to read and write—among English speakers in the United States and England have never been as high as they are at the moment.

The second comparison, regarding the quality of writers now versus those in the past, is more open to interpretation, but at the least, the playing field must first be leveled before any comparison can be made. Though there are no objective criteria for what constitutes a "notable writer," comparing the number of notable British writers listed on Wikipedia.org in the three centuries between Chaucer and Milton with those in the three centuries following Milton reveals a substantial advantage in numbers for the modern group. This advantage is even more dramatic if American and other English-language writers are included.

Moreover, shifting the advantage even more firmly in the direction of modern authors, it might be worth including in our comparison group screenwriters or theater performers/writers (such as Stanley Kubrick, Ingmar Bergman, or Lin-Manuel Miranda), who in many ways are the modern equivalent of Renaissance playwrights. The point is not to malign great writers of the past so much as it is to demonstrate that their greatness does not imply a subsequent decline in language usage. Not only is the extent of English literacy at its apex, but also the prevalence of great writers, good writers, and even mediocre writers has increased over time. Despite the conventional wisdom, texting, Twitter, and other media have not caused widespread decline in writing ability. To the contrary, they have only increased the linguistic participation of modern language users, whose English varies along the lines described in the previous chapters. The most careful studies of the effects of texting and online chat applications have all concluded that engaging in these media improves children's and adult's overall literacy and knowledge of standard language conventions (e.g., Drouin, 2011; Kemp, 2010; Plester, Wood, & Joshi, 2009; Wood, et al., 2011).

Finally, just for fun, it is worth imagining how Shakespeare might fare as a student in modern classrooms. The Bard is currently credited in the *Oxford English Dictionary* with the first written attestation of some 1,513 words (www.oed.com). Certainly, some of these were slang terms used around London, but others were likely his own creation, made up of roots, prefixes, and suffixes that had not previously been combined. Either way, it is hard to imagine his plays not being marked up by teachers with notes such as "*Amazing* isn't a word," "What is *applause* supposed to mean?", "Don't use *chew* metaphorically," "Two negatives make a positive," and "*Juvenile* is an adjective, not a noun." All this is before, of course, young student Will started to lose points for his use of clichés, inconsistent pronoun usage, and poor punctuation, not to mention his blatant plagiarism (aside from retelling stories recorded in earlier sources, he sometimes used passages from those sources verbatim, as in the case of the famous six-line description of Cleopatra on her royal barge, which was taken directly from Plutarch's *Mark Antony*). Without suggesting that the quality of product is comparable, observers note that Shakespeare's playfulness and inventiveness with language is not unlike that of hip hop artists today (see, e.g., Emery, 2009). His retelling of tales is in line with cinematic retellings of famous stories. We aim to make two points here: 1. Norms change. What we celebrate from the past, we might punish today. 2. Language norms exist separately from judgments about literary quality and importance, or creativity. Enforcing prescriptive language norms in unprincipled ways might thwart the next Shakespeare.

Norms and Texting

One of the most dramatic examples of changing norms for writing is the case of electronically mediated communication (EMC) that takes place in texting, messaging, and other current written forms of communication typically done on mobile phones. Since the explosion of instant messaging in the 1990s, a new set of norm-governed writing practices particular to this medium (and related to the constraints of digital space) has emerged. These developments include punctuation (no periods following sentences), no capitalization (other than "shouting"), spelling abbreviations (such as *ppl* for "people"), homophones (such as *u* for "you"), lexical shortening (e.g., clipping such as *tom* for "tomorrow"), acronyms (such as *LOL* for "laugh out loud," *OMG* for "oh my god'), emoticons (e.g., ☺), emojis, and other specialized practices largely restricted to this writing genre. Though these practices have sometimes been assailed as random and haphazard, they are, in fact, quite coherent and shaped by regularized conventions—norms—that are transmitted informally rather than formally. The change is led by young adult writers, as smartphone ownership is the highest among young adults; young adults use text messaging more than ten times as much as their parents (Schneier & Myrick, 2016). Younger texters also appear more selective in their deployment of some of these electronic features. For example, while older texters may vary randomly between *u* and *you* or *2* and *two/to/too*, this difference has become stylistically important to younger texters, who use the shortened forms only to convey a specific tone of voice or style. Research suggests that younger texters have greater stylistic range and are far more selective in their use of EMC features (Tagliamonte & Denis, 2008; Thurlow & Brown, 2003). Even though these practices are fairly recent developments, some EMC features seem to be dropping out of modern texting and online interaction, underscoring the dynamic nature of these conventions. For example, the abbreviation LOL has been found to be nearly absent in the EMC of younger Americans (Nguyen, 2015). These findings contradict popular depictions of generational norms, as it is the older generations who employ more text-speak shortenings and acronyms, while younger speakers employ such features selectively as "expressive punctuation," which contrasts with standard usages (McCulloch, 2015, personal communication, August 16, 2016).

Like other modes of communication, texting is subject to variation based on the relationship of the people messaging. For example, a parent might be addressed with "How u doin" while a peer might be addressed with "sup." The purpose of the communication, the background of the texter, and other factors can affect the way someone composes in this medium. For example, women tend to use more emoticons than men (Baron & Ling, 2011). Older users tend to employ more punctuation than younger speakers (Baron & Ling, 2011). Like all variation in language, differences carry social significance. As with other forms of interaction, there is a set of expectations, or *maxims*, that guide text conversations. These can be summarized as 1) be quick; 2) be brief; 3) imitate speech; and 4) find ways to communicate tone or mood (Thurlow, 2006). As a venue for examining language variation, texting and instant messaging are ideal for students and teachers to explore together. Students' implicit knowledge of the norms can help practitioners who learned to communicate in the pre-texting era as they learn and accommodate the norms of new writing modes that students have internalized. The fact that these norms are not codified makes them especially worthy of exploration and description.

The Specialized Language of Schools

Schools focus keenly on language practices and language norms. Traditionally, attention to language and responsibility for promoting students' language development has been vested primarily in English language arts and ESL departments. But the importance of speaking, listening, reading, and writing in all of the content areas is now acknowledged. For example, the content standards for math developed by the National Council of Teachers of Mathematics (NCTM) emphasize that students need to be able to explore ideas collaboratively and to explain their thinking as they do math at all grade levels. Furthermore, the National Council of Teachers of English (NCTE) and the National Council for the Social Studies (NCSS) both list dialect knowledge in their standards for what students should know and be able to do.

Clearly, more attention is being paid to language and language variation in school than in the past, and most state curricula (many of which are based on the Common Core State Standards) now spread the responsibility for teaching language and literacy to all content area teachers, which means that these teachers must now begin to consider how variable language patterns in their students' speech affect their work. Further, it becomes even more important for all teachers to examine their own attitudes toward students' language. Working together across disciplinary areas, teachers and administrators can identify the language use goals and the language development goals mentioned in the content area standards, and devise ways to share responsibility for addressing them. In doing so, they can focus on language variability in their own school.

Fields of study typically develop specialized vocabulary and repurpose other words to specific technical meanings. Such vocabulary is termed *jargon*. All students, regardless of dialect background, must acquire the "language of mathematics" or the "language of science," in the sense that they must learn the crucial special vocabulary and norms for language use peculiar to various disciplines. Neither standard dialect nor vernacular dialect speakers go around uttering comparisons such as "one fifth as many as" or "the sum of five squared and three cubed is equal to" in ordinary conversation, yet such language structures and vocabulary must be processed and produced in learning fundamental math operations. Recognizing that all students must learn a special set of language conventions for the various content areas, it is still reasonable to expect that the differences between math language and ordinary, everyday language may be greater for the vernacular speaker than they are for the standard dialect speaker. At this point we do not know whether the extent of the dialect difference is great enough to present a significant obstacle. Only careful, matched, comparative studies of vernacular and standard dialect speakers processing the special conventions of math language and science language, for example, can answer this question.

English language arts certainly has its own jargon as well, including words for literary and grammatical analyses. The former range from the familiar (*analogy*) to the obscure (*adynaton*), while the latter are used with varying degrees of specificity and accuracy. It is not uncommon, for example, for language gatekeepers to describe inaccurately some grammatical structures, as Strunk and White do with three of the four examples of passive voice in their well-known *Elements of Style* (Pullum, 2009). While schools would not tolerate such inexact description of math or science terminology, the terminology related to language often flies under the radar, primarily because many people are unsure of the appropriate field-specific technical usages. This issue suggests that a school's language experts should play an important role as leaders in defining language policies in the school and perhaps even leading professional development efforts related to reading and writing across the curriculum.

This chapter has shown that language norms have shifted over time, both the implicit norms that linguists uncover and the explicit norms of language prescription. Ultimately, norms are arbitrary in the sense that they do not derive from some sort of logic or standard of purity from which English has strayed. The fact that they are arbitrary, however, does not mean that they are pointless. Recall, for example, the points made above regarding politically responsive prescriptivism. Words mean more than their literal definitions, and the social environment in which we use words shapes meaning. In society in general, and in educational settings especially, it is worth seriously considering the rationales (or lack thereof) for our language norms.

Each educator can benefit from examining his or her language attitudes. Every teacher and every language user has pet peeves. And each of us has our own prescriptivist tendencies. It is wise to investigate whether personal pet peeves are related to forms that all users must learn (e.g., commas are not a part of any spoken dialect—no one acquires comma rules naturally) or forms that are only found in a stigmatized dialect (e.g., *aks*). And are we committing the etymological fallacy when we endorse or prohibit a particular usage? Do we pick and choose randomly what usages should be restored and the time period from which previous usages should be restored? The answers to these questions may well be "yes."

One of the more challenging aspects of thinking about what language norms will be accepted in various school settings is that many decisions about language norms are made at levels beyond the classroom or even the school through text adoption or assessment choices. Because of the ramifications for student, teacher, and school evaluations, standardized testing is perhaps the most ominous form of externally imposed language norms influencing the classroom. This topic is explored in the next chapter. It is critical to understand that accepting scientific information about language variation and change does not mean that teachers should never enforce prescriptive language norms. Instead, having an understanding of how language norms originated and what effects they have should help teachers avoid deficit perspectives as they approach language differences in their classrooms.

Discussion Questions

1. During a *Science Friday* radio interview (www.sciencefriday.com/segments/how-hashtags-texts-and-tweets-are-influencing-digital-language/) with linguist Gretchen McCulloch and psychologist Celia Klin, a middle school teacher calls in to recount how he encourages his students to practice Standard English conventions in their text messaging. What do you think about this teacher's suggestion? Is this teacher helping or hurting his students? Is this teacher a prescriptivist?

2. Analyze a few of your own pet peeves about the way people use language. What norm do they violate? Consider the possibility that this norm is changing. If so, what do you think is driving the change?

3. The chapter points out errors in Strunk and White (1959) concerning the passive voice. The intention is not to devalue this highly regarded resource. What is the value of this and other guides to language norms? Why are they called "style guides"?

4. Have you ever encountered a difference in text-users' norms for communication? Was it serious?

5. Argue that the ability to understand the meaning differences among the response options in the chapter's opening scenario demonstrates high level literacy.

6. How important is it for schools to focus on the new language use demands of the curriculum? If it's important, who is it important for? Just English learners? How might a school-wide effort to enhance students' language skills be organized? Should it focus solely on the norms of Standard English for vernacular dialect speakers? Why not?

Links of Interest

1. Learn why you shouldn't end your texts with a period: www.chicagotribune.com/bluesky/technology/ct-texting-period-terrible-study-20151210-story.html

2. Listen to linguist Gretchen McCulloch and psychologist Celia Klin talk about evolving texting norms on *Science Friday*: www.sciencefriday.com/segments/how-hashtags-texts-and-tweets-are-influencing-digital-language/

3. Explore the website and writings of a linguist who studies language on the internet and in other electronic forms: https://gretchenmcculloch.com/

4. Delve into a range of linguistic topics at Language Log: http://languagelog.ldc.upenn.edu/nll/

5. Check out this education blog's take on how Shakespeare's language usage is similar to the language play found in hip hop. The link also includes a TED talk on the topic: www.nosweatshakespeare.com/blog/hip-hop-shakespeare/

6. Read Geoffrey Pullum's discussion of what many grammar guides get wrong: www.chronicle.com/blogs/linguafranca/2014/06/05/new-book-same-old-grammar-babble/

7. Test your knowledge of "41 grammar rules to follow to make you sound smarter": www.msn.com/en-us/lifestyle/smart-living/41-little-grammar-rules-to-follow-to-sound-smarter/ss-BBw1EQM?ocid=DELLDHP15#image=1

8. Explore the American Dialect Society's annual "Words of the year" ballots and discussions from 1998 to the present: www.americandialect.org/woty

Further Reading

Adams, M. (2009). *Slang: The people's poetry.* Oxford, UK: Oxford University Press.
An academic exploration of slang written for a general audience, this engaging volume considers the history and cultural significance of slang in American society.

Curzan, A. (2014). *Fixing English: Prescriptivism and language history.* Cambridge, UK: Cambridge University Press.
Though academic in tone, this book details different forms of prescriptivism and shows how prescriptive forces have (and have not) shaped the development of the English language. The book looks at a variety of prescriptive sources, including computerized spelling and grammar checkers.

Lakoff, R. T. (2000). *The language war.* Berkeley, CA: University of California Press.
An investigation of language and power in modern American society, this book examines questions like who holds power? How do they use it? And how do they keep it? For data, the author examines well-known court cases, politicians, comedians, and media outlets.

Shea, A. (2014). *Bad English: A history of linguistic aggravation*. New York, NY: Penguin.
Adopting a humorous tone, this book shows how people have responded to language change throughout the centuries. It also reveals the lack of consistency in determining which norms are followed and which are abandoned.

References

Baron, N. S., & Ling, R. (2011). Necessary smileys & useless periods. *Visible Language, 45*(1/2), 45–67.

Bereiter, C., & Engelmann, S. (1966). *Teaching disadvantaged children in the preschool*. Englewood Cliffs, NJ: Prentice-Hall.

Bernstein, B. (1960). Language and social class. *British Journal of Sociology, 11*(3), 271–276.

Blake, R., & Cutler, C. (2003). AAE and variation in teachers' attitudes: A question of school philosophy? *Linguistics and Education, 14*(2), 163–194.

Buringh, E., & Van Zanden, J. L. (2009). Charting the "rise of the West": Manuscripts and printed books in Europe, a long-term perspective from the sixth through eighteenth centuries. *The Journal of Economic History, 69*(2), 409–445.

Comly, J. (1803). *English grammar; Made easy to the teacher and pupil*. Philadelphia, PA: John H. Oswald for Emmor Kimber.

Cross, J. B., DeVaney, T., & Jones, G. (2001). Pre-service teacher attitudes toward differing dialects. *Linguistics and Education, 12*(2), 211–227.

Curzan, A. (2014). *Fixing English: Prescriptivism and language history*. Cambridge, UK: Cambridge University Press.

Drouin, M. A. (2011). College students' text messaging, use of textese and literacy skills. *Journal of Computer Assisted Learning, 27*(1), 67–75.

Dyson, A. H., & Smitherman, G. (2009). The right (write) start: African American language and the discourse of sounding right. *The Teachers College Record, 11*(4), 973–998.

Emery, A. (2009, April 15). Shakespeare: How do I compare thee to hip-hop? *The Guardian*. Retrieved from www.theguardian.com/stage/2009/apr/15/shakespeare-hip-hip-rap

Fairbanks, C. M. (1998). Nourishing conversations: Urban adolescents, literacy, and democratic society. *Journal of Literacy Research, 30*(2), 187–203.

Godley, A. J., Carpenter, B. D., & Werner, C. A. (2007). I'll speak in proper slang: Language ideologies in a daily editing activity. *Reading Research Quarterly, 42*(1), 100–131.

Grimm, J. (1819). *Deutsche grammatik, part I*. Göttingen, Germany: Dieterichsche Buchhandlung.

Hairston, M. (1981). Not all errors are created equal: Nonacademic readers in the professions respond to lapses in usage. *College English, 43*(8), 794–806.

Hazen, K. (2015). *An introduction to language*. Malden, MA: Wiley Blackwell.

Johnson, S. (2005). *Johnson's dictionary: A modern selection*. Mineola, NY: Dover.

Kemp, N. (2010). Texting versus txtng: Reading and writing text messages, and links with other linguistic skills. *Writing Systems Research, 2*(1), 53–71.

Lareau, A. (2011). *Unequal childhoods: Class, race, and family life* (2nd ed.). Berkeley, CA: University of California Press.

Luntz, F. I. (2007). *Words that work: It's not what you say, it's what people hear*. New York, NY: Hyperion.

MacNeil/Lehrer Productions. (2005). *Do you speak American?* [Video]. Arlington, VA: Author.

McCulloch, G. (2015, June 22). A linguist explains how we write sarcasm on the internet. *The Toast*. Retrieved from http://the-toast.net/2015/06/22/a-linguist-explains-how-we-write-sarcasm-on-the-internet/

National Center for Education Statistics. (n.d.). *National assessment of adult literacy: A nationally representative and continuing assessment of English language literacy skills in American adults*. Retrieved from http://nces.ed.gov/naal/lit_history.asp

Nguyen, T. (2015, Aug. 10). Facebook data indicates that "LOL" is dead. *Vanity Fair*. Retrieved from www.vanityfair.com/news/2015/08/facebook-data-lol-dead

Orwell, G. (1946). Politics and the English language. *Horizon, 13*, 252–265.

Paris, G. (1862). *Etude sur le rôle de l'accent latin dans la langue française*. Paris, France: A. Franck.

Plester, B., Wood, C., & Joshi, P. (2009). Exploring the relationship between children's knowledge of text message abbreviations and school literacy outcomes. *British Journal of Developmental Psychology, 27*(1), 145–161.

Pullum, G. K. (2009, April 17). 50 years of stupid grammar advice. *The Chronicle of Higher Education.* Retrieved from http://chronicle.com/article/50-Years-of-Stupid-Grammar/25497

Schatzman, L., & Strauss, A. (1955). Social class and modes of communication. *American Journal of Sociology, 60*(4), 329–338.

Schneier, J., & Myrick, C. (2016). Wuts up w Txting? *Tar Heel Junior Historian, 55*(3), 32-33.

Steffensen, M. S. (1978). Bereiter and Engelmann reconsidered; The evidence from children acquiring Black English vernacular. Urbana, IL: Center for the Study of Reading. Technical Report; no. 082.

Strunk, Jr., W. (2009). *The elements of style: Everything you need to know to write well.* New York, NY: WLC Books.

Strunk, Jr., W., & White, E. B. (1959). *The elements of style, first expanded edition.* London, UK: Macmillan.

Swift, J. (1712). *A proposal for correcting, improving and ascertaining the English tongue: In a letter to the Most Honourable Robert, Earl of Oxford and Mortimer, Lord High Treasurer of Great Britain.* Dublin, Ireland: Benjamin Tooke.

Tagliamonte, S. A., & Denis, D. (2008). Linguistic ruin? LOL! Instant messaging and teen language. *American Speech, 83*(1), 3–34.

Thurlow, C. (2006). From statistical panic to moral panic: The metadiscursive construction and popular exaggeration of new media language in the print media. *Journal of Computer-Mediated Communication, 11*(3), 667–701.

Thurlow, C., & Brown, A. (2003). Generation txt? The sociolinguistics of young people's text-messaging. *Discourse Analysis Online, 1*(1), 30.

Vizetelly, F. H. (1906). *A desk-book of errors in English: Including notes on colloquialisms and slang to be avoided in conversation.* New York, NY: Funk & Wagnalls Company.

Walsh, B. (2015, December 4). The *Post* drops the 'mike' – and the hyphen in 'e-mail.' *The Washington Post.* Retrieved from www.washingtonpost.com/opinions/the-post-drops-the-mike--and-the-hyphen-in-e-mail/2015/12/04/ccd6e33a-98fa-11e5–8917–653b65c809eb_story.html?tid=a_inl

Watson, J. S. (trans. and ed.). (1871). *Cicero on oratory and orators with his letters to Quintus and Brutus.* London, UK: Bell and Daldy.

Weigel, H. (1974). *Die Leiden der jungen Wörter: ein Antiwörterbuch* (The sorrows of young words: An anti-dictionary). Zurich, Switzerland: Artemis.

Wolfram, W., & Reaser, J. (2014). *Talkin' Tar Heel: How our voices tell the story of North Carolina.* Chapel Hill, NC: University of North Carolina Press.

Wood, C., Meachem, S., Bowyer, S., Jackson, E., Tarczynski-Bowles, M. L., & Plester, B. (2011). A longitudinal study of children's text messaging and literacy development. *British Journal of Psychology, 102*(3), 431–442.

Yáñez-Bouza, N. (2008). Preposition stranding in the eighteenth century: Something to talk about. In I. Tieken-Boon van Ostade (Ed.), *Grammars, grammarians and grammar-writing in eighteenth-century England* (pp. 251–278). Berlin, Germany: Mouton de Gruyter.

6

Dialects and Language Assessment

Scenario

The following five items are constructed in the form of a standardized language assessment. The twist here is that the only correct answers are words or phrases from the dialect of Pittsburgh. See how you would score on the test; there is just one correct answer for each question (the Pittsburghese option).

Select the word or phrase that best completes the sentence.

1. That girl needs to know everything that's going on even though it is none of her business. She sure is _____

   a. Inquisitive
   b. Meddlesome
   c. Nosy
   d. Nebby

2. Bill: What kind of sandwich did you get?
   Matt: I got a jumbo.
   Matt's sandwich _____

   a. Was large
   b. Had bologna
   c. Had a dipping sauce
   d. Had turkey

3. Little brown rodents with stripes have been digging up my garden. I have a problem with _____

   a. Grinnies
   b. Marmots
   c. Ground squirrels
   d. Minibears

4. I can't go to the game Saturday because my dad said I needed to _____ the house

   a. Pick up
   b. Redd up

    c.   Clean up

    d.   Nebb up

5. The carpenter did a terrible job on that wall! It's all _____, not even close to square!

    a.   Cattywampus

    b.   Crooked

    c.   Antigogglin

    d.   Sigogglin

The answers to these questions are (1) d. nebby; (2) b. had bologna; (3) a. grinnies; (4) b. redd up; and (5) c. antigogglin. It is very possible that you deduced a few correct answers based on your familiarity with the other answers available. For example, in question 1, you might have selected the only nonstandard word in the list. Perhaps some of the others were more difficult unless you have some familiarity with the dialect the quiz is based on. Though this task reflects a relatively superficial assessment of vocabulary knowledge, it is worth thinking about what can be learned from the number of questions you got correct. On the most basic level, getting many of these answers right might merely identify you as a speaker of this dialect. Certainly no one could conclude the test is a reasonable assessment for children across the country, unless the goal of the test was merely to gauge familiarity with Pittsburghese. While it is easy to reject these test items as absurd, many standardized assessments include questions that are culturally specific, or are normed on populations with certain linguistic backgrounds. The covert biases of these tests are insidious because they might go unnoticed by people who have mainstream language norms that are most likely to be the ones reflected in the tests.

The previous chapter explored prescriptive language norms in some detail. It examined how they are formed, how they change, and what effects they can have on classroom pedagogies and policies. This chapter builds on that theme by examining the role of language norms in standardized testing, arguably one of the most pervasive and influential aspects of modern education. Federal regulations require schools to collect data on students' performance, analyze it according to various demographic categories, and report the results. Many schools and school districts elect to examine their data further, find explanations for the patterns that emerge, and use these findings to adjust and modify their programs. In the context of such efforts to improve schools, there are opportunities to consider the role that language and language variation play in students' performance, instructional practice, and school policy.

For tests of language development, language variation presents a challenge because different dialects have different rules of grammar, vocabulary, and pronunciation. Variation is problematic in other kinds of tests too because language standards are unavoidable in testing; that is, tests rely on language for instructions and questions, and the language used for those purposes can be problematic in subtle ways because it may be less familiar to some students or because some students' cultural backgrounds result in them interpreting directions differently. The reality is that it is impossible to create a language assessment task that does not privilege certain language norms. Assessing reading comprehension, writing, speech, and other language skills always requires an endorsement of some set of language norms, which can result in test bias. Some of these biases can be minimized through informed test creation, interpretation, or manipulation. The following chapters examine language standards related to oral language instruction, writing, and reading. This chapter is dedicated to formal language assessments in school contexts, namely through high stakes standardized tests including speech and language assessments, in which language variation is not typically taken into account—to the detriment of vernacular dialect speakers.

Assessing Students' Literacy Skills

Although literacy rates in the United States are at an all-time high (National Center for Education Statistics, n.d.), some critics maintain that the reading and writing skills of today's students lag behind those in previous generations. They most commonly cite declining SAT scores as evidence, but the story of the SAT reveals that this trend has been affected by demographic diversity in ways that cast doubt on this simplistic conclusion.

First introduced in 1926, the SAT has traditionally been the test most widely used for college admissions. Originally dubbed the Scholastic *Aptitude* Test, the exam was intended to assess inherent ability as opposed to learning. From 1926 until 1941, the scores for each test section were scaled so that each one had a mean of 500 out of a maximum of 800 and a standard deviation of 100. As a result, comparisons between years—or even between different sittings of tests during a year—are impossible because there is no common reference point.

Between 1941 and 1995, all tests were equated to the one test given in April, 1941, making scores comparable from year to year; however, since the format of the test changed during this time, even these scores can only roughly track trends in literacy. By the 1950s, the mean on the reading/verbal section had climbed to around 550 (out of 800), suggesting some overall improvement of literacy skills (or, in this case, aptitude).

From this high water mark, scores began to decline, hovering at or just below 500 from 1990 to 1994. This pattern offered skeptics the data they needed to claim that literacy skills were declining. But that interpretation is far too simplistic. Examining the data closely shows that the downward trend is largely explained by what is known as Simpson's paradox or the Yule–Simpson effect (Goltz & Smith, 2010): Instead of a decrease in literacy skills among the population, the decline is attributable to the increase in the number of test-takers (see analysis in Bracey, 2004), as more and more secondary school students took the exam. Beginning in 1961, the number of test-takers increased rapidly, more than doubling by 1977. As the pool of test-takers increased, it increasingly included many more low-achieving students and students from demographics that typically fare worse on such exams. Thus, the higher mean scores in the earlier years can be explained by the more restricted population of test-takers.

The mid-1990s brought substantial changes to the test and a re-centering of the mean to 500, a move widely decried as "lowering the bar" by those who took the test under the previous scoring arrangements. In reality, the re-centering merely demonstrates the importance of test norming. In this case, the population of test-takers had changed dramatically, and, therefore, the test needed to be re-normed. This process is critical for standardized assessments, as will be seen below.

Another interesting change occurred during this period. In 1994, the test's moniker changed from Scholastic Aptitude Test to Scholastic Assessment Test, a concession after decades of external critique saying that the test did not measure any inherent ability. Previously, some researchers who were convinced of the test's ability to measure aptitude had interpreted differences in means between racial groups as evidence that some races were cognitively inferior to others. The name change was intended to end any notion that the SAT claimed to demonstrate that. The name was changed again in 2004 so that now SAT is not an acronym, and the official test description suggests nothing specific about aptitude or even achievement: "The SAT and SAT Subject Tests are designed to assess your academic readiness for college" (https://sat.collegeboard.org/about-tests).

Another factor in the decreasing SAT scores in the modern era is that a number of states have adopted a policy of requiring all high school students to take the test—though not necessarily to achieve any specific score—in order to graduate. Predictably, students without college ambitions may not take the exam seriously, and their very low scores disproportionately affect the mean—again, complicating the notion that SAT data demonstrate any real decline in literacy skills.

Given the lack of a stable population of SAT takers, a better source of data for tracking literacy skills is the National Assessment of Educational Progress (NAEP), dubbed "The Nation's Report Card," which shows that fourth and eighth graders' reading performance actually improved between 1971 and 2013 (the most recent year for which there are data), and that there was no difference during that time for twelfth graders (NAEP, n.d.). These changes are even more impressive given the demographic shifts in schools over the past decades. For example, between 1978 and 2012, the proportion of whites—the group that has performed best on the assessment—dropped from 80% to 56% of test-takers even while scores overall rose; furthermore, the gap between white and black students and that between white and Hispanic students shrank (NAEP, n.d.). This result suggests that reading comprehension skills in all ethnic groups have improved over the past decades, although there remains a significant gap between the reading scores of whites and non-whites. Writing assessments have followed similar trajectories over this period.

Diversity and Standardized Testing

Despite common refrains to the contrary, most evidence points to American public schools as doing as good a job as ever teaching children literacy skills. However, a pattern of lower outcomes remains for some groups, including American Indian, African American, Hispanic, Appalachian, and Southern students. Among the possible hypotheses about the cause of this disparity, a few emerge as most plausible. Some have argued that the pattern is explained by differences in school readiness. However, longitudinal data from NAEP suggest that the gap between white and African American students increases with age, so the explanation of a difference in starting point does not account for all of the discrepancy. This observation points to a second possibility: namely, that school systems are not meeting the needs of minority students. In fact, as Jonathan Kozol has documented, per-pupil spending in majority white districts is often twice that for districts where a majority of students are from minority backgrounds (2005, pp. 321–326). Combining these two accounts suggests that children who perform less well on the assessments enter school poorly prepared and then fall further behind because they are in schools with less funding, so that they do not receive the sorts of educational enrichment and support that other students receive. Another possibility is that the tests used to evaluate achievement are culturally biased. Or, perhaps the explanation lies in the fact that once children are labeled as low-achieving, they may be tracked into educational programs that do not challenge them or, because of their labels, teachers may unconsciously treat them differently, resulting in self-fulfilling prophecies about achievement (Rosenthal & Jacobson, 1968).

Teasing out the effects on student performance of economic, family, social, and educational factors is an ongoing and complicated process. One of the difficulties in studying the effects of various groupings is that these influences are not independent; for example, being poor and African American is not merely a combination of those two conditions, but rather a unique category that may incorporate a set of challenges not included in either category by itself. Other characteristics, such as age, sex, sexual orientation, regionality, and rural-ness, may further result in unique combinations of factors that relate to differences in performance, as do diverse factors from caretaker literacy to teacher expectations to testing bias.

Many of the factors that have been shown to relate to lower levels of academic performance are associated with language differences as well. Students from vernacular dialect backgrounds (based on social class, ethnicity, and/or region) tend to be less familiar with language rituals privileged in school settings. In order to understand and address the needs of linguistically diverse students at school who may not be achieving as well as other groups, it is important to consider the possible role of language and culture differences in both instruction and assessment. In this section, we examine some of the language and culture-related dimensions of standardized assessments and the impact of such assessments on diverse students.

Test Norming

The fundamental consideration in the relationship of test scores to ethnic and cultural diversity is that tests are not always appropriate for all the groups to whom they are administered. The practice of using standardized, norm-referenced tests arose when the school population was more homogeneous than it is now and when there was more acceptance of norms that imposed the dominant group's language and culture on other segments of society. The 1916 Stanford–Binet intelligence test was normed on "1000 white children of average social status born in California" (Weinberg, 1983, p. 60). The test revealed "enormously significant racial differences in general intelligence" (Weinberg, 1983, p. 60). The results of the test and others like it allowed numerous institutions to operate on the premise that different races had different genetic predispositions to intelligence. This kind of thinking drove the eugenics programs of the 1930s. Problems of test interpretation related to race are magnified when differences between languages are included. Recall the quotation from Florence Goodenough in Chapter 1, in which she concluded, based on her standardized tests, that "The use of a foreign language in the home is one of the chief factors in producing mental retardation" (1926, p. 393). In retrospect, it is clear that her interpretation arose because her tests were inappropriate or, at least, they were not normed on a population that was appropriate for children whose native language was not English.

Test norming remains a critical topic for teachers and language practitioners. Norm-referenced tests are based on the assumption that children fall into a regular distribution, often called a bell curve. This assumption and the methodologies that extend from it allow these tests to be used to compare students with each other. However, these tests are not able to judge whether students have met certain learning goals. A few of the influential norm-referenced education tests include the California Achievement Test, the Iowa Test of Basic Skills, the Stanford Achievement Test, and the Clinical Evaluation of Language Fundamentals (CELF). These tests contrast with criterion-referenced tests in which students are assessed against a fixed set of standards. Many graduation tests or end-of-course tests are criterion-referenced tests that define success as meeting a pre-defined threshold. An analogy is useful in illustrating the difference between these tests. Imagine students are running a timed mile. A criterion-referenced scoring system might be set up such that times under 9 minutes are passing but times above 9 minutes are failing. Thus, in theory, all students could pass a criterion-referenced test. A norm-referenced scoring system will result in a ranking that allows for comparisons among all runners. Half of the test-takers will fall below the norm and half above the norm. The added twist is that the norm-referenced test relies on some other group, not those currently running the race, as the norm on which the bell curve is built. Consider the different ranking criteria that would be established if those in the norm group were somehow privileged (for example, only cross-country runners). Privileging Pittsburghese norms in the opening scenario created a norm-referenced metric for which speaking only Standard English was a disadvantage. Privileging white Californian speech on the original Stanford–Binet test created a norm-referenced metric for which speaking any vernacular dialect was a disadvantage.

Because norm-referenced tests are still commonly used in educational settings, it is important to examine why small biases can produce large discriminatory effects. It is possible for all test-takers to pass a criterion-referenced test but impossible for all students to achieve highly on a norm-referenced test as the scoring is based on variation among students, so even small differences in performance can land students on opposite sides of the bell curve. Both types of tests can have linguistic biases, though such biases may appear in different ways. However, a linguistically biased question on a norm-referenced assessment will make vernacular-speaking students individually and collectively appear inferior to mainstream English-speaking students. For example, a linguistically biased question on a criterion-referenced assessment may make the test more difficult to pass for vernacular speakers when compared to mainstream English-speaking students. The following two sections examine some aspects of how question and test design can affect outcomes for groups of diverse language users. Because norm-referenced tests rely on past performance to calibrate scoring, past inequities can contribute to injustice for future test-takers. Careful consideration of the groups a test is normed on is critical when analyzing the data generated from the assessment.

Question Design

While test development has improved dramatically since the early intelligence tests, there are indications that insidious cultural and linguistic biases continue to underlie many common tests. Seemingly little things can make big differences in how different groups of students respond to assessment items. For example, studies have found that boys and minorities do worse on essay questions that require drawing on personal experiences in the response (Engelhard, Gordon, & Gabrielson, 1992). Other studies have indicated a strong discomfort with personal essays compared to other types of writing for some English language learners (Leki, 1992) and students in remedial college writing classes (Haviland & Clark, 1992). Another study found that children of different cultural backgrounds understood the intention of the word *summarize* in quite different ways (Minami & McCabe, 1995). And English language learners may apply non-Western rhetorical styles from their native languages to their standardized test essays, favoring, for example, indirectness over directness (Leki, 1992).

There are countless documented instances of culturally insensitive or otherwise inappropriate questions on tests. For example, a 2006 New York State Regents practice exam for third graders included a reading passage on Venus and Serena Williams that relied on students' knowledge of unstated details about the workings of private tennis clubs (Woestehoff, 2011). That same year, on the New York State Regents global history exam, students were asked to analyze a series of historical quotes to describe how Africa benefitted from imperialism (www.nysedregents.org/GlobalHistoryGeography/Archive/2006 0124exam.pdf). In addition to the highly controversial premise that is presented as a priori truth (i.e., that Africa benefitted from imperialism), many of the historical quotations reflected problematic imperial depictions of non-Europeans as savages, uneducated, and heathens to be saved. A 2011 SAT sample writing prompt asked students to evaluate the authenticity of reality television shows and their impact on people. Critics pointed out that not every family has a television, and not every student watched reality shows (Strauss, 2011). The embarrassment caused when these biased questions were made public increased the pressure on developers to hire bias reviewers during test construction, but it has also increased their reluctance to share standardized test items for public scrutiny. These examples may seem obvious and isolated, but they arise from a lack of awareness that stems from (false) assumptions about shared cultural knowledge and mores. Broader biases that impact testing are more difficult to observe, making them more insidious.

Test Design

One outspoken critic of bias in standardized testing is Jay Rosner, an admissions test expert who has studied the biases in tests such as the SAT, ACT, GRE, MCAT, and LSAT. In his examination of the October 1998 SAT exam, he found that all 138 questions (60 math and 78 verbal) favored whites over African Americans (Rosner, 2003, p. 24). This bias stems from the test-making procedures. He notes:

> Each individual SAT question ETS chooses is required to parallel the outcomes of the test overall. So, if high-scoring test-takers—who are more likely to be white—tend to answer the question correctly in pretesting, it's a worthy SAT question; if not, it's thrown out.
>
> *2003, p. 24*

He also cites a verbal question that was excluded from the test because, according to ETS (the company that makes the SAT), when it was tested, 8% more African Americans than whites got the question right. In other words, as a norm-referenced test, the means by which a question is evaluated as appropriate or not depends on the extent to which is elicits responses that mirror previous performance by various groups, which "reproduces racially disparate test results in an internally reinforcing cycle" (Rosner, 2003, p. 24). So, while NAEP data have shown minorities improving faster than white students (NAEP, n.d.), the methodology underlying the creation of the SAT assumes a static gap between groups. Theoretically, higher achievement by African Americans and Hispanics in schools may not be reflected on some norm-referenced assessments (or at least improved scores on such tests will lag compared to other educational indicators) because of the design parameters of the test. Test design bias may underlie the divergent trends of rising NAEP scores but level SAT scores for African American and Hispanic students. Subsequent research on ethnic differentiation of SAT questions revealed that on the most difficult verbal questions, elite African American students outpaced elite white students, suggesting that cultural bias may be lessened in questions that use obscure vocabulary that must be learned rather than just absorbed (Freedle, 2003).

Although many test-makers have endeavored to accommodate diversity, many testing situations have underestimated the importance of linguistic and cultural diversity in the processes of test development, validation, and norming. As Mountford noted:

> Although cultural anthropology has again and again shown that cultural difference underlies schisms between European American and African American patterns of speech and writing, and between men's and women's speech patterns in many American subcultures, our academic policies—particularly on writing [assessment]—have largely worked to ignore or erase such differences.
>
> *1999, p. 373*

Mountford then describes aspects of large-scale writing prompts that "pass what I call the 'cultural anthropology' test" (1999, p. 385), including prompts that draw on universal human experiences, avoid prior knowledge, orient the writer to the intended purpose and audience, and provide clues to the intended genre of the response. The most recent test development practices have certainly improved in these areas, but teachers and language practitioners should remain vigilant in critically evaluating the assessments their students and clients are exposed to. Even the best test design practices merely minimize, not erase, cultural and linguistic biases.

What is Being Measured?

When a test measures something different from what it claims to measure, it is said to have "labeling bias." Labeling bias is another critical issue for educational professionals to be aware of, because knowing what is measured is critical to understanding how to interpret and use data. For example, some IQ tests still claim to measure innate aptitude, the results of which might then justifiably be used to track children at an early age. However, "almost all psychologists now agree that intelligence tests measure developed rather than innate abilities" (Jencks & Phillips, 1998, p. 13). Interpreting test results as an indication of innate ability results in "a racially biased estimate" of student potential (Jencks & Phillips, 1998, p. 13). Therefore, a more disturbing result of labeling bias is that such tests can be used to support deficit views of certain cultural groups.

Labeling bias affects other tests as well. Rather than measuring what they claim to measure, some test items instead measure test-takers' knowledge of standard forms of the language (Wolfram, 1976, 1983). This means that the standardized test may contain biases against various groups of students in the test population, resulting in somewhat lower scores for those groups. A practice SAT item that was intended to indicate the test-taker's ability to identify sentence errors illustrates the issue: "The other delegates and him immediately accepted the resolution drafted by the neutral states." (www.college board.com/student/testing/sat/prep_one/sent_errors/pracStart.html, retrieved June 18, 2005). For speakers of a standard dialect, the preferred response would be obvious, based on the knowledge of language that they have acquired unconsciously. For speakers of other dialects, however, this sentence might reflect a linguistically well-formed language pattern, in that it follows a regular pattern of the test-taker's dialect. Items such as this one can introduce *linguistic bias* to the test. To respond correctly to the question, these students must suppress an answer that is based on their own knowledge of language and appeal instead to knowledge of external language norms or prescriptive rules. This is parallel to the questions in the opening scenario, in which a non-Pittsburgher must suppress their own language knowledge in order to answer correctly.

Questions like the one above might be said to measure students' familiarity with Standard English conventions. Such an evaluation may be appropriate if the test, like the modern SAT, is "designed to assess your academic readiness for college" (https://sat.collegeboard.org/about-tests). However, the item would not be appropriate if the goal of the assessment were to measure students' *educational aptitude*, which, recall, was the original claim of the SAT. Questions of this form can still be found on educational aptitude tests, including the Stanford–Binet and Woodcock–Johnson tests, both of which are commonly used with even very young students; the former is normed for children as young as 2 years of age. In the most recent versions of these tests, a number of changes were made in order to limit the potential for linguistic bias.

For example, for the first time, the current Stanford–Binet Intelligence Scales 5 incorporates nonverbal components (such as pointing or assembling items) for each domain it assesses and provides support for separating verbal IQ from nonverbal IQ scores for each domain. Researchers have noted that while this methodology is an improvement, the only moderate correlation between nonverbal and verbal scores suggests some linguistic bias persists, especially in the evaluation of younger test-takers (ages 2–11) (Canivez, 2008).

Given the importance of Standard English in classroom settings, it is not unreasonable to assess a student's ability to operate within that code; however, that ability is very different from *educational aptitude*. One's native dialect or language in no way determines their educational aptitude, and therefore Standard English proficiency should be tested separately from their ability to learn the full range of skills associated with schooling.

Perhaps one of the most obvious examples of test questions not measuring what they were intended to involves the following disclosed items (meaning they are no longer in use) from the Language Use section of a California Achievement Test. Third grade students taking the assessment were instructed to choose which option in the brackets "you think is correct."

(1) Beth $\left\{ \begin{array}{l} \text{come} \\ \text{came} \end{array} \right\}$ home and cried.

(2) Can you $\left\{ \begin{array}{l} \text{went} \\ \text{go} \end{array} \right\}$ out now?

(3) When $\left\{ \begin{array}{l} \text{can} \\ \text{may} \end{array} \right\}$ I come again?

In each case, the "correct" form is the one associated with Standard English. The incorrect option involves different types of considerations. In question 1, the incorrect choice is a form that would be expected in many vernacular dialects. In question 2, the choice is between a form that is acceptable in all dialects and one that is not found in American English dialects. *Can you went out now* is not a well formed sentence in any dialect of American English. Question 3 is testing the difference between a formal prescription and an informal usage that is found in all dialects. In informal conversations, most Americans would be more likely to say, "When can I come again?" because in present-day English, the form *can* has expanded its range to include both ability and permission. Insisting that *may* is the correct response is buying into a form of *restorative prescriptivism*, which was examined in the previous chapter. In response to these three items, it is probable that mainstream English speakers would answer correctly for 1 and 2, but incorrectly for 3. Vernacular speakers, on the other hand, might very well answer incorrectly for 1 and 3. Test item 1 becomes a diagnostic of the student's dialect. In the disclosed version of this test, 14 of the 25 items were in the style of question 1; over half the test items only assessed dialect.

This kind of bias is not confined to language assessments. Since most tests of academic knowledge rely on language for instructions and questions, it is possible that certain forms or phrasings might be problematic for some dialect speakers. One study that reveals the subtle effects of linguistic bias found that certain features caused African American English speakers more difficulty on math word problems (Terry, Hendrick, Evangelou, & Smith, 2010). The carefully designed study found that second grade African American students struggled on word problems that included third-person -*s* forms (e.g., "James walks to school"). Applying a sophisticated statistical method to account for other factors (e.g., ability in math, achievement test performance, etc.) revealed that the relative incidence of -*s* third-person forms (e.g., "A train goes. . .") in a word problem correlates with difficulty in processing the test item for readers who have higher rates of third-person -*s* absence (e.g., "A train go. . .") in their spoken language. Linguistic bias can operate in extremely subtle ways.

Overcoming linguistic bias is not easy to do. One innovative assessment strategy that attempts to circumvent the language issue in testing scientific and mathematical reasoning is found in the ONPAR project, developed by the Center for Applied Linguistics and the University of Wisconsin (see http://iiassessment.wceruw.org/). Designed primarily for elementary and middle school English language learners, the assessment program uses technology to replace virtually all linguistic content typical of test questions. Most questions unfold as a series of visuals and include only a few words required to answer them; students can click on these words to translate them into various languages (including Spanish, Russian, Arabic, Hmong, and Mandarin). In one question, from the elementary school test, students watch a demonstration involving variously shaped and colored objects being put into balance, after which they are told (in translatable language) "The scales are balanced." Students then see a green block in balance with two purple spheres. Next to the balance, a scale with the green cube reads "10 pounds." Below, a scale with a purple sphere reads "? pounds." Students are expected to recognize that the purple sphere weighs half as much as the green block, or 5 pounds. Students use a number pad to input their answer. The tests measure a range of mathematical and scientific knowledge, including notions of balance, surface area, volume, mass, velocity, acceleration, force, causation, buoyancy, and a variety of other concepts. The results of early pilots of ONPAR tests in fourth grade math and science, seventh grade math, eighth grade science, high school chemistry, and high school biology all suggest that the innovative method can completely close the testing gap between mainstream students, English language learners, and students with a variety of learning disabilities (see, e.g., Kopriva, 2009). Innovative tests like this one foreground the fact that other standardized assessments are testing both content knowledge *and* English literacy, and so claims that they are purely content exams are inaccurate. Of course, avoiding language in a language assessment is impossible, but the ONPAR system demonstrates that with innovative development and careful testing, linguistic bias can be reduced or eliminated in math and science evaluations.

Difference versus Disorder

A mismatch between assessments of all kinds and students' language can put children at a disadvantage quite early in their academic careers. For example, classroom teachers may refer young children for screening for a possible language problem because they misinterpret the students' use of vernacular grammatical forms as evidence of disorder, including, for example, multiple negation, or vernacular pronunciation, such as *f* for the sound represented by the spelling "th" (e.g., pronouncing *birthday* as "birfday," *tooth* as "toof," *bath* as "baf," and *mouth* as "mouf"). Following standard screening procedures, the children could be found to have developmental delays or other disorders if those procedures are not sensitive to vernacular dialect norms. Children from Standard English-speaking communities may also use some of these same language features in the early years, but for them these forms are considered to indicate only immature language when they persist past the age of 5 or so. In other words, identical linguistic features give different evidence about children's language development depending on which dialect the children are acquiring. Features that are developmentally inappropriate for standard dialect speakers may be developmentally appropriate for vernacular dialect speakers, given the adult norms of the vernacular.

Teachers who are aware of dialect differences can avoid inappropriate refer-ral by carefully noting the details of young children's speech. The dialectally knowledgeable teacher could make certain observations that would clarify the situation. Consider again the student from the previous paragraph who says words like *mouth* as "mouf." The dialectally knowledgeable teacher might notice that in the child's speech, the *f* pronunciation is used only in the middle and at the ends of words, never in the beginning (e.g., never "fick" for *thick*). Thus, there is a restricted pattern to the student's pronunciation, not a general substitution of *f* for *th*. Second, the teacher might notice that other children from that child's speech community have a similar pronunciation pattern. Considering these facts in conjunction with other knowledge about dialect differences, the teacher could conclude that the student was using a regular rule of the speech community's dialect and was not a candidate for language dis-ability screening. The key consideration in distinguishing between a language difference and a disorder is the language norm of the student's own speech community or dialect.

Because some features of vernacular varieties of English might resemble features that also might indicate speech-language delay, traditional tests normed on mainstream children may misdiagnose dialect as disorder for vernacular dialect speakers. Innovative tests in early child development, however, recognize the importance of using a local norm rather than Standard English. An early example was the Minimal Competence Core approach, which uses a set of features expected at a specific development age (Stockman, 1996). A second example ignores morphological endings (e.g., plural -*s*, past tense -*ed*, etc.) altogether, focusing instead on complex sentence structure for evidence (Craig & Washington, 1994). Although both of these approaches were ultimately abandoned, they demonstrate the types of strategies that can be considered, based on research into language structure.

Another promising attempt to develop a non-biased language assessment involved a number of speech pathologists who created a diagnostic tool normed on African American children that, among other things, avoided linguistic forms that might lead to a misdiagnosis (Seymour, Roeper, & de Villiers, 2005). Their instrument, named the Diagnostic Evaluation of Language Variation – Norm Referenced (DELV-NR), represents an important shift in standardized language assessment, and while it still was not as accurate as careful analysis of language samples, it was found to be an improvement over past models of assessment (Pearson, Jackson, & Wu, 2014). The tool is built on the premise that individuals whose speech and language are not appropriate according to the norms of their own speech communities are the ones who may be showing genuine disorders. In other words, the DELV-NR seeks to separate vernacular speakers whose language is not disordered from vernacular speakers who have speech disorders. There is no question that the most effective basis for discriminating dialect difference from language disorder comes from an understanding of normal language variation and specific knowledge about local dialects.

Oral Language Assessment

Other aspects of language screening may put non-middle-class children at a disadvantage. Some of the most innocuous-appearing procedures for getting children to produce a language sample for diagnostic purposes may be fraught with sociolinguistic values that discriminate against their speech. For example, as demonstrated in Box 6.1, in a classic example from the sociolinguistic literature, a friendly invitation by an adult to a child to "tell me everything you can about the fire engine on the table" is laden with implicit values about verbosity (the more you tell, the better), telling obvious information (describe the object even though you know the adult knows all about it and can also see it), and the consequences of information sharing (what a child tells the adult will not be held against the child).

Other seemingly straightforward test prompts can cause confusion in children of different cultural backgrounds. Some speech/language assessments have the practitioner ask children to "repeat after me," which seems clear enough, but some children are confused by the purpose of the request and misinterpret it. "Repeat after me" has no place in natural communication—other than marriage

BOX 6.1: EXCERPTS FROM "THE LOGIC OF NONSTANDARD ENGLISH," BY WILLIAM LABOV

Copyright 1969 by Georgetown University Press. "The Logic of Nonstandard English." From *Georgetown University Round Table on Languages and Linguistics (GURT) 1969: Linguistics and the Teaching of Standard English to Speakers of Other Language*, James E. Alatis, Editor, pp. 5–6. Reprinted with permission by www.press.georgetown.edu

In the past decade, a great deal of federally sponsored research has been devoted to the educational problems of children in ghetto schools. In order to account for the poor performance of children in these schools, educational psychologists have attempted to discover what kind of disadvantage or defect they are suffering from. The viewpoint that has been widely accepted and used as the basis for large-scale intervention programs is that the children show a cultural deficit as a result of an impoverished environment in their early years. Considerable attention has been given to language. In this area, the deficit theory appears as the concept of "verbal deprivation": Negro [stet] children from the ghetto area receive little verbal stimulation, are said to hear very little well-formed language, and as a result are impoverished in their means of verbal expression: They cannot speak complete sentences, do not know the names of common objects, and cannot form concepts or convey logical thoughts.

Unfortunately, these notions are based upon the work of educational psychologists who know very little about language and even less about Negro children. The concept of verbal deprivation has no basis in social reality. In fact, Negro children from the urban ghettos receive a great deal of verbal stimulation, hear more well-formed sentences than middle-class children, and participate fully in a highly verbal culture; they have the same basic vocabulary, possess the same capacity for conceptual learning, and use the same logic as anyone else who learns to speak and understand English.

The notion of "verbal deprivation" is part of the modern mythology of educational psychology, typical of the unfounded notions that tend to expand rapidly in our educational system. In past decades, linguists have been as guilty as others in promoting such intellectual fashions at the expense of both teachers and children. But the myth of verbal deprivation is particularly dangerous because it diverts attention from real defects of our education system to imaginary defects of the child; and . . . it leads its sponsors inevitably to the hypothesis of the genetic inferiority of Negro children, which it was originally designed to avoid.

Verbality

The most extreme view that proceeds from this orientation—and one that is now being widely accepted—is that lower class Negro children have no language at all. . . . On many occasions, we have been asked to help analyze the results of research into verbal deprivation in . . . test situations.

Here, for example, is a complete interview with a Negro boy, one of hundreds carried out in a New York City school. The boy enters a room where there is a large, friendly White interviewer who puts on the table in front of him a block or a fire engine and says, "Tell me everything you can about this." (The interviewer's further remarks are in parentheses.)

[12 seconds of silence]
(What would you say it looks like?)
    [8 seconds of silence]
A space ship.
(Hmmmmm.)
    [13 seconds of silence]
Like a je-et.
    [Like a plane.]
    [20 seconds of silence]
(What color is it?)
Orange. [2 seconds] An' whi-ite. [2 seconds] An' green.
    [6 seconds of silence]
(An' what could you use it for?)
    [8 seconds of silence]
A je-et.
    [6 seconds of silence]
(If you had two of them, what would you do with them?)
    [6 seconds of silence]
Give one to some-body.
(Hmmmm. Who do you think would like to have it?)
    [10 seconds of silence]
Cla-rence.
(Mm. Where do you think we could get another one of these?)
At the store.
(Oh ka-ay!)

We have here the same kind of defensive, monosyllabic behavior that is reported in [a psychologist's] work. What is the situation that produces it? The child is in an asymmetrical situation where anything he says can literally be held against him. He has learned a number of devices to <u>avoid</u> saying anything in this situation, and he works very hard to achieve this end. . . . If one takes this interview as a measure of the verbal capacity of the child, it must be as his capacity to defend himself in a hostile and threatening situation. But unfortunately, thousands of such interviews are used as evidence of the child's total verbal capacity or, more simply, his "verbality."

The view of the Negro speech community that we obtain from our work in the ghetto areas is precisely the opposite from that reported by [psychologists]. We see a child bathed in verbal stimulation from morning to night. We see many speech events that depend on the competitive exhibition of verbal skills: sounding, singing, toasts, rifting, louding—a whole range of activities in which the individual gains status through his use of language. We see the younger child trying to acquire these skills from older children—hanging around on the outskirts of the older peer groups and imitating this behavior to the best of his ability. We see no connection between verbal skill at the speech events characteristic of the street culture and success in the schoolroom.

vows, where the parties are afraid they might forget their lines. In the contrived language situation of screening, lack of familiarity with the instruction can result in children second-guessing the purpose of the task: "Why would I say the exact same words back? Maybe I am supposed to convey the same meaning but say it differently?" Such a response actually involves more advanced linguistic skills, but it would be scored incorrect according to standard protocols. A good guideline is "The more superficial and limited the scope of language capability tapped in a testing instrument, the greater the likelihood that the instrument will be inappropriate for speakers beyond the immediate population on which it was normed" (Wolfram & Schilling, 2016, p. 319).

Language assessment situations are inherently different from natural conversations, introducing the potential for task/instruction confusion. Further, the dynamic of (often) an adult stranger interacting with a child during the assessment can lead to a level of discomfort, particularly when there are mismatches in cultural backgrounds between examiner and student (Argeton & Moran, 1995; Franco & LeVine, 1985; Fuchs & Fuchs, 1986). Such situational factors are important.

Various kinds of bias undermine the validity of standardized tests used in speech and language assessment and throughout education. Values biases occur when a test question incorrectly assumes a cultural stance (such as the example of the New York Regents exam asking about the benefits of imperialism). Bias can also be introduced through norming. When a test is normed on a primarily Northern middle-class population, for instance, these norms may not be at all appropriate for students from a Southern working-class community due to language and culture differences. Some tests do provide alternative scoring guidelines to accommodate vernacular speakers. However, these guidelines are intended to account for speakers of that social group nationwide, and not all responses are locally appropriate. And, of course, the format of the test and the language used in the test can introduce additional bias. Bias at all these levels is part of the reason why it is difficult to rely on standardized test results for diagnosis of oral language disorders. While we do not wish to suggest that standardized language assessments and testing have no place in modern education, we hope it is clear that standardized assessment scores should not be used as an objective measure, but rather as one that requires interpretation. One of the most damning interpretations of modern standardized testing in general comes from researcher Harold Berlak:

> Standardized tests are a particularly invidious form of institutionalized racism because they lend the cloak of science to policies that have denied, and are continuing to deny, persons of color equal access to educational and job opportunities. An educational accountability system based on standardized testing — though predicated on "standardized" measurements which are purportedly neutral, objective, and color-blind — perpetuates and strengthens institutionalized racism.
>
> *2009, p. 71*

Since there can be no standardized assessment that is truly neutral with respect to language, teachers and language practitioners must seek a work-around. The following list of questions can help them select, use, and interpret assessments:

1. What does the test claim to be testing? Does it actually test what it claims to test?
2. What assumptions about language underlie the test both in terms of the questions that test-takers must answer and in terms of the test instructions?
3. What kinds of language-related tasks may be central to participating in the test?
4. What demographic group(s) was the test normed on?
5. How must the results be interpreted for different dialect groups?

Looking back at the constructed language test in this chapter's opening scenario, we can use a few of these questions to see why the test is so absurd. With regard to question 1, the instructions state that it is a language assessment, but all it does is establish whether or not the test-taker is a speaker of Pittsburghese. Concerning question 4, the correct answers were normed on a very unrepresentative regional and social group.

Most standardized assessments of oral language fail to account for all dialect forms, leaving vernacular speaking students at increased risk of being misdiagnosed with speech and communication disorders. In recognition of the potential problems, especially for ethnic minorities, that might arise during speech evaluation, the American Speech-Language-Hearing Association has since 1983 maintained a Position Statement on Social Dialects that reads in part as follows:

It is the position of the American Speech-Language-Hearing Association (ASHA) that no dialectal variety of English is a disorder or a pathological form of speech or language. Each social dialect is adequate as a functional and effective variety of English. Each serves a communication function as well as a social solidarity function. It maintains the communication network and the social construct of the community of speakers who use it. Furthermore, each is a symbolic representation of the historical, social, and cultural background of the speakers. For example, there is strong evidence that many of the features of Black English represent linguistic Africanisms.

reprinted with permission; available at
www.asha.org/policy/PS1983–00115/

Because knowledge about sociolinguistics is not always a part of the training of speech pathologists, ASHA includes in the position statement six recommendations that can help teachers and language practitioners better understand and meet the needs of their diverse students. Though written for speech-language pathologists, these recommendations are applicable to all educators. Everyone who formally serves in some capacity as a language gatekeeper should have the following:

1. Knowledge of the particular dialect as a rule-governed linguistic system,
2. Knowledge of nondiscriminatory testing procedures,
3. Knowledge of the phonological and grammatical features of the dialect,
4. Knowledge of contrastive analysis procedures,
5. Knowledge of the effects of attitudes toward dialects,
6. Thorough understanding and appreciation for the community and culture of the nonstandard speaker.

Cole, 1983, p. 25

Various kinds of bias undermine the validity of standardized tests used in speech and language assessment and throughout education. Since the ASHA position statement, misdiagnosis of dialect as disorder has decreased; however, it is still the case that African American students are two to three times more likely to be diagnosed with a language disorder than white students (Aud, Fox, & Kewal-Ramani, 2010, p. 40). While a tremendous amount of progress has been made, the remaining biases persist because they are so covert. Eliminating these biases requires vigilance at every level, from classroom teachers to speech-language pathologists to test designers.

Formal diagnoses are just one dimension of the testing challenge. There is no question that most of the language assessment in schools happens outside of standardized testing situations. The routine literacy and other language-based assessments associated with teaching can have implications as powerful as formalized assessments. More specifics about teachers' responses to students' oral language, writing, and reading are examined in the following three chapters.

Discussion Questions

1. Standardized test development is remote from practitioners. What is the value of focusing on it here?
2. How can classroom teachers take dialect into account in classroom assessment?
3. The excerpt from "The Logic of Nonstandard English," by William Labov, has been widely reprinted. It was published in 1969. Is it still important? What parts are outdated (if any) and what are still relevant after all these years?
4. The final sentence of the Labov excerpt says that his research team sees "no connection between verbal skill at the speech events characteristic of the street culture and success in the schoolroom." Why don't schools assess this kind of verbal skill?
5. What other points in this excerpt are particularly important for practitioners?
6. With the chapter's opening parodic assessment of the Pittsburgh dialect as the backdrop, examine the list below of language-related skills and knowledge, and decide which of them might be reasonably assessed through a standardized test. How might you design a test to assess people's grasp of one of these skill and knowledge domains? What other sets of skills or knowledge might affect how someone performs on that test? Recall that the vocabulary test at the start of the chapter merely identified whether or not you were familiar with the dialect of Pittsburgh.

General vocabulary	Antonyms	Synonyms
Verb endings	Apostrophe usage	End punctuation
Academic vocabulary	Subject–verb agreement	Word associations
Dialect spoken	Writing ability	Reading comprehension
Drawing inferences	Summarizing a text	Word meaning from context

Links of Interest

1. See the ONPAR test items for science: http://iiassessment.wceruw.org/projects/ONPAR-science-tasks.html
2. See the ONPAR test items for math: http://iiassessment.wceruw.org/projects/ONPAR-math-tasks.html

3. Visit former Assistant Secretary of Education turned educational activist Diane Ravitch's blog about educational standards, money, and standardized testing: https://dianeravitch.net/

4. Read about the education testing and assessment initiatives at the Center for Applied Linguistics: www.cal.org/areas-of-impact/testing-assessment

5. Look at ETS's guidelines for assessing English language learners: www.ets.org/s/about/pdf/ell_guidelines.pdf

6. Examine a list of resources compiled by the American Speech-Language-Hearing Association for assessing language disorders in schools: www.asha.org/SLP/Assessment-and-Evaluation-of-Speech-Language-Disorders-in-Schools/

7. Read information about reading and writing assessments at the website of the National Council of Teachers of English: www.ncte.org/standards/assessmentstandards/introduction

Further Reading

Charity Hudley, A. H., & Mallinson, C. (2011). *Understanding English language variation in U. S. schools.* New York, NY: Teachers College Press.
> This book provides an overview of issues in education related to English language variation. It focuses mostly on Southern and African American English, though other dialects are included.

Craig, H. K., & Washington, J. A. (2006). *Malik goes to school: Examining the language skills of African American students from preschool-5th grade.* Mahwah, NJ: Lawrence Erlbaum.
> This volume presents the findings from a major study of the language skills of young African American children. Though technical in nature, the book's discussions and conclusions are important for teachers and speech-language practitioners.

Fecho, B. (2004). *"Is this English?": Race, language, and culture in the classroom.* New York, NY: Teachers College Press.
> This book offers students and teachers methods for applying critical inquiry to language issues within the classroom context.

References

Argeton, E., & Moran, M. (1995). Effects of race and dialect of examiner on language: Samples elicited from southern African-American preschoolers. *Journal of Childhood Communication Disorders, 16*(2), 21–25.

Aud, S., Fox, M. A., & Kewal-Ramani, A. (2010). Status and trends in the education of racial and ethnic groups. NCES 2010–15. *National Center for Education Statistics.* Available online at http://nces.ed.gov/pubs2010/2010015.pdf

Berlak, H. (2009). Race and the achievement gap. In W. Au (Ed.), *Rethinking multicultural education: Teaching for racial and cultural justice* (pp. 63–73). Milwaukee, WI: Rethinking Schools.

Bracey, G.W. (2004). Simpson's paradox and other statistical mysteries. *American School Board Journal, 191*(2), 32–34.

Canivez, G. L. (2008). Orthogonal higher order factor structure of the Stanford–Binet Intelligence Scales—for children and adolescents. *School Psychology Quarterly, 23*(4), 533.

Cole, L. (1983). Implications of the position on social dialects. *Asha, 25*(9), 25–27. Retrieved from www.asha.org/policy/PS1983–00115.htm#AP1

Craig, H. K., & Washington, J. A. (1994). The complex syntax skills of poor, urban, African-American preschoolers at school entry. *Language, Speech, and Hearing Services in Schools, 25*(3), 181–190.

Engelhard Jr., G., Gordon, B., & Gabrielson, S. (1992). The influences of mode of discourse, experiential demand, and gender on the quality of student writing. *Research in the Teaching of English, 26*(3), 315–336.

Franco, J., & LeVine, E. (1985). Effects of examiner variables on reported self-disclosure: implications for group personality testing. *Hispanic Journal of Behavioral Sciences, 7*(2), 199–210.

Freedle, R. (2003). Correcting the SAT's ethnic and social-class bias: A method for reestimating SAT scores. *Harvard Educational Review, 73*(1), 1–43.

Fuchs, D., & Fuchs, L. (1986). Test procedure bias: A meta-analysis of examiner familiarity effects. *Review of Educational Research, 56*(2), 243–262.

Goltz, H. H., & Smith, M. L. (2010). Yule–Simpson's paradox in research. *Practical Assessment, Research & Evaluation, 15*(15), 1–9.

Goodenough, F. L. (1926). Racial differences in the intelligence of school children. *Journal of Experimental Psychology, 9*(5), 388–397.

Haviland, C. P., & Clark, J. M. (1992). What can our students tell us about essay examination designs and practices? *Journal of Basic Writing, 11*(2), 47–60.

Jencks, C., & Phillips, M. (1998). The Black-White test score gap: An introduction. In C. Jencks & M. Phillips (Eds.), *The Black-White test score gap* (pp. 1–51). Washington, DC: Brookings Institute.

Kopriva, R. J. (2009). Assessing the skills and abilities in math and science of ELs with low English proficiency: A promising new method. *AccELLerate!! The Quarterly Newsletter of the National Clearinghouse for English Language Acquisition, 2*(1), 7–10.

Kozol, J. (2005). *The shame of the nation: The restoration of apartheid schooling in America.* New York, NY: Random House.

Labov, W. (1969). The logic of nonstandard English. In J. Alatis (Ed.), *20th Annual Round Table. Linguistics and the teaching of Standard English to speakers of other languages and dialects* (pp. 1–44). Washington, DC: Georgetown University Press.

Leki, I. (1992). *Understanding ESL writers: A guide for teachers.* Portsmouth, NH: Boynton/ Cook.

Minami, M., & McCabe, A. (1995). Rice balls and bear hunts: Japanese and North American family narrative patterns. *Journal of Child Language, 22*(2), 423–445.

Mountford, R. (1999). Let them experiment: Accommodating diverse discourse practices. In C. Cooper & L. Odell (Eds.), *Evaluating writing: The role of teachers' knowledge about text, learning, and culture* (2nd ed.) (pp. 366–396). Urbana, IL: National Council of Teachers of English.

National Assessment of Educational Progress (n.d.). *Top stories in NAEP long-term trend assessments 2012.* Retrieved from www.nationsreportcard.gov/ltt_2012/

National Center for Education Statistics. (n.d.). *National assessment of adult literacy: A nationally representative and continuing assessment of English language literary skills in American adults.* Retrieved from http://nces.ed.gov/naal/lit_history.asp

Pearson, B. Z., Jackson, J. E., & Wu, H. (2014). Seeking a valid gold standard for an innovative, dialect-neutral language test. *Journal of Speech, Language, and Hearing Research, 57*(2), 495–508.

Rosenthal, R., & Jacobson, L. (1968). *Pygmalion in the classroom: Teacher expectation and pupils' intellectual development.* New York, NY: Holt, Rinehart and Winston.

Rosner, J. (2003, March 27). On white preferences. *The Nation.* Retrieved from www.thenation. com/article/white-preferences/

Seymour, H. N., Roeper, T., & de Villiers, J. G. (2005). *DELV-NR (diagnostic evaluation of language variation) norm-referenced test.* San Antonio, TX: The Psychological Corporation.

Strauss, V. (2011, March 15). SAT question on reality TV stirs controversy. *The Washington Post.* Retrieved from www.washingtonpost.com/blogs/answer-sheet/post/sat-question-on-reality-tv-stirs-controversy/2011/03/15/ABjNyCY_blog.html

Stockman, I. J. (1996). The promises and pitfalls of language sample analysis as an assessment tool for linguistic minority children. *Language, Speech, and Hearing Services in Schools, 27*(4), 355–366.

Terry, J. M., Hendrick, R., Evangelou, E., & Smith, R. L. (2010). Variable dialect switching among African American children: Inferences about working memory. *Lingua, 120*(10), 2463–2475.

Weinberg, M. (1983). *The search for quality integrated education: Policy and research on minority students in school and college.* Westport, CT: Greenwood Press.

Woestehoff, J. (2011, May 30). Rahm as "Da Bachelor" and other reality TV ideas for Chicago's schools. *Huffington Post*. Retrieved from www.huffingtonpost.com/julie-woestehoff/rahm-as-da-bachelor-reality-tv_b_842268.html

Wolfram, W. (1976). Sociolinguistic levels of test bias. In T. Trabasso & D. Harrison (Eds.), *Seminar in Black English* (pp. 265–267). Hillsdale, NJ: Lawrence Erlbaum Associates.

Wolfram, W. (1983). Test interpretation and sociolinguistic differences. *Topics in Language Disorders, 3,* 21–34.

Wolfram, W., & Schilling, N. (2016). *American English: Dialects and variation* (3rd ed). Malden MA: John Wiley & Sons.

7

Dialect Policy and Oral Language Program Development

Scenario

In his autobiography, basketball legend Kareem Abdul-Jabbar recounted the distress he experienced as a result of being labeled different in fourth grade based on his advanced reading ability:

> When the kids found this out [his reading ability] I became a target. . . It was my first time away from home, my first experience in an all-black situation, and I found myself being punished for everything I'd ever been taught was right. I got all A's and was hated for it; I spoke correctly and was called a punk. I had to learn a new language simply to be able to deal with the threats. I had good manners and was a good little boy and paid for it with my hide.
>
> *Abdul-Jabbar & Knobler, 1983, p. 16*

What sorts of things are revealed by how you speak and read? What do you interpret "punk" to mean in this example? Can speaking a vernacular ever earn you the label, "punk"? What do teachers need to know about dialects in order to create the sorts of environments where all dialects are valued? How was Abdul-Jabbar's success in school-related activities viewed by some of his peers? How do you explain that? What sort of "new language" is meant when he writes, "I had to learn a new language simply to be able to deal with the threats"?

Many people argue, notwithstanding the linguistic equality of all dialects, that the social realities of American society dictate that all students be proficient in speaking Standard English. This position raises fundamental educational issues concerning language differences between groups of students. One serious issue is the expectation that this position imposes on vernacular-speaking students: They are expected to communicate complex thoughts in a language code that they are less comfortable using than their native dialects. If it were possible to teach Standard English quickly and successfully to members of communities where other dialects are used, doing so might provide a rather simple solution to all the problems involving language diversity mentioned in this volume. If there were truly a clear-cut social advantage to speaking Standard English, then, after a short time, all students would share the same advantage. Problems of language interference in test-taking, writing, and reading would be eliminated. However, as might be expected, the answer to questions about how schools should address dialect diversity is not nearly as simple as teaching all students to speak Standard English. This chapter explores the issues related to Standard English and suggests some principles for policy and program development. Emphasis is placed in this chapter on oral language, but issues of Standard English policy, curriculum, and instruction involve written language as well, as demonstrated in Chapters 8 and 9. Thus this chapter also deals to some extent with dialects and writing.

Standard English and Social Reality

One of the central questions in any discussion of teaching Standard English concerns the broad-based influence of the dialect that children have learned in their home and neighborhood. Can classroom instruction in a standard dialect succeed despite the influence of the speech of parents, siblings, and friends outside of school? Children in families that move from one English-speaking area to another often adapt quickly to the regional dialect spoken in the new location, even when their parents maintain the dialect of their backgrounds. Similarly, children whose home language is not English can succeed in learning English and using it at school and with friends while maintaining a different language with their family. These kinds of experiences clearly suggest that children should be able to learn mainstream varieties of English—if the issue is simply language learning. So we have to look at the kinds of social and educational conditions that surround learning Standard English.

The social situation inside the school can be an important factor in dialect learning. If relationships between groups are harmonious and if the vernacular dialect and its associated culture are not devalued in the school and classroom, students may not experience a disjunction between language outside of school (e.g., in peer groups and communities, at home) and language in school. In this case, studying Standard English may not have a negative symbolic value that interferes with learning. However, if tensions between standard and vernacular speakers are high, then an opposition is established and students may have reason to resist the standard variety. In fact, there is evidence that white and African American English dialects diverged more rapidly in the United States following school integration than before (Labov, 2009), demonstrating that exposure does not necessarily lead to language convergence.

For years, debate on teaching Standard English has ebbed and flowed in education and linguistic forums, and in the popular press. Just as interest in dialect issues seems to be waning, debate flares up again when a school district introduces an instructional program or policy related to dialects, as happened in 1996 and 1997 when Oakland (CA) Unified School District drew attention to its program through a school board action. More recently, the debate has emerged again in response to the release of the Common Core State Standards (2010a). These standards include both "Speaking and Listening" and "Language" strands, which some interpret as requiring instruction in standard oral language.

Fundamentally, teachers have three options to choose from in deciding how to deal with oral use of vernacular dialects in their classrooms: 1. insist that they not be used (the eradication position); 2. teach code-switching or code-meshing between the vernacular dialect and a standard variety (the additivist position); or 3. permit all dialects (the linguistic pluralism position). Proponents of the eradication and additivist positions might argue that teaching Standard English is necessary because, given society's attitudes, it is associated with success at school and in the workplace. Because implicit attitudes are extremely difficult to change, they might argue, schools should provide high-quality instruction in Standard English rather than waiting for social attitudes to be altered. Indeed, parents from vernacular-speaking communities typically expect that schools will teach Standard English because they are likely to hold some of the same entrenched language prejudices found in the society at large. They recognize the instrumental value of Standard English and expect schools to equip their children with the tools they need for economic success.

Among those who favor teaching Standard English, however, eradication-ists and additivists differ fundamentally in how they value the nonmainstream dialect. The first group, eradicationists, might suggest that the dialect used outside of school has no value, whereas those in the additivist group would argue that because vernacular dialects can be important to social function and identity, it is better to increase students' linguistic repertoires (by adding a Standard English variety to the existing vernacular) rather than limit them (by replacing the vernacular with a standard variety).

Additivists typically endorse one of two contrasting approaches to building and using students' English language repertoires. These approaches are termed *code-switching* and *code-meshing*. In *code-switching*, students are taught through contrastive analysis how to switch between vernacular and Standard English patterns based on situation. This approach acknowledges that the vernacular code may be the appropriate choice for interactions in which social solidarity is critical, such as in the home or community (Wheeler & Swords, 2006, 2010). The Standard English code, often termed "formal English" or "school English," is generally expected in most school contexts. One study that employed code-switching as part of an instructional intervention found that, combined with other dialect awareness instruction, this approach improved the performance of urban upper elementary school children on writing assessments (Sweetland, 2006).

Critics of the code-switching approach to instruction argue that it still mar-ginalizes vernacular varieties by setting them up as unworthy for educational and other purposes. They note also that appropriate language choice is not governed strictly by broad context or domain (e.g., classroom vs. playground) (Young & Martinez, 2011; Young, Barrett, Young-Rivera, & Lovejoy, 2013). Instead, speakers may employ multiple language varieties in a single conversation as they negotiate stances and identities (Schilling-Estes, 2004). This more fluid deployment of multiple codes within an exchange is called *code-meshing*. This construct more accurately reflects the shifting and negotiated language choices that characterize successful communication in which a person's identity fluctuates: "Speakers use different combinations of language features from a variety of sources to index various types of identities and stances in everyday interaction in a wide variety of interactions and contexts" (Wolfram & Schilling, 2016, p. 327).

A type of code-meshing can be seen in the speech of people in positions of power, who will sometimes evoke a nonstandard or vernacular form for effect in formal contexts. Barack Obama occasionally incorporated African American English features into formal addresses as President, such as when he said, "You ain't seen nothin' yet" at a fundraising event (Youngman, 2009). White politicians may do similar things. Newspaper columnist Barry Saunders noted of North Carolina Governor Pat McCrory that he exaggerated some Southern pronunciations, despite the fact that he grew up in Ohio and urban North Carolina, places where such features are rare (reported in Wolfram & Reaser, 2014, p. 89). Fluid dialect use helps speakers negotiate communication effectively, and, for vernacular speakers, successfully meshing vernacular and standard codes can be highly effective. A code-meshing approach to instruction does not devalue the vernacular in the way that the code-switching approach can, the latter of which sets up a school-home dichotomy that is operationally unrealistic and that subordinates the home variety in contrast to the school variety.

Code-meshing is not without criticism, though. Peter Elbow, well-known for his writing pedagogies, generally finds the approach appealing, but also points out some limitations. First, he notes that minority children will typically have to earn the license to integrate code-meshing into their writing:

> Since student writing is so commonly read through a teacher-lens that looks for problems, student code meshing probably won't be so successful unless the student has convinced the teacher that she is skilled and sophisticated and in control of the written language.
>
> *2012, p. 331*

Essentially, Elbow argues that in present-day classrooms, control of Standard English norms is required before a writer has the freedom to consciously violate those norms. As a result, code-meshing may be a skill more appropriate for refining the tone of advanced writers rather than a method that can help emergent writers. Elbow is also critical of highlighting the inclusion of vernacular features, as in the President Obama example in the previous paragraph. He notes, "This kind of racially marked code meshing can only work in our present culture if the writer has some authority" (2012, p. 331). Elbow suggests that students must be given opportunities to write with "*wholly unplanned* vernacular language usage—with *no* need for linguistic sophistication or control" (2012, p. 331, italics in original) as a way of building the language competence that might lead them to becoming effective at code-meshing. This methodology can manifest in various ways, including vernacular dialogue journals.

Adherents of the third position listed above—the linguistic pluralism position that permits all dialects—have differing rationales for their approach. Some teachers may decide to simply ignore oral language differences while other teachers might embrace or celebrate linguistic diversity in their classroom. Proponents of this approach point out that there is no linguistic reason to ask people to change the way they speak. The only solution, they maintain, is to change society's attitudes toward various dialects so that all varieties of English are accepted (see, e.g., Conference on College Composition and Communication/National Council of Teachers of English, 1974; Smitherman, 2000). Some observers have opposed teaching Standard English at all, arguing that doing so is discriminatory because certain students would be singled out for instruction—those who do not already speak Standard English (Alim & Smitherman, 2012; Sledd, 1969). The argument is that it is classist and/or racist to allow some but not all students to communicate complex ideas in the linguistic code they are most comfortable with and to require students who speak vernacular dialects—by definition, those whose backgrounds are less congruent with the demands of school—to learn curriculum content and the standard variety while mainstream children are required to learn only the curriculum. Another concern is that, given the social realities about which dialects are privileged and which are stigmatized, Standard English instruction often appears to be remediation, opening vernacular dialect speakers to potentially devastating deficit views and low expectations in school.

Group Reference and Dialect Learning

The three positions presented above on how dialects can be handled in schools are more theoretical than actual. The fact of the matter is that for many years, schools have attempted in one way or another to ensure that all students speak Standard English. Yet many people who have gone to school continue to use vernacular forms in situations that call for a standard variety, according to mainstream language norms. The evidence thus suggests that we need to confront the relative lack of success that has typified both formal and informal strategies of teaching Standard English. Why hasn't instruction in Standard English been more successful?

As with all learning, the factor that is probably most responsible for success (or lack of it) in teaching someone to speak a standard dialect is relevance. People are motivated to learn a dialect that they need for daily interaction. When this need is understood from the speaker's perspective, rather than from the observer's, group reference becomes a key element. The desire to belong to a group whose members speak a particular language variety is a critical motivational factor for learning another dialect. If students from vernacular-speaking communities identify with Standard English speakers, the chances are good that they will learn Standard English; but if identifying with Standard English speakers and learning Standard English leads to rejecting the non-school culture, undesirable consequences can occur for the individual, the community, and the society. Students who have no desire to identify with Standard English-speaking groups will probably resist attempts to teach them Standard English.

Age and linguistic role models can play an important role, too. In a longitudinal study, 70 African American students were interviewed at least every other year for the first 20 years of their lives (Van Hofwegen, 2015a; Van Hofwegen & Wolfram, 2010). Detailed analysis of the students' speech data found that they arrived at school with varying levels of African American English features—often similar to that of their primary caregivers. In their early elementary years, however, they became more standardized in both speech and writing, presumably due to the influence of more standard linguistic role models—teachers (Abrams, 2011; Van Hofwegen & Wolfram, 2010). Beginning in about fifth grade and continuing through middle school, almost all of the students began to use more vernacular features in their speech, suggesting a shift in orientation from teacher to peers. The high school years saw greater variability in the students' dialect paths, with some becoming increasingly vernacular while others became increasingly standard. This research underscores the fact that there is no single trajectory in terms of increasing or reducing vernacular forms.

Sometimes it can be hard for mainstream speakers to understand why, given the obvious importance of Standard English in educational and professional settings, some children do not value learning it in schools. However, the association of Standard English with white, middle-class culture means that embracing it can be interpreted as selling out in some communities. In fact, derogatory labels are common for members of minority groups who are seen as too white—including *Oreo, Aunt Jemima,* and *Bounty Bar* for African Americans; *banana* or *Chonky* for those of East Asian origin; *apple* for American Indians; and *coconut* or *pocho/pocha* for Hispanics. Of course, the term *wigger* is sometimes used for a Caucasian who attempts to identify with African American culture, but it tends to not carry the same stigma as the other terms listed. While dress, academic orientation, and interests affect who is determined to be "acting white," there is, perhaps, no greater indicator of cultural identity than language

(Fordham & Ogbu, 1986). John Rickford has collected numerous anecdotes from interviews with African American students in working-class areas of California. One of the more succinct and revealing statements about the social consequences of acting white comes from a student who noted "Over at my school . . . first time they catch you talkin white, they'll never let it go. Even if you quit talkin like that, they'll never let it go" (Rickford & Rickford, 2002, p. 223). The social costs for African Americans who are judged to be acting white are quite stiff, and outcomes can range from "being deemed a social outcast, to being beaten, or killed" (Austen-Smith & Fryer, 2003, p. 3). This is, in fact, the sentiment expressed by Kareem Abdul-Jabbar in the opening scenario of this chapter. Given the stigma of acting and talking white, it is no surprise that African American students in an urban high school were found to resist speaking Standard English (Fordham, 1998).

School environments are often assumed to be places where Standard English is the de facto best language choice; but schools are a social environment, and as a result, students' language choices are affected by more than just the preferences of their teachers. Good language choices in school settings might serve multiple purposes, including placating a teacher without incurring a social penalty. Robert Pooley offers this understanding of appropriate language choices: "'Good English' is marked by success in making language choices so that the fewest number of people will be distracted by the choices" (1946, p. 5). Using a vernacular dialect in educational settings can sometimes be understood as students making a socially appropriate, albeit controversial, language choice, given the complex social environment of the school.

In his book, *Is This English?: Race, Language and Culture in the Classroom* (2004), Bob Fecho tells the story of a speech made by one of his students, Kenya, an African American student in an overwhelmingly black school. The speech included features of African American English. The other students in the class described Kenya's speech as "lively, natural, and engaging" (p. 54). Fecho notes that:

> The syntax, grammar, and vocabulary choices matched the expectations of this audience for that speaker. In this community of students, being one's self rather than "frontin'" or putting up a façade was valued.

> *p. 54*

However, the use of African American English, which was essential to the positive evaluation by the class, was also criticized:

> One student noted that Kenya had spoken in what he termed as Black English and that, when it came time for her to present for graded evaluation, she needed to switch to standard usage.

> *p. 54*

Following that comment, Fecho wrote "Black English" on the board under the "Needs Improvement" category on a chart he was keeping to annotate the session. When someone noticed this, the class erupted into a lively discussion that highlights the academic double jeopardy that speakers of vernacular dialects find themselves in every day in schools. One student argued:

> If we saw how natural Kenya sounded and her audience is Black students, why shouldn't she be allowed to speak Black English? Now she sees [her usage] listed as needing improvement. The idea is that's something that she should change. And that's a problem.
>
> *p. 54*

To extend the point this student is making, if the speech was natural and appropriate to the audience and the language allowed Kenya to speak with confidence, it would seem appropriate to evaluate the strength of Kenya's argument in this version of her speech, since it is likely that translating the speech into a standard code would result in the speech seeming less natural and the speaker less confident. Fecho reported that some members of the class were so absorbed in debating these points that they stayed after the session ended to continue the discussion. Discussions of language, culture, and power can become moments of rich learning.

Apart from allowing students to express themselves in the codes they are most comfortable with, there are other rationales for accepting or even encouraging oral vernacular usage in the classroom. Showing solidarity with one's social and/or ethnic group can be an important motivation for using a vernacular dialect. A powerful anecdote illustrating this principle comes from June Jordan, who tells the story of a student, Willie Jordan, whose brother Reggie had been an innocent victim of a police shooting. Jordan's class, which had been studying African American English, decided to write a letter to the police department in memory of Reggie Jordan. The class wrestled with whether to write the letter in Standard English, "the language of the killer," or "in our own language, the language of the victim," which would mean that the letter was likely to be dismissed (Jordan, 1988, p. 372). The decision was made to write the letter in African American English, after the students described the choice of Standard English as "suicide on top of Reggie's murder" (1988, p. 372). Jordan describes the aftermath of this decision: "It was heartbreaking to proceed, from that point. Everyone in the room realized that our decision in favor of Black English had doomed our writings" (1988, p. 372). In fact, the power of language choice in conveying solidarity is so strong that people who are not fully proficient in a vernacular dialect may use certain highly salient structures, intonation patterns, vocal quality, or vocabulary to signal their social loyalties. For example, people of Southern origin living outside the South may continue to use regional dialect vocabulary (e.g., "y'all" for the plural *you*; "fixin' to" instead of *about to*) to show affinity with other Southerners.

Decisions about how to handle language variation at school must take social facts into account. Students' relationships with their communities outside of school play an important role in language learning and language resistance. Students must continue to interact and participate appropriately in non-school settings and with peer groups. To maintain these important ties, they need to retain the ability to interact in the native dialect.

Professional Organizations' Positions on Dialects and Dialect Education

Chapter 5 explored the danger of viewing vernacular speech as evidence of cognitive deficit instead of students' social identity. The examples above suggest that even when using a vernacular dialect is not interpreted as evidence of cognitive deficit, contrasting expectations about language use in homes, communities, and schools may create tensions in the social environment of the school. Therefore, it is paramount that teacher education programs, speech-language practitioner training programs, and schools be guided by linguistically informed principles in their policy and professional development decisions. Linguistic research has consistently demonstrated that language variety in and of itself does not cause learning difficulties. In fact, even though deficit positions still assume that a relationship holds between language variety and cognition, linguistic scholarship has been unified on this matter for many years:

> There is no reason to believe that any nonstandard vernacular is in itself an obstacle to learning . . . As linguists we are unanimous in condemning this view as bad observation, bad theory, and bad practice . . . That educational psychology should be so strongly influenced by a theory so false to the facts of language is unfortunate, but that children should be the victims of this ignorance is intolerable.
>
> *Labov, 1969, p. 34*

In response to these issues, several professional organizations have issued position statements to guide educators as they take action with respect to dialect differences. A subdivision of the National Council of Teachers of English (NCTE), the College Composition and Communication Conference (CCCC), adopted a strong position on students' dialect rights, which was modified and adopted by the larger group. The 1974 CCCC/NCTE statement is reproduced in Box 7.1.

Although the statement asserts the rights of students to their own language and dialect, it also asserts that teachers will give them the opportunity to learn written *edited American English*, which is another term for Standard English. Here the need for linguistic adjustment falls disproportionately on vernacular speakers, which is, in part, why James Sledd once called code-switching

BOX 7.1: COLLEGE COMPOSITION AND COMMUNICATION
CONFERENCE/NATIONAL COUNCIL OF TEACHERS OF
ENGLISH POSITION STATEMENT, "STUDENTS'
RIGHT TO THEIR OWN LANGUAGE"

Resolved, that the National Council of Teachers of English affirm the students' right to their own language—to the dialect that expresses their family and community identity, the idiolect that expresses their unique personal identity;

That NCTE affirm the responsibility of all teachers of English to assist all students in the development of their ability to speak and write better, whatever their dialects;

That NCTE affirm the responsibility of all teachers to provide opportunities for clear and cogent expression of ideas in writing, and to provide the opportunity for students to learn the conventions of what has been called written edited American English; and

That NCTE affirm strongly that teachers must have the experiences and training that will enable them to understand and respect diversity of dialects. . . .

That NCTE promote classroom practices to expose students to the variety of dialects that comprise our multiregional, multiethnic, and multicultural society, so that they too will understand the nature of American English and come to respect all its dialects.

programs "the linguistics of white supremacy" (1969, p. 1307). But the mainstream population bears the responsibility to alter its prejudices and respect dialect differences for what they are—a natural manifestation of cultural and linguistic diversity. Linguistic scholars and professional education associations can provide leadership in making this case.

Other language-related organizations have also issued position statements regarding dialects. The American Association for Applied Linguistics (see Box 7.2), the American Speech-Language-Hearing Association (previous chapter), the Linguistic Society of America, and Teachers of English to Speakers of Other Languages all affirm that language variation is normal and natural.

At the same time, the right of individuals to maintain their own dialect must be balanced with the need for language standardization in the society. This conclusion comes not just from examining the situation in the United States or in English-speaking areas, but from surveying language situations throughout the world (Fasold, 1984). In all speech communities, there is a drive for standardization and a tendency toward social evaluation based on language

BOX 7.2: AMERICAN ASSOCIATION FOR APPLIED
LINGUISTICS RESOLUTION ON APPLICATION
OF DIALECT KNOWLEDGE TO EDUCATION

WHEREAS, The American Association for Applied Linguistics recognizes the legitimacy of African American language systems, variously referred to as African-American Vernacular English, Black English, or Ebonics, and their pedagogical importance in helping students acquire Standard English;

WHEREAS, Public discussion of the Oakland School Board's decision on the legitimacy of Ebonics and its usefulness in teaching Standard English demonstrates a lack of public aware-ness and understanding of the nature and naturalness of different varieties of language;

and WHEREAS, Students' competence in any dialect of English constitutes an important resource for learning Standard English as an additional dialect;

THEREFORE BE IT RESOLVED at the general business meeting of the American Association for Applied Linguistics, convened on this 11th day of March, 1997:

1. THAT, All students and teachers should learn scientifically-based information about linguistic diversity and examine the social, political, and educational consequences of differential treatment of dialects and their speakers;
2. THAT, Teacher education should systematically incorporate information about language variation and its impact on classroom interaction and about ways of applying that knowledge to enhance the education of all teachers;
3. THAT, Research should be undertaken to develop and test methods and materials for teaching about varieties of language and for learning Standard English; and
4. THAT, Members of the American Association for Applied Linguistics should seek ways and means to better communicate the theories and principles of the field to the general public on a continuing basis.

Reprinted with permission. Retrieved from:
http://aaal.site-ym.com/?page=Resolutions&hh
SearchTerms=%22resolutions%22#March 1997

differences. Resolving the Standard English debate involves balancing the inevitability of dialect diversity, the benefits of language standardization, and the sociopolitical realities that lead to negative evaluations of nonstandard usage and vernacular-speaking groups. This balancing act is nowhere more consequential than in our diverse schools and classrooms.

Language Policy and Curriculum Development

National position statements on dialect diversity are intended to guide policy and program development in schools. But a school's response to dialect differences in the student population ultimately depends on the values, goals, and resources of the school district, the school, the teachers, and the community. Each link in this chain is vital to implementing any programmatic decision about teaching spoken Standard English. Some school districts have developed language policy and Standard English instructional programs that use children's implicit knowledge of another dialect to teach the standard dialect.

More often, however, Standard English instruction proceeds either haphazardly, without any formal policy guidance, or from non-research-based curricula that treat vernacular dialect features as errors and attempt to eradicate them. This latter approach is common in "no excuse" style charter schools, such as KIPP or Uncommon Schools. In fact, the director of Uncommon Schools, Doug Lemov, endorses this approach in his best-selling book for teachers, *Teach Like a Champion*, publically endorsed by David Levin, co-founder of KIPP, and Wendy Kopp, CEO and founder of Teach for America. One of the teaching techniques advocated in this book instructs teachers to "correct slang, syntax, usage, and grammar in the classroom even if you believe the divergence from standard is acceptable, even normal in some settings, or even if it falls within a student's dialect" (Lemov, 2010, p. 47). In other words, the approach maintains that there should be only one acceptable form of language in these classrooms, and students who deviate from that standard in any way are to be corrected immediately, despite substantial evidence that this method of teaching is not appropriate (e.g., Piestrup, 1973). Such approaches are problematic for reasons related to social identity, political power, and pedagogical effectiveness. To break this curricular mold, educators and communities need to develop policies that are scientifically based and socially equitable. To do so, they can examine professional organizations' position statements as well as the current dialect policies and instructional programs of states and districts that have confronted diversity directly. Toward this end, we offer two guidelines for policy development and then a series of recommendations for curriculum development.

Recommendations for Policy Development

Districts should develop explicit policies on teaching and learning Standard English. It is likely that school districts have some policies, implicit or explicit, on teaching Standard English. Typically, these policies derive from the states' content area standards, many of which in turn have been built on the Common Core State Standards (CCSS). CCSS contain strands describing standards for the four domains of language use: reading, writing, speaking, and listening. There is also a language strand, which specifies the language students are to use in demonstrating competency in the four domains. In the language strand of the English Language Arts/Literacy CCSS, the first standard is "Demonstrate command of the conventions of standard English grammar and usage when speaking or writing" (CCSS, 2010a, p. 25). This standard is problematic with regard to language variation in several ways. In the first place, because it mentions a single correct norm, schools would need to teach Standard English to students who use vernacular dialects. In addition, the standard blurs the distinction between expectations for spoken language use and those for written language use, to the detriment of vernacular dialect speakers. Many nonstandard oral language patterns may be accepted in classrooms while those same patterns may be discouraged or prohibited in school writing. The undifferentiated approach that the standard implies is unfortunate for the reasons discussed above.

An example clearly demonstrates these concerns. In the CCSS, each standard has a series of subpoints related to grade levels to further specify it. One of the grade 9–10 subpoints of standard 1 is "Use various types of phrases (noun, verb, adjectival, adverbial, . . .) and clauses . . . to convey specific meaning" (CCSS, 2010a, p. 54). According to that standard, without considering the question of Standard English, the following sentence would be considered acceptable: "I be chillin' at my dad house." This sentence uses noun and verb phrases following the patterns of the writer's dialect. If usage of language structures were the intent of this standard, no instructional time would be needed to accomplish this standard. As linguist Kristin Denham notes, "All students are, of course, already *using* phrases and clauses to convey meaning and have been since they were toddlers. They have also been doing so in their writing since a very young age" (2015, p. 140). Thus the reference to Standard English in the general language standard, which governs this subpoint and which applies from kindergarten to grade 12, demonstrates an orientation in the CCSS toward Standard English usage in speech as well as in writing.

The CCSS and framing documents contain only a few overt acknowledgments of language variation. For example, a language standard for fifth grade reads "Compare and contrast the varieties of English (e.g., *dialect, registers*) used in stories, drama, or poems" (CCSS, 2010a, p. 29). However, there is no indication that students might also make use of their own diverse linguistic abilities or that students might need to study language variation as a means of better understanding language. Appendix A to the CCSS (2010b) details the research that underlies the standards. With regard to language variation, the CCSS authors discuss examining dialect only as a way of better understanding literature, which circumscribes the role language should play in the school curriculum:

> Learning the grammatical structures of nonstandard dialects can help students understand how accomplished writers such as Harper Lee,

Langston Hughes, and Mark Twain use various dialects of English to great advantage and effect, and can help students analyze setting, character, and author's craft in great works of literature.

CCSS, 2010b, p. 29

In general, the CCSS do not offer substantive guidance for developing differentiated policies governing oral language use and written language use. Given the role of formal written Standard English in classrooms, it might make sense to impose prescriptive guidelines for that domain; however, as noted above, the lack of clear benefit for requiring spoken Standard English makes dubious applying the same prescriptive standard to this domain. A standard that endorses a single language usage standard across both modes of communication will always privilege mainstream dialect-speaking students.

Prior to the development of the CCSS, the most influential document for designing language arts standards was a set of curriculum recommendations by NCTE and the International Reading Association (now International Literacy Association). These guidelines acknowledged and promoted the value inherent in different varieties of language, as in these two standards: "Students adjust their use of spoken . . . language . . . to communicate effectively with a variety of audiences for different purposes" and "Students develop an understanding of and respect for diversity in language use, patterns, and dialects across cultures, ethnic groups, geographic regions, and social roles" (NCTE/IRA, 1996, p. 3). Instead of being expected merely to conform to a standard variety in their speech, students were expected to learn about language in many social and regional contexts, which would lead them ultimately to becoming more informed and effective language users. Despite the lack of similar guidance in the CCSS, Denham concludes that their emphasis on learning about grammatical structure does open opportunities for language analysis for linguistically savvy teachers:

The Common Core can offer an opportunity to introduce discussions about the role of language in society when materials . . . are chosen thoughtfully by teachers who know that language can and must be studied scientifically, and that language study should not be used to reinforce linguistic inequality.

2015, p. 147

The sorts of conversations Denham proposes need to occur at the level of policy-making as well as in the classroom. These discussions may be difficult because language variation is linked to ethnicity, social class, and power—topics that communities may find hard to talk about. Nonetheless, policy development requires discussion, and various stakeholders should be involved, including administrators, teachers, principals, parents, students, and employers. Whatever decision is reached about teaching a variety of Standard English, those who establish policy and set curriculum goals should be aware, as Denham notes, of findings from the science of language study, as well as facts about local language variation and culture situations that might affect local policy.

Policy development should consider curricular priorities. Because vernacular grammatical forms are perceived much more negatively than most variations in pronunciation, a school district might decide that grammatical structure, not pronunciation, should be the focus for oral language instruction. Alternatively, the focus for Standard English instruction might not fall on oral language at all, but on writing, because the ability to speak a standard dialect may not be as crucial for students' success as the ability to use standard forms in writing. Burling (1973) describes a number of academic language skills that students need to succeed in school, beginning with listening skills and extending into oral and written communication skills. For English learners, and to a lesser extent vernacular-speaking students, learning to understand the spoken language of the teacher is an important language skill to master early on (although in the case of English learners, teachers are typically expected to make instruction understandable, as in sheltered instruction [Echevarria, Vogt, & Short, 2016]). Burling then describes the importance of students being able to make themselves understood to the teacher, which is a very different goal than having the ability to speak in Standard English. Similar patterns occur with printed forms of the language; the ability to read conventional English precedes the ability to write it. Bearing in mind the various language abilities required and desired by schools, perhaps the least important goal would be to ensure that students have standard pronunciation. Considering the relative importance of oral Standard English for a given district, school, and community is an important step in deciding how, or if, it will be emphasized in district policies and programs. In addition, it is essential to recognize the disproportionate burden such programs place on vernacular speakers and English language learners as these choices are made. At the least, it is important for districts to prioritize and strategically sequence the language skills students must be taught, which will be discussed next.

Recommendations for Curriculum Development

If the policy decision is made to teach spoken Standard English, it is important to develop an explicit, articulated curriculum to guide teachers and provide a coherent, relevant learning experience for students. General principles for curriculum development reflect the considerations outlined earlier:

1. *Teaching Standard English must take into account the importance of group reference factors.* Students will not be motivated to learn a dialect that they cannot imagine themselves using for purposes that are important to them;

if they see that their own social group uses that dialect for certain purposes or that groups they would like to belong to use the dialect, they are more likely to regard dialect learning as a natural objective. Instructional approaches consistent with code-meshing (mentioned earlier in this chapter) emphasize adding competence in a standard dialect to a speaker's repertoire without denigrating the language variety of the speaker's reference group. Appealing to external sources of motivation for the students (e.g., Standard English can help them become a member of a group that makes it easier to get a good job) is potentially another way of dealing with this factor, so long as such presentations are framed so that they do not require an abandonment of a student's reference group. Convincing students to learn a dialect with which they do not identify at all is a tall order.

2. *An instructional program for teaching spoken Standard English should be based on expanding, not limiting, students' linguistic repertoires.* This principle takes a stand on the language policy possibilities outlined at the beginning of this chapter. Two opposing goals are additivism— adding Standard English while maintaining the native dialect—and eradicationism—learning Standard English to replace the native dialect. The ability to use more than one dialect in conversations is sometimes called *bidialectalism* by analogy to *bilingualism*. This model is often presented as the most reasonable goal for an oral language instruction program that deals with dialect differences. Speakers of vernacular dialects learn a standard variety of English in school and maintain their non-school dialects as well. This proposal for bidialectalism mirrors the pedagogical position for English language learners that promotes bilingualism by adding English to a speaker's repertoire rather than replacing the heritage language with English.

3. *A Standard English instructional program should incorporate scientific information on the nature of dialect diversity.* Any focus on dialect learning needs to counter the misinformation about language variation that often goes unchallenged in schools by including a robust, scientifically based program of dialect knowledge in the instructional program. In teaching another dialect, it is essential to establish that both the native and the target dialect are full-fledged linguistic varieties, with social and political histories and large numbers of users. To ground second dialect teaching and learning, teachers and students need a solid understanding of the natural sociolinguistic principles that lead to the development and maintenance of language varieties, including a linguistically informed perspective on the history of English.

Providing students with background information on dialect diversity will underscore the social basis for evaluating speech patterns and strengthen the pragmatic rationale for developing skills in a standard variety.

Furthermore, because most people find dialect diversity inherently interesting, information about different language varieties will engage students. Having students investigate different ways of speaking, including their own, can amplify their understanding of dialect diversity and demonstrate the integrity of their own and others' dialects as full-fledged language systems. Furthermore, students, like teachers, need to understand that a dialect difference in no way represents an inherent linguistic or cognitive deficit. An outline of a language awareness program, with sample activities, appears in Chapter 10.

4. *Instruction should draw on sociolinguistic research.* In addition to defining which language skills will be prioritized and the sequence in which they will be taught, it is important to determine what will guide instructional choices at each level. For example, for improving students' writing abilities, arguments can be made for starting instruction with the most stigmatized features and the features that occur most commonly. Unfortunately, these lists are not the same. Hairston (1981) compiled a ranking of the severity of writing errors, which could inform programs that wish to start with highly stigmatized features. Connors and Lunsford (1988) compiled a similar list based on frequency. Though these two studies concern writing rather than speaking, they offer teachers and administrators a research basis for making their decisions.

5. *The dialect of spoken Standard English that is to be taught should reflect the language norms of the community.* Standard English varies regionally. What is considered standard in the South is not the same as in the Midwest, New England, or the West. In eastern New England, the standard variety may include the absence of *r* in words like "cah" for *car* and "pahty" for *party;* in many Southern dialect regions, the lack of contrast between words like *pin* and *pen* or *tin* and *ten* is part of the regional standard, as is the ungliding of the PRICE vowel in *time* ("tahm") and *tide* ("tahd"). The goal of instruction should be learning the informal standard dialect of the local community, not some formal dialect of English that is external to the area. This is particularly true for pronunciation features, where local standards may exist along with standards for grammatical features that characterize a wider area. Since any program must be tailored to the community in which the students live, it becomes crucial to identify the local norms for both standard and vernacular dialects in order to present students with accurate, credible information about the language they hear around them. In Chapter 2, we outlined a method for investigating local dialect features.

6. *Language instruction should address interactive norms that typify mainstream speakers, at the same time that it respects culturally-based differences in interactive style.* Speaking a mainstream language variety includes using particular conversational strategies as well as the

pronunciation and grammatical forms that distinguish standard from vernacular dialects. In particular, conversational routines for specialized uses of language, such as providing constructive criticism via peer review or disagreeing with another student or teacher, involve behaviors that extend beyond language structures per se; and, as English language learners can attest, they are some of the most difficult aspects of language to master. These ways of using language, characteristic of academic discourse, involve more than just using standard grammatical and pronunciation features, and they are important to success in school (Gutierrez, 1995; Schleppegrell, 2004).

7. *Language instruction must be age-appropriate.* A final issue for developing a Standard English instructional program concerns when to introduce it. The optimum age for beginning second dialect learning has not been established. Studies conducted on foreign language learning may provide some guidance. Because of the common assumption that children can learn some aspects of a new language system more easily than adults can, many programs advocate beginning second language instruction as early as possible. There may be some language learning advantage in early childhood due to certain characteristics of brain development, but there are other significant factors that affect language learning in which older learners are at an advantage. Older learners can be more analytic and may be better able to monitor their speech. For second dialect learning, the influence of peer groups, particularly strong among adolescents, may be an important factor in inhibiting or favoring the learning of a variety of Standard English. Longitudinal research on the use of vernacular features in childhood and early adolescence suggests that children may lose some of their vernacular forms during early schooling only to reacquire and intensify them as they enter middle school (Van Hofwegen & Wolfram, 2010). In the trajectory of Standard English use among African American English-speaking students, we see increasing amounts of Standard English forms during the first four years of exposure to the school environment, but then an increase in vernacular forms over the middle grades when peer-group influence becomes greater (Craig & Washington, 2006; Van Hofwegen, 2015b). Some investigators advocate postponing instruction in a second dialect until students can appreciate the social significance of different dialects of English, at about grade 4 (Burling, 1973). However, with this approach, there is the risk of negative evaluation early on when children use the vernacular, especially in writing, unless teachers are well aware of school policy and gear their expectations to the curriculum.

Language awareness instruction in the primary grades provides a good basis for Standard English instruction in upper elementary. In kindergarten, children can begin to pay attention to different dialects in the stories that they hear and read. Even at that early age, they can talk about the general notion of suiting language to the situation and identify ways that language varies from situation to situation in the stories. Building on that foundation, students may be introduced to learning Standard English for some situations and then expand contexts and forms.

Methods of Teaching Spoken Standard English

In the past, some approaches to teaching spoken Standard English as a second dialect borrowed heavily from techniques used for teaching foreign languages. In some ways, teaching a second dialect and teaching a foreign language are similar because in both cases the aim is to support students' access to another language system for use in certain circumstances. The learning contexts differ significantly, however, in that two varieties of English have almost everything in common, whereas two separate languages may have little in common. To help build bidialectal competence, standard dialect instruction should focus on the particular areas of difference between the standard and vernacular varieties used in the school's community. This approach is called *contrastive analysis* because it involves analyzing the differences, or contrasts, between the varieties. A systematic comparison of the local vernacular dialect with the local standard variety will reveal particular areas of difference.

Put another way, there is no need to learn an entirely different language system in second dialect programs as there is in learning a new language. However, the similarity between the learner's native dialect and the dialect to be added does not necessarily mean that learning the second dialect will be easier than learning a second language. The fact is that native dialect items are thoroughly habituated, a condition that may make it more difficult to modify a small set of thoroughly entrenched items within a pattern of overall similarity. It is easier to learn an entirely new pattern because modifying habituated items may require unlearning as well as learning. For example, in a second language learning situation, where students know that every part of their communication in the second language must be, effectively, switched into that language, students can focus their attention on how to accomplish the switches. In a bidialectal situation, the student must first identify forms that require shifting, and then recall how to shift them.

Two telling examples are found in the documentary *Do You Speak American?* (MacNeil/Lehrer Productions, 2005). Minority children in Daniel Russel's fifth grade class are playing a game that requires them to translate vernacular sentences into Standard English. In one example, a student is asked to translate the sentence "Last night, we bake cookies." Responding to Russel's prompts, the student identifies the vernacular feature as "past-tense marker -*ed*," demonstrating that he has identified the form to shift. But when the student offers an oral translation of the sentence into Standard English, the *t* sound that completes the past-tense marker is imperceptible. Even when the student is acutely aware of the standard pattern, articulating the consonant cluster -*kt* at the end of a word as it is done in Standard English is extremely difficult. The effect is that despite the student's grammatical knowledge, his speech might still be deemed ungrammatical.

A second example from this segment of the documentary demonstrates the difficulty in recognizing nonstandard forms if they are a part of one's native dialect. In this example, the sentence to be translated is "We don't have nothin' to do," which contains two nonstandard features, negative concord ("don't . . . nothin'") and nasal fronting (final sound of "nothin'"), both of which are part of the responding student's native dialect. Presumably drawing on the instruction he has received related to Standard English pronunciation, the student focuses his attention on the nasal, stressing it and even adding a *g* sound for emphasis as he says, "We don't have nothinG to do." This student's response demonstrates how difficult it is for vernacular speakers to recognize the ways in which their own grammar differs from that of Standard English. The good news is that contrastive analysis is not hopeless; the student is given another chance to translate the sentence, which he does flawlessly. This example indicates that through intensive contrastive analysis work, students are able to begin independently making the types of shifts required for the academic environment. Specific attention to the structural details of dialect differences may prove useful when conscious attention to speech is heightened. Thus, attention to contrasts, either directly through contrastive analysis or indirectly through some other approach, is useful in second dialect instruction.

Instruction is likely to be most effective when it is clearly tied to situations in which authentic Standard English is expected, and when it is part of short mini-lessons intended to promote performance in real situations. Consider a situation in which middle-school students are preparing oral presentations. Several students use the vernacular "Here go my speech." Regardless of whether anyone mentions the structure during class critique of the practice session, the teacher can seize the opportunity for a mini-lesson contrasting vernacular "Here go" with standard "Here is" or "Here's." Focusing directly on language structures is more likely to be effective when it is embedded within such authentic situations.

One method of teaching spoken Standard English that does not work is simply "correcting" vernacular features. Piestrup (1973) found that vernacular speakers who were corrected when they used vernacular features actually used more, not fewer, vernacular features over time.

A more positive strategy is reinforcing and augmenting students' existing knowledge of the standard dialect. Activities can include role play and dramatization that require students to think consciously about the effects of different language choices and then decide on the appropriate dialect patterns in order to act out a part. They may plan scenarios in advance, or they may act them out on the spur of the moment. They can assume adult roles like that of a teacher, school administrator, salesperson, doctor, newspaper reporter, or office worker in which they must try to approximate the speech styles of people from different backgrounds as realistically as possible. Scenarios may come from real life or from texts the students have read. This activity gives the student the opportunity to vary verbal styles and deliberately switch to alternate dialect patterns. It can also spur discussions about the appropriateness of the language choices students made for each character and language use by register or genre (see Dean, 2011, for a detailed account of this approach). Finally, it gives students practice for real-life contexts outside of school where using Standard English forms may be crucial, such as in a job interview.

From an additivist perspective, realistic role playing might also include situations where a vernacular dialect is important for all or part of an exchange, such as in peer group and family conversations. In order to identify appropriate situations, however, some observational research would be needed, because intuitions may not match language practice. When role play uses standard and vernacular English, the important function of each is demonstrated realistically, along with the fact that they coexist in the community. Students tend to be more willing to learn a standard variety when they see clearly that the solidarity functions of their vernacular variety are not necessarily threatened by the addition of a standard variety. One caution is in order: In instructional settings that include students who are monodialectal in Standard English, those students should not be asked to speak in a vernacular dialect unless they have studied the pronunciation and grammar patterns of the dialect and are being careful to apply this knowledge rather than reproducing stereotyped structures that are not grammatical in that dialect. Using role playing and dramatization, combined with a small amount of explicit instruction in Standard English structures, is a practical approach to giving specific attention to the use of spoken Standard English.

Identifying situations in which students naturally use Standard English features can show them that Standard English is already an important medium for them. They can identify Standard English situations at school—probably those in which they speak with authority on some topic (Adger, 1998). Identifying natural sites for Standard English in the classroom has several instructional implications. In some cases, the teachable moment occurs in situations where students implicitly agree to use standard features, but encounter difficulties, and the context allows for suggestions from the teacher or fellow students. In other cases, rather than interrupt with edits, the teacher can note potential problem structures and then conduct mini-lessons at an appropriate future time.

In sum, teaching oral Standard English should incorporate several components. Some activities should be directed at sharpening students' awareness of the nature of dialects and developing motivation for enhancing their proficiency in a second dialect. Other activities can be focused on particular language forms, with students learning which structures have standard and nonstandard alternates, and practicing their use in appropriate social contexts. It is important to use the local standard variety as the reference point and to embed any language practice in authentic situations.

Learning the Language of School

As mentioned earlier in this chapter, all children, regardless of their native language or dialect, need linguistically rich classrooms in all subject areas to develop expertise in academic talk, the language used in teaching and learning and testing. This need is heightened by the implementation of standards like the Common Core State Standards, which emphasize the ability to use academic language, as in the sixth grade language arts speaking/listening standard that calls for students to "Present claims and findings, sequencing ideas logically and using pertinent descriptions, facts, and details to accentuate main ideas or themes" (CCSS, 2010a, p. 49). Because of the sociolinguistic context of academic English, it is primarily based on Standard English language forms. But it extends beyond form, to encompass how language is used to accomplish functions, such as supporting a point of view, analyzing a problem, or making a presentation, that are inherent in classrooms and similar settings (Bunch, 2009; Schleppegrell, 2004). These functions are primarily learned at school from teachers and texts, and students benefit from attention to academic language by teachers in all content areas, not just in language arts.

Academic language contrasts with the language of interpersonal communication not only in terms of dialect but also in terms of how meaning is expressed. Academic talk is more decontextualized—less elliptical, less dependent on the surrounding talk and other aspects of the context. Meanings are usually made more fully explicit through words in academic talk, and academic vocabulary includes technical terms. Particular words tend to occur more frequently in academic discourse than in casual social interaction, including words like *elliptical, decontextualized, aspects,* and *explicit.* Complex syntactic structures typify academic language, as demonstrated by many sentences in this text, including this one. Patterns of language use also differ. For example, the request for a display of known information (when a teacher asks students to provide information that the teacher already knows, as in a question like "At what temperature does water boil?") may be more common at school. Just as the curriculum may require instruction in Standard English, instruction about these academic language conventions may be necessary, especially in the early years and especially for children from nonmainstream communities. It is important, of course, to adopt the additivist perspective discussed earlier and to teach academic language conventions, including Standard English, as an addition to community language use and to ground instruction in authentic situations.

Linguistically rich classrooms provide many opportunities for children to talk on academic topics, which in turn promotes expansion of their linguistic repertoire. To make this possible, social interaction structures need to be varied. Teachers can take advantage of the fact that "Instead of thinking of their school as an academic institution, most learners regard their school as a *social organization*" (Andrews, 2006, p. 51, italics in original). When students are empowered by group-based learning, they can become content experts within the organization. That in turn can help break the traditional classroom social structure which is dominated by teacher talk. Group-based learning can engage all students in discussions rather than merely involving the few who can produce desired information at specific moments in whole-class instruction (Erickson, 1996). In the absence of opportunities for real engagement, students become less and less likely to self-nominate in whole-class discussion, and they may pay less and less attention, so that when the teacher does call on them they have little to say. For these students, classroom communication is a listening occasion at best. Many opportunities to talk and practice academic language are essential for students to develop these valuable oral language skills for success in school.

This chapter has taken up the issue of whether students who come from vernacular dialect backgrounds should be expected to add oral Standard English to their linguistic repertoires and has looked at issues related to policy formulation and program planning. School district policy in this domain needs to be informed by social realities within the community and the school and guided by the positions of professional language-related organizations that are grounded in linguistic knowledge. As oral language is addressed in language arts and other content areas, it needs to be done thoughtfully and with an additive orientation, so that students are positively engaged in expanding their linguistic skills. Principles articulated in this chapter should help. In addition to providing access to Standard English forms, teachers should help students learn the conventions of academic language. The chapters that follow will move from oral to written language, considering the interaction of dialects with writing and reading.

Discussion Questions

1. The chapter says that the answer to questions about how schools should address dialect diversity isn't as simple as teaching all students to speak Standard English. Do you agree? Explain.

2. The chapter explains why some vernacular dialect speakers might not want to learn Standard English. Recap the argument, providing examples if possible.

3. Do you believe that schools need to have formal dialect policies, or should they be guided by informal policies? In either case, where could such policies be found and who could enforce them?

4. If you have been part of a Standard English instructional program, as a learner or a teacher, what insights have you gained about the quality of this

program? Do you have ideas about how to improve it? In making your critique, use the principles for curriculum development presented in this chapter.

5. What do you think of the assertion that Standard English varies regionally? Does it seem problematic? Can you think of any examples of differences in regional standard varieties?

6. How can teachers support their students' development of academic talk in the various content areas?

7. A common maxim with many variations and sources reads "Know the rules well so you can break them effectively." This notion is sometimes applied to evaluations of students' oral language and writing. Some even claim that "Authors don't violate rules out of ignorance." Do you agree or disagree with this notion in regard to writing and speaking? What does this position say about code-meshing vs. code-switching?

Links of Interest

1. Watch a clip on contrastive analysis from *Do You Speak American?*: www.youtube.com/watch?v=xX1-FgkfWo8

2. Read an article on teaching oral language endorsed by the National Council of Teachers of English: www.ncte.org/library/NCTEFiles/Resources/ Journals/EE/1968/EE1968–2Preparing.pdf

3. Consider a position paper on the role of English teachers in educating English language learners: www.ncte.org/positions/statements/teachers educatingell

4. Read the full "Students' right to their own language" statement with additional commentary: www.ncte.org/library/NCTEFiles/Groups/CCCC/ NewSRTOL.pdf

Further Reading

Dyson, A. H., & Genishi, C. (Eds.). (1994). *The need for story: Cultural diversity in classroom and community*. Urbana, IL: National Council of Teachers of English.

This collection looks at reading, writing, and oral stories and storytelling as personal, cultural, and social practice. Chapters are organized into sections: Connections Between Story, Self, and Others: Why Do We Tell Stories?; Ways With Stories: Whose Stories Are Told? Whose Stories Are Heard?; and Weaving Communities Through Story: Who Are We?

Heath, S. B. (1983). *Ways with words: Language, life, and work in communities and classrooms*. Cambridge, UK: Cambridge University Press.

Heath, S. B. (2012). *Words at work and play: Three decades in family and community life*. Cambridge, UK: Cambridge University Press.

The first book listed is a classic ethnographic study of two different Southern communities, telling how language functions in the community and in the school. It provides important background for understanding attitudes and approaches to language by children from vernacular-speaking backgrounds. The second volume offers an analysis of the roles of literacy practices in the occupations and interpersonal lives of the original study's participants based on 30 years of ethnographic observation.

Hewitt, R. (1986). *White talk Black talk: Inter-racial friendship and communication amongst adolescents.* Cambridge, UK: Cambridge University Press.

This classic ethnographic study examines the sociolinguistics of adolescent race relations. Though it is based on research in England, the themes and discussions raise important questions for teachers in all areas.

Gee, J. P. (2014). Decontextualized language: A problem, not a solution. *International Multilingual Research Journal, 8*(1), pp. 9–23.

In this theoretical article with practical applications, the author argues that all discussions of language should be situated within the context of authentic classroom discourse as opposed to literary contexts or hypothetical examples. Specifically, he shows that the most beneficial data for such discussions involve language that might be misinterpreted if the hearer were not highly familiar with the context.

Wheeler, R. S., & Swords, R. (2006). *Code-switching: Teaching Standard English in urban classrooms.* Urbana, IL: National Council of Teachers of English.
Wheeler, R. S., & Swords, R. (2010). *Code-switching lessons: Grammar strategies for linguistically diverse writers, grades 3–6.* Portsmouth, NH: Firsthand Heinemann.

University professor Rebecca Wheeler and urban elementary teacher Rachel Swords describe teaching students about contrastive analysis and code-switching as a way to foster Standard English mastery among African American dialect speakers. The second book listed offers the lesson plans and other resources for teachers to implement contrastive analysis in their classrooms.

References

Abdul-Jabbar, K., & Knobler, P. (1983). *Giant steps: The autobiography of Kareem Abdul-Jabbar.* New York, NY: Bantam Books.

Abrams, K. D. (2011). *Comparing codes: Dialect density measurements of oral and written codes in African American English.* Unpublished master's thesis, North Carolina State University.

Adger, C. T. (1998). Register shifting with dialect resources in instructional discourse. In S. Hoyle & C. T. Adger (Eds.), *Kids talk: Strategic language use in later childhood* (pp. 151–169). New York, NY: Oxford University Press.

Alim, H. S., & Smitherman, G. (2012). *Articulate while black: Barak Obama, language, and race in the U.S.* Oxford, UK: Oxford University Press.

Andrews, L. (2006). *Language exploration and awareness: A resource book for teachers* (3rd ed.). Mahwah, NJ: Lawrence Erlbaum Associates.

Austen-Smith, D., & Fryer, R. G. (2003). *The economics of 'acting white'* (No. w9904). Cambridge, MA: National Bureau of Economic Research.

Bunch, G. C. (2009). "Going up there": Challenges and opportunities for language minority students during a mainstream classroom speech event. *Linguistics and Education, 20*(2), 81–108.

Burling, R. (1973). *English in black and white.* New York, NY: Holt, Rinehart & Winston.

Common Core State Standards Initiative (CCSS). (2010a). *Common Core State Standards for English language arts & literacy in history/social studies, science, and technical subjects.* Washington, DC: National Governors Association Center for Best Practices, Council of Chief State School Officers. Available online at: www.corestandards.org/wp-content/uploads/ELA_Standards1.pdf

Common Core State Standards Initiative (CCSS). (2010b). *Appendix A: Research supporting key elements of the standards, glossary of key terms.* Washington, DC: National Governors Association Center for Best Practices, Council of Chief State School Officers. Available online at: www.corestandards.org/assets/Appendix_A.pdf

Conference on College Composition and Communication (CCCC)/National Council of Teachers of English (NCTE). (1974). *Resolution on students' right to their own language.* Retrieved from www.ncte.org/positions/statements/righttoownlanguage

Connors, R. J., & Lunsford, A. A. (1988). Frequency of formal errors in current college writing, or Ma and Pa Kettle do research. *College Composition and Communication, 39*(4), 395–409.

Craig, H. K., & Washington, J. A. (2006). *Malik goes to school: Examining the language skills of African American students from preschool-5th grade.* Mahwah, NJ: Lawrence Erlbaum Associates.

Dean, D. (2011). "EJ" in focus: Shifting perspectives about grammar: Changing what and how we teach. *English Journal, 100*(4), 20–26.

Denham, K. (2015). Examining linguistics in the language strand of the Common Core State Standards. *Language and Linguistics Compass, 9*(3), 139–149.

Echevarria, J., Vogt, M. E., & Short, D. J. (2016). *Making content comprehensible for English Learners: The SIOP Model* (5th ed.). Boston, MA: Pearson.

Elbow, P. (2012). *Vernacular eloquence: What speech can bring to writing.* Oxford, UK: Oxford University Press.

Erickson, F. (1996). Going for the zone: The social and cognitive ecology of teacher–student interaction in classroom conversations. In D. Hicks (Ed.), *Discourse, learning, and schooling* (pp. 29–62). Cambridge, UK: Cambridge University Press.

Fasold, R. (1984). *The sociolinguistics of society.* Malden, MA: Basil Blackwell.

Fecho, B. (2004). *"Is this English?": Race, language, and culture in the classroom.* New York, NY: Teachers College Press.

Fordham, S. (1998). Speaking standard English from nine to three: Language as guerrilla warfare at Capital High. In S. Hoyle & C. T. Adger (Eds.), *Kids talk: Strategic language use in later childhood* (pp. 205–216). New York, NY: Oxford University Press.

Fordham, S., & Ogbu, J. U. (1986). Black students' school success: Coping with the "burden of 'acting white'". *The Urban Review, 18*(3), 176–206.

Gutierrez, K. D. (1995). Unpackaging academic discourse. *Discourse Processes, 19*(1), 21–37.

Hairston, M. (1981). Not all errors are created equal: Nonacademic readers in the professions respond to lapses in usage. *College English, 43*(8), 794–806.

Jordan, J. (1988). Nobody mean more to me than you and the future life of Willie Jordan. *Harvard Educational Review, 58*(3), 363–375.

Labov, W. (1969). The logic of nonstandard English. In J. Alatis (Ed.), *Georgetown monograph series on language and linguistics, 22* (pp. 1–44). Washington, DC: Georgetown University Press.

Labov, W. (2009). *Dialect diversity in America: The politics of language change.* Charlottesville: University of Virginia Press.

Lemov, D. (2010). *Teach like a champion: 49 techniques that put students on the path to college (K–12).* San Francisco, CA: John Wiley & Sons.

MacNeil/Lehrer Productions. (2005). *Do you speak American?* [Video]. Arlington, VA: Author.

National Council of Teachers of English, & International Reading Association. (1996). *Standards for the English language arts.* Urbana, IL: National Council of Teachers of English.

Piestrup, A. M. (1973). *Black dialect interference and accommodations of reading instruction in first grade.* Berkeley, CA: University of California, Language and Behavior Research Lab. (Monograph 4, ED119113).

Pooley, R. C. (1946). *Teaching English usage.* New York, NY: Appleton-Century-Crofts.

Rickford, J. R., & Rickford, R. J. (2002). *Spoken soul: The story of black English.* New York, NY: John Wiley & Sons.

Schilling-Estes, N. (2004). Constructing ethnicity in interaction. *Journal of Sociolinguistics, 8*(2), 163–195.

Schleppegrell, Mary J. (2004). *The language of schooling: A functional linguistics perspective.* Mahwah, NJ: Lawrence Erlbaum Associates, Inc.

Sledd, J. (1969). Bi-dialectalism: The linguistics of white supremacy. *The English Journal, 58*(9), 1307–1329.

Smitherman, G. (2000). *Talkin that talk: Language, culture, and education in African America.* London, UK: Routledge.

Sweetland, J. (2006). *Teaching writing in the African American classroom: A sociolinguistic approach.* Unpublished doctoral dissertation, Stanford University.

Van Hofwegen, J. (2015a). The development of African American English through childhood and adolescence. In S. Lanehart, (Ed.), *Oxford handbook of African American language* (pp. 454–474). Oxford, UK: Oxford University Press.

Van Hofwegen, J. (2015b). Dyadic analysis: Factors affecting African American English usage and accommodation in adolescent peer dyads. *Language & Communication, 41*(1), 28–45.

Van Hofwegen, J., & Wolfram, W. (2010). Coming of age in African American English: A longitudinal study. *Journal of Sociolinguistics, 14*(4), 427–455.

Wheeler, R. S., & Swords, R. (2006). *Code-switching: Teaching Standard English in urban classrooms.* Urbana, IL: National Council of Teachers of English.

Wheeler, R. S., & Swords, R. (2010). *Code-switching lessons: Grammar strategies for linguistically diverse writers, grades 3–6*. Portsmouth, NH: Firsthand Heinemann.

Wolfram, W., & Reaser, J. (2014). *Talkin' Tar Heel: How our voices tell the story of North Carolina.* Chapel Hill, NC: University of North Carolina Press.

Wolfram, W., & Schilling, N. (2016). *American English: Dialects and variation* (3rd ed.). Malden MA: John Wiley & Sons.

Young, V. A., Barrett, R., Young-Rivera, Y., & Lovejoy, K. B. (2013). *Other people's English: Code-meshing, code-switching, and African American literacy.* New York, NY: Teachers College Press.

Young, V. A., & Martinez, A. Y. (Eds.). (2011). *Code-meshing as world English: Pedagogy, policy, performance.* Urbana, IL: National Council of Teachers.

Youngman, S. (2009, May 27). Obama in L.A., "You ain't seen nothing yet." *The Hill.* Retrieved from http://thehill.com/homenews/news/19845-obama-in-la-you-aint-seen-nothing-yet

8
Dialects and Writing

Scenario

The following paragraph was composed by a ninth grader from an African American working-class community. As you look at the passage, think about how you would mark/evaluate the student's work and discuss it with him. List what you see as his most pressing writing issues. Are there any nonstandard usages that would cause you little or no concern? If you were going to have a 10-minute one-on-one conference with this student about his writing, what topics would you want to address? You can download from this book's companion website a printable version of the passage if you would like to actually mark the text.

> I would prefer living the way the Hunzakuts live. because they live a whole lot longer and they don't have no crime and they don't get sick and if you are the age of 60, or 80 you still can play many game like you the age of 6 or 9 and don't have to worry about Cancer or Heartattacks. Its would be a whole lot better living their way.

What was your first reaction upon reading the paragraph? Did you feel the urge to correct? Were you overwhelmed? Certainly a range of reactions would be appropriate, depending on your own language background and experiences of having your own writing evaluated. One critical question that you might consider is the extent to which your past experiences are useful in guiding your reaction to this student's writing. If you came to school with a mainstream dialect, some of the sorts of markings that your teachers put on your papers might not be effective with a student who comes to school speaking a vernacular dialect. As the school population continues to diversify (Boser, 2014; Putman, Hansen, Walsh, & Quintero, 2016), it is critical that researchers and teachers interrogate inherited writing pedagogies that have been used for more homogeneous classrooms. In this chapter, we explore some of the ways that dialect impacts student writing and some ways teachers can respond to students' written language in sociolinguistically informed ways. As you go through the rest of this chapter, keep in mind this passage and your initial reactions to it.

Some important issues related to writing and vernacular dialect speakers will be considered in our discussion.

Teaching students to write is one of the most important functions of schools. But teaching writing is hard work, in part because students bring a range of language skills to the task. For speakers of vernacular dialects, there are some special factors for teachers to consider in writing instruction, largely because the contrasts between the language of speaking and the language of writing are greater for them than for speakers of a Standard English dialect. This chapter does not engage the vast body of research on general pedagogy for teaching writing; rather, it considers a range of issues in teaching writing to vernacular dialect speakers in K–12 classrooms. It also expands on the discussion of the dialect-related issues in standardized writing assessment that were addressed in Chapter 6.

Oral and Written Language

It is commonly but incorrectly assumed that writing is fundamentally speech coded into orthography. But research has shown that there are substantial differences between writing and speaking, and people have to learn a range of different skills for writing. It turns out that writing and speaking are supported by different parts of the brain. Studies of people with various brain injuries provide stunning evidence of just how distinct these capabilities are. For example, many stroke victims, depending on where damage occurs to their brains, lose either the ability to speak grammatically or the ability to write grammatically, but they retain grammaticality in the other medium (see, e.g., Rapp, Benzing, & Caramazza, 1997). The cognitive independence of these tasks allows speakers to maintain distinct systems of parsing and deploy them appropriately when engaging with language orally (speaking and listening) and when engaging with the written form (reading and writing) (Rapp, Fischer-Baum, & Miozzo, 2015). It is critical for language practitioners and teachers to recognize this cognitive separation.

The contrast between the spoken language medium and the written language medium presents challenges for all writers regardless of their dialect. Before examining the challenges that are specific to vernacular dialect speakers, it is important to consider this contrast in language modalities that all writers must learn to handle. One challenge concerns the need to distinguish between features and structures that are particular to writing and those that are generally restricted to speaking. Another challenge is accommodating the special communicative demands associated with particular writing situations.

Differences between Oral and Written Language

A key element of the contrast between spoken and written language relates to formality. While speech varies in formality according to situation, written language tends to be more formal than spoken language. In classroom contexts, expectations generally privilege a more formal written style over an informal style. Thus classroom writing is more formal than both the speech styles that students use most frequently and the writing style that they may use in other settings, including journals, emails, and texts. For example, the phrase "a good deal of difficulty" might be preferred in an essay or report over "a lot of trouble," which is common in informal speech and appropriate for a note or an email message. Since school is the context in which students are expected to be most formal with their language style, it is the context in which some students are expected to use language in ways that are most dissimilar from their dialects.

Developing written language expertise involves learning to make choices about style at different levels of language, including vocabulary, grammar, and text structure. Some conventions of written language style that are tied to formality come to students more naturally than others; for example, they could be expected to know that the use of informal conversational features like *you know* and *like* is quite restricted in formal writing. In contrast, they might need to learn to write without the first-person perspective for school contexts: Rather than observing "I think soccer is very popular," a writer might express the thought as "Soccer seems to be very popular" or "It seems that . . ." and so forth. To become successful writers, students must eventually master such contrasts in style and understand the connotations of alternative ways of expressing the same thought.

A second dimension of the contrast between written language and speech stems from the circumstances surrounding the acts of writing and speaking. The two media place differing demands on the communicator. The fact that writing is received visually rules out the kind of information that can be conveyed in speech through vocal shifts in stress and intonation. In writing, that kind of meaning has to be provided in another way. For example, in speech, the difference between a compound word (e.g., *a blackbird*) and a phrase (*a black bird*) is conveyed by stress; in writing, the difference is conveyed by spacing (spoken words have no gap between them, so spacing is a convention peculiar to written language). Similarly, questions can be indicated by intonation in speech, but they have to be marked by punctuation in writing (e.g., "Malcolm took the train?").

The most significant contrast between writing and speaking situations lies in the role of the recipient. In face-to-face interaction, the hearer (or viewer, in the case of sign language) provides feedback to the speaker through gestures, facial expressions, body orientation, and oral feedback cues like *Uh-huh, Yeah*, commenting and questioning. The speaker and hearer align to each other in a kind of conversational ballet, each following the other's lead, getting and giving news about whether the interaction is succeeding (Johnstone, 2002; Tannen, 1993). If something goes wrong, they can negotiate meaning. In most writing contexts, though, the receiver of the communication is not present in the same way, and immediate feedback is unavailable (texting and internet chatting are exceptions). As a result, the writer must carefully consider the perspective of this absent reader when making assumptions about things like shared knowledge, topic orientation, or word connotations. Both for the child who is beginning to write and for the experienced writer, taking the perspective of the absent reader(s) into account can be one of the most difficult aspects of writing. A young writer might report on vacation activities with "We went to visit grandma. Ginger went too . . .," without making it explicit that Ginger is a dog. One of the central tasks of writing instruction is helping children develop an awareness of the reader's needs and ways to accommodate them.

The grammatical patterns used for spoken and written communication differ in important ways too. For example, sentence fragments are common, even pre-ferred, in oral communication. (Think of an exchange like: "Enjoy the game?" "Yeah, especially the end.") Verbs often differ in speaking versus writing as well. Common verbs like *show, see, mean,* and *know,* and phrasal verbs, includ-ing *look up, deal with,* and *get along,* tend to occur more in speech. In writing, it is often preferable to replace—sometimes via editing—such verbs with more formal alternatives, such as *demonstrate, observe, denote, understand,* or *research* (see, e.g., Carter & McCarthy, 2006). Differences have also been found in the use and frequency of nominalizations (words that are other parts of speech are made into nouns, as in *allotment, legalization, proliferation,* etc.), passives, and grammatical patterns that contribute to more complex sentences, such as appositives (e.g., the bit between the commas in, "The Nile, the longest river in the world, is in Egypt") and conjunctions (Biber, 1991). From his detailed inves-tigation of the grammars of speech and writing, Biber concludes that they "are different systems, both deserving of careful analysis" (p. 7).

Writing also involves a set of conventions unique to this medium—the mechanics of writing—that govern when to capitalize, place periods, insert commas, and so forth. These conventions are quite arbitrary, as indicated by the fact that writing systems vary around the world, and different languages—and, indeed, English at different times in its history—use different mechanical conventions. Since English is not spelled phonetically, spellings also fall into the category of writing conventions. When speaking, it is not possible to use the wrong spelling of *there, their,* and *they're* or other homophones, including those that include punctuation, like *it's* and *its.* All writers need to master the features and conventions that are particular to written language in order to convey the meaning they intend.

Vernacular Dialect and Writing

Although speakers of all dialects have to develop writing skills, writing instruc-tion should not ignore students' dialects. In fact, vernacular speakers may face challenges in several areas due to differences between their oral language skills and those required for writing. It is important for teachers to be able to distinguish dialect influence from difficulty with writing conventions or other writing skills, since the pedagogical responses to these different features should be different.

Vernacular Influence in Writing

Although there is limited research on the precise role that a student's dialect background plays in the writing process (but see Abrams, 2011; Ball, 1995; Craig & Washington, 2006; Dyson & Smitherman, 2009; Smitherman, 2000), some observations on the dimensions of dialect influence are useful for teachers. Vernacular dialect speakers may encounter at least three different types of problems in writing.

Organization of an Argument or Narrative. Judgments about appropriate text organization may relate to culturally-based expectations for how to tell a story or make an argument. Divergent narrative structures were examined in Chapter 5, along with the deficit theory advanced from students' retellings of a tornado in Arkansas. The researchers concluded that the students from lower social-class backgrounds "literally cannot tell a straight story or describe a simple incident coherently" (Schatzman & Strauss, 1955, p. 336). Another study found differences in narrative structures between different cultural groups (Michaels, 1981). Working-class African American children's stories were likely to include several episodes rather than one, with shifting scenes, and more narrative markers, such as "and then" (meaning *also* or a shift from one temporal moment to another) linking the episodes. Since the children's language norms did not match those of their European American, middle-class teachers, the teachers found the stories disjointed. European American students in these classrooms, who did employ the linear narrative style that teachers expected, received helpful feedback for refining storytelling, but the African American students were directed to restructure their stories. Such judgments illustrate the general problem of viewing some culturally-based practices as deficient rather than different. Misunderstandings like this may widen the gap between in-school and out-of-school experiences. As children learn that their language skills are less valuable at school, they may learn to devalue their own abilities and distance themselves from school expectations. If children write in an episodic style or follow other culturally-based styles of oral narrative or argumentation, which is likely, teachers might reach similar conclusions about their students' writing.

Grammar. Grammatical differences between Standard English and the student's dialect interfere in producing the kinds of written language products that contribute to school success. The use of nonstandard verb forms, as in "The girl knowed the answer," may come from a spoken dialect that regularly uses these grammatical rules. Depending on the grammar of the student's dialect, any of the inflectional morphemes described in Chapter 3 may vary from the standard expected in the classroom. One study found African American English features in the writing of 62% of the third graders surveyed (Thompson, Craig, & Washington, 2004). Among the grammatical patterns that might well occur in the writing of African American English speakers are third-singular -*s* absence ("My sister live_ with me"), possessive -*s* absence ("my dad_ house"), plural -*s* absence ("The park has two basketball hoop_"), absence of copula verb ("He __ funny"), absence of modal auxiliaries ("I hope you __ be a good teacher"), and regularization of past-tense *be* ("we was"). For vernacular Appalachian English speakers, the following forms might occur in writing: regularization of past tense ("We growed squash"), bare root verb forms ("She come home yesterday"), different irregular verb forms ("It riz up from the water"), -*s* added to verbs following collective nouns ("People goes"), and absence of -*s* plural with nouns of measure ("four pound"). Similarly, the use of expletive or existential *it* for "there" in written sentences such as "It was a new student in the class yesterday" may come from a vernacular speaker's normal use of this form in spoken language. Other students may show similar dialect influences in their writing whenever their dialect's grammar differs from that of Standard English.

English language learners may exhibit some of these same features, but they may struggle more with grammatical features that are unusual or used inconsistently in Standard American English (de Kleine, 2006). While this issue is not technically a function of vernacular dialect influence, it does represent language patterns that affect the writing of certain groups of students whom teachers encounter in their classes. For example, *do*-support, where a form of *do* is used with questions or negatives, is a tricky pattern to learn. Questions in English are often formed through subject–verb inversion (the statement "It's Thursday" becomes the question "Is it Thursday?"). However, since not all verbs can be moved, some questions must be formed by adding a form of *do* as an auxiliary verb. For example, the statement "You like milk" becomes the question "Do you like milk?" instead of *"Like you milk?" Negating sentences like this one also requires *do* ("You don't like milk") while other types of sentences do not require *do* ("You shouldn't eat that"). Other inconsistent patterns in English can also cause confusion for English language learners.

More broadly, English language learners may experience grammatical influence from their native language (L1) anytime the grammar systems between the two languages are different. In fact, resources exist that detail these contrasts between English and other languages (e.g., Swan & Smith, 2001).

Grammatical patterns typical of English learners may occasionally be encoded in the native English dialects of social groups whose English is influenced by another language: For example, Latino English speakers may maintain the negative agreement patterns of Spanish (e.g., "We didn't do nothing") even if they learned English as their first language. This pattern should be seen not as an error but rather as a feature of a Latino English dialect.

Grammatical forms from—or similar to—vernacular language patterns are the most highly stigmatized features in written language (Hairston, 1981). Even when items are similar in type to errors in mainstream English, the association with vernacular dialects results in their being treated more harshly. For example, the subject–verb agreement pattern in "We was planning a party" is similar in form to "Enclosed is his transcript and resume." But because the first is more strongly linked to vernacular dialects, it was more negatively evaluated than the latter example (Hairston, 1981).

Pronunciation. As with grammar, pronunciation can potentially interfere in writing wherever there are differences between Standard English and a vernacular dialect or L1, although most studies find that there is less phonological influence than grammatical influence in student writing (e.g., Craig & Washington, 2006). The fact that English spelling does not map onto the sounds of the language consistently in a one-to-one relationship makes spelling challenging for everyone, but dialect differences introduce an additional set of possibilities for spelling errors. For example, spelling the first vowel sound of *tinder* and *tender* the same way relates to the fact that these words are pronounced the same in Southern dialects. This would be quite similar to a Standard American English speaker confusing "t" and "d" spellings in a word like *therapeutic* (sounds like "therapeudic") because the consonant spelled with "t" is pronounced as a *d* in this position. This confusion would not arise for speakers of British English who pronounce *t* and *d* between vowels differently (as in *latter* and *ladder*). A student may write *a* as the form of the indefinite article before both a consonant and a vowel (e.g., "a teacher" and "a aunt") if the article can be used this way in speech. However, some phonological differences do not manifest themselves often or at all in student writing. Vernacular dialects often replace the voiced sound spelled with "th" with a *d* sound ("dese" and "dem" for *these* and *them*) but despite the difference, vernacular-speaking children typically have no trouble using the "th" letter sequence in writing.

One important phonological influence is common in vernacular speakers' and some English language learners' writing. Word-final consonant clusters, described in detail in Chapter 3, are commonly reduced to a single consonant in the speech of vernacular dialect speakers and English learners. It is unfortunate that these less usual—at least among the languages of the world— phonological features play such an important grammatical role in English, since they make up the majority of regular past tense verb forms. Verbs such as *faced* and *loved* are pronounced as a single syllable, ending with consonants -*st* and -*vd*, respectively. Leaving off the second consonant in oral language is likely to affect writing (Craig & Washington, 2006; DeStefano, 1972; Kligman & Cronnell, 1974). Because this feature is perceived as a grammar error rather than a phonological influence on writing, it is more heavily stigmatized than other phonological influences in writing.

Difference and Error in Written Language

In the strictest sense, the examples given above are not errors. Instead, they are the reflection in writing of differences in communicative norms, grammar, and pronunciation between the student's dialect and the normative standard against which writing is judged at school. One of the dangers of teachers treating the predictable reflection of verbal expression as "error" is that students may infer that their general writing skills are inadequate and hesitate to use them. Also, they may make real errors in an attempt to avoid certain usages from their spoken dialect, a phenomenon known as *hypercorrection*. For instance, after numerous experiences with correction in the use of indefinite articles, a student might begin using structures like "an car" or "an city," hypercorrecting by using *an* regardless of how the following word begins. Such usages, which may also occur to a lesser extent in speech, represent an effort to catch potential errors by thwarting the natural tendency to use the form *a* everywhere.

Departures from the standard forms that schools expect in student writing can be classified into three categories: problems with the *conventions* that distinguish written and spoken language, *influences* from the oral vernacular ways of speaking, and *mistakes*. Mistakes occur when a writer knows the written standard but simply errs in adhering to it through a typo or a lapse in concentration, or falls victim to an overzealous autocorrect feature. For example, if a student makes an error one time with respect to a convention (e.g., confuses *its* and *it's*) or a dialect pattern (e.g., omits a plural -*s*) but uses the standard form elsewhere in the piece where a dialect form is possible, it is likely that the student understands the standard pattern, but just made a mistake. Distinctions among mistakes, conventions, and dialect influence are important: Teachers should approach each category differently in the process of instructive editing. All writers struggle with conventions, but dialect influence may require more individualized attention. If teachers examine an item in the context of a student's written work, looking for other instances of the feature, they can determine whether the student needs additional help on a feature or not. In this way, the role of the grader is changed from evaluator to scientist: Instead of merely reacting to errors, the teacher will be looking for patterns, hypothesizing about them, collecting additional data, and interpreting the data.

Given the three kinds of departure from the standard written language that schools expect, we can return to the writing sample in the opening scenario of this chapter. Detailed knowledge about the student's spoken dialect allows us to identify some instances of direct influence in this passage. For example, "They don't have no crime" is an instance of multiple negation, a common feature in vernacular dialects of English. The absence of the plural ending in "many game_" is also a candidate for dialect influence, as is copula absence, the absence of *be* in "You still can play many game like you ___ the age of 6 or 9." These dialect influences can be contrasted with writing convention errors. For example, if the writer had written "your" for *you're*, as in "Your the age of 6," this would be an error related to convention. All speakers of English share the problem of writing words that sound alike but are spelled differently.

This sample of student writing also shows indirect influence from spoken dialect. Hypercorrection is a likely source of the construction "its would be." It may be that copula absence had appeared previously in the student's writing and been corrected rather frequently, resulting in the student's becoming sensitive to the problem of leaving out forms of the *be* verb. The unnecessary addition of *s* on *its* in the case of "its would be" may represent an unconscious effort to avoid omitting *is* or *are*, but without a full understanding of the structure in question. This likely hypercorrection shows that a dialect can influence production of written forms both directly and indirectly.

Writing samples from vernacular dialect speakers reflect only selected features from the spoken dialect, since some frequently occurring characteristics of speech are seldom found in writing. Some of those that do occur are apparently related to development patterns in the acquisition of general writing skills. A study that compared a large amount of spoken and written data from both standard and vernacular dialect speakers at all age levels found that all writers, regardless of dialect background, omitted certain grammatical suffixes to some extent in early writing (Farr & Daniels, 1986). These included the verbal -*s* ending (e.g., "He walk"), the plural ending (as in "many game" from the sample composition), and the past ending -*ed* ("Last summer she move to Texas"). For all groups in the research sample, the suffixes were sometimes absent, but the frequency was much higher for vernacular dialect speakers who also use these features in their speech to varying extents. Thus, the influence from dialect combines with a general tendency in writing development to produce non-normative structures in early writing.

Paradoxically, some of the vernacular features that count as errors in school writing are used in now-popular instant messages (IM) and texting modes of communication. This practice lends a certain flair or efficiency and modernity to the media, mirroring the tradition of using vernacular features to indicate distance from the mainstream. Some have worried that the language of IMing and texting would be a threat to acquiring proficiency in written Standard English for students, but the research shows overwhelmingly that these communication modes have either a neutral or a positive effect on students' reading (see, e.g., Drouin, 2011; Kemp, 2010) and writing abilities (for studies on IMing, see, e.g., Squires, 2010; Tagliamonte & Denis, 2008; for studies on texting see, e.g., Crystal, 2008; Plester, Wood, & Joshi, 2009). Engaging in literacy practices, even with nonstandard language use, can improve students' standard language writing abilities. Furthermore, smartphones' predictive language engines may actually help students learn standard syntax and spelling, because the options shown to the user during the composition of a message subtly reinforce standard language norms.

Teaching Writing

How can teachers support the development of writing skills in their vernacular-speaking students? Farr and Daniels (1986) suggest a set of 15 research-based factors in effective writing instruction for secondary school students from vernacular dialect backgrounds, which appear to be readily adaptable for students at any level. According to them, students should have:

1. Teachers who understand and appreciate the basic linguistic competence that students bring with them to school, and who therefore have positive expectations for students' achievements in writing.
2. Regular and substantial practice in writing, aimed at developing fluency.
3. The opportunity to write for real, personally significant purposes.
4. Experience in writing for a wide range of audiences, both inside and outside of school.
5. Rich and continuous reading experience, including both published literature of acknowledged merit and the work of peers and instructors.
6. Exposure to models of the process of writing and writers at work, including both teachers and classmates.
7. Instruction in the process of writing: that is, learning to work at a writing task in appropriate phases, including prewriting, drafting, and revising.
8. Collaborative activities involving other students that provide ideas for writing and guidance for revising works in progress.
9. One-to-one writing conferences with the teacher.
10. Direct instruction in specific strategies and techniques for writing.
11. Reduced instruction in grammatical terminology and related drills, with increased use of sentence combining activities.
12. Teaching of writing mechanics and grammar in the context of students' actual compositions, rather than in separate drills or exercises.
13. Moderate marking of surface structure errors, focusing on sets of patterns of related errors.
14. Flexible and cumulative evaluation of student writing that stresses revision and is sensitive to variations in subject, audience, and purpose.

15. Practice in using writing as a tool of learning in all subjects in the curriculum, not just in English.

Farr & Daniels, 1986, pp. 45–46

Several important conclusions can be drawn from these guidelines for teaching writing. One is that writing instruction for vernacular speakers should include all of the elements of effective writing instruction, and that attention to vernacular forms should be embedded within it. Another conclusion is that decontextualized, skills-based instruction in written Standard English should be avoided, just as with teaching spoken Standard English. It does not lead to competent writing, and it alienates students who seek to improve their writing. For example, a longitudinal study in New Zealand tested a traditional decontextualized grammar curriculum against a curriculum that involved intensive reading and writing; it found that by the end of three years, not only did students in the grammar curriculum have worse written grammatical abilities than the reading and writing group, but they also had a much more negative view of their school (Elley, Barham, Lamb, & Wyllie, 1976).

One study that found remarkable success teaching African American English-speaking children to write well seems counterintuitive at first. Julie Sweetland designed a 10-week curriculum for upper elementary students that sought to improve student writing through teaching them sociolinguistic approaches to language and reading. The curriculum included dialect awareness lessons (similar to those in Chapter 10), contrastive analysis, literature that used African American English, and opportunities for students to use African American English in their writing. The unit was taught to urban students in a Midwestern city. At the end of the unit, the students who had experienced the sociolinguistically informed curriculum outscored their peers who had participated in a writing process curriculum on a standardized writing test (Sweetland, 2006). How is it that students exposed to nonstandard writing opportunities and literature improved more than students who received explicit instruction in writing? Sweetland found that the teachers who taught the sociolinguistic curriculum changed their approaches to writing errors, and that adjustment had a positive effect on the students. Further, in discussing literature, they talked about character identity and authors' decisions to use the vernacular in their writing, which led students to better understand how writers accomplish voice, tone, and mood, while also reframing writing as a process rather than an event. The conclusion, ultimately, is not as counterintuitive as it seems at first: In order to teach children to write well, teachers need to engage students in discussions of the language in varying kinds of literature rather than simply giving them a formula, such as the five-paragraph essay, for writing.

It is important to note that none of the recommendations put forth by Farr and Daniels (1986) are incompatible with the Common Core State Standards (CCSS, 2010), the framework for language arts and mathematics adopted in many states. In fact, viewed collectively, these recommendations can help reinforce or complement the standards. For example, the CCSS Writing Standard 10, "Write routinely over extended time frames . . . and shorter time frames. . . for a range of tasks, purposes, and audiences" (CCSS, 2010, p. 18), echoes recommendations 2 and 4 in Farr and Daniels' list. Other recommendations on the list are less about curricular decisions and more about pedagogical support (e.g., those for holding student–teacher conferences and marking written work). They can be seen as complementary since the Common Core State Standards make no recommendations about *how* writing should be taught.

Teaching students to consider language choices can be empowering. One approach encourages teachers and students to consider how to deploy multiple language codes in one literacy event instead of compartmentalizing them by context. Code-meshing, described and critiqued in the previous chapter, is about making and evaluating language choices rather than following a prescriptive procedure (Young, Barrett, Young-Rivera, & Lovejoy, 2013; Young & Martinez, 2011). Proponents of this approach report dramatic improvement in student engagement with writing and literature. We do not mean to suggest that teachers should not teach Standard English forms to students who use vernacular forms in their writing or that there are no writing events in which teachers should expect standard usage. There is fairly widespread agreement among educators and researchers that the ability to use Standard English for written work is an important skill (Smitherman, 1995). But writing instruction for speakers of vernacular dialects should not be reduced to a focus on contrasting forms. Vernacular speakers should be afforded opportunities for writing appropriately in different codes, including exclusively in their vernacular, exclusively in a standard dialect, and with deliberate meshing of standard and vernacular codes. Even unplanned and unintentional code-meshing can serve as the basis for rich guided discussion of the effects of language on the audience. Allowing students the opportunity to write without fear of correction can result in the type of language data that teachers can use to turn unsuccessful and unintentional instances of vernacular influence into deliberate, skillful code-meshing (Elbow, 2012).

Editing

The process approach to writing, which emphasizes language skills that all students can be presumed to have in rich abundance, deals with dialect influence only after the writing is drafted and does so in ways that are linguistically informed. Because vernacular features such as the absence of suffixes do not signal lack of conceptual knowledge, writers can make changes during the revision phase rather easily if dialect interference is pointed out to them. As a practical matter, it may be difficult for teachers who learned to write in a sea of red ink to postpone editing, and students may be concerned with dialect features in their own and others' writing when they are supposed to be focusing on content. However, commitment to producing authentic, high-quality writing, rather than writing for evaluation or remedial skill-learning purposes, suggests that editing be relegated to the back burner during the composing phase. This recommendation should not be interpreted as advice to ignore or downplay editing, but to convey to students that attention to the form of language is distinct from and secondary to conceptualizing and drafting. However, because editing is most focused on language structures that are unique to writing, it is a skill that must be learned; and students are likely to benefit from explicit instruction in effective self- and peer-editing.

Approaches to Editing

The categories of writing challenges suggested earlier—writing conventions; dialect influence (including text structure, grammar, and pronunciation); and mistakes—may be useful in identifying problems in students' writing. Students might focus on these categories as they learn the process of self-editing. Understanding precisely what kind of difficulty a writer is experiencing in these categories, students and teachers can move more deliberately toward achieving proficiency in using appropriate written forms. Teachers and students might, for example, prioritize their areas of difficulty and systematically focus on different kinds of writing misfires at different points in the process of developing proficient Standard English writing skills.

Another technique is to focus on a set of related items rather than on every instance of dialect influence and technical mistake in each piece of writing. If possessives become a target of attention, for example, then attending to both singular and plural forms makes sense because these items are related. In this context, issues of dialect influence on plural formation can be addressed too. Focusing on a few forms at a time can keep students from feeling overwhelmed. It can also help teachers approach marking in more systematic ways.

To help vernacular speakers learn to edit their writing into written Standard American English, teachers need to know the structure of their students' home dialect so that they can understand the reasons for the forms that students produce and help their students understand them as well. For example, a teacher in a Southern setting might have to teach the spelling of *tin* and *ten* like other homophonous words, such as *too*, *to*, or *two*. The problems associated with sounding out words to arrive at their spellings do not appear to be that much greater for speakers of vernacular dialects than for other speakers. All speakers are faced with the challenges of English spelling in which the sound and spelling relationship is not regular: For example, *could, tough,* and *though* cannot be spelled on the basis of sound. It seems likely, then, that a child who pronounces "toof" can adjust to the standard spelling *tooth* as well as another child who says "tuff" learns to spell it *tough*. Vernacular dialect speakers may make different mistakes in attempting spellings at various stages of development, which may draw undue attention to a spelling "problem." The Appendix offers a compendium of vernacular features that teachers can use in developing a profile of the local dialect(s).

Peer Editing

Peer interaction can contribute to developing writing skills when students have been trained to critique each other's writing and to help edit out errors, when the purpose and the nature of the evaluation task is clear, and when editing is directly tied to a whole-class project. Peer editing can generate topics for targeted instruction on mechanics and standard dialect features. For example, if it becomes clear to students from peer editing sessions that many of them have trouble with possessives, as in writing "John hat" for *John's hat* (a problem shared to some extent by both standard and vernacular speakers at certain stages of learning to write), then this feature can become the focus of direct instruction and student attention for a time. This approach has at least two advantages: Contrasting dialect and mechanics are explained in context, and students share in identifying their writing problems for explicit instruction.

Evaluation of Students' Writing

In standardized writing tests, evaluation takes place outside of the classroom teacher's purview. Nevertheless, it is important for teachers to be aware of how the prompts and grading policies for such tests can disproportionately affect students from vernacular dialect backgrounds so that they can prepare students for the tests and advocate for fair practices. In Chapter 6, we examined briefly the sorts of linguistic biases that can affect standardized writing test prompts. This section critiques the process of evaluation in these standardized writing exams as a prelude to considering sociolinguistically informed evaluation procedures that can be deployed in the classroom.

District-level guidelines may include a linguistically sound policy on language variation (see Chapter 7), encouraging the teaching of writing with a primary focus on important skills like developing writing fluency, voice, and organization. But on state-mandated standardized assessments, among others, dialect features and mechanics are likely to be accorded major importance in formal evaluation of writing ability, putting the speakers of vernacular dialects at a disadvantage. The New York Regents exam is one such high stakes test that requires students to write essays. The different types of essays are scored according to different criteria. The textual analysis essay, for example, includes criteria for "command of evidence" and "content and analysis," while the critical lens essay includes criteria for "meaning" and "development." However, all essays include at least one language criterion, and in order to be scored above average, essays must have no errors that "hinder comprehension."

(www.nysedregents.org/comprehensiveenglish/). On the surface this metric seems like a reasonable approach, since most dialect errors in writing do not hinder comprehension. Yet, examining the sample scored essays reveals that dialect influence is evaluated quite severely.

According to the August 2015 Scoring Key and Rating Guide, the following dialect influences are judged as hindering comprehension. The suggestion is that the students' writing should be rated below the median score:

1. "She first **begin** to tell a story" – third-person singular -*s* absence (p. 26)
2. "This is **apparen** through time" – consonant cluster reduction (p. 26)
3. "People treat her **bad**" – adjective for adverb (p. 56)
4. "Lily and Rayona's **life** changes" – unmarked plural (p. 56)
5. "Lily wants to move away from her father that she thinks **don't** love her" – third-person singular -*s* absence (p. 58)
6. "Lily thought it **will** be fine to just set out" – present tense for past tense (p. 59)

While the meaning seems clear in each sentence, the writers are penalized for dialect influence. By contrast, the errors that are cited as examples of not hindering comprehension include various agreement issues (e.g., "a child looks at **their** parents" [p. 5]; though never third-person singular -*s* absence), significant misspellings (well beyond consonant cluster reductions), comma absences, and the lack of an apostrophe to denote possessive. The message is clear: Errors related to convention are expected of all writers, so these are not remarkable; but errors related to dialects are something unusual and should be treated punitively.

During timed writing tests, students may well not have a chance to deploy their editing skills thoroughly. Thus, the tests place value on the skill of composing—specifically composing without dialect influence—above all other writing skills even though it is only one part of the writing process. They privilege Standard English speakers and discriminate against speakers of vernacular dialects. Furthermore, such metrics place teachers in a very difficult situation. Though research suggests that students become better writers through exposure to diverse language uses and information about each step of the writing process (i.e., pre-writing, composing, editing, and proofreading), the high stakes test environment frames writing as an event, not a process (e.g., Villanueva & Arola, 2011).

Researchers have advocated for a number of changes to large-scale testing that might help alleviate such biases. One researcher offers the following suggestions for the assessment of writing:

1. States must confront the question of what is to be evaluated: the ability to write correctly in Standard English or the ability to communicate effectively in writing.

2. Grading anchor exemplars (papers that serve as benchmarks for grading) must include proficient papers that exhibit dialect influence. Exemplars must also include non-proficient papers written in Standard English.

3. No test materials, test evaluation materials, or test evaluation training should include the words "standard writing conventions" or "standard English."

4. The pool of test evaluators should reflect the diversity of the state.

5. Training for evaluators must contain information to thaw "the chilly attitudes found toward dialectal language use" among many teachers and educational professionals. Training should also help evaluators move away from "language policing."

adapted from Harmon, 1994, pp. 21–22

Classroom-Based Assessment

Classroom-based assessment can avoid many of the pitfalls of large-scale testing. The classroom teacher is in a much better position to assess student writing development than scorers of large-scale tests, because the teacher can track individual progress across time and know precisely which dialect differences the student is managing. Moreover, classroom-based assessment is instructionally useful. Informal classroom diagnostic assessments that acknowledge that writing "errors are a necessary concomitant of growth" (Weaver, 1996, p. 59) can help teachers particularize writing goals for students and plan subsequent instructional activities.

Portfolio assessment has gained a wide following as a way of evaluating student progress. Students select some of their writings for teacher evaluation and defend them in a conference with the teacher, explaining why they value these writings. Evaluation often involves rubrics, which may include items particular to the student's personal goals. When this approach is used as intended, students play an active role in assessing their own work and articulating their personal view of excellent writing, and teachers can track individual development. Teachers and students can address controlling dialect influence as one element of development.

Classroom-based assessment typically involves documenting student progress in some detail so that teachers can see patterns in students' development. They may notice, for example, that error reduction in students' writing does not follow a linear path. An early recognition of this fact came from Roger McCaig:

> By literal count, good sixth grade writing may have more errors per word than good third grade writing. In a Piagetian sense, children do not master things for once and for all. A child who may appear to have mastered sentence sense in the fourth grade may suddenly begin making what adults

call sentence errors all over again as he attempts to accommodate his knowledge of sentence to more complicated constructions.

1977, pp. 50–51

With vernacular-speaking students, similar patterns arise. Certain vernacular features may be eliminated from formal writing at one stage only to appear again when students attempt to write in more complex styles (Abrams, 2011). This finding should help teachers pivot from seeing writing errors as persistent problems to seeing writing errors as opportunities for further learning. This perspective coincides with using evaluation as a form of understanding development, rather than just a means of evaluating what standards have been met.

Marking

It is worth asking how marking students' written products can be made more valuable to students and less routine for teachers, and how dialect influence can be handled. Consider a common response to a student error. If a student writes *there* for *their*, many teachers would cross out the student's form and write in the correct form. The message is that the student made an error. Because there is no explanation of why one word is wrong and the other right, there is no meaningful feedback to the student. This method of marking—error correction—is ineffective for furthering learning. Rosen (1987) offers some other options, all of which can be critiqued. The first is for teachers to ignore errors on a final draft. This approach is only appropriate if students understand that errors will not be marked, and engage with questions of usage and style throughout the writing process. It places high value on the student's language choices by respecting the final draft as a result of intentional choices. Some teachers employ this approach because they believe it allows them to focus more completely on the argument or narrative rather than on errors. A second option is for teachers to respond only to certain errors. Teachers may elect to inform students of the type of error that will be evaluated and the justification for selecting this type. This approach can be useful for teachers who are knowledgeable about the differences among dialect influence, writing conventions, and mistakes, and their relative frequency (Connors & Lunsford, 1988), as well as the public's evaluation of different types of errors (Hairston, 1981). A final approach offered by Rosen (1987) is to merely draw attention to errors by marking them with a checkmark or a circle. Students can work on their own to understand and correct as many errors as possible, and the teacher can use any misunderstood errors as the basis for further, often individual, instruction.

Reframing assessment from evaluation to opportunity should allow teachers to help their students improve every aspect of their writing. Doing so requires that criteria and processes for evaluation be developed intentionally and shared. Teachers might want to discuss grading criteria along with the writing assignment.

As schools and school districts wrestle with accountability requirements, teaching writing becomes a more public and consequential issue. At the individual level, students are writing across the curriculum, and their writing in subject matter classes and tests can impact their educational pathways. Given the high stakes associated with writing at all levels, vernacular dialect speakers may not reach their full potential unless writing instruction explicitly addresses the contrast between their language and written Standard English. It is important for schools and teachers to develop policies and practices that support writing skill development coherently across the school years and that take students' diverse language experiences into account in doing so.

Writing in the Vernacular Dialect

Vernacular dialect should not be viewed as a threat to developing writing skills and producing high quality work. It has a natural role to play.

Writing to Extend Thinking

Teachers are urged to give their students frequent and varied writing activities for different purposes across the content areas. Jotting down ideas for a structured discussion, annotating written text, and taking class notes are all important kinds of writing that do not need to be refined into a final draft for publication and assessed. There is no need to demand that these forms of writing avoid vernacular features. Extensive experience with various forms of writing can help make students comfortable with writing and, perhaps, more likely to feel capable of producing polished written text with Standard English.

Choosing the Vernacular in Writing

Students who speak vernacular dialects can be invited to write in their dialect if they wish to and to preserve these features through the editing process. For example, in writing personal narratives, students may find that vernacular features lend authenticity, just as they do in the writing of accomplished authors such as Alice Walker, Lee Smith, Sandra Cisneros, or Silas House. By inviting students to use vernacular features in this kind of writing, teachers reinforce the notion that writers suit language style to genre (Bean, et al., 2003; Sweetland, 2006; Young, et al., 2013; Young & Martinez, 2011).

In an account of a writing course that involved occasional writing in the vernacular, Irvine and Elsasser (1988) explain that they first created a climate that helped students understand the value of vernacular writing. Their method involved building students' awareness that their dialect was structured, not deficient, and providing direct instruction in some of the structural contrasts between the vernacular and standard dialects. Similar approaches appear in June Jordan's account of African American college students in a writing class (1988) and, more recently, in the literature on code-meshing pedagogy (Young & Martinez, 2011).

One formal educational program that embraces vernacular voices is the Appalachian Writing Project, which works with educators throughout the region to implement practices that help their students develop as writers while also learning about differences between their grammar and that of Standard English. The program also helps teachers and students examine the language usage expectations of the Virginia Standards of Learning exam, the state's standardized testing program for grades K–12 content areas, including English language arts. For example, for one test question from a disclosed exam, a sentence correction task that features multiple negation, "The model did not look like no sailboat I have ever seen" (Clark, 2013, p. 118), vernacular speakers must recognize that their intuitions on "what sounds right" would backfire. In the Appalachian Writing Project, program participants determine which vernacular patterns are most prevalent in local classrooms so that teachers can focus instruction precisely. At one point in the program, students collected local language usages for class discussion. The goal was to examine authentic language use and consider the rhetorical power of using the vernacular. Students also wrote poetry and prose in the vernacular, which led to discussions about the role of dialect in constructing strong characters and vivid settings, as well as discussions about outsiders' attitudes toward the local dialect. A two-year study of nearly 200 students in middle grades and high school classrooms participating in the Appalachian Writing Project found that students improved their formal writing assessment scores by 72%, while control groups improved only 9% (Clark, 2013, p. 121). Pedagogies that affirm and preserve culture like those included in the Appalachian Writing Project are effective in helping vernacular-speaking students attain the literacy skills that schools require of them.

Dialogue Journals

One effective strategy to encourage writing without dwelling on form and dialect for both mainstream and nonmainstream children is the dialogue journal (Peyton & Reed, 1990): a "sustained written interaction between students and teachers" (https://en.wikipedia.org/wiki/Dialogue_journal). Students can write as much as they want about topics of their choice. The teacher writes back each time the student writes—often responding to the student's topics, but also introducing new topics, making comments and offering observations and opinions, requesting and giving clarification, asking questions, and answering student questions. There is no overt correction of the student's writing, although the

teacher may model particular linguistic features or probe for missing information. The advantage of this method is that students experience writing as an
interactive communicative experience in a nonthreatening atmosphere. They
write about topics that are important to them and explore topics in a genre that
accommodates their current level of proficiency in writing. Many teachers have
found that dialogue journals encourage students from quite different backgrounds and with quite different experiences in terms of traditional academic
success to feel confident in expressing themselves in writing (Peyton, 1990).
As an added benefit, dialogue journals "are not only a way to improve student
writing, but also a means for teachers to get to know their students and their
learning processes, which helps teachers to better serve their learners' needs"
(Denne-Bolton, 2013, p. 5).

Traditionally, dialogue journals used notebooks, but now they are being
done online. This updated approach has revealed exciting results with both
native English speakers and English language learners. In one study, college-
level English language learners developed a stronger writing voice as a result
of the computer mediated dialogue journals (Wang & Ruhl, 2011). Another
study found that the electronic journals (in the form of emails) helped English
language learners with the writing conventions most commonly expected in
education settings more than peer students who engaged in pen-and-paper
dialogue journals (Foroutan, Noordin, & bin Hamzah, 2013). In other cases,
using the journals led to students being better able to demonstrate agency in
their own education (Miller, 2007), become more aware of their own learning
process (Carroll & Mchawala, 2001), improve critical thinking (Mizokawa &
Hansen-Krening, 2000), and ask more thoughtful questions (Kim, 2005).
All of these results are possible because dialogue journals encourage fluency
over accuracy, which is essential to building confidence:

> It is not unusual in the language classroom to see learners struggling to
> find something to write about an assigned topic of little relevance to their
> lives, but when learners can write about what they know, they find they
> have a lot more to say. This engagement leads them to grapple with
> expressing new and complex ideas in English.
>
> *Denne-Bolton, 2013, p. 4*

While dialogue journals are just one approach to helping students from
diverse language backgrounds become better and more confident writers, the
research on this pedagogical technique reflects many of the key conclusions
about dialects and writing presented in this chapter. First, as with approaches to
oral language norms discussed in the previous chapter, additivist approaches
to helping students develop written language skills are far more effective and
reasonable than eradicationist approaches. Second, developing fluency is the
most critical writing goal. As students gain fluency, the number and type of

errors in their writing may change and even increase; however, errors are a predictable feature of learning to write well and responding to them in ways that foreground learning over assessment helps students continue to grow as writers. Vernacular-speaking students face the same challenges as other students with regard to mastering written English practices, including word choice, punctuation, capitalization, and spelling; however, they require specialized instruction that helps them understand the differences between Standard English grammar and the grammar of their dialects. They also need to learn how their pronunciation patterns relate to spelling. Finally, students from nonmainstream cultures may need explicit instruction regarding expectations for narrative structure and other language functions.

Discussion Questions

1. Do you agree that teaching students to write is one of the most important functions of schools? Provide examples showing what happens when people do learn to write well, as well as examples showing what happens when people don't learn to write well.
2. Explain why the term *dialect influence* is preferred, and *dialect error* is not preferred.
3. Reflect on the list of recommendations from Farr and Daniels (1986) for teaching writing to students from vernacular dialect backgrounds. Does it seem right, based on what you know about language variation and about teaching writing? Does it seem practical? Does it seem important? Explain.
4. How valuable is it that vernacular-speaking students be given opportunities to use their dialects in writing? How can teachers who don't share a dialect with their students ensure that the vernacular is being used appropriately and well in student writing?
5. Critique Rosen's three options for marking student papers from the standpoint of how well each one would meet the particular needs of vernacular dialect speakers.

Links of Interest

1. Read about dialogue journals: https://en.wikipedia.org/wiki/ialogue_journal
2. Learn more about the Appalachian Writing Project: http://awp.uvawise.edu/
3. Consider a statement arguing against the use of writing as a form of punishment: www.ncte.org/positions/statements/writingaspunishment
4. Watch an interview with Vershawn Young about code-meshing: www.youtube.com/watch?v=OIrED9k5tmM
5. Check out Grammar Girl's tips to writing accents and dialects: www.quickanddirtytips.com/education/grammar/writing-accents-and-dialects

Further Reading

Ball, A. F., & Lardner, T. (2005). *African American literacies unleashed: Vernacular English and the composition classroom.* Urbana, IL: National Council of Teachers of English.
> The focus here is on the college composition class, but the recommendations for teachers of writing are broadly applicable. The authors show how teachers can help African American students capitalize on their linguistic skills.

Crystal, D. (2008). *Txtng: The gr8 db8.* Oxford, UK: Oxford University Press.
> This short volume offers an accessible overview of some of the early fears about and research on the effect of texting on the English language.

Dean. D. (2008). *Bringing grammar to life.* Newark, DE: International Reading Association.
> A guide for teachers, this volume uses *To Kill A Mockingbird* as the basis for discussions about ethnic dialects and for teaching Standard English grammar and writing skills.

Elbow, P. (2013). *Vernacular eloquence: What speech can bring to writing.* Oxford, UK: Oxford University Press.
> Elbow makes the case that not only should students be permitted to write in their natural dialects, but that doing so is a critical aspect of developing as a writer. He offers practical approaches so that all writing teachers can turn vernacular dialects into important classroom resources.

Farr, M., & Daniels, H. (1986). *Language diversity and writing instruction.* Urbana, IL: National Council of Teachers of English.
> This resource offers both a theoretical framework and practical suggestions to educators who wish to improve writing instruction for secondary school students who speak vernacular dialects.

Hampton, S. (1995). Strategies for increasing achievement in writing. In R. W. Cole (Ed.), *Educating everybody's children: Diverse teaching strategies for diverse learners: What research and practice say about improving achievement* (pp. 99–112). Alexandria, VA: Association for Supervision and Curriculum Development.
> Clear and practical, this summary of thinking on writing instruction does not focus on students' dialect, but it does concern teaching writing to students from outside the mainstream.

Shaughnessy, M. P. (1977). *Errors and expectations: A guide for the teacher of basic writing.* New York, NY: Oxford University Press.
> This classic work provides a helpful approach to the systematic study of writing errors. It is not specifically targeted for writers from vernacular dialect backgrounds, but many aspects of the approach will prove useful to teachers of these students.

Young, V. A., Barrett, R., Young-Rivera, Y., & Lovejoy, K. B. (2013). *Other people's English: Code-meshing, code-switching, and African American literacy.* New York, NY: Teachers College Press.
> This volume illustrates the potential of pedagogies that allow African American English to exist alongside Standard English in classrooms. Though the discussion focuses solely on African American English, the methodology is adaptable for other vernacular dialects.

References

Abrams, K. D. (2011). *Comparing codes: Dialect density measurements of oral and written codes in African American English.* Unpublished master's thesis, North Carolina State University.

Ball, A. F. (1995). Text design patterns in the writing of urban African American students: Teaching to the cultural strengths of students in multicultural settings. *Urban Education, 30*(3), 253–289.

Bean, J., Cucchiara, M., Eddy, R., Elbow, P., Grego, R., Haswell, R., Irvine, P., Kennedy, E., Kutz, E., Lehner, A., & Matsuda, P. K. (2003). Should we invite students to write in home languages? Complicating the yes/no debate. *Composition Studies, 31*(1), 25–42.

Biber, D. (1991). *Variation across speech and writing.* Cambridge, UK: Cambridge University Press.

Boser, U. (2014). *Teacher diversity revisited.* Washington, DC: Center for American Progress.

Carroll, M., & Mchawala, C. (2001). Form or meaning? Academic writing with a personal voice. In J. Burton and M. Carroll (Eds.), *Journal writing,* (pp. 47–58). Alexandria, VA: TESOL.

Carter, R., & McCarthy, M. (2006). *Cambridge grammar of English: A comprehensive guide; spoken and written English grammar and usage.* Stuttgart, Germany: Ernst Klett Sprachen.

Clark, A. D. (2013). Voices in the Appalachian classroom. In A. D. Clark & N. M. Hayward (Eds.), *Talking Appalachian: Voices, identity, and community* (pp. 110–124). Lexington, KY: University of Kentucky Press.

Common Core State Standards Initiative (CCSS). (2010). *Common Core State Standards for English language arts & literacy in history/social studies, science, and technical subjects.* Washington, DC: National Governors Association Center for Best Practices, Council of Chief State School Officers. Available online at: www.corestandards.org/wp-content/uploads/ELA_Standards1.pdf

Connors, R. J., & Lunsford, A. A. (1988). Frequency of formal errors in current college writing, or Ma and Pa Kettle do research. *College Composition and Communication, 39*(4), 395–409.

Craig, H. K., & Washington, J. A. (2006). *Malik goes to school: Examining the language skills of African American students from preschool–5th grade.* Mahwah, NJ: Lawrence Erlbaum Associates.

Crystal, D. (2008). *Txtng: The gr8 db8.* Oxford, UK: Oxford University Press.

Denne-Bolton, S. (2013). The dialogue journal: A tool for building better writers. *English Teaching Forum, 51*(2), 2–11.

DeStefano, J. S. (1972). Productive language differences in fifth grade black students' syntactic forms. *Elementary English, 49*(4), 552–558.

Drouin, M. A. (2011). College students' text messaging, use of textese and literacy skills. *Journal of Computer Assisted Learning, 27*(1), 67–75.

Dyson, A. H., & Smitherman, G. (2009). The right (write) start: African American language and the discourse of sounding right. *The Teachers College Record, 111*(4), 973–998.

Elbow, P. (2012). *Vernacular eloquence: What speech can bring to writing.* Oxford, UK: Oxford University Press.

Elley, W. B., Barham, I. H., Lamb, H., & Wyllie, M. (1976). The role of grammar in a secondary school English curriculum. *Research in the Teaching of English, 10*(1), 5–21.

Farr, M., & Daniels, H. (1986). *Language diversity and writing instruction.* New York, NY: ERIC Clearinghouse on Urban Education; Urbana, IL: ERIC Clearinghouse on Reading and Communication Skills.

Foroutan, M., Noordin, N., & bin Hamzah, M. S. G. (2013). Use of e-mail dialogue journal in enhancing writing performance. *Asian Social Science, 9*(7), 208.

Hairston, M. (1981). Not all errors are created equal: Nonacademic readers in the professions respond to lapses in usage. *College English, 43*(8), 794–806.

Harmon, M. R. (1994). Standardized tests for non-standard speakers/writers: State-wide writing assessment and dialects. *Language Arts Journal of Michigan, 10*(1), 19–22.

Irvine, P., & Elsasser, N. (1988). The ecology of literacy: Negotiating writing standards in a Caribbean setting. In B. Rafoth & D. Rubin (Eds.), *The social construction of written communication* (pp. 304–320). Norwood, NJ: Ablex.

Johnstone, B. (2002). *Discourse analysis.* Malden, MA: Blackwell.

Jordan, J. (1988). Nobody mean more to me than you and the future life of Willie Jordan. *Harvard Educational Review, 58*(3), 363–375.

Kemp, N. (2010). Texting versus txtng: Reading and writing text messages, and links with other linguistic skills. *Writing Systems Research, 2*(1), 53–71.

Kim, J. 2005. A community within the classroom: Dialogue journal writing of adult ESL learners. *Adult Basic Education, 15*(1), 21–32.

de Kleine, C. (2006). West African World English speakers in U.S. classrooms: The role of West African Pidgin English. In S. J. Nero (Ed.), *Dialects, Englishes, creoles, and education* (pp. 205–232). Mahwah, NJ: Lawrence Erlbaum.

Kligman, D., & Cronnell, B. (1974). *Black English and spelling.* Washington, DC: Office of Education.

McCaig, R. A. (1977). What research and evaluation tells us about teaching written expression in the elementary school. In C. Weaver & R. Douma (Eds.), *The language arts teacher in action* (pp. 46–56). Kalamazoo, MI: Western Michigan University Press.

Michaels, S. (1981). "Sharing time": Children's narrative styles and differential access to literacy. *Language in Society, 10*(3), 423–442.

Miller, J. (2007). Inscribing identity: Insights for teaching from ESL students' journals. *TESL Canada Journal, 25*(1), 23–40.

Mizokawa, D. T., & Hansen-Krening, N. (2000). The ABCs of attitudes towards reading: Inquiring about the reader's response. *Journal of Adolescent and Adult Literacy, 44*(1), 72–79.

Peyton, J. K. (Ed.). (1990). *Students and teachers writing together: Perspectives on journal writing*. Alexandria, VA: Teachers of English to Speakers of Other Languages.

Peyton, J. K., & Reed, L. (1990). *Dialogue journal writing with nonnative English speakers: A handbook for teachers*. Alexandria, VA: TESOL.

Plester, B., Wood, C., & Joshi, P. (2009). Exploring the relationship between children's knowledge of text message abbreviations and school literacy outcomes. *British Journal of Developmental Psychology, 27*(1), 145–161.

Putman, H., Hansen, M., Walsh, K., & Quintero, D. (2016). *High hopes and harsh realities: The real challenges to building a diverse workforce*. Washington, DC: Brookings Institution.

Rapp, B., Benzing, L., & Caramazza, A. (1997). The autonomy of lexical orthography. *Cognitive Neuropsychology, 14*(1), 71–104.

Rapp, B., Fischer-Baum, S., & Miozzo, M. (2015). Modality and morphology: What we write may not be what we say. *Physiological Science, 26*(6), 892–902.

Rosen, L. M. (1987). Developing correctness in student writing: Alternatives to the error-hunt. *The English Journal, 76*(3), 62–69.

Schatzman, L., & Strauss, A. (1955). Social class and modes of communication. *American Journal of Sociology, 60*(4), 329–338.

Smitherman, G. (1995). Students' right to their own language: A retrospective. *English Journal, 84*(1), 21–27.

Smitherman, G. (2000). *Black talk: Words and phrases from the hood to the amen corner* (revised edition). New York, NY: Houghton Mifflin.

Squires, L. (2010). Enregistering internet language. *Language in Society, 39*(4), 457–492.

Swan, M., & Smith, B. (Eds.). (2001). *Learner English. A teacher's guide to interference and other problems*. Cambridge, UK: Cambridge University Press.

Sweetland, J. (2006). *Teaching writing in the African American classroom: A sociolinguistic approach*. Unpublished doctoral dissertation, Stanford University.

Tagliamonte, S. A., & Denis, D. (2008). Linguistic ruin? LOL! Instant messaging and teen language. *American Speech, 83*(1), 3–34.

Tannen, D. (Ed.). (1993). *Framing in discourse*. New York, NY: Oxford University Press.

Thompson, C. A., Craig, H. K., & Washington, J. A. (2004). Variable production of African American English across oracy and literacy contexts. *Language, Speech, and Hearing Services in Schools, 35*(3), 269–282.

Villanueva, V., & Arola, K. L. (Eds.). (2011). *Cross-talk in comp theory: A reader* (3rd ed.). Urbana, IL: National Council of Teachers of English.

Wang, A. L., & Ruhl, D. M. (2011). Discovering students' real voice through computer-mediated dialogue journal writing. In R. Katarzyniak, T. F. Chiu, C. F. Hong, & N. T. Nguyen (Eds.), *Semantic methods for knowledge management and communication: Studies in computational intelligence, 38* (pp. 241–251). Berlin, Germany: Springer-Verlag.

Weaver, C. (1996). *Teaching grammar in context*. Portsmouth, NH: Boynton/Cook Publishers.

Young, V. A., Barrett, R., Young-Rivera, Y., & Lovejoy, K. B. (2013). *Other people's English: Code-meshing, code-switching, and African American literacy*. New York, NY: Teachers College Press.

Young, V. A., & Martinez, A. Y. (Eds.). (2011). *Code-meshing as world English: Pedagogy, policy, performance*. Urbana, IL: National Council of Teachers of English.

9

Language Variation and Reading

Scenario

Early grade teachers typically read aloud to their students from trade books that they know will engage the children. Often they choose books that include settings, characters, language, and values that students will recognize. Eloise Greenfield's *She Come Bringing Me that Little Baby Girl* (1974) tells the story of a boy who wanted his mother to bring home a brother from the hospital. It begins with:

> I asked Mama to bring me a little brother from the hospital, but she come bringing me that little baby girl wrapped all up in a pink blanket. Me and Aunt Mildred were looking out the window when Daddy brought them home.

Do you consider this kind of activity an important element of literacy instruction? In this context, consider the following:

- The role of prior knowledge or experience in reading comprehension
- The role of vernacular dialect in text
- The value of listening to text being read vs. the need for children to read text independently
- The importance of fostering a love of reading
- The connection between social class and literacy.

There is a strong correlation between families' socioeconomic status and children's literacy. Children from poor families on average perform more poorly on tests of reading in the early grades, and this pattern usually intensifies across the grades (Murnane, Sawhill, & Snow, 2012). We infer that the likelihood of reading problems is increased if a person is a member of a vernacular English-speaking population because vernacular speakers tend to cluster in the lower socioeconomic classes. NAEP results for 2015 confirm this assumption; for both grades 4 and 8, African American and Hispanic students' reading scores continue to lag behind those for white students (National Center for Educational Statistics, n.d.). Despite this correlation, it should not be concluded that speaking a vernacular dialect causes reading failure. Following her thorough survey of the academic literature, Sweetland concludes,

> It is becoming increasingly clear that dialect difference does not cause educational difficulty in and of itself—dozens of studies have looked for linguistic barriers, especially in the reading process, and have failed to find convincing evidence of a direct relationship (Schwartz, 1982). On the other hand, there is ample evidence of an *indirect* relationship between dialect and academic failure—and it is one mediated through the teacher.
>
> *2006, p. 71*

There are many successful readers who come from vernacular English-speaking backgrounds. Speaking a vernacular variety does not inevitably lead to reading failure, and speaking a standard variety does not guarantee reading success.

The relationship between spoken dialect and the acquisition of reading skills has been explored from a number of perspectives. For many years, it was assumed that a mismatch between features of spoken dialect and print representations of language led to difficulty in learning to read (the "linguistic interference" hypothesis). As will be discussed below, all children face a mismatch between spoken and written language, but vernacular dialect speakers may find the interference to be greater.

More recently, research has indicated that African American children who have a higher familiarity with Standard English and who are more adept at code-switching performed better on tests of reading achievement (Charity, Scarborough, & Griffin, 2004; Craig, Zhang, Hensel, & Quinn, 2009). This has led to another hypothesis, the "linguistic awareness/flexibility hypothesis," which posits that differences in metalinguistic knowledge contribute to degree of success in learning to read, including phonological awareness, a key component in reading (Mitri & Terry, 2013). According to this line of thinking, students who use vernacular features in contexts where a standard language variety would be expected (as in a test) may not have developed the metalinguistic awareness to be sensitive to these patterns of language variation. This lack of sensitivity and metalinguistic awareness contribute to reading difficulty for students who use vernacular features in a way that is less direct than the relationship suggested by the linguistic interference hypothesis (Terry, 2014). It suggests that, since learning to read involves metalinguistic awareness about relating sounds to print, students with less developed metalinguistic skills may have difficulty in early reading. Another hypothesis that has been suggested is "teacher bias," which proposes that negative views of vernacular speech held by teachers lead them to interact with students who use those varieties differently, in ways that may affect their reading achievement (Terry, 2012).

It is likely that the underlying factors represented by these hypotheses are all in play to some extent in explaining reading difficulty for speakers of vernacular dialects. Because the correlation between social class and reading achievement has been so durable, it is important to consider how dialect differences may relate to the reading process and how reading specialists, literacy mentors, teachers, and other practitioners can take the differences into account, since, as Sweetland notes, the relationship between dialect and academic failure, including reading, can be influenced by educators. This chapter addresses questions about what teachers need to know and do in order to help vernacular dialect speakers develop reading proficiency.

Written Language and Spoken Language

Learning to read involves learning skills beyond the oral language skills that young children acquire unconsciously. At the same time, however, readers automatically apply their general linguistic skills to the task of reading. To get meaning from the printed page, readers must be able to recognize the words they see there and employ their tacit understandings of grammar and semantics. Reading involves interpreting the grammatical relationships among the words on the page and figuring out the meanings of sentences and longer stretches of text, drawing on both implicit linguistic knowledge and general background knowledge. Theorists, however, have disagreed about just how linguistic knowledge and oral language skills are applied in the reading process. There is disagreement about the role that relating print to sound plays in the process of reading, although it is clear that it does play some role.

Because the language of most reading materials is closer to Standard English than to other varieties, we might predict that it would be easier for a Standard English speaker to learn how to read these materials. However, the language of the printed text is not as similar to the spoken language of Standard English speakers or as different from the spoken language of vernacular English speakers as is sometimes assumed. There are differences between written and spoken English that transcend dialect. One obvious difference is that spoken language lacks punctuation, and so all readers must learn how to interpret the various punctuation marks. Then, too, grammatical structures in written texts differ from spoken language: Certain constructions used in early reading materials are unlikely to be used in natural conversation. For example, adverb phrases are sometimes placed at the beginning of the sentence in books for young children, both basal readers and trade books, as in this sentence from *The Hungry Giant of the Tundra*: "On the other side of the river stood a crane dancing on her long legs" (Sloat, 1993, p. 18). Similarly, primers sometimes show peculiar patterns such as the repetition of noun phrases in "The boy has a boat. The boy likes the boat. The boat is red." This construction is quite unlike spoken discourse, where pronouns and other anaphoric devices are used for successive references (e.g., "The boy has a boat that he likes. It's red."). Regardless of their spoken dialect, then, everyone learning to read English encounters language structures that differ from the structures of speech.

It is still true though that the language of reading materials may differ more for the speaker of a vernacular variety than for the speaker of a standard variety (following the "linguistic interference" hypothesis mentioned earlier). The vernacular speaker will find that written language consistently uses certain structures that are less common in vernacular dialects. For example, beginning reading materials use standard negation ("He didn't hit anything") rather than multiple negation ("He didn't hit nothing"), which is frequent in spoken vernacular dialects. Thus, there is a contrast between spoken and written language for all readers, but the contrast is greater for the speaker of a vernacular dialect.

What Do Teachers Need to Know about Dialects to Teach Reading?

The Common Core State Standards have embraced a "Reading and Writing across the Curriculum" approach in which all teachers, regardless of content area, are expected to facilitate the literacy development of all students:

> The Standards insist that instruction in reading, writing, speaking, listening, and language be a shared responsibility within the school ... This division reflects the unique, time-honored place of ELA [English Language Arts] teachers in developing students' literacy skills while at the same time recognizing that teachers in other areas must have a role in this development as well.
>
> *CCSS, 2010, p. 4*

While English language arts teachers are expected to assume a leadership role in teaching reading, all teachers need research-based information about reading in order to serve their students well.

What particular knowledge about dialect differences will help a teacher work effectively to promote literacy learning with students from a spectrum of regional, ethnic, and social class communities? Researchers who have looked at language variation and reading have suggested, either explicitly or implicitly, several types of information. First, general knowledge about the nature of language diversity is required. Without understanding the systematic and patterned nature of differences, it is difficult to appreciate dialects for what they are—natural subgroupings within a language. Second, knowledge about the physiology of reading (factors such as eye movement and how the eyes perceive what is on the page) helps teachers make better sense of dialect influence and reading mistakes. A third requirement is insight into how cultural differences in background knowledge can affect reading comprehension.

The Nature of Language Diversity

Teachers' knowledge about particular structures in the dialects that their students speak is as necessary for teaching reading as it is for teaching writing. This kind of information helps teachers understand why certain forms occur, where they occur, and how they should be viewed in the context of teaching and assessing reading skills. For example, understanding a student's oral reading performance might require knowing about the vernacular pronunciation rule that explains why a speaker would pronounce *sell* and *sale* the same (the absence of contrast between DRESS and FACE vowels before *l*) and the grammatical rule that explains why *done* may be used as a simple past-tense form (as in "She done a good job"). Consider the following example of oral reading by a child who speaks a vernacular variety of English:

Text: Ruth's brother missed a game, and the coach doesn't like it.
Oral reading: Ruf brovuh miss' a game, and da coach don' like it.

Several items are noticeable in the oral rendition of the passage: the pronunciations of *Ruth* and *brother*, the absence of the possessive -*s*, the absence of the -*ed*, and the form "don'" for *doesn't*. All of these contrasts are perfectly predictable in terms of the reader's spoken dialect. Thus, this rendition could actually signal appropriate decoding and accurate comprehension because none of the differences changes the meaning of the text. It is important for reading teachers to know how dialect differences might be manifested in oral reading so that they can anticipate dialect-related miscues that do not affect comprehension. The term "miscue" contrasts with "error" to signal that these departures from the written text in oral reading are not random. Rather, they reveal strategies that readers use to process text.

Mismatches between written Standard English and vernacular dialects can occur at all linguistic levels. But not all differences have the same impact on reading. For example, while teachers would likely notice phonological or grammar influences, a cultural difference might go unnoticed during the reading process. Such cultural differences might only become apparent by checking reading comprehension. As a result, the phonological influence might be more salient to the teacher, but the cultural difference might result in difficulty on reading comprehension tests.

The Role of Physiology

All readers make mistakes in word identification; good readers do it in predictable ways. Miscue patterns include substituting one word for another when it does not violate syntactic patterns (e.g., "Jack" instead of "Teddy" or "She said sweetly" instead of "She said softly"); transposing words, especially when they occur in formulaic usages (e.g., "Annie said" vs. "said Annie"); or substituting morphologically equivalent forms (e.g., "funner" for "more fun"). Given the predictable dialect influence just discussed, it is reasonable to assume that vernacular speakers might produce these and other types of miscues when encountering texts written in the standard variety, like the omission or leveling of helping verbs (e.g., "She __ going" or "We is having fun"). Although miscues are common, dialect-related miscues can baffle teachers and language practitioners who are less familiar with vernacular features. Miscues are explained partly by the fact that during the reading process of semi-fluent and fluent readers, the eyes do not actually come to rest on each word, nor do they progress smoothly from left to right in a typing sort of motion. Understanding a little about how the eyes work throughout the reading process can help teachers better interpret reading miscues and dialect influence in reading.

Assuming newspaper print size, most people can see with 100% acuity about five printed letters at normal reading distances (see, e.g., Rayner, Slattery, & Bélanger, 2010) through the part of the eye with the sharpest vision, or *fovea centralis*. Letters outside the focal point are visible, but they are perceived with increasing blurriness toward the periphery of the eye. Most people can perceive with enough clarity anywhere from 6 to 20 characters of normal text at any one time.

A second critical aspect of reading physiology is eye movement during reading. It is commonly assumed that the eyes move continuously and smoothly, like a laser beam cutting through metal. In reality, the fovea centralis jumps around the page through a series of saccades, meaning that the eyes do not fixate or fixate equally on all parts of a text. It is only in the brief moments where the eyes are fixated—that is, still—that they can transfer information to the brain. Generally, emergent readers have more and longer fixations per unit of text than proficient or fluent readers (see, e.g., Rayner, Foorman, Perfetti, Pesetsky, & Seidenberg, 2001). Emergent readers might fixate every five to seven characters, while proficient readers might have saccades of more than 20 characters. Thus, emergent readers literally have a larger percentage of the text perceived by the brain than fluent readers. Because of that, they are less likely to make the sort of reading mistakes described above. The irony is that more proficient readers are more likely to make these mistakes—which encompass both general miscues and dialect influence—than emergent readers because as the brain "sees" less of the text, it relies on its linguistic knowledge to fill in the gaps between the eyes' fixations. Readers who did not struggle with unmarked past tense or copula absence while learning to read might start to produce these dialect features as they become more proficient, which teachers may interpret as a decline in reading competence or even a lack of effort or focus. In fact, such miscues can actually be a sign of improving reading proficiency.

Some Effects of Misunderstanding Reading Miscues

If teachers are not well versed in the physiology of reading and the specifics of how vernacular dialect-speaking children interpret sound/print correspondences in different ways than Standard English speakers do, they may conclude that a decoding problem exists and place students in low reading groups. Once they are placed in low reading groups, children may fall even farther behind because the nature of the reading experience in those groups may actually make it more difficult for students to continue to learn to read. Children in low reading groups are more likely to receive phonics skills instruction exclusively, rather than the phonics and comprehension strategy instruction that higher groups receive, and to be corrected for "errors" that are attributable to dialect influence instead of decoding or comprehension difficulty (Collins, 1988). Interrupting reading to target a dialect pronunciation works against the development of reading fluency, a critical dimension of skilled reading that underlies comprehension.

Furthermore, the teacher may be more likely to be distracted by other activities in the classroom when working with the low-achieving group, including controlling behavior not related to the reading process. Because other students recognize the low social status of poor readers, they may feel free to interrupt (Borko & Eisenhart, 1989). As a result, children in the lower reading groups may experience reading as fragmented and boring, and progress at a slower rate than children for whom reading is more interesting. These students are often assumed to have less experience with print outside of school; and as a member of a low reading group, they may have less rich experiences with print inside school as well (Charity, Scarborough, & Griffin, 2004). In this unproductive pattern, vernacular dialect speakers may find themselves repeating skills lessons and basal readers, falling further and further behind other students. Eventually they may be diagnosed as learning disabled.

Knowledge about dialect differences, then, should inform instruction as well as assessment in reading for those who do not speak standard varieties of English. In fact, this conclusion has been supported by the judicial system. In a landmark court decision in Ann Arbor, MI, in 1979 that still resonates today, the presiding judge ruled that a school district was at fault for not taking the dialect of students from vernacular-speaking backgrounds into account in teaching reading. As part of the ruling, the district was required to implement a program that would educate reading teachers about dialect difference and to devise a reading program that would incorporate information about spoken language varieties into effective reading instruction for students from certain communities (Smitherman, 2000). This judicial decision underscores the importance of understanding dialect differences for those who teach reading.

Another kind of contrast playing a central role in reading and reading instruction has to do with cultural traditions for language use and literacy, as well as the cultural dimensions of literature that were exemplified in the opening scenario. This contrast, the focus of the next section, is alluded to throughout this chapter.

Language and Culture

Information about children's cultural backgrounds is indispensable in teaching reading, as it is in teaching writing, especially when there is a cultural or social class difference between the teacher and the students. Cultural and linguistic differences are closely intertwined in distinguishing vernacular and mainstream communities.

Differences among cultural groups in early language routines may impact how children respond to texts once they begin reading. Many classroom literacy activities build on literacy skills that children are assumed to have acquired at home (see Chapter 8). Middle-class children typically have a variety of experiences with reading and writing before they come to school, such as having books read aloud to them daily. However, in some communities, storytelling is more common than reading aloud. As a result of different experiences with narrative forms, children may have different ideas about the structure of narratives that can affect their literacy development at school.

In the early school years, an important literacy-related activity is "sharing time" (or "show and tell"). In this speech event, students gain experience in producing cohesive narratives, considering the audience, and using other skills that figure in literacy development. But students may not all profit equally from this experience. In a well-known study of sharing time in urban elementary school classrooms, researchers found that children's storytelling styles affected their success in the sharing time activity and their chance to gain literacy-related skills from it (Michaels, 1981). Specifically, European American, middle-class teachers expected a linear narrative style like that used in books where events are linked sequentially. The presentation style of European American children generally matched this expectation much more closely than that of working-class African American children. As a result, the European American students received helpful feedback for refining their narrative style, but the African American children often experienced frustration. Their stories were likely to include several episodes rather than one, with shifting scenes, and they used more narrative markers, such as "and then" (meaning *also*), to link the episodes. European American teachers treated these episodic narratives as poorly formed and attempted to guide the students toward the literate discourse model by telling them to talk about "just one thing" (topic-centered discourse). Such judgments illustrate the general problem of viewing some culturally-based practices as deficient rather than different.

Community traditions of literacy may extend to the definition of reading. Purcell-Gates (1995) told the story of one urban Appalachian family in which the parents' lack of literacy skills resulted in their children having different experiences with reading than their schools anticipated. In this family, reading books involved inventing stories to match the pictures. As a result, the children did not understand the cuing function of print. Early reading instruction that assumed this knowledge did not meet these children's needs. Understanding the role that reading and writing play or do not play in students' homes and communities can help a teacher make reading experiences more congruent with students' experiences and thus more meaningful and successful.

Another area of contrast between student experience and teacher expectations pertains to the background knowledge that students bring to reading comprehension. Researchers investigating this connection asked urban African American children and rural white children to read a passage about a sounding episode—an African American speech event involving ritual insults (Reynolds, Taylor, Steffensen, Shirey, & Anderson, 1982). Clearly, the reading was culturally biased in favor of the African American readers: As anticipated, this group scored considerably higher in comprehension than the rural students—an outcome that suggests that some reading problems may relate to differences in background knowledge. As the researchers discussed the experiment with the African American readers, they explained that some of the rural students might not understand the story. An African American student exclaimed, "What's the matter? Can't they read?"

In a classic ethnographic comparison of communicative styles in the classroom and in the Warm Springs Indian reservation community, Sue Philips (1983/1993) identified a number of kinds of cultural conflict between classroom and community norms that alienate students and affect learning. For example, a common pedagogy that teachers employ to build reading competence is learning through public mistakes. Philips showed that this pedagogy resulted in Warm Springs Indian children developing a reluctance to read aloud as well as resisting reading in general. Studies of other American Indian groups have shown that enculturated tribal reading and literacy norms are at odds with the norms expected in schools (e.g., Cazden & John, 1971; Wax, Wax, & Dumont, 1964; Wolcott, 1967).

Children's background experience with language and literacy remains a crucial variable in educational success, but one that may not be adequately explored in teacher education (Fillmore & Snow, 2002). Teachers encounter a wide range of language and cultural differences among their students in early childhood and primary classrooms. When they share cultural identity with their students, teachers are more likely to perceive students' language use as appropriate and to know how to support development of the academic language skills that count for success at school and in other mainstream institutions. When they and their students are ethnically different, it becomes crucial for teachers to investigate the possibility that their students' classroom performance is rooted in community practice. Investigation, including teacher and student research as outlined in Chapters 2 and 3, can help educators ascertain whether students' performance that does not meet school expectations is due to cultural norms with which they are unfamiliar, or whether there might be other factors at work.

One approach to bridging cultural differences between teachers and students involves teachers actively interacting with families outside the school. Some teachers whose cultural backgrounds are different from their students' have been getting first-hand experience with the "funds of knowledge" in their students' homes and communities to improve their understanding of the background knowledge that students bring to reading and other school tasks (Gonzalez, et al., 1993; Moll, Amanti, Neff, & Gonzalez, 2005). Investigating funds of knowledge involves teacher-researchers visiting their students' homes to talk with parents and other family members. Their goal is to become acquainted with the knowledge and skill areas that families control and the social networks in which they participate. Teachers engaged in this research meet in study groups to compare findings from their visits and reflect together on the match between students' background knowledge and classroom practices.

In sum, teachers of reading need general knowledge about linguistic and cultural differences among the students they teach and detailed knowledge about their students' dialects and culturally-based literacy practices. Beyond that, they should be aware of the status of each student's emergent literacy. To this end, school districts need to provide continuing professional development about the role of language and culture in students' school performance.

Teaching Children to Relate Sound to Print

Teaching beginning readers to relate written language to the sounds of oral language may be more complicated because of dialect variation. But the implications of dialect differences vary somewhat for different instructional approaches as demonstrated below.

There are two general approaches to teaching children the relationship between the sounds of oral English and the alphabetic symbols on the printed page: an approach centered on explicit and systematic phonics instruction and an approach centered on meaning. Phonics instruction focuses students' attention on the relationship of print to sounds, with the intent of helping them learn to decode the combinations of printed letters and blend the sounds to make words (e.g., as seen in the materials for Open Court Reading). It uses children's phonemic awareness as a foundation (Adams, 1990; Chall, 1996). Contrasting instructional approaches include meaning-based reading (whole language) and learning sight words (Routman, 1991). These approaches integrate phonics instruction into meaning-based activities or address the sound/print connection after children have learned sight words (Weaver, 1994). Sight word instruction emphasizes understanding words both individually and in the context of the sentence.

The Common Core State Standards embrace a blended approach to foundational skills for reading. Beginning in kindergarten, for example, children are expected to read high-frequency words (e.g., *the, of, to, you, she, my*) "by sight" and decode other words by using "basic knowledge of one-to-one letter-sound correspondences" (CCSS, 2010, p. 15). We return to the matter of instructional approaches after a look at the effects of dialect on oral reading.

Effects of Dialect Differences on Reading Aloud

When students deviate from what the teacher expects while reading aloud, it may be thought to signal a failure to decode and comprehend what was read. But since dialects may play a role in such deviations, it is important to draw a distinction between dialect influence and dialect interference. *Dialect influence* refers to an oral rendition of text that differs from the written form in line with vernacular features but has no consequence for understanding; *dialect interference* refers to renditions in which dialect contrast may affect comprehension of the passage. For example, in dialects with identical pronunciations for different words (e.g., *find* and *fine*; *Mary, merry, marry*), not differentiating the words has the potential to interfere with meaning in oral reading, but in most cases the reader does not misinterpret the meaning, so the effect is limited to an *influence* on oral reading (i.e., pronunciation).

Dialect differences in grammatical forms also have the potential for influence or interference. In oral reading, producing the text *five cents* as "five cent" shows dialect influence, but probably not interference: It is unlikely that the basic meaning of the text would have been lost by the omission of the final *-s*. However, some deviations from the text are actual reading errors because they do not preserve the author's meaning. If a student sees *He's done trying to please everyone* and reads it as "He done tried to please everyone," the meaning of the text is not preserved, and it is likely that the student has misunderstood. In the written sentence, the verb indicates present completed action. The text might be interpreted as "He's done trying to please everyone for the time being." But in the substituted sentence, the reader seems to have comprehended a completed past action (roughly equal to "He completely tried to please everyone").

When a student substitutes a vernacular structure in oral reading, it is not always possible to distinguish dialect influence from true interference. For a study conducted by William Labov and his colleagues at the University of Pennsylvania, researchers developed a process for estimating whether a vernacular substitution is a reading error or simply a case of dialect influence (Labov & Baker, 2010). The method involves observing what follows the substitution. If the reader has made a reading error, then what follows may be in error too. But if a substitution is only a case of dialect influence, what follows is likely to be consistent with the text. For example, a third grader read *I played it cool and took a sip of my coke* as "I play it cool and took a sip of my coke" (Labov & Baker, 2010, p. 739). It appears that the reader deleted the final sound of *played* (and thus the past-tense marker *-ed*), but understood it as a past-tense verb: The next verb in the sentence, *took,* was not altered. Understanding the past tense of *played* seems to have contributed in some way to reading *took* correctly.

Labov and Baker (2010) found that certain dialect substitutions were more likely than others to be errors (i.e., interference, not just dialect influence). This varied according to the reader's ethnolinguistic group. For example, deletion of the plural marker by African American English speakers was unlikely to be a reading error, but deletion of this feature by Latino vernacular dialect speakers was likely to be an error. But comparison between group speech patterns and reading substitutions revealed uneven patterns. For example, the more a group deleted the agreement marker on a verb in speech (e.g., "Kevin usually go to work early"), the more likely that its deletion in reading would not constitute an error. But the more a group deleted the possessive marker (e.g., "Kevin cat is missing"), the more likely that its deletion in reading *would* constitute an error. Thus, how vernacular dialects affect oral reading is quite complex and still not fully understood.

One goal of this research program, which became the basis for the Penn Reading Initiative, was to find ways to improve the decoding skills of speakers of vernacular dialects (see www.ling.upenn.edu/pri/). Among the recommendations offered is that teachers of struggling readers who are vernacular dialect speakers should provide direct instruction on certain grammatical features that strongly correlate with reading errors: the possessive marker ("Kevin's cat"), the copula ("Kevin's late today"), and irregular past-tense verbs.

Comprehension Strategies

Teachers are well aware of the need to actively teach new vocabulary to enhance students' facility with text. They also employ various strategies to help students comprehend as they read, strategies that mimic aspects of comprehension or function as aids to comprehension. For example, teachers may describe their own practices in comprehending a piece of text by reading and "thinking aloud" about their inferential processes, and they may ask students to do the same, to strengthen the understanding that reading involves thought, prediction, speculation, and rereading (see the collection of essays in Plaut, 2009, for examples of this method from researchers and practitioners across the disciplines). In thinking aloud about a piece of text, teachers of vernacular speakers could mention predictable dialect influence on the reading process. For example, teachers might analyze the sentence considered earlier, *He's done trying to please everyone*, anticipating possible dialect interference and referring to context to resolve ambiguity. This sort of demonstration has the effect of demystifying the reading process for children who may have had less exposure to reading or different experiences with it before coming to school.

Strategies to support reading comprehension often call for students to write or talk about their understanding of a text. If in doing so they use vernacular features, "correcting" these features could well confuse them. The point of activities such as summarizing and mapping out story elements is understanding the text, not producing Standard English.

Dialects and Meaning-Based Reading Instruction

Meaning-based literacy instruction, including the whole language approach, typically integrates reading with writing and speaking, uses trade books, and embeds phonics instruction in these activities. In this approach to teaching reading, the teacher's role is to facilitate students' experiences with literacy by providing materials and opportunities for rich, authentic encounters with written and spoken language. Some have expressed a concern about de-emphasizing explicit and systematic phonics instruction, feeling that this may lead to a haphazard approach to reading skills (Adams, 1990; Clay, 2013). Delpit (1988) observes that because middle-class children are more likely to have acquired literacy skills outside school, instruction that de-emphasizes phonics puts those who need to learn sound/print skills, including vernacular speakers, at a disadvantage.

Whether instruction addresses phonics systematically (as in the phonics approach) or incidentally (as in the whole-language approach), dialect differences are likely to influence learning sound/symbol relationships unless the teacher's dialect matches that of every student in the class. Dialect pronunciation may not be as problematic with the sight word approach to early reading (also called *look–say*), in which children begin to read by learning to recognize 50 to 100 words and then learn details flowing from the alphabetic principle—that print relates to sound. Sight word instruction emphasizes understanding the words both individually and in the context of the sentence. But it is important for teachers using this approach to be aware of dialect-specific pronunciations that differ from Standard English. For instance, when the printed word is *then* and the student pronounces it like "den" or "din," or when the student who speaks African American English pronounces *stream* as "skream," it should not be assumed that the word has been misidentified.

Teaching Children to Comprehend Text

Comprehension, of course, is the point of reading. For expert readers, comprehension usually occurs fairly effortlessly as long as the text is clearly written, and the reader knows the vocabulary and is somewhat familiar with the topic. Adult readers may not realize that comprehension is a skill that beginning readers need to learn. But comprehension stitches together many aspects of reading, including accuracy, fluency, and contextualization. In teaching comprehension, it is critical to be sensitive to the potential influence of language differences.

Vocabulary

Deriving meaning from text is a cognitive process: The reader processes chunks of text thoughtfully using knowledge of language and the world, and constructs some meaning for them. The meaning of words plays an essential role in constructing the meaning of texts. But in this domain, dialect differences may interfere with the automatic comprehension of text that practiced readers take for granted. Encountering words that are unexpected, including those that result from dialect vocabulary differences, interrupts the fluent flow of reading. For example, readers outside of Louisiana may not be familiar with the term *lagniappe* (meaning *small gift*), or those outside of the Southwest might not be familiar with the term *arroyo* for a type of gully. Authors sometimes help with definitions and translations. The popular *Clovis Crawfish* series for early elementary school children includes some Cajun English and many Cajun French idioms and phrases as a means of honoring the region's culture. The books often provide translations in the text. For example, in one story, Clovis saves his butterfly friend's baby. When Clovis asks the butterfly what the baby's name will be, she responds "His name is *Petit Papillon*," and the story goes on to say "which is the way to say 'little butterfly' in south Louisiana" (Fontenot, 2009, unpaginated). Recognizing the language differences between Cajun French, Cajun English, and Standard English, the series also includes a pronunciation and translation guide. Teachers need to be knowledgeable about students' dialects and watchful for potential vocabulary mismatches that cause readers— especially young readers who may not recognize such variants—to stumble.

But sometimes vocabulary differences are more subtle than these examples where the denotation of a word is unfamiliar. Language variation can have an impact on connotative differences (as in the difference between the terms *childlike* and *childish*). Many figurative uses of language employ less familiar connotations, which can cause comprehension difficulties, especially for non-native English speakers. Consider the following passage from the popular middle grades book *Where the Lilies Bloom*, which is set in the South: "Don't pay her any mind. She's cloudy-headed. Why did you say you had been to Sugar Boy and Old Joshua [two hills] for the memory? That wasn't a real answer, was it?" (Cleaver, 1969, p. 2). Phrases like "pay her any mind" and "cloudy-headed" may be less familiar to non-Southerners than to Southerners, but the figurative meanings are generally transparent enough for readers to work through. More regionally specific phrases, like "a real answer" meaning "a true answer" might be too opaque for non-Southern students to understand without help.

These types of difficulties might exist with unfamiliar dialects at any level of reading. The Appalachian picture book *Fearless Jack* includes the simile, "Jack puffed up like a banty rooster," which includes a dialect pronunciation of (the possibly unfamiliar word) *bantam* (Johnson, 2001, p. 4). Later, the phrase "You still drawing air, son?" is used to mean "Are you still catching your breath?" (Johnson, 2001, p. 6). Further, the use by a stranger of the term of address "son" may be interpreted by speakers of other dialects more negatively than it is intended. Teachers might want to preteach dialect-contrasting terms in advance of reading a text and ensure that children see and hear them often enough to understand different connotations, while being careful not to imply that the new variant is correct and the familiar one incorrect.

Background Knowledge and Comprehension

Texts that assume background knowledge more strongly associated with mainstream culture can make reading comprehension problematic for readers from other backgrounds. For example, urban students having little direct experience with mountain biking or mowing lawns might find passages that presume knowledge about these topics somewhat difficult, just as students living in tropical climates might have trouble understanding narratives involving blizzard conditions. As mentioned in Chapter 6, a passage in a New York State practice examination about tennis stars Venus and Serena Williams assumes readers understand how private tennis clubs operate, a setting that would be quite foreign to many students. Consider an example that demonstrates how students who grew up in an urban area may struggle to understand a text due to a lack of background knowledge. The illustrated novel *Trampoline* (Gipe, 2015) is about the effects of strip-mining on a town in the Appalachian Mountains. Along with local vocabulary that may be unfamiliar to English speakers from other regions, the book requires some familiarity with mineral rights, land contracts, and a number of rural customs.

Teachers can accommodate students' background knowledge in a number of ways when they recognize what their students' funds of knowledge consist of. There are excellent trade books from which teachers may select readings that closely match students' cultural background, such as the book mentioned in the opening of this chapter. Including work by authors who share the students' cultural background and who incorporate vernacular dialect in their writing can entice children who might otherwise experience literacy as focusing exclusively on other people's cultures and other people's language.

Teachers can also select instructional strategies to build the background knowledge that students need to comprehend text. Thematic approaches to reading can build up an informational store so that children have the resources they need to become interested in a text and to write and talk about the content of texts that may be distant from their experience. Prereading experiences for students of any age can help them activate and build relevant knowledge. After reading, students may engage in response-to-literature tasks that lead them into the text again from a different perspective. For example, they may rewrite a part of the story or enact a sequel to it.

Reciprocal teaching (Palincsar & Brown, 1987; Pilonieta & Medina, 2009), a strategy that groups children with diverse abilities and achievement levels for reading and writing tasks, is often mentioned as being particularly appropriate for children whose language and cultural backgrounds may be different from their teachers'. Teachers work with the groups, helping children talk and write about what they have read and how they understood the text. This process engages students in talk about literacy and literature in order to scaffold reading development. It invites vernacular dialect-speakers to use their oral language abilities in literacy activities.

Expert teachers have a repertoire of instructional strategies that is continually refreshed through professional development experiences. When teachers understand and value students' language abilities and previous literacy learning, and when they acknowledge and accommodate low literacy levels appropriately, they are able to continually adapt reading instruction to their students' needs. In their classrooms, students engage with text in ways that build reading abilities throughout the school years.

Reading Materials and Dialect Differences

One of the issues that has been raised by linguists and educators alike with respect to dialects is the nature of the reading materials used in schools in teaching children to read. Are the same reading materials appropriate for students from middle-class, Standard English-speaking communities and for vernacular-speaking students from non-middle-class communities? In light of the fact that the language of texts is closer to Standard English than it is to any vernacular dialect, should adjustments be made so that reading materials are more accessible for vernacular speakers?

Two basic positions have been taken regarding the language of reading materials that are written especially for beginning readers (texts with controlled vocabulary and sentence structure). Some researchers have advocated changing the language in the text because it is a poor match for speakers of vernacular dialects; others maintain that texts written in Standard English can be used for everyone because speakers of other dialects can accommodate to them. Both positions acknowledge a concern about the mismatch between those students' oral language and the language of reading materials, but the strategies for addressing this issue differ. The alternatives also seem to be based on different assumptions about the significance of the mismatch.

Matching Materials and Dialects

Those who advocate changing the materials focus on reducing the mismatch between reader and materials by making the language of the materials more closely resemble the student's language. This change can be accomplished in several ways. One strategy is to remove (or avoid) constructions that are points of dialect difference. For example, in standard varieties, an indirect question can be formed as "He asked if he could go"; other dialects might use "He asked could he go." In striving for more dialect-neutral materials, this structure would be avoided, and a structure common to all dialects of English could be used instead (in this case, a direct question such as "He asked 'Can I go?'"). Such grammatical changes in the texts are intended to make the materials as neutral as possible with respect to dialect differences.

Dialect Readers

Another text modification approach advocated involves incorporating vernacular English constructions. Thus, using the indirect question example just mentioned, the text would use the vernacular form "He asked could he go" instead of "He asked if he could go." Similarly, multiple negatives (e.g., "He didn't do nothing"), vernacular subject–verb agreement patterns (e.g., "We was here"), and alternative tense markings (e.g., "In those days, we went to the fiesta and we have a good time") would be used in texts designed for communities where these patterns are the norm. Such texts would be used to build early literacy skills using the oral language skills of vernacular speakers. They would not be intended to replace other reading materials.

In the dialect reader approach illustrated below, the African American English passage in Version 2, taken from an early experiment with dialect readers, represents a deliberate attempt to incorporate grammatical and vocabulary features of this dialect. Changes in spelling to capture pronunciation contrasts are generally considered nonessential.

Version 1: *Standard English*

> "Look down here," said Suzy.
> "I can see a girl in here.
> The girl looks like me.
> Come here and look, David.
> Can you see that girl?"

Version 2: *African American Vernacular English*

> Susan say, "Hey you-all, look down here!
> I can see a girl in here.

The girl, she look like me.
Come here and look, David!
Could you see the girl?"

Wolfram & Fasold, 1969, pp.147–148

The use of dialect readers is intended to be transitional. Once decoding skills are well established, the learner begins a transition to reading Standard English, using texts that gradually eliminate vernacular constructions and eventually conform to the patterns of Standard English. The original intent was that dialect readers would be written for a variety of vernacular English dialects, but the only materials ever prepared are in African American English.

The use of dialect readers has always met with mixed reactions. Many people, including educators and community leaders, view anything written in a dialect other than Standard English as educationally unsound and socially offensive (McWhorter, 1997). They consider dialect readers patronizing and unnecessary educational accommodations (Labov, 1995). But a small group of people have enthusiastically advocated their use.

Some research was conducted on the effectiveness of dialect readers as compared to traditional reading materials. *Bridge: A Cross-Culture Reading Program* (Simpkins, Holt, & Simpkins, 1977) was field-tested with secondary students receiving remedial reading instruction. Gains made by these students on the Iowa Test of Basic Skills exceeded those of students who used the regular reading materials (6.2 months of gain for a 4-month period for students using the *Bridge* program vs. 1.2 months of gain for those using the regular reading materials). Separating out the influence of the text's being written in vernacular dialect from factors such as students' increased interest in text themes is a difficult task, and even the authors of the *Bridge* program speculate that the latter might account for a substantial part of the students' improvement (Simpkins & Simpkins, 1981). Nonetheless, research on the effectiveness of dialect readers has been limited due to widespread negative reactions.

Later on, linguist John Rickford and educational researcher Angela Rickford contended that it was a mistake to discard dialect readers prematurely and that experimental research on their effectiveness should be resumed (Rickford & Rickford, 1995). Accordingly, they conducted three small-scale studies investigating the *Bridge* curriculum. Older students preferred the bidialectal readers more than younger students did, and boys preferred them more than girls did, but no impact on reading achievement was found. They recommended experimenting with new ways of introducing and using dialect readers that would allay doubts about them. But parents and other community members would need to be convinced that dialect readers represent a scaffolded approach to reading Standard English, and that teachers share with parents the goal of supporting children's Standard English development. This argument has so far been hard to make.

Language Experience

Dialect readers attempt to be true to the general language patterns of a particular group of speakers. In the language experience approach, teachers record what a student says, and those texts are used as reading materials (Dorr, 2006; Hall, 1976; Stauffer, 1970). Thus, the texts reflect the language patterns of an individual speaker. The rationale for this approach is that the greatest asset of beginning readers is their ability to use and understand language. In using a language experience approach with vernacular dialect speakers, transcribing can become problematic. If teachers edit students' stories into Standard English, the written version is not a fully accurate rendition of what the child said. In translating the children's stories into what the teacher considers proper English or school language, she or he communicates an attitude about the worth of the children's language. The message for students is that their language is wrong or inadequate. Teachers who are knowledgeable about dialect differences may decide to write down what students say and use this text as one source for reading instruction. The language of the written text is closer to the child's own language experience than that found in either basal reading texts or reading materials written for vernacular dialect speakers. Moreover, the content reflects familiar contexts and activities. New technologies allow teachers and students to incorporate images, videos, and audio files into their personalized literacy environment (Labbo, Eakle, Jonathan, & Montero, 2002). This approach has been found to benefit a wide range of students, including English language learners (Parrish, 2004).

Despite the differences between them, dialect readers and student-created texts that incorporate dialect differences may be lumped together if people react negatively to the use of nonstandard linguistic patterns in print.

Vernacular Dialect for Rhetorical Purpose

People seem willing to suspend their objections to printed vernacular dialect in literature where it is used to evoke cultural identity or social reality. The audience in this case is readers from all language backgrounds rather than only those who are vernacular speakers, and the works are selected for their literary value rather than their language form. Reading work by established writers such as Sandra Cisneros, Richard Wright, Virginia Driving Hawk Sneve, Jade Snow Wong, Amy Tan, Silas House, Lee Smith, and Zora Neale Hurston can present the opportunity for high school students to extend their knowledge about language in society and for teachers to introduce language study into the study of literature.

When such literature is taken up in the classroom, discussion might focus on the authors' purposes for using vernacular features in writing, a medium in which readers are more accustomed to seeing standard dialect. Students could consider whether the features seem to be an accurate rendition of speech or a general means of conveying a character's social identity. They might investigate whether the language of the text matches dialects in their own area. They might compare vernacular dialect in fiction with that in poetry and recent works with older ones. Is dialect used similarly in Richard Wright's *Native Son* and Toni Morrison's *Beloved*, important novels written nearly 50 years apart? How does Lee Smith, who uses versions of Appalachian English in her novels, represent the dialect of some of her mountain personalities in *Oral History*? How does Charles Chesnutt, a highly educated, bi-racial nineteenth-century writer, who spent time in Ohio and North Carolina and identified as white or African American depending on the situation, use his characters' dialects to explore aspects of region, ethnicity, morality, and culture? How do Sandra Cisneros, Amy Tan, and Bharati Mukherjee capture different aspects of languages and cultures in contact in their books *The House on Mango Street, The Joy Luck Club,* and *Jasmine*? Studying dialects in written text can be a valuable route to enhancing students' knowledge about their own dialects as well as those of others.

Reading and the Acquisition of Standard English

Would it be easier to learn to read if young vernacular dialect speakers were first taught to speak Standard English, then taught to read? If this strategy worked, then the question of dialect mismatch and reading would be moot. But there are several reasons why making Standard English a prerequisite for reading instruction is not feasible. In the first place, the mismatch between speaking and reading would remain: As we noted, all speakers of English confront differences between written and spoken language, regardless of their dialect. Furthermore, many speakers of vernacular dialects show little difficulty in overcoming the mismatch. There is no clear-cut indication that learning Standard English will, in itself, ease learning to read. On top of that, there is little evidence that spoken Standard English can be taught successfully on a wide scale. Most important, however, is timing. If Standard English could be taught successfully, and reading instruction were postponed until children achieved Standard English fluency, learning in other academic areas that are dependent on reading skills would be significantly delayed.

Another possibility would be to teach Standard English at the same time as teaching reading by "correcting" a student's vernacular English rendition to Standard English. But such a practice has serious pedagogical flaws (Delpit, 2006). Piestrup (1973) found that correcting students' reading actually led to more "errors," not fewer. It is confusing to mix teaching Standard English with teaching reading because the two goals are not necessarily linked. If a rural Appalachian dialect speaker reads *cliff* as "clifft," a southwestern Latino or American Indian student reads *sing* as "sin," or an African American English speaker reads *find* as "fine," there is no reason to suspect a letter/sound correspondence problem. Such a problem would be indicated, of course, if the same students read *cup* as "sup" or *big* as "dig." The first set of examples involves accurate reflections of sound/letter correspondences in particular dialects, whereas the second set does not reflect the patterns of any of the dialects. Correcting both types of production as if they were the same phenomenon would only confuse the learner because readers depend on their tacit knowledge of language to figure out sound/print relationships. A New England child might similarly be confused if told that the only correct way to read *car* is with an *r* at the end or that *caught* and *cot* must contain different vowel sounds to be read accurately. Learning a spoken Standard English dialect requires different skills from those involved in learning sound/letter correspondence. If the two sets of skills are addressed at once, students are unlikely to learn either one very well.

Accommodating Social and Cultural Identity in Teaching Reading

Research has shown that the literacy-related experiences that children have in their homes and communities may differ from those presumed by school programs, which more easily accommodate the literacy experiences of white middle-class children (Hammer, 2001; Labov, 1972). A literacy-rich classroom culture that supports children's transition into the school culture has been shown to support children from vernacular dialect-speaking backgrounds who come to school with limited literacy experiences of the type the school expects (Purcell-Gates, McIntyre, & Freppon, 1995). In this setting, children engaged in frequent, informal writing tied to reading; regular journal writing; literacy activity across the curriculum; silent reading; oral story reading; and story performance: in short, the classroom was a highly participatory, highly literate environment. By the end of first grade, children in such classrooms were performing in reading on par with children who had been read to extensively at home. They also scored higher than other children from similar backgrounds in skills-based curricula.

Other teachers use practices that reduce the discontinuities between home and school. In a classic study, Au and Jordan (1981) documented the practice of teachers at the Kamehameha Early Education Program in Hawai'i who were incorporating a language strategy from their students' home culture. To address the problem of poor reading by Hawaiian students, they made reading lessons more like important language events in Hawaiian culture called "talk story" and "storytelling." Rather than taking turns at talking during teacher-led discussion to support comprehension, children jump in to extend each other's ideas in talking about the text. They volunteer responses, rather than waiting for the teacher to call on them. The program also incorporates forms of classroom organization that support informal learning situations. Students work together in small groups at learning centers. By responding to narrative and social conventions of the students' background, this approach helps to narrow the gap between home and school learning and promote text comprehension.

Reading performance, reading problems, and reading failure for different dialect and cultural groups have a complex explanation. The kinds of materials that children read play a role. Language structure, text content, and readers' background knowledge and cultural values regarding literacy all may influence reading success. Teachers will want to continue observing their students' performance, reflecting on their practice, and refining instruction.

Reading Tests and Dialect Differences

A final issue regarding reading and vernacular-speaking populations concerns reading assessment. There has been debate for some time as to whether standardized tests, especially standardized reading tests, reflect the linguistic and cultural realities of vernacular English speakers and what difference that makes. Some test-takers who score low on these tests do, in fact, have genuine reading problems, and this diagnosis holds up through multiple measures of reading ability. Concern about the quality, form, and context of the tests is not meant to deny the seriousness of actual reading problems. The question is whether the tests can accurately measure reading performance for all students.

In some cases, serious misclassifications may occur on the basis of test scores; some students may be classified as overall poor readers even if they are not, due to the kinds of language and cultural items included in the test. In other cases, what seem to be reading problems may instead be a function of language differences, and certain speakers may be penalized because their native dialect is different from that used as the norming sample on standardized tests. For example, a deficiency in word recognition skills might be diagnosed when, in fact, the test-taker has simply applied the pronunciation rules of the native dialect in responding to test items. The possibility of language bias in standardized reading tests must be taken into account along with other factors in order to make an accurate assessment of reading skills.

Pronunciation, Grammar, and Vocabulary Differences

As discussed in Chapter 6, dialect differences may affect scores on standardized reading tests in several ways. First, some reading tests may contain sections that depend on Standard English pronunciations. A decoding exercise that relies on the ability to distinguish *pen* from *pin* and *death* from *deaf* clearly contains a bias against speakers of Southern-based dialects, in which these pairs of items may be pronounced the same. In responding to test items, the child sounds the words out according to the dialect's pronunciation rules and does not note a difference. Because the norms for the test reflect the Standard

English pronunciation distinction, the child's responses are marked as incorrect, even though they accurately follow precise rules of the native language variety.

In some elementary level tests, students may be required to choose the correct word to complete a sentence. For example, a test item may ask for a choice between *them* and *those* in a sentence such as *I have read (them, those) books* or between *no* and *any* in a sentence such as *I didn't hear (no, any) noise.* According to the Standard English norm, one correct form is predicted (*those* and *any*, respectively) in these sentences, but the grammatical rules of the test-taker's home dialect may predict the other choice (*them* and *no*). Responses that follow native dialect rules show accurate word recognition and thus demonstrate reading skill. If those responses are judged to be wrong, dialect differences may lead to faulty assessment of reading ability.

In another testing task, students are asked to match words to pictures, to demonstrate their word recognition skills. For example, for a drawing that shows trees with falling leaves, the options are *aunt, autumn, summer,* and *town.* This test item holds several potential difficulties. First, the term *autumn,* which the test developers consider correct for this scene, may not be familiar to some children because it is associated more with written language than spoken language. Children with less written language experience may expect the word *fall* to name the season. Thus, this item may be more difficult for them than for others.

Another difficulty with this item concerns students' cultural experiences with seasons. Elementary schools typically emphasize seasons as a school topic, thus establishing the relationship between leaves and *autumn* as background knowledge that is relevant to school tasks. For children in rural and suburban areas in the North, this emphasis is congruent with out-of-school experience. But for children living in the inner city, wearing jackets may have a stronger association than falling leaves with autumn/fall. In areas that do not have deciduous trees, such as South Florida and Southern California, or where seasons are marked in a different way, such as rainy and dry seasons in the U.S. Virgin Islands, the test item makes a different semantic demand than it does for children in the East and Midwest.

Tests assume that vocabulary items have the same meaning associations for all readers, but that is not the case. A reading test can inaccurately assess a reader from a region, social class, or cultural group that uses a vocabulary form different from the response required by the test. (This phenomenon underlies any number of web applications that can determine where you have lived based on your responses to a small number of vocabulary and pronunciation items, for example, the *New York Times'* version of this test: www.nytimes.com/interactive/2013/12/20/sunday-review/dialect-quiz-map.html.)

People may have some sense that different dialects use different words for the same thing, such as a long sandwich (*torpedo, hoagie, grinder, sub,* etc.), a public water dispenser (*water fountain, drinking fountain, bubbler,* etc.), or any number of other objects or ideas. It is common for people to assume that vernacular dialect speakers have both the vernacular and the mainstream terms readily available. However, this is often not true. In an illustrative exchange from the documentary *American Tongues* (Alvarez & Kolker, 1987), a middle-aged woman from Pittsburgh identifies a *gumband*. When asked if she has ever heard another word for this item she responds, "Rubber band? I think some people call it a rubber band? Not here, though." The hesitancy in her response is telling, and it is apparent that the term might cause her trouble if she were taking an assessment which had determined *rubber band* to be the only acceptable response. Likewise, mainstream English speakers would be hurt on assessments that deemed the following vernacular usages as the only correct response: *whopperjawed* ("crooked"), *shore* ("beach"), *cabinet* ("milkshake"), *meehonkey* ("hide and seek"), or *rotary* ("roundabout"). Such a test may be able to diagnose which dialect someone speaks, but it cannot tell much about the person's reading ability. A low score on a test of reading vocabulary might merely mean that the person taking the test speaks a vernacular dialect, not that there are any reading problems per se.

Background Knowledge

Tests of reading comprehension entail language processes beyond the literal meaning of a passage. It is virtually impossible to construct a reading comprehension test that pertains only to the literal meaning of words. Comprehension tests assess the student's ability to make inferences—the ability to connect explicitly stated information with other information believed to follow naturally from it.

Background knowledge is among the factors that contribute to inferring meanings from text. We have pointed out that what constitutes a person's background knowledge is constrained to an enormous extent by considerations of culture and ethnicity, social class, gender, race, age, geographical location, and other factors. Consider the following description of redwood trees in terms of the background information that a child from New York City and a resident of Northern California near the redwood forests might bring to the test:

> They are so big that roads are built through their trunks. By counting the rings inside the tree trunk, one can tell the age of the tree.
>
> *From the Metropolitan Reading Test for third graders,*
> *cited in Meier, 1973*

If an urban child is less familiar with the use of the terms *rings* and *trunk* in connection with trees, this passage might conjure up a fairy tale image. In contrast, a child raised in proximity to the forest might find such a description almost trivial by the third grade. Background knowledge plays an essential role in reading comprehension, and what readers bring as background knowledge to reading may vary according to group.

Consider another account, also taken from a disclosed version of the Metropolitan Reading Test:

> "Good afternoon, little girl," said the policeman. "May I help you?"
> "I want to go to the park. I cannot find my way," said Nancy. "Please help me."

After reading this passage, the child is supposed to select the one right ending for the story:

> The policeman said,
>
> **a.** Call your mother to take you.
> **b.** I am in a hurry.
> **c.** I will take you to the park.
>
> *From Meier, 1973, p. 22*

Quite obviously, cultural values about the role of the police influence the answer: Readers with different value orientations might select different answers.

Background knowledge can impact the way a person interprets the words on the page, but even more profoundly, it can impact the way that person fills in gaps in a passage. The inferences a reader makes throughout reading are, fundamentally, what makes the text coherent for the reader (Kintsch & van Dijk, 1978). A number of studies have found that the fewer inferences required of the reader—through employing a process called textual repair—the better young students performed on reading comprehension tasks (see, e.g., Britton & Gülgöz, 1991; Linderholm, Everson, van den Broek, Mischinski, Crittenden, & Samuels, 2000). Yet no amount of textual repair has been able to eliminate the impact of background information on reading comprehension (McNamara, Kintsch, Songer, & Kintsch, 1996), suggesting that it is impossible to remove all bias from reading comprehension tests.

Other Fairness Factors

It is important, then, to consider systematic characteristics of social and ethnic groups, including language patterns, in scoring test responses. But other factors bear on fairness in testing as well. Certain aspects of the testing situation favor social and behavioral traits typically associated with middle-class children. For example, values about displaying abilities through paper-and-pencil tasks or performing for unfamiliar adults, working quickly, concentrating on the test topic, among others, can be quite culture-specific.

The techniques used to obtain information in many standardized reading tests also presume particular kinds of skill training that may be culture-specific. For example, phonemic awareness and phonics skills are often measured through tasks that focus on rhyming words, words sounding the same, or parts of a word rather than the whole word—activities that may not be familiar to all students. Reading vocabulary may be measured by tasks that call for identifying word association types: same meanings (synonyms such as *proprietor* and *owner*), opposite meanings (antonyms such as *tall* and *short*), specific and general category relationships (e.g., *python* and *snake*), or descriptive, dictionary-like definitions (e.g., a *linguist* is a person who studies the patterning and organization of language). These assessment tasks for getting at meaning are, of course, different from real-life language use where meaning is derived from words in context. A specialized set of skills may be needed to succeed in tests of such facets of reading; and the test-taker's failure to interpret the tasks in the intended way can lead to a diagnosis of reading failure where it may not be warranted.

Equity in assessment is a complex issue, and no simple approach emerges as best. Test responses could be analyzed in ways that take into account the systematic differences between dialects. If a working-class African American child marked *mile* and *mild* as sounding the same because of the regular pronunciation rule that can eliminate the *d* sound in *mild,* or a Southern rural child noted that *tire* and *tar* sound the same, this response would be interpreted as a legitimate reflection of a dialect difference, not a reading error. Similarly, if a native Philadelphian marked items such as *ran* and *ban* as not rhyming because of the distinct vowels in these items (the *a* in *ran* as the vowel in TRAP, and the *a* in *ban* as something closer to the vowel in DRESS), this, too, would be interpreted as a legitimate reflection of the Philadelphia pronunciation system, and not as a reading error. An interpretation of responses that takes into account dialect differences can help the evaluator see what effect dialect may be having by identifying responses that are legitimate in terms of the language system of the test-taker, but differ from the standardized norms of the test. To make such an interpretation, the evaluator must be thoroughly familiar with the systematic differences between the various dialects of test-takers, whether they are rural Southern, urban African American, or Southwestern Chicano. Naturally this principle holds for informal assessment as well, understanding why certain forms might occur in the oral reading of passages in contrast to the actual forms written in the passage. It is crucial, however, to determine the test-taker's dialect and not to assume it based on race or ethnicity.

Schools often use multiple methods of assessing reading achievement so that scores from standardized reading tests are not the exclusive measure of reading skills. Both informal assessments and criterion-referenced tests are recommended. Performance-based assessments, in which test-takers are required to produce a product or a process based on their understanding of a text, have been used in progressive situations. Asking students why they chose particular answers is also useful. Getting a glimpse of the reasoning behind the child's answer can be quite enlightening. In the comprehension test item about the police officer mentioned earlier, a child could supply an appropriate rationale for selecting the alternative "I am in a hurry," instead of "I will take you to the park." The child's background knowledge might suggest that police officers are doing their job when they are hurrying from one place to another, taking care of troublesome situations. Checking on that background knowledge may reveal that there are different cultural perceptions regarding officers' responsibilities. Certain answers that are wrong according to the norms of a test might be reasonable indications that the child is, in fact, reading with considerable understanding, even if it involves a perspective different from that assumed by the author or test constructor. For educators who are concerned with a genuine understanding of students' reading skills, specific information of this type may be considerably more useful for placement and instruction than objective scores.

This chapter argues, as the other chapters do, that educators need to have broad understanding about variation in language and culture. Beyond that, they need to know the details about their own students' dialects and cultural backgrounds. It is not enough to have a general respect for group-based differences. Specific understanding of students' dialects and cultures makes it possible for teachers to understand their students' reading performance and support reading development in concrete, informed ways as they engage students from diverse communities and language varieties.

Discussion Questions

1. The quote from Sweetland at the beginning of the chapter points to an indirect relationship between dialect and academic failure that is mediated through the teacher. What are the implications for teacher learning?

2. Find some sentences in books for young children that seem more typical of book language than spoken language. Would they be hard for young children to understand when listening to an adult read the book? Would they be hard for children to read? Would they be harder for vernacular dialect speakers than for Standard English speakers? Explain. If you think they are hard for any children to understand, why do you think the author used those constructions? How could teachers help children understand such sentences?

3. Chapters 8 and 9 tie teacher learning about language variation to literacy, a traditional primary focus of schooling. The chapters argue that all teachers must support literacy learning (Chapter 7 says the same about supporting oral language development). Does that mean that all teachers need detailed understanding of the dialects in the community where they teach? Or just some teachers? Explain.

4. How could the funds of knowledge approach to learning about children's communities help teachers improve literacy instruction? How could the demands it places on teacher time be accommodated?
5. Recap the difference between dialect influence and dialect interference. Why is the distinction important?

Links of Interest

1. Read the National Council of Teachers of English statements on learning to read: www.ncte.org/positions/statements/onreading
2. Explore the Penn Reading Initiative program and materials: www.ling. upenn.edu/pri/
3. Find out about the Appalachian Prison Book Project: https://aprison bookproject.wordpress.com/
4. Discover a project that aims to improve access to reading materials for at-risk children: www.firstbook.org/

Further Reading

Hammond, B., Hoover, M. E. R., & McPhail, I. P. (Eds.). (2005). *Teaching African American learners to read: Perspectives and practices.* Newark, DE: International Reading Association.
    Contributors to this book include researchers and practitioners with a deep understanding of how dialects can affect learning to read. The chapters feature accounts of how schools have used children's home dialect in building their reading skills.

Harris, J., Kamhi, A. G., & Pollock, K. E. (Eds.). (2001). *Literacy in African American communities.* Mahwah, NJ: Lawrence Erlbaum Associates.
    The chapters in this volume present a broad view of literacy-related practices in linguistic, cultural, historical, and political contexts.

Meier, T. (2008). *Black communications and learning to read: Building on children's linguistic and cultural strengths.* New York, NY: Erlbaum.
    Meier combines research summary and classroom experience to describe effective literacy instruction for young African American English speakers. The book takes into account the forms of the dialect as well as interactional style, and it includes many examples.

Purcell-Gates, V. (1995). *Other people's words: The cycle of low literacy.* Cambridge, MA: Harvard University Press.
    This case study tells the compelling story of the author's work with a nonliterate mother and her young son, who are urban Appalachians. The title comes from the mother's assessment of her difficulty in learning to read books written in a language that was not her own. The writer shows how she took into account the home literacy traditions and dialect difference in supporting the mother's and son's literacy development.

References

Adams, M. J. (1990). *Beginning to read: Thinking and learning about print.* Cambridge, MA: MIT Press.
Alvarez, L., & Kolker, A. (Producers). (1987). *American tongues* [Video]. New York, NY: Center for New American Media.
Au, K., & Jordan, C. (1981). Teaching reading to Hawaiian children: Finding a culturally appropriate solution. In H. Trueba, G. P. Guthrie, & K. H. Au (Eds.), *Culture and the bilingual classroom: Studies in classroom ethnography* (pp. 139–152). Rowley, MA: Newbury.

Borko, H., & Eisenhart, M. (1989). Reading ability groups as literacy communities. In D. Bloome (Ed.), *Classrooms and literacy* (pp. 107–133). Norwood, NJ: Ablex.

Britton, B. K., & Gülgöz, S. (1991). Using Kintsch's computational model to improve instructional text: Effects of repairing inference calls on recall and cognitive structures. *Journal of Educational Psychology, 83*(3), 329–345.

Cazden, C. B., & John, V. P. (1971). Learning in American Indian children. In M. L. Wax, S. Diamond, & F. O. Gearing (Eds.), *Anthropological perspectives on education* (pp. 252–272). New York, NY: Basic Books.

Chall, J. (1996). *The great debate.* New York, NY: McGraw-Hill.

Charity, A. H., Scarborough, H. S., & Griffin, D. M. (2004). Familiarity with school English in African American children and its relation to early reading achievement. *Child Development, 75*(5), 1340–1356.

Clay, M. M. (2013). *An observation survey of early literacy achievement* (3rd ed.). Portsmouth, NH: Heinemann.

Cleaver, B. (1969). *Where the lilies bloom.* New York, NY: Harper Collins.

Collins, J. (1988). Language and class in minority education. *Anthropology & Education Quarterly, 19*(4), 299–326.

Common Core State Standards Initiative (CCSS). (2010). *Common Core State Standards for English language arts & literacy in history/social studies, science, and technical subjects.* Washington, DC: National Governors Association Center for Best Practices, Council of Chief State School Officers. Available online at: www.corestandards.org/wp-content/uploads/ELA_Standards1.pdf

Craig, H. K., Zhang, L., Hensel, S. L., & Quinn, E. J. (2009). African American English-speaking students: An examination of the relationship between dialect shifting and reading outcomes. *Journal of Speech, Language, and Hearing Research, 52*(4), 839-855.

Delpit, L. (1988). The silenced dialogue: Power and pedagogy in educating other people's children. *Harvard Educational Review, 58,* 280–298.

Delpit, L. (2006). What should teachers do? Ebonics and culturally responsive instruction. In S. J. Nero (Ed.), *Dialects, Englishes, creoles, and education* (pp. 93–101). New York, NY: Routledge.

Dorr, R. E. (2006). Something old is new again: Revisiting language experience. *The Reading Teacher, 60*(2), 138–146.

Fillmore, L. W., & Snow, C. (2002). What teachers need to know about language. In C. Adger, C. Snow, & D. Christian (Eds.), *What teachers need to know about language.* McHenry, IL: Delta Systems and Washington, DC: Center for Applied Linguistics.

Fontenot, M. A. (2009). *Clovis crawfish and petit papillon.* Gretna, LA: Pelican.

Gipe, R. (2015). *Trampoline: An illustrated novel.* Athens, OH: Ohio University Press.

Gonzalez, N., Moll, L. C., Floyd-Tenery, M., Rivera, A., Rendon, P., Gonzales, R., & Amanti, C. (1993). *Teacher research on funds of knowledge: Learning from households.* Santa Cruz: National Center for Research on Cultural Diversity and Second Language Learning, University of California, Santa Cruz.

Greenfield, E. (1974). *She come bringing me that little baby girl.* New York, NY: Harper Collins.

Hall, M. (1976). *Teaching reading as a language experience.* Columbus, OH: Charles E. Merrill.

Hammer, C. S. (2001). "Come sit down and let mama read": Book reading interactions between African American mothers and their infants. In J. L. Harris, A. G. Kamhi, & K. E. Pollock (Eds.), *Literacy in African American communities* (pp. 21–44). Mahwah, NJ: Lawrence Erlbaum Associates.

Johnson, P. B. (2001). *Fearless Jack.* New York, NY: Margaret K. McElderry Books.

Kintsch, W., & van Dijk, T. A. (1978). Toward a model of text comprehension and production. *Psychological Review, 85*(5), 363–394.

Labbo, L. D., Eakle, A. J., Jonathan, A., & Montero, M. K. (2002). Digital language experience approach: Using digital photographs and software as a language experience approach innovation. *Reading Online, 5*(8), n8.

Labov, W. (1972). *Language in the inner city: Studies in the Black English Vernacular.* Philadelphia, PA: The University of Pennsylvania Press.

Labov, W. (1995). Can reading failure be reversed: A linguistic approach to the question. In V. L. Gadsden & D. A. Wagner (Eds.), *Literacy among African-American youth* (pp. 39–68). Cresskill, NJ: Hampton.

Labov, W., & Baker, B. (2010). What is a reading error? *Applied Psycholinguistics, 31*(4), 735–757.

Linderholm, T., Everson, M. G., van den Broek, P., Mischinski, M., Crittenden, A., & Samuels, J. (2000). Effects of causal text revisions on more-and less-skilled readers' comprehension of easy and difficult texts. *Cognition and Instruction, 18*(4), 525–556.

McNamara, D. S., Kintsch, E., Songer, N. B., & Kintsch, W. (1996). Are good texts always better? Interactions of text coherence, background knowledge, and levels of understanding in learning from text. *Cognition and Instruction, 14*(1), 1–43.

McWhorter, J. H. (1997). Wasting energy on an illusion. *The Black Scholar, 27*(1), 9–14.

Meier, D. (1973). *Reading failure and the tests* (Occasional Paper). New York, NY: Workshop for Open Education.

Michaels, S. (1981). "Sharing time": Children's narrative styles and differential access to literacy. *Language in Society, 10*(3), 423–442.

Mitri, S. M., & Terry, N. P. (2013). Phonological awareness skills in young African American English speakers. *Reading and Writing, 27*(3), 555–569.

Moll, L., Amanti, C., Neff, D., & Gonzalez, N. (2005). Funds of knowledge for teaching: Using a qualitative approach to connect homes and classrooms. In N. Gonzalez, L. Moll, & C. Amanti (Eds.), *Funds of knowledge: Theorizing practices in households, communities, and classrooms* (pp. 71–88). Mahwah, NJ: Lawrence Erlbaum Associates, Inc.

Murnane, R., Sawhill, I., & Snow, C. (2012). Literacy challenges for the twenty-first century: Introducing the issue. *The Future of Children, 22*(2), 3–15.

National Center for Educational Statistics. (n.d.). *Reading assessment.* Retrieved from https://nces. ed.gov/nationsreportcard/reading/

Palincsar, A. S., & Brown, A. L. (1987). Instruction for self-regulated reading. In L. B. Resnick & L. E. Klopfer (Eds.), *Toward the thinking curriculum: Current cognitive research* (pp. 19–39). Alexandria, VA: Association of Supervision and Curriculum Development.

Parrish, B. (2004). *Teaching adult ESL: A practical introduction.* New York, NY: McGraw-Hill.

Philips, S. U. (1983/1993). *The invisible culture: Communication in the classroom and community in the Warm Springs Indian Reservation.* Long Grove, IL: Waveland.

Piestrup, A. M. (1973). *Black dialect interference and accommodations of reading instruction in first grade.* Berkeley, CA: University of California, Language and Behavior Research Lab. (Monograph 4, ED119113).

Pilonieta, P., & Medina, A.L. (2009, October). Reciprocal teaching for the primary grades: "We can do it, too!" *The Reading Teacher, 63*(2), 120–129.

Plaut, S. (Ed.) (2009). *The right to literacy in secondary school: Creating a culture of thinking.* New York, NY: Teachers College Press.

Purcell-Gates, V. (1995). *Other people's words: The cycle of low literacy.* Cambridge, MA: Harvard University Press.

Purcell-Gates, V., McIntyre, E., & Freppon, P. A. (1995). Learning written storybook language in school: A comparison of low-SES children in skills-based and whole language classrooms. *American Educational Research Journal, 32*(3), 659–685.

Rayner, K., Foorman, B. R., Perfetti, C. A., Pesetsky, D., & Seidenberg, M. S. (2001). How psychological science informs the teaching of reading. *Psychological Science in the Public Interest, 2*(2), 31–74.

Rayner, K., Slattery, T. J., & Bélanger, N. N. (2010). Eye movements, the perceptual span, and reading speed. *Psychonomic Bulletin & Review, 17*(6), 834–839.

Reynolds, R. E., Taylor, M., Steffensen, M. S., Shirey, L., & Anderson, R. C. (1982). Cultural schemata and reading comprehension. *Reading Research Quarterly, 17*, 357–366.

Rickford, J. R., & Rickford, A. E. (1995). Dialect readers revisited. *Linguistics and Education, 7*(2), 107–128.

Routman, R. (1991). *Invitations: Changing as teachers and learners: K–12.* Portsmouth, NH: Heinemann.

Schwartz, J. I. (1982). Dialect interference in the attainment of literacy. *Journal of Reading, 25*(5), 440–446.

Simpkins, G. A., Holt, G., & Simpkins, C. (1977). *Bridge: A cross-culture reading program.* Boston, MA: Houghton-Mifflin.

Simpkins, G. A., & Simpkins, C. (1981). Cross-cultural approach to curriculum development. In G. Smitherman (Ed.), *Black English and the education of Black children and youth* (pp. 221–240). Detroit, MI: Center for Black Studies.

Sloat, T. (1993). *The hungry giant of the tundra.* New York, NY: Dutton's Children's Books.

Smitherman, G. (2000). *Talkin that talk: Language, culture, and education in African America.* London, UK: Routledge.

Stauffer, R. G. (1970). *The language-experience approach to the teaching of reading*. New York, NY: Harper & Row.

Sweetland, J. (2006). *Teaching writing in the African American classroom: A sociolinguistic approach*. Unpublished doctoral dissertation, Stanford University.

Terry, N. P. (2012). Examining relationships among dialect variation and emergent literacy skills. *Communication Disorders Quarterly, 33*(2): 67–77.

Terry, N. P. (2014). Dialect variation and phonological knowledge: Phonological representations and metalinguistic awareness among beginning readers who speak nonmainstream American English. *Applied Psycholinguistics, 35*(1), 155–176.

Wax, M. L., Wax, R., & Dumont, R. V. (1964). *Formal education in an American Indian community*. Kalamazoo, MI: Society for the Study of Social Problems.

Weaver, C. (1994). *Understanding whole language: From principles to practice*. Portsmouth, NH: Heinemann.

Wolcott, H. (1967). *Oregon State College Warm Springs research project, vol. 2: Education*. Corvallis, OR: Oregon State College.

Wolfram, W., & Fasold, R. W. (1969). Toward reading materials for speakers of Black English: Three linguistically appropriate passages. In J. C. Baratz & R. W. Shuy (Eds.), *Teaching black children to read* (pp. 138–155). Washington, DC: Center for Applied Linguistics.

10

Dialect Awareness for Students

Scenario

When asked to comment on a dialect awareness curriculum that was being pilot tested, some ninth grade students in North Carolina gave the following written responses (Reaser, 2006, pp. 128–139). As you read through them, think about what knowledge students and teachers gained from learning about dialects. Also think about how this knowledge helped reshape their attitudes toward language variation.

(Student responses are verbatim. Only spelling errors are corrected.):

Question:	Do you think it is important to study different dialects? Why or why not?
Student response:	"Yes, because you'll have more respect for people with different dialects and it will give you an open mind. You'll probably judge people on things beside their dialect and the stereotypes attached to that dialect."
Student response:	"Yes, I do, because it makes me see that it's ok to have a different dialect. It doesn't make me any less smart. I also have respect for others who have a dialect."
Question:	What was the most surprising thing that you learned about dialects?
Student response:	"I learned that a dialect doesn't tell anyone if the person is smart or dumb or anything like that."
Student response:	"I learned that dialects aren't sloppy versions of Standard English. They follow specific patterns that are logical."
Question:	Why do people have negative attitudes about dialects?
Student response:	"I think people have such negative opinions of dialects because they judge too quickly. They think that if someone can't speak Standard English they are ignorant

Student response: "or something. What can be done to change attitudes and opinions is teach this to children who can share it with their parents."

Student response: "Many people think that they don't have a dialect, thus leading them to think others who do are uneducated. This program could help them learn too."

What do you make of these responses? Are you surprised? What sorts of feelings do you think the students had about vernacular dialects before they took the course? What kinds of information do you think were most important in changing their attitudes? Why might being exposed to information about dialect variation evoke such strong reactions?

Not only is language variation an essential topic for professional educators, it is also an intriguing area of study for students at all levels as shown by the reactions in the opening scenario. Studying language variation helps students understand how language is structured and how it figures in regional and social diversity. Unfortunately, this important topic does not receive enough attention. In K–12 schools, multicultural education has moved ahead, but the study of language diversity has lagged behind. Understanding language patterns and the social role of language can help students become more tolerant of language variation (Reaser, 2006) and even improve their mastery of Standard English conventions (Sweetland, 2006; Wheeler & Swords, 2006, 2010; Young, Barrett, Young-Rivera, & Lovejoy, 2013). Educating students about language diversity should be an essential component of education at all levels because it can increase students' awareness of the role that language plays in social identity and prejudice. And it is never too early to develop dialect awareness, as indicated in the experiment with pre-school children summarized in Box 10.1.

BOX 10.1: LANGUAGE ATTITUDES IN PRESCHOOL

In a telling experiment conducted by Marilyn Rosenthal (1977), children aged 3 to 5 were asked to accept a box of crayons and a drawing pad from one of two "magic boxes." The boxes looked identical, but the voices that played from a hidden speaker within each box were different: Steve spoke Standard American English and Kenneth spoke African American English. The interviewer played the same message from the different boxes, followed by questions such as "Which box has nicer presents?" and "Which box sounds nicer?"

The responses were revealing:

"I like him [points to Steve] cause he sound nice. I don't like him [pointing to Kenneth]."

"I think I want my present from Kenneth, if he doesn't bite."

"Cause Steve is good, Kenneth is bad."

The experiment demonstrates that children acquire attitudes about language differences early and these attitudes quickly become entrenched. Linguist Rosina Lippi-Green notes in her book *English with an Accent: Language, Ideology, and Discrimination in the United States*, that "Accent discrimination can be found everywhere in our daily lives. In fact, such behavior is so commonly accepted, so widely perceived as appropriate, that it must be seen as the last back door to discrimination. And the door is still wide open" (2012, p. 74). While other forms of inequality, prejudice, and discrimination have become more widely recognized and exposed in recent decades, language prejudice is often overlooked and even unintentionally promoted.

One of the central keys to overcoming language prejudice and discrimination is the direct study of language diversity. Reaser (2006) investigated the effects of a unit on dialects on middle-school students. The curriculum unit, parts of which are excerpted in this chapter, focused on prejudice about language differences and the orderly nature of dialect patterning. Findings indicated that more than 85% of the students felt that it was important to study dialects. Furthermore, they found the subject highly interesting, as indicated by the fact that more than 90% of those in one classroom noted in an end-of-year course review that this unit was their favorite topic of study.

Investigating the structure of vernacular dialects and their role in speech communities has additional advantages for students from vernacular-speaking backgrounds. When dialect diversity becomes an object of serious study for students, rather than merely a problem or an obstacle to be overcome, the gap between community and school that vernacular-speaking children frequently encounter is diminished. Exploring local dialect patterns becomes a natural activity.

More educators and linguists are now encouraging the active study of dialects—including vernacular ones—as a regular part of the curriculum for all students. Indeed, as noted in Chapter 7, the standards for the English language arts developed jointly by the International Reading Association (IRA) and the National Council of Teachers of English (NCTE) include dialect in one of the essential language arts standards: "Students develop an understanding of and respect for diversity in language use, patterns, and dialects across cultures, ethnic groups, geographic regions, and social roles" (NCTE/IRA, 1996, p. 3). Though less explicitly rooted in sociolinguistic tradition, the Common Core State Standards (CCSS) include in the speaking and listening strand some standards that seem to underscore the importance of knowledge about language diversity. For example, Speaking and Listening Standard 1 asks in part that students "Participate effectively in a range of conversation and collaborations with diverse partners" (2010, p. 22), which seems to acknowledge the value of exposure to language diversity.

In the following sections, we expand on why dialect diversity should be integrated into the school curriculum and illustrate how it can be implemented in English language arts, social studies, and elsewhere. We present excerpts from dialect awareness curricula that have been used successfully in several locations, including a Northern metropolitan area and several areas in the rural and urban South. We exemplify the sort of information about dialects that students need to know and that they enjoy learning as they examine the languages of their own community and other communities.

Investigating Dialects

Traditionally, curriculum materials for both primary and secondary school levels have virtually ignored dialect diversity. If they treat it at all, materials focus on dialect in literature or regional differences in vocabulary and do not address systematic pronunciation and grammatical differences in any detail. Matters of social dialect contrasts are usually taken up from a deficit perspective, particularly with regard to grammar. A few notable exceptions to this are Brown (2009), which is a workbook that helps students build competency in academic writing and grammar by studying language variation, and Dean (2008), which offers teachers an approach to using dialect differences in literature to build student competence in grammar and understanding of the social importance of vernacular dialects. Other approaches to incorporating study of language diversity in schools are described in Denham and Lobeck (2010).

While materials may be lacking, every school has nearby communities that are linguistically interesting both in their own right and in how they compare with other communities. They can be valuable sources of data, giving students an opportunity for first-hand observation of dialect diversity and helping to build their dialect awareness. Diversity can, of course, be observed within the school, but going out into the community will seem more like authentic language research.

Data from local speech communities can help students understand concepts related to language patterns and language variation. Data collection and analysis activities can be designed to deal with particular features of a dialect along the lines of the dialect study procedures outlined in Chapter 2. Consider, for example, a student in New York City. For the most part, New Yorkers are aware of dialect differences within the city and between speakers from their region and other regions of the United States. Unfortunately, such diversity is often seen in terms of unwarranted stereotypes, rather than as a valid object of study (consider "Brooklynese"). Carefully collected data from some New York communities can provide a base for developing an understanding of the systematic nature of dialects (consider the availability of ethnic [e.g., Jewish, Italian, Puerto Rican] and social class language varieties that may be in proximity to the school).

Even in a locale that seems homogenous socially and ethnically, there will be diversity according to age, generation, social practice, and status. There are also likely to be some residents who have moved from other areas and retained some contrasting linguistic features. Both individual introspection by students about their own speech and samples of speech from other residents in the area may serve as a database for empirical research.

Such activities have added value for students as experience with scientific investigation. Examining how speakers in their community use language provides a natural laboratory for the students to make generalizations based on an array of data. Their own knowledge of the language can form the basis for hypothesizing rules that govern the use of particular linguistic items. These hypotheses can then be checked against additional data that they gather from other speakers. In a sense, then, the process of hypothesis construction and testing that is fundamental to scientific inquiry can be practiced in the unique laboratory of current language use.

Student investigation of dialects serves other functions, too. It is a central way to get at the attitudes about language held by all students, to enhance self-awareness, and to gain insight into the nature of culturally-based behavior. Students can explore attitudes toward language differences among people and examine how they themselves feel about other students' language and about their own language use. It is not uncommon, for example, for students who speak socially favored varieties to view their dialectally different peers as linguistically deficient. Worse yet, speakers of socially disfavored varieties may come to accept this viewpoint about their own variety of language, feeling like they do not talk "right," "proper," or "correct." Students need to understand that a dialect difference is not an inherent linguistic or cognitive deficit. Only when this understanding is commonly accepted in the community and the school will there be a change in the current practice of discrimination on the basis of dialect.

Using the community as a language resource can also help to preserve the region's cultural and oral traditions. Sending students into the community to gather language data is an opportunity to gather and record information about traditions and oral history. The SKILLS program at the University of California, Santa Barbara, serves working-class high school students, on the premise that "Young people have a wealth of linguistic knowledge and cultural expertise that is typically not used, valued, or even recognized in traditional schooling" (Bucholtz, 2014, p. 113). In the program, which is supported by the university, secondary-level student-researchers work in communities to answer linguistic questions. In describing the results of the program, Bucholtz notes that "Not only do [students] build on their existing linguistic expertise to acquire important academic skills but they also undergo the transformative experience of appreciating the crucial role of language in their own and others' lives" (p. 115). Another way to use the community as a resource is to invite its members to visit the classroom for specific purposes, including discussions about older traditions and ways of doing things. Students can interview them and then write up what they learned about the life and language of these community figures.

If sending students into the community is impossible, the media and internet can provide data for analysis of language variation. Brown (2009) outlines exercises in which students discover nonstandard uses of *like* and patterns of *ain't* usage in print and television media. He also suggests using dictionaries as sources of data for such an analysis. For example, Brown cites information in various online dictionaries to highlight how a word like *dog* has changed over time (p. 43). In this case, the word shifted from a specific breed of dog to the generic animal. From there, it took on other meanings, including those in such usages as "you lucky dog," "He's a lazy dog," "going to the dogs," and "She's a dog" (the last one being a reference to physical attractiveness). Students can think of other usages of *dog*, such as to refer to a good friend, and amend the dictionary entry to reflect these changes. They could also use the internet to find data to support their impressions.

The concept of using dialect diversity and the cultural diversity that accompanies it as a curriculum resource proceeds from a viewpoint that is different from traditional educational practices with respect to language. Instead of seeing differences as problems, proponents of this approach have found that the differences are fascinating topics for study that expand what students know about their environment.

Components of Dialect Awareness Programs

To build the knowledge that students need to understand linguistic diversity and its social implications, schools can offer dialect awareness units. Linguists and educators have developed dialect units related to a variety of themes and tested them in various locations (Bucholtz, et al., 2014; Charity Hudley & Mallinson, 2011, 2014; Denham & Lobeck, 2010; Hazen, forthcoming; Reaser & Wolfram, 2007a, 2007b; see Links of Interest at the end of this chapter for others).

Because few teachers have had extensive training in linguistics, they are likely to require background explanation and teaching tips for a dialect awareness unit. Over the past decade, linguists have been engaged in conversations about how to bridge this knowledge gap either through curriculum design (Henderson, 2016; Reaser, 2010a, 2010b; Reaser & Adger, 2007; Sweetland, 2006; Wolfram, Reaser, & Vaughn, 2008) or professional development (Charity Hudley & Mallinson, 2014; Reaser, 2016; Sweetland, 2010). However, this lack of sociolinguistic education among teachers (see, e.g., Cross, DeVaney, & Jones, 2001; Godley, Sweetland, Wheeler, Minnici, & Carpenter, 2006) remains a challenge to incorporating programs in schools. One dialect awareness curriculum designed for North Carolina that was carefully constructed for use by teachers without a linguistic background included an extensive teacher's manual (Reaser & Wolfram, 2007a) so that any social studies teacher could teach it without prior training in linguistics or sociolinguistics.

Introduction to Language Diversity

One essential component of any program or curriculum on dialect awareness is a unit that considers the naturalness of dialect variation in American English. This is probably best done inductively. An easy method involves having students listen to representative speech samples of regional, class, and ethnic varieties. They need to compare the speech of mainstream American English speakers in diverse regions such as New England, the rural South, and the urban North in order to appreciate the reality of spoken regional standards, just as they need to recognize the difference between standard and vernacular varieties in these regions. In particular, students in the Midwest need to consider some of the traits of their own variety as it compares with others in order to understand that everyone really does speak a dialect (Niedzielski & Preston, 2000; Reaser, 2006). There are a variety of online resources that can be consulted for recordings of diverse speakers, including national collections (such as the American English Dialect Recordings Collection at the Library of Congress) and documentaries on specific regions such as *Voices of North Carolina* (Hutcheson, 2005), *Yinz* about Pittsburghese (www.youtube.com/watch?v=A1eSQ2u0STQ), and *Pidgin: The Voice of Hawai'i* (http://sls.hawaii.edu/pidgin/filmsAboutPidgin.php). There are also lots of examples on YouTube, such as the "Accent Tags," though they have to be used with some caution since they are self-selected and may not always be the ideal representative of a particular dialect. Some vignettes from the video production *American Tongues* (Alvarez & Kolker, 1987) are effective for having students confront the affective parameters related to dialect diversity. Although the film is dated, its message is still quite current. Some entertaining clips from the film that appear on YouTube expose basic prejudices and myths about language differences. Passages from the documentary *Do You Speak American?* (MacNeil/Lehrer Productions, 2005) are also useful in this regard. A website related to the production (www.pbs.org/speak) addresses issues related to dialect diversity, language norms, and different regional and ethnic varieties. The travelogue's length (3 hours) precludes watching it in a single session, but useful vignettes can be extracted from the program for classroom use (www.pbs.org/speak/education) or professional development (www.pbs.org/speak/education/training/).

Language Attitudes

Although students can be introduced to language prejudice by viewing film clips, they also need to be exposed to language discrimination and prejudice directly (Reaser, 2010a). In one of the early exercises in the North Carolina dialect curriculum for middle school, students confront language prejudice in a 1-minute ad titled "Accents – Fair Housing PSA" on linguistic profiling and housing discrimination (see Baugh, 2003) prepared by the National Fair Housing Alliance, U.S. Department of Housing and Urban Development, and

Leadership Conference on Civil Rights Education (Ad Council, 2003; see Links of Interest). A viewing activity from the student workbook (Reaser & Wolfram, 2007b) is presented in Box 10.2.

The teacher's manual for the dialect curriculum (Reaser & Wolfram, 2007a) provides background data that is helpful in guiding students' discussion, including estimates of how many cases of linguistic profiling occur each day and each year. Box 10.3 reproduces the instructions and background information for the classroom teacher. Notice how much additional information the teacher's manual contains to support those who may not have previously been exposed to sociolinguistics. It also contains pedagogical support regarding how to teach about the example, the time required, and contextualized answers with ideas to further probe student responses.

BOX 10.2: STUDENT WORKBOOK VIDEO EXERCISE: EXAMINING LANGUAGE PREJUDICE (FROM REASER & WOLFRAM, 2007B, P. 2). REPRINTED WITH PERMISSION

During phone conversations, it is often possible to tell a number of things about a person based on the characteristics of his/her voice. You will see a 1-minute commercial produced by the U.S. Department of Housing and Urban Development (HUD) [https://languageandlife. org/vonc/vonc02.mp4]. The purpose of this commercial is to raise awareness of how discrimination can occur over the phone. As you watch the video, think of answers to the following:

1. How common do you think it is for people to be discriminated against on the phone?
2. How strong are people's prejudices about language?
3. Why do you think people have such strong prejudices about language?

BOX 10.3: TEACHER'S MANUAL: EXAMINING LANGUAGE PREJUDICE (FROM REASER & WOLFRAM, 2007A, P. 2). REPRINTED WITH PERMISSION

(Approximate time: 10 minutes)

During phone conversations, it is often possible to tell a number of things about a person based on the characteristics of his/her voice. But identifying characteristics about a person isn't the problem. The problem occurs when we act in a biased manner toward someone because of a perceived characteristic. Bias can be overt or covert. That is, people may openly say things like, "I don't like the way kids talk today," or they may comment on a language variety or group indirectly by saying things like, "People from up North are always in a hurry," which may indicate that they consider Northerners to be rude. Everybody has linguistic bias whether they are aware of it or not. Oftentimes, people project perceived characteristics of a group onto the language variety that the group speaks (as in the example above). Ask students to think about situations in which someone can be discriminated against based on the information carried by his or her voice. After a brief discussion, have students watch the 1-minute commercial produced by the U.S. Department of Housing and Urban Development (HUD) [https://languageandlife.org/vonc/vonc02.mp4]. After students watch the advertisement, ask them to write answers to or discuss the questions [that appear in Box 10.2].

1. How common do you think it is for people to be discriminated against on the phone?
   [Answer key] This is an opinion question but students may be interested to learn that it is estimated that there are approximately 2 million cases of linguistic profiling every year in the United States. That is nearly 5,500 instances per day. Of course, many of these may not be the result of a conscious desire to discriminate. The fact of the matter is that we have unconscious reactions to the people we interact with and language does convey a lot of information about us.
2. How strong are peoples' prejudices about language?
   [Answer key] Because so much information about us is conveyed in our voices, any prejudice that a person has about another person or group can be projected onto the language of that group. In fact, prejudice about language may be even more intense than prejudice against groups: People are generally quite aware that it is wrong to discriminate against people based on, for example, the color of their skin or religion, but discrimination based on language is widely accepted. Language becomes the screen upon which our prejudices are projected. Most people filter their prejudices when describing groups but not necessarily when describing language. While no one would think it is appropriate to say something like, "Group X is dumb," it is very common to hear a statement such as "They can't be smart, just listen to the way they talk," when, in fact, a person's speech is independent of that person's intelligence.
3. Why do you think people have such strong prejudices about language?

[Answer key] As long as people are aware of differences between groups, they will continue to be aware of differences between the way groups talk and will continue to treat the speech of stigmatized groups as incorrect. Because language stereotypes are so commonly ignored or accepted as appropriate, the prejudice that goes along with these stereotypes is intense. Related to this is the fact that people don't have to learn about language in order to use it (contrast this with, say, math). Language is simply acquired from birth, and we use it without much effort; therefore, we assume people who speak differently from us must not be as smart as us.

This video exercise has proven to be effective with students from grade 4 through graduate school and in workshops conducted for the general public as well. One of the most consistent responses in Reaser's (2006) post-curriculum survey and questionnaire for middle-school students concerns the inappropriateness of language prejudice.

Levels of Dialect

The dialect curriculum also engages students in examining dialect diversity. To do this, it is essential to understand that language is organized simultaneously on various levels and that variation can occur at every one of them. Students can engage in activities that help them recognize different levels of language organization. Box 10.4 includes excerpts from sample exercises on levels of dialect difference from the North Carolina program's teacher's manual.

Local vocabularies are a rich resource for engaging students in examining dialect differences. Vocabulary is also one of the levels of language that people are naturally curious about, which makes local vocabulary an ideal level of language for students to engage in their community investigations. The excerpt of the activity in Box 10.5 is taken from the Ocracoke dialect unit in the North Carolina curriculum (Wolfram, Schilling-Estes, & Hazen, 1997), which has been taught for more than two decades to middle-school students who attend school on the island. It has always succeeded in drawing students into dialect study. Activities of this type help students become aware of the culturally specific, relative nature of vocabulary. It is offered here as a prototype for student involvement in gathering data. Local adaptations of the activity can be constructed based on vocabulary variation in the community around the school.

BOX 10.4: SAMPLE EXERCISES ON LEVELS OF DIALECT (ADAPTED WITH PERMISSION FROM REASER & WOLFRAM, 2007A, PP. 3–4; COMPLETE EXERCISES AVAILABLE AT THE COMPANION WEBSITE)

Language is organized on several different levels. One level of organization is *pronunciation*, which concerns how sounds are used in a language. Different dialects may use sounds in quite different ways. Sometimes this is referred to simply as accent. For example, some people from New England pronounce the words *car* and *far* without the *r*. Also, some people from the South may say *greasy* with a *z* sound in the middle of the word, so they pronounce it "greazy."

Another level of language organization is *grammar*. Grammar concerns the particular ways in which speakers arrange words in sentences. Different dialects may arrange words in different ways. For instance, in some parts of western Pennsylvania, speakers may say "The car needs washed," whereas other speakers say "The car needs washing." Also, some people from the Appalachian Mountains may say "The man went a-hunting," whereas other people say "The man went hunting." When a person from the Outer Banks says "It weren't me," as opposed to "It wasn't me," we have an example of dialect grammar.

A third level of language involves how different words are used; this is called the *vocabulary* or *lexicon* of the language. Speakers of different dialects may use different words to mean the same thing. Thus, some people in Philadelphia, Pennsylvania, use the word "hoagie" in reference to the same kind of sandwich that other people call a *sub—* or a *grinder, torpedo, hero, poor boy*, and so forth. Also, a common word might be used with different meanings across dialects. Thus, in some areas, "soda" is used for a carbonated drink with ice cream; whereas in other areas, "soda" is used just to refer to a carbonated drink without anything added to it.

Levels of Dialect: Practice

(Teaching time: 20–30 minutes)

This discussion and exercise requires students to apply the definitions discussed earlier. Ask students to review by defining the terms *dialect vocabulary, dialect pronunciation,* and *dialect grammar.*

In this exercise, students look at the components that make up a dialect, or *dialect levels.* In doing this, they examine dialect features from the Outer Banks to Appalachia. In the sentence pairs given next, have students decide whether the difference between the sentences in each pair is at the vocabulary, pronunciation, or grammar level. In the blank provided beside each pair, have them place a V for vocabulary, a P for pronunciation, or a G for grammar to indicate which level is exemplified.

Worksheet Answer Key and Explanations

1. __P__ That feller sure was tall
   That fellow sure was tall

   Background information: This feature, common in many rural Southern dialects, can affect all words that end with an unstressed o sound, including *yellow, potato, tomato, mosquito, window, elbow, burrito*, and so forth. These words would be pronounced with an r sound instead of the o sound: "yeller," "potater" (or simply "tater"), "tomater" (or simply "mater"), "mosquiter" (or simply "skeeter"), "winder," "elber," and "burriter." This pattern does not apply when the o sound is stressed, as in *throw, go,* or *bestow*. Thus, there is a pattern that determines when this feature can operate and when it cannot.

2. __V__ That road sure is sigogglin
   That road sure is crooked

   Background information: The word *sigogglin* is found in the speech of people who live in the Appalachian Mountain region of North Carolina. It can mean *crooked, askew,* or *not plumb*. Roads, houses, and walls can all be sigogglin. This word is sometimes written *sygogglin* and sometimes pronounced as "sigoggly." In other parts of the South, the word *catawampus* or *catterwampus* can be used to mean crooked. In other places, such as the South Midland region, some speakers use the word *antigogglin*. All of these are examples of dialect vocabulary.

3. __G__ They usually be doing their homework
   They usually do their homework

   Background information: There is a special use of *be* in African American English. The uninflected form of *be* is used in place of conjugated *am, is,* or *are* in sentences that describe habitual or recurring action. In this sentence, the habitual context is denoted by the word *usually*. In nonhabitual contexts, African American English speakers would use either regularly inflected forms such as *am, is,* and *are*, or they would omit the verb altogether.

4. __G__ I weren't there yesterday
   I wasn't there yesterday

   Background information: This feature, common in many dialects, is a result of an irregular pattern being made regular. Linguists refer to this as *regularization* or *leveling*. Leveling is a natural process that may take place whenever there is an irregularity in a particular pattern. Because the verb *to be* is irregular in English, there is a natural tendency to favor regularization or leveling of this pattern. Thus, vernacular dialects may use *was* for all past-tense forms—"I was," "you was," "he was," and so forth. In some dialects in North Carolina, affirmative past-tense forms of *to be* may be leveled to *was*, but negative past-tense forms are often leveled to *weren't* (as in "I was," "you was," "he was," "we was," and "I weren't," "you weren't," "he weren't," "we weren't").

[Remainder of exercise can be found at link above]

BOX 10.5: EXAMPLE OF DIALECT VOCABULARY ACTIVITY (ADAPTED WITH PERMISSION FROM WOLFRAM, SCHILLING-ESTES, & HAZEN, 1997, N.P.)

VOCABULARY IN OCRACOKE

There are lots of vocabulary differences that can be described for Ocracoke. Each of the uses has a unique history. We can trace back some uses in the English language more than 1,000 years, and some go back just a few years. For example, words like *token* (in "token of death"), *mommuck*, and *quamish* were used centuries ago in ways related to how they are used in Ocracoke today. Other terms such as *dingbatter*, *scud*, and *up the beach* are relatively recent uses. We can trace certain vocabulary forms confidently, but we can make only educated guesses about the origins of other words. For example, a unique Ocracoke use of the phrase *call the mail over* may be traced to the earlier custom of distributing mail by calling aloud the names of those who received letters at the dock when the mail boat arrived. We're not exactly sure how *meehonkey* came into use, but we guess that it had something to do with the attempt to imitate the call of a goose.

Most of the dialect words found in Ocracoke occur in other dialects as well, but a few are unique to Ocracoke. Also, the use of vocabulary in Ocracoke differs according to age and background.

Following are some words that are part of the Ocracoke dialect vocabulary. For each of the words, do the following:

- Figure out what the word means, if you don't already know. You can usually do this by asking island residents of different ages about the words.
- Use the word in a sentence and try to figure out what part of speech it is.
- Identify the type of people who know the word and who use it: Is it used by older people, by younger people, by nonislanders?
- Which of the words do you think are used ONLY in Ocracoke or in the Outer Banks?

Write your answers below.

slick cam _____

puck _____

across the beach _____

Make a chart that summarizes the group of people who know the words in the list. On top of the chart, list the groups. Here is an example:

	Older Ocracokers	Younger Ocracokers	Outsiders
Word		✓	
Word		✓	✓
Word	✓		

Dialect Patterning

Language, including dialects, is a unique form of knowledge, in that speakers know a language simply by virtue of the fact that they speak it. Much of this knowledge is not conscious, but it is still open to systematic investigation. Examining dialects opens a fascinating window through which we can see how language works. Furthermore, the inner patterning of language is just as readily observed in examining dialect patterning as through the exclusive study of a single standard variety.

Making generalizations from carefully described sets of data, students can hypothesize about the patterning of language features and then check their hypotheses on the basis of actual usage. This process, of course, is an important kind of scientific inquiry, and it is well within the grasp even of younger students. In fact, students in the upper elementary grades have been able to work through the steps of hypothesis formation and testing by using exercises involving dialect features, like those in Boxes 10.6 and 10.7. The exercises in Box 10.6 illustrate patterning in pronunciation and those in Box 10.7 illustrate patterning of grammatical differences.

Pronunciation patterns. It is helpful to do pronunciation exercises with supportive audio recordings of the actual pronunciation. The exercises in Box 10.6, samples taken from the teacher's manual in Reaser and Wolfram (2007a), represent both regional and social dimensions of dialects, ranging from Southern regional speech to New England speech, as well as Appalachian and vernacular African American speech. They allow students to experience inductively how patterned all varieties of language are regardless of their social valuation.

BOX 10.6: ILLUSTRATIVE EXERCISES IN PRONUNCIATION
PATTERNING (ADAPTED WITH PERMISSION FROM REASER
AND WOLFRAM, 2007A, PP. 5–6, 10–13; COMPLETE
EXERCISES AVAILABLE AT THE COMPANION WEBSITE)

PRONUNCIATION LESSON

This lesson asks students to examine language data, and to formulate
and test hypotheses about how dialects pattern. These hypotheses
are refined as students gain authentic knowledge of language patterns.

Overview

Many people are shocked to learn that dialects are patterned and
systematic. Even speakers of dialects who conform to the patterns
may not be aware of the patterns that govern their speech. The following activities examine a few linguistic patterns from different dialects
of English, including New England English, Southern English, and
Appalachian English. These activities demonstrate the systematic
nature of language variation and help students see language as a
topic worthy of scientific study.

Key Ideas

1. All dialects have patterns that govern their use, just as Standard
   English does.
2. Some individual dialect features pattern in relatively simple ways,
   whereas others follow multiple rules that govern their use.
3. Linguists study language patterns.
4. Some language patterns can be discovered with help from our
   linguistic intuitions, whereas others require examining data from
   dialect speakers.

How Dialects Pattern

Dialects are patterned and rule-governed, not haphazard. What this
means is that the dialects of a language follow their own patterns. The
rules that dialects follow state the regular, predictable patterns that
dialect forms follow. Sometimes these patterns can be complicated
and difficult to figure out. However, the human mind has the capacity
to learn all of these intricate patterns unconsciously and follow them.
The ability to absorb language patterns and follow them without
thinking about the patterns is one of the most amazing things about
the human mind.

   In this lesson, the class will try to figure out some patterns for
different dialect forms. The challenge is to come up with a rule that
accurately describes all the examples. If the rule is correct, it should
predict how new language forms will be treated.

How Pronunciation Differences Work: Southern Vowel Merger

In some Southern dialects of English, words like *pin* and *pen* are pronounced the same. Usually, both words are pronounced as "pin." This pattern of pronunciation is also found in other words. Examining data from a native speaker of this dialect demonstrates how linguists uncover linguistic patterns. List A has words in which the *i* and *e* are pronounced the same in these dialects. Play a recording of a native speaker with this vowel merger for the students.

LIST A: *I* AND *E* PRONOUNCED THE SAME [https://languageandlife.org/vonc/vonc12.mp4]

1. *tin* and *ten*
2. *kin* and *Ken*
3. *Lin* and *Len*
4. *windy* and *Wendy*
5. *sinned* and *send*

Although *i* and *e* in List A are pronounced the same, there are other words in which *i* and *e* are pronounced differently. List B has word pairs in which the vowels are pronounced differently.

LIST B: *I* AND *E* PRONOUNCED DIFFERENTLY [https://languageandlife.org/vonc/vonc13.mp4]

1. *lit* and *let*
2. *pick* and *peck*
3. *pig* and *peg*
4. *rip* and *rep*
5. *litter* and *letter*

Ask students to examine the word pairs in the two lists and offer hypotheses about when *i* and *e* are pronounced the same and when they are pronounced differently. If they are having trouble discovering the pattern, ask them to examine the sounds that are next to the vowels. The pattern is determined by the presence or absence of an *n* sound. If an *n* sound follows the vowel, the words are pronounced the same. If there is no *n*-sound following the vowel, the words are pronounced differently.

Have students use what they have learned about this pronunciation pattern to predict the word pairs in List C that are pronounced the same and those that are pronounced differently in this Southern dialect. Have them mark the word pairs that are pronounced the same with S and the word pairs that are pronounced differently with D. Answers are supplied here.

List C: Same or Different? [https://languageandlife.org/vonc/vonc14.mp4]

__D_ *bit* and *bet*
__D_ *pit* and *pet*
__S_ *bin* and *Ben*
__D_ *Nick* and *neck*
__S_ *din* and *den*

How Pronunciation Differences Work: Dropping r in English Dialects

In some dialects of English, the *r* sound of words like *car* or *poor* can be dropped. In these words, the *r* is not pronounced, so that these words sound like "cah" and "po." However, not all *r* sounds can be dropped. In some places in a word the *r* sound may be dropped, and in other places it may NOT be dropped. By comparing lists of words where the *r* may be dropped with lists of words where it may NOT be dropped, the students can figure out a pattern for *r*-dropping.

List A gives words where the *r* may be DROPPED.

List A: Words That Can Drop r [https://languageandlife.org/vonc/vonc15.mp4]

1. car
2. father
3. card
4. bigger
5. cardboard

List B gives words where the *r* sound may NOT be dropped. In other words, speakers who drop their *r*s in List A pronounce the *r* in the words in List B.

List B: Words That CANNOT Drop r [https://languageandlife.org/vonc/vonc16.mp4]

1. run
2. bring
3. principal
4. string
5. okra

To find a pattern for dropping the *r*, look at the type of sound that comes before the *r* in Lists A and B. Does a vowel or a consonant come before the *r* in List A? What comes before the *r* in List B? How can you predict where an *r* may or may not be dropped?

In List C, pick those words that may drop their *r* and those that may not drop their *r*. Use your knowledge of the *r*-dropping pattern that you learned by comparing Lists A and B. Put Y for "Yes" if the word can drop the *r* and N for "No" if it cannot drop the *r*.

LIST C: APPLYING THE RULE FOR *r*-DROPPING [https://languageandlife.org/vonc/vonc17.mp4]

1. _____ bear
2. _____ program
3. _____ fearful
4. _____ right

Think of two new words that may drop an *r* and two new words that may NOT drop an *r*.

Can drop *r*	Cannot drop *r*
1. _____	1. _____
2. _____	2. _____

MORE ABOUT *r*-DROPPING PATTERNS

In the last exercise, you saw that *r*-dropping only takes place when the *r* comes after a vowel. Now look at the kinds of sounds that may come AFTER the *r* in some dialects of English. This pattern goes along with the one you already learned. Now see if you can figure out the pattern.

Here are some words where the *r* may NOT be dropped even when it comes after a vowel.

LIST A: WORDS THAT DO NOT DROP R [https://languageandlife.org/vonc/vonc18.mp4]

1. bear in the field
2. car over at the house
3. garage
4. caring
5. take four apples

What kinds of sounds come after the *r* in List A? Are they vowels or consonants?

In List B, the *r* MAY be dropped. What kind of sounds come after the *r* in this list?

LIST B: WORDS THAT DROP R [https://languageandlife.org/vonc/vonc19.mp4]

1. bear by the woods
2. car parked by the house

3. parking the bus
4. fearful
5. take four peaches

What does the sound that comes after *r* do to *r*-dropping?

Use what you know about the pattern for *r*-dropping to pick the *r*s in List C that can be dropped. Say why the *r* can or cannot be dropped. Write Y for "Yes" if the *r* can be dropped and N for "No" if it cannot be dropped. Remember that the *r* must come after a vowel to be dropped, but it cannot have a vowel after it.

LIST C: WORDS THAT MAY OR MAY NOT DROP R [https://languageandlife.org/vonc/vonc20.mp4]

1. pear on the table
2. pear by the table
3. park in the mall
4. program in the mall
5. car behind the house

LIST D: PRACTICING THE R-DROP PATTERN

Try to pronounce the two sentences given here according to the *r*-drop pattern that you learned.

1. The teacher picked on three students for an answer.
2. Four cars parked far away from the fair.

Grammatical Patterns. Exercises on grammatical patterning can go a long way toward dispelling the notion that vernacular dialects are simply imperfect renditions of the standard variety. Working with them sets the stage for generating a genuine respect for the complexity of systematic differences among dialects.

Box 10.7 presents excerpts from two exercises. The first one looks at the pattern in *a*-prefixing. The advantage of examining this form is that its patterning is intuitive to both those who use the form in their own vernacular dialect and those who do not. This fact makes the exercise appropriate for English-speaking students regardless of their native dialect (although English language learners may well not have intuitions about this form simply because they have had little exposure to it). The second exercise in Box 10.7 is part of an activity on habitual *be* in vernacular African American English. These two grammatical patterns highlight the need to employ different pedagogical approaches to language analysis based on whether students are likely to have intuitions about the feature or not. Most English-speaking students have little trouble select-ing the *a*-prefixing sentence that sounds better, but relatively few have intuitions about the habitual aspect encoded by the uninflected form of *be*. In the former, the forced choice method leads to discovering the rules of the pattern. In the second, students can derive the pattern only through analysis of student response data.

BOX 10.7: TWO ILLUSTRATIVE EXERCISES OF GRAMMATICAL PATTERNING

The use of *a*-prefix (adapted with permission from Reaser & Wolfram, 2007b, pp. 7–9; complete exercise available at the companion website)

In some traditional rural dialects of the South, some words that end in *-ing* can take an *a-*, pronounced as "uh," in front of the word, as in "she went a-fishing." This pattern is called *a-* prefixing. But not every *-ing* word can have an *a-* prefix. There are patterns or rules that determine when the *a-* prefix can be used and when it cannot be used. You will try to figure out these rules by using your inner feelings about language. These inner feelings, called *intuitions*, tell you when you CAN and CANNOT use certain forms. The job of linguists is to figure out the reason for these inner feelings and state the exact pattern or rule.

Read each pair of sentences in List A. Decide which sentence in each pair sounds better. For example, in the first sentence pair, does it sound better to say, *A-building is hard work* or *She was a-building a house*? For each pair of sentences, place a check next to the sentence that sounds better with the *a-*.

List A: Sentence Pairs for A- Prefixing

1. a. _____ *A*-building is hard work.
   b. _____ She was *a*-building a house.
2. a. _____ He likes *a*-hunting.
   b. _____ He went *a*-hunting.
3. a. _____ The child was *a*-charming the adults.
   b. _____ The child was very *a*-charming.

Look at your choices for the *a-* prefix in each pair of sentences and answer the following questions.

Do you think there is some pattern that guided your choice of an answer? You can tell if there is a definite pattern by checking with other people who did the same exercise on their own. Do you think that the pattern might be related to parts of speech? To answer this, see if there are any parts of speech where you CANNOT use the *a-* prefix. Look at *-ing* forms that function as verbs and compare those with *-ing* forms that operate as nouns or adjectives. For example, look at the use of *charming* as a verb (The child was *a*-charming the adults) and adjective (*The child was very *a*-charming) in Sentence 3.

The first rule of the pattern for a- prefix is related to the part of speech of the -ing word, but there is more to the pattern. To discover the second rule, read the sentences in List B, insert the a- before the -ing word, and decide which sentence in each pair sounds better. For each pair of sentences, place a check next to the sentence that sounds better with the a-.

List B: A Further Detail for A- Patterning

1. a. _____ They make money by a-building houses.
   b. _____ They make money a-building houses.
2. a. _____ People can't make enough money a-fishing.
   b. _____ People can't make enough money from a-fishing.

The second rule of the pattern for a- prefix is related to prepositions. But there is still another rule to the pattern for a- prefix use. To discover the third rule, read the sentences in List C, insert the a- before the -ing word, and decide which sentence in each pair sounds better. To help you figure out this rule, the stressed or accented syllable of each word is marked with the symbol ´. For each pair of sentences, place a check next to the sentence that sounds better with the a-.

List C: Figuring out a Pronunciation Pattern for A- Prefix

1. a. _____ She was a-discóvering a trail.
   b. _____ She was a-fóllowing a trail.
2. a. _____ They were a-fíguring the change.
   b. _____ They were a-forgétting the change.
3. a. _____ The baby was a-recognízing the mother.
   b. _____ The baby was a-wrécking everything.

Say exactly how the three rules determine the pattern for attaching the a- prefix to -ing words.

Rule 1: _____
Rule 2: _____
Rule 3: _____

Using your rules, try to predict whether the sentences in List D may use an a- prefix. Use your understanding of the pattern to explain why the -ing word may or may not take the a- prefix.

List D: Applying the A- Prefix Rule

1. She kept a-handing me more work.
2. The team was a-remémbering the game.
3. The team won by a-playing great defense.
4. The team was a-playing real hard.

Be in African American English (adapted with permission from Reaser & Wolfram, 2007b, pp. 36–37; complete exercise available at the companion website)

The next task concerns a form in a dialect that is sometimes used by young African American speakers in large cities. The form *be* is used where other dialects use *am*, *is*, or *are*, except that it has a special meaning. A group of 35 young speakers of this dialect of English in Baltimore, Maryland, chose the sentence that sounded better to them in the following sentence pairs, like you did for *a-* prefixing. Notice that they had a definite preference for one sentence over the other.

Why do you think that was the case?

The number before each sentence indicates how many of the young people chose that sentence as the best one in the pair:

1. <u>32</u> a. *They usually be tired when they come home.*
   <u>3</u> b. They be tired right now.
2. <u>31</u> a. *When we play basketball, she be on my team.*
   <u>4</u> b. The girl in the picture be my sister.
3. <u>3</u> a. My ankle be broken from the fall.
   <u>32</u> b. *Sometimes my ears be itching.*

Try to figure out the pattern that led the young people to make their choices. To do this, look at the type of action that is involved in each sentence. Does the action take place at just one time, or does the action take place more than once? Try to state the regular pattern in terms of the action.

Now that you know how the form *be* is used, predict which of the following sentences follow the rule for using *be* in the African American English dialect and which do NOT. Write Y for "Yes" if the sentence follows the dialect pattern and N for "No" if it does not.

1. _____ The students always be talking in class.
2. _____ The students don't be talking right now.
3. _____ Sometimes the teacher be early for class.
4. _____ At the moment the teacher be in the lounge.

As you can see, African American English has rules that determine when you can and cannot say *be*. In other words, there are rules for using *be* just as there are rules for using *a-* prefixing (*he went a-fishing*). Despite the fact that African American English is rule-governed and patterned like all dialects, it is often viewed negatively.

A Video Exercise

As you watch a video (8-minute vignette on African American English from *Voices of North Carolina* [https://languageandlife.org/vonc/vonc 27.mp4]) about African American English, think about the following questions:

1. Why do you think that these African Americans feel they have to change the way they speak sometimes?
2. Do you ever feel that you have to change the way you speak? Why?
3. Think about the different situations in which you change your speech. In what situation(s) do you think you have to talk most formally? In what situation(s) do you think you can talk more casually?

The exercise on habitual *be* is used along with a video of African American speakers demonstrating that patterning can be unique to a particular dialect and that we cannot make assumptions about other dialects based on our own dialect. The exercise on systematic use of habitual *be* may be coupled with a reflective activity on the use of language in different situations, as indicated in the set of follow-up questions. This excerpt comes from the student materials. Working through exercises of this type is an effective way of confronting the myth that dialects have no rules of their own; at the same time, the activity demonstrates the underlying cognitive patterning of language.

These exercises show students how linguists collect and organize data to formulate rules, and they demonstrate that linguistic rules are statements about patterns that speakers follow, not prescriptions about what speakers should do. They also provide a model for analyzing data that students collect from their own community. To emulate this process, students should record language data, extract particular examples from the recordings, formulate linguistic rules, and then test those formulations on more examples. In this way, they can learn first-hand to examine language scientifically.

Language Change

Dialects play an essential role in the change that languages inevitably undergo. As a part of dialect study, it is important for students and instructors to understand that language change is natural. Understanding the processes of change involves recognizing that change involves orderly cognitive and behavioral processes. For example, languages tend to "level" irregular patterns over time: Regularization is a normal and natural process in language change. When students from vernacular-speaking backgrounds regularize the past tense of irregular verbs such as "knowed" for *knew* and "growed" for *grew*, they are simply following a time-honored and natural tradition of leveling irregular verb forms—the same processes that gave Standard English *worked* (once *wrought*) and *helped* (once *holp*). Many of the regular verbs we now accept as part of Standard English were, in fact, once irregular forms. Changes at all levels are part of a continuously changing language, and current changes in progress in English follow the principles that have guided language change forever. An appreciation for the evolution of the English language over time should promote more tolerance for the types of changes it is currently undergoing.

Box 10.8 is a simple comparative activity that shows how dramatically English has changed over the centuries. By examining a familiar passage, in this case the Lord's Prayer, students can see radical change in the language at every level—from the sounds and the words, to the orderly arrangement of words within sentences.

BOX 10.8: AN ILLUSTRATIVE EXERCISE IN LANGUAGE CHANGE (ADAPTED WITH PERMISSION FROM WOLFRAM, SCHILLING-ESTES, & HAZEN, 1997, N.P.)

English has changed quite dramatically over the centuries. In fact, early English is barely recognizable today. Compare the versions of English at various stages in its history, as found in the first verse of the Lord's Prayer.

Old English (about 950 A.D.)
Fader urer ðu bist in heofnas, sie gehalgad noma ðin

Middle English (about 1350 A.D.)
Oure fadir þat art in heuenes, halwid be þi name

Early Modern English (about 1550 A.D.)
oure father which arte in heven, hallowed be thy name

Modern English (about 1985 A.D.)
Our father, who is in heaven, may your name be sacred

1. Try pronouncing the different versions of English. In the older versions (Old and Middle English), "silent letters" do not exist, so you will need to pronounce *all* the letters. The symbol ð is pronounced something like the *th* of *this*, and the þ is pronounced like the *th* of *think*.

2. Try to identify some of the older versions of modern words. For example, trace the words that became the current words *father*, *heaven*, *name*, *is*, and *our*. *Hallow* is still used in formal English, but it also became *holy* (a synonym, *sacred*, appears in the Modern English Lord's Prayer). What other modern English word did *hallow* become?
3. What does this comparison tell you about the way the English language has changed over the centuries?

Implementing Dialect Awareness Curricula

Implementing new curricular programs is easier said than done. To our knowledge, there are not many dialect awareness programs in the United States and thus there are limited models for introducing them. In our experience, marketing skills, bureaucratic finesse, and a good sense of timing have proved to be essential for introducing dialect awareness curricula into schools. The argument has to be made that the programs are consonant with the educational objectives of statewide and local curricula and that they are readily implemented by practitioners (Lord & Klein, 2010; Reaser, 2010b). Dialect curriculum developers have to identify specific competencies in the course of study (e.g., social studies, language arts, communication skills) as set forth by the State Board of Education and align lessons with these competencies (Reaser, 2010b). For example, the North Carolina Standard Course of Study for eighth grade social studies includes this objective: **1.01** Assess the impact of geography on the settlement and developing economy of the Carolina colony. The objective is met by the dialect curriculum's examination of how isolation caused by ocean, swamps, and mountains shaped dialects. Further, geography explains the Great Wagon Road, which has had a lasting impact on North Carolina dialects.

Another important part of implementing dialect awareness programs is preparing teachers for the challenge of teaching about language variation, a formidable task in its own right. Workshops, webinars, and other online programs are needed to support these efforts, and linguists are developing best practices for such experiences (Reaser, 2016; Sweetland, 2010).

Dialect Awareness Beyond K–12

Although dialect awareness programs in schools help introduce students to knowledge about language beyond the classroom, better informed language views cannot be achieved solely through the K–12 education sector. There is obviously a critical need for dialect awareness to spread. Efforts to promote dialect awareness in recent years have included community-based programs such as television and video documentaries (e.g., www.talkingnc.com), trade books on dialects for general audiences (Rickford & Rickford, 2002; Wolfram & Reaser, 2014), museum exhibits, and presentations to a wide range of community organizations such as civic groups, churches, preservation societies, and other local institutions and agencies. However, it is clear that much work remains to be done creating materials that both celebrate and teach about the vast language diversity in the United States.

Most institutions in the United States have recognized the importance of diversity in the workplace and in education, and many now have dedicated organizational programs focused on promoting diversity. These efforts are intended to affirm a wide range of cultural and individual lifestyles and behaviors. Although these efforts extend to a range of groups and behavior—based on race/ethnicity, sexual orientation, religious affiliation, gender, and so on—they rarely address language variation, which can index all of those characteristics (Lippi-Green, 2012). Dunstan's (2013) study of Appalachian students' experiences in a Southern urban university, for example, found that students who use a variety of Appalachian English or "mountain speech" experienced social consequences in a number of domains, including in class participation, perceptions of intelligence expressed by professors and other students, and to an extent, in their own sense of belonging on campus. These adverse effects did not necessarily align with traditional sociopolitical ideologies found in different fields: Some students perceived that there was less tolerance of language variations in the social sciences and humanities than in disciplines such as economics or the physical sciences. A blog associated with *The Economist* (no author, 2015) summarized the irony of this situation:

> The collision of academic prejudice and accent is particularly ironic. Academics tend to the center-left nearly everywhere, and talk endlessly about class and multiculturalism. (. . .) And yet accent and dialect are still barely on many people's minds as deserving respect.

As the importance and benefits of diversity training programs become recognized, it is unfortunate that language diversity is not typically represented (Dunstan, Wolfram, Jaeger, & Crandall, 2015). At the same time, studies of dialect diversity education suggest that such programs can ameliorate some of the negative attitudes and beliefs about vernacular varieties, and by extension, the people who speak them (Dunstan, Jaeger, & Crandall, 2014; Murphy, 2012). For higher education, Dunstan, et al. (2014) found that, although students and professors alike may subscribe to the principle of linguistic subordination (Lippi-Green, 2012), it is possible to intervene to change these beliefs and develop appreciation and tolerance. Language diversity can be added to any institutional program on diversity, but it is also essential to see how language issues intersect with traditional topics in the diversity canon such as race, ethnicity, religion, gender, and sex. For example, issues of sexist language,

language discrimination, and the language of sexual consent intersect with our understanding of sex and gender. In the process of considering these issues, it becomes important to challenge sexist and homophobic discourses and to recognize the ways in which language and gender interact.

Although there are only a few examples of such language diversity programs, North Carolina State University, the home institution of two of this book's co-authors, has recently established a campus-wide program on language called Educating the Educated. The program addresses the lack of institutional language diversity programs and advances knowledge of the effectiveness of dialect diversity training. It is comprehensive, multidisciplinary, and cross-organizational, involving collaboration across the colleges and administrative units on campus in order to reach the entire university community, providing information about language diversity to students, faculty, administration, and staff. The conceptual framework underlying the program is based on Pedersen's (1988) Multicultural Development Model, and it addresses awareness, knowledge, and skill.

The model's first stage, addressing the affective domain, is awareness. Because language is rarely given attention as an element of diversity in college and because standard language ideology and linguistic hegemony are so pervasive in American society, members of the campus community remain largely unaware of the attitudes and assumptions they hold about language and, by extension, speakers of those dialects/languages. This program seeks to raise awareness through an inductive process that asks participants to think critically about their beliefs. The second stage, knowledge (the cognitive domain), involves providing factual, scientific linguistic evidence to dispel common myths and fallacies associated with language and language variation. Finally, the program moves to the third stage, skill (the behavioral domain), by offering strategies for being inclusive and for considering language and dialect when interacting with others from different linguistic backgrounds on campus and in society. The program coordinators of Educating the Educated represent different colleges and faculty/administrative roles at the university, thus offering different perspectives, disciplinary affiliations, and administrative networks to the program, which enables a "campus-infusion model" for implementation.

The program's language diversity awareness materials take a variety of forms. For example, there is a 6-minute vignette on language and dialect diversity at the university, which was filmed on campus and features spontaneous student responses to questions about their speech and about dialect diversity on campus (www.youtube.com/watch?v=eQYNEHwDFhE). This vignette has become a key component of presentations about the program as well as a resource for diversity training/programming. It is now shown routinely to incoming students, staff, and faculty as a part of orientation. Other materials were created for distribution on campus to raise awareness, such as buttons and posters highlighting the NC State Wolfpack mascot (shown in Figure 10.1),

FIGURE 10.1 "Howl with an accent" button and campus diversity poster (NC State trademarks used with permission by North Carolina State University)

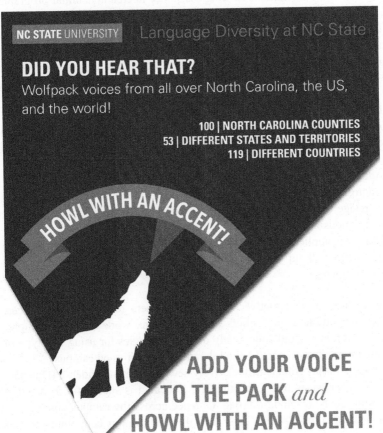

which are placed in locations such as in residence halls, and classroom and administrative buildings, and in digital format on digital campus bulletin boards.

Another strategy used in Educating the Educated is a student ambassador program in which graduate students in sociolinguistics receive training and then engage in peer education by delivering workshops and developing resource materials. For example, some ambassadors with interests in language variation and composition sought out a workshop opportunity with a campus writing program, while ambassadors with an interest in education became involved in a workshop for pre-service teachers. Diversity ambassadors have also worked to create an online digital repository of resource materials (PowerPoint presentations, audiovisual materials, assessment materials, etc.), which all team members can access. These online resources are available for sharing with other institutions seeking assistance in creating similar programs (http://howl.wordpress.ncsu.edu/).

The campus infusion model highlights major organizational divisions on campus: student affairs units, academic affairs, human resources, faculty affairs, and campus diversity. Workshops are offered throughout the campus following this format:

1. Defining what a dialect is.
2. Addressing three common myths/truths about dialects (everyone speaks a dialect; the "standard" is a social construct; all dialects are rule-governed and systematic).
3. Addressing issues of linguistic discrimination.
4. Addressing issues of language variation contextually for the audience (how language variation might impact you, your discipline, work environment, interactions with others, etc.).
5. Drawing implications for practice (how audience members can use information about dialect diversity to create inclusive and respectful environments).

The workshops are interactive: Audience members reflect on experiences, explore their attitudes and beliefs about language, work through examples of dialect patterning, and collectively discuss strategies for using this type of diversity to facilitate respectful and tolerant communities on campus.

Although this program is still relatively new, assessment evidence (Dunstan, et al., 2015) suggests that Educating the Educated is successful in meeting its learning goals, reaching a broad audience across the campus community, and addressing a topic that is both critical to the campus community and of interest to most participants. Participants have provided overwhelmingly positive feedback. Much of this success is owed to the multidisciplinary nature of the team behind the program and the subsequent ability to make use of strategic connections across disciplines and levels of administration. Institutions seeking to create similar programs should be open to interdisciplinary, cross-organizational collaborations and be intentional in planning, seeking out, and gaining the support of leaders and key gatekeepers on campus. Similar programs could readily be established for other public and private institutions, including K–12 schools. In conducting such programs, it is essential to begin with a limited set of learning outcomes and to engage participants in a *positive* manner with examples and activities that are easily relatable and applicable to their daily lives.

The Importance of Dialect Awareness for All Students

Thanks to recurrent national language controversies and the inherent curiosity most people have about language differences, we have witnessed a growing interest in language issues. These often create "a teachable moment of national proportion" (Getridge, 1997, p. 2)—an occasion to provide accurate information about dialect diversity to counter some of the misguided, popular interpretations that surround it. But it is time to move beyond these spurts in interest to ensure long-term sociolinguistic education to the American public. We need to implement concrete public programs in addition to the campus- and school-based programs examined here in order to guide our society at large to replace widespread, destructive myths about language variation with scientific, factually based evidence on the nature of dialect diversity. There is simply no other insurance against the kinds of controversies and misunderstandings that continue to arise over language variation. More important, there is probably no other road to an authentic understanding of the role of dialect diversity in American society.

Happily, the programs described here have been effective. Students' responses in the opening scenario suggest that they find dialect information to be interesting and important for a number of reasons. When more than 85% of the pilot study students reported that it is important to study dialects and more than 90% of those in one classroom reported that the dialect curriculum was the most memorable part of their year, it is hard to imagine another academic topic being seen as more engaging and critical than language awareness. Teachers can generate this enthusiasm when they have the appropriate materials and information.

Two teachers involved in the pilot study of the North Carolina curriculum wrote about their experiences, revealing how they perceived the value of dialect awareness. Ms. Leatha Fields-Carey writes (Fields-Carey & Sweat, 2010, pp. 272–274) as follows:

As the unit progressed, I realized that not only had I underestimated the students' ability to understand the material, I also had no idea how fascinated they would become with the study of dialects.

> I have found the study of language variations to be a wonderful way to address differences between people, and this aspect of [the dialect curriculum] has been the most valuable part to me and my students. . . Discussing bias in relation to language is a non-threatening way to begin thinking and talking about biases in general.

> Through the study of dialects and language differences, my views of what it means to truly teach about the "art of language" has broadened significantly. I now realize that to understand language is not only to know how to speak and write "standard English" correctly, but also to value the rich tapestry of language in all its forms.

Ms. Fields-Carey's testimony is powerful. The themes in these passages and throughout her account suggest that this study transformed her class and her students. She describes typically reticent students who became engaged and animated, students who were transformed when their heritage or culture was validated, and students whose stereotypes dissipated as they confronted the realities of language variation.

There is no question that speakers of socially stigmatized dialects benefit most when speakers of mainstream dialects come to learn the patterns, history, and cultural significance of vernacular speech. One teacher noted that studying African American English "has proven to be empowering for my minority students. For many of them, this is the first time they have been told in a school setting that their dialect is not 'broken'" (Fields-Carey & Sweat, 2010, pp. 273–274). Perhaps it is for this reason that linguists have most commonly created materials specifically examining African American English (e.g., Baratz & Shuy, 1969; Fasold & Shuy, 1970; Sweetland, 2004; Wheeler & Swords, 2006, 2010) and have begun to address other varieties, such as Latino English (e.g., Henderson, 2016).

One long-standing concern has been that such programs have been taught only to speakers of the dialects in question, perpetuating the unequal burden of language knowledge and accommodation for vernacular-speaking students (Sledd, 1969). Such a model is not desirable for several reasons. First, placing the burden of language accommodation entirely on one group is not aligned with American ideals of fairness. Second, the people most likely to be in a position to effect social or policy change with respect to language variation are mainstream English speakers, and therefore exposing them to information about language diversity may help change policy. Third, all students benefit from studying scientific information about language variation (Charity Hudley & Mallinson, 2014; Henderson, 2016; Sweetland, 2006; Wheeler & Swords, 2006). Finally, studying language variation broadly can result in transference of understanding from one language context to another. The pilot study examined in this chapter (Reaser, 2006) was taught at the height of the Hispanic immigration to North Carolina, and popular rhetoric suggested that the immigration was an invasion. English-only sentiments were widely apparent. Though the students participating in the dialect awareness intervention did examine Latino English as part of the curriculum, it was actually their study of Cherokee that led many of them to change their minds about whether Spanish posed a threat to English. One of the participating teachers, Suzanne Sweat, described this transference of understanding:

> When we discussed personal language biases as a class, one belief that was communicated by several students was that Hispanic students should not be allowed to speak Spanish in our American schools. . . After discussing how the culture of the Cherokee Indians was intertwined with their language, we discussed how the language of Hispanic students was also an important part of their culture. Students began to realize that forcing Hispanic students to only speak English was analogous to asking them to give up part of their culture. I began to see the beliefs and prejudices once held by some of my students slowly begin to dissipate.
>
> *Fields-Carey & Sweat, 2010, p. 275*

Dialect awareness programs, therefore, need to include many dialects to represent the wide range of language diversity in American society. In fact, experience with programs in schools and communities indicates that they are most effective and least threatening when they do not isolate a single language variety in the discussion of language variation.

There are few facts of life more misrepresented in the public sector than those involving language variation; it seems only appropriate that a wide-scale, dedicated effort be made to counter this miseducation by using a full range of formal and informal public education venues. Elementary and secondary schools are clearly at the center of this effort.

Discussion Questions

1. How do you explain the fact that so little attention has been paid to dialect diversity in education? Do you have experience with a dialect awareness curriculum? If your own education has included accurate information on language variation, how do you explain your exceptional experience?

2. How might student investigation of local dialects be structured? Do you think teachers need advanced knowledge about language to lead such an undertaking? How could they get expert help, if they need it?

3. Which of the dialect curriculum materials excerpted in this chapter seem to be readily usable? Which would need to be modified for regions outside North Carolina, and how could that be done?

4. Which exercises strike you as must intriguing? Explain.
5. The chapter suggests that whether to teach a dialect awareness unit might not be at the teacher's discretion. Does this seem right? Where should the impetus for teaching such a unit come from? The approval?
6. What would be the value of developing and implementing a program akin to Educating the Educated in high schools and middle schools? What resources would be needed and where would leadership come from?

Links of Interest

1. Watch and read more about the housing discrimination advertisement featured in this chapter: www.civilrights.org/fairhousing/ads/accents.html
2. Explore the dialect awareness materials created by the Language and Life Project at NC State University: http://linguistics.chass.ncsu.edu/thinkand do/dialecteducation.php
3. Discover a curriculum on the dialect, history, and culture of West Virginia: http://dialects.english.wvu.edu/outreach/dialects_in_schools
4. Examine materials and links related to the PBS documentary *Do You Speak American?* www.pbs.org/speak/education/
5. Mine the linguistic lesson plan resources compiled at TeachLing: https://teachling.wwu.edu/
6. Explore a curriculum on the Pidgin spoken in Hawai'i: http://sls.hawaii.edu/pidgin/materialsForEducators.php
7. Learn how to speak Jamaican Patois, part of a curriculum project designed to celebrate Jamaica's creole language: http://jamaicanpatwah.com/b/how-to-speak-jamaican-patois#.V7c0rfkrJph
8. Listen to selections from the American English Dialect Recordings at the Library of Congress: www.loc.gov/collections/american-english-dialect-recordings-from-the-center-for-applied-linguistics/about-this-collection/
9. Watch the "Language Diversity at NC State" educational video: www.youtube.com/watch?v=eQYNEHwDFhE
10. Review the language lessons created by the North Carolina Civic Education Consortium that support the book *Talkin' Tar Heel: How our voices tell the story of North Carolina*: http://linguistics.chass.ncsu.edu/thinkanddo/cec.php

Further Reading

Andrews, L. (2006). *Language exploration and awareness: A resource book for teachers* (3rd ed.). Mahwah, NJ: Lawrence Erlbaum.
  An engaging overview of the importance of language exploitation pedagogy, this book also offers teachers dozens of lesson ideas for engaging their students in the study of language variation and change.

Brown, D. W. (2009). *In other words: Lessons on grammar, code-switching, and academic writing.* Portsmouth, NH: Heinemann.

> This book provides a detailed curriculum of 35 classroom-ready lessons on topics that include grammar, prescriptivism, language change, academic writing, and language variation. The book also contains additional support for teachers who may not be familiar with the methods and vocabulary of language research.

Charity Hudley, A. H., & Mallinson, C. (2014). *We do language: English language variation in the secondary English classroom.* New York, NY: Teachers College Press.

> A follow-up to their 2011 book, *Understanding English language variation in U.S. schools,* this volume focuses on strategies, models, and vignettes developed for English instructors. The book also contains activity and discussion ideas used by the featured classroom teachers.

Denham, K., & Lobeck, A. (Eds.). (2013). *Linguistics at school: Language awareness in primary and secondary education.* Cambridge, UK: Cambridge University Press.

> This collection brings together the major developers of curricula on language and language differences in the schools, considering both theoretical and practical issues.

Devereaux, M. D. (2015). *Teaching about dialect variations and language in secondary English classrooms: Power, prestige, and prejudice.* New York, NY: Routledge.

> This book offers practical ideas for teaching about language variation and language ideologies in secondary classrooms through canonical texts and language exploration. The suggestions are designed to help all students learn Standard English conventions.

Reaser, J., & Wolfram. W. (2007). *Voices of North Carolina: From the Atlantic to Appalachia.* Student workbook and instructors manual. Raleigh, NC: Language and Life Project. http:// linguistics.chass.ncsu.edu/thinkanddo/vonc.php.

> This 450-minute dialect awareness curriculum, endorsed by the North Carolina Department of Public Education for use in the eighth grade social studies curriculum, includes many video- and audio-based activities. Although the material is designed for North Carolina students, many of the activities and exercises can be used more broadly. Other curricula for dialect awareness in secondary school literature classes are also available at this website.

References

Ad Council. (2003). Accents – Fair housing PSA. Available from: www.civilrights.org/fairhousing/ads/accents.html

Alvarez, L., & Kolker, A. (Producers). (1987). *American tongues* [Video]. New York, NY: Center for New American Media.

Baratz, J. C., & Shuy, R. W. (Eds.). (1969). *Teaching black children to read.* Washington, DC: Center for Applied Linguistics.

Baugh, J. (2003). Linguistic profiling. In S. Makoni, G. Smitherman, A. Blake, & A. K. Spears (Eds.), *Black linguistics: Language, society, and politics in Africa and the Americas* (pp. 155–168). London, UK: Routledge.

Brown, D. W. (2009). *In other words: Lessons on grammar, code-switching, and academic writing.* Portsmouth, NH: Heinemann.

Bucholtz, M. (2014). A sociolinguist's vignette: Teaching students the SKILLS of linguistic research. In A. H. Charity Hudley & C. Mallinson, *We do language: English language variation in U.S. schools* (pp. 113–115). New York, NY: Teachers College Press.

Bucholtz, M., Lopez, A., Mojarro, A., Skapoulli, E., VanderStouwe, C., & Warner-Garcia, S. (2014). Sociolinguistic justice in the schools: Student researchers as linguistic experts. *Language and Linguistics Compass, 8*(4), 144–157.

Charity Hudley, A. H., & Mallinson, C. (2011). *Understanding English language variation in U.S. schools.* New York, NY: Teachers College Press.

Charity Hudley, A. H., & Mallinson, C. (2014). *We do language: English language variation in the secondary English classroom.* New York, NY: Teachers College Press.

Common Core State Standards Initiative (CCSS). (2010). *Common Core State Standards for English language arts & literacy in history/social studies, science, and technical subjects.* Washington, DC: National Governors Association Center for Best Practices, Council of Chief State School Officers.

Cross, J. B., DeVaney, T., & Jones, G. (2001). Pre-service teacher attitudes toward differing dialects. *Linguistics and Education, 12*(2), 211–227.

Dean, D. (2008). *Bringing grammar to life.* Newark, DE: International Reading Association.

Denham, K., & Lobeck, A. (Eds.). (2010). *Linguistics at school: Language awareness in primary and secondary education.* Cambridge, UK: Cambridge University Press.

Dunstan, S. B. (2013). *The influence of speaking a dialect of Appalachian English on the college experience.* Unpublished doctoral dissertation, NC State University.

Dunstan, S. B., Jaeger, A. J., & Crandall, R. E. (2014, April). Exploring the efficacy of dialect diversity workshops in higher education. Paper presented at the annual meeting for the American Educational Research Association. Philadelphia, PA.

Dunstan, S. B., Wolfram, W., Jaeger, A. J., & Crandall, R. E. (2015). Educating the educated: Language diversity in the university backyard. *American Speech, 90*(2), 266–280.

The Economist. (2015, July 29). The last acceptable prejudice. Retrieved from www.economist. com/blogs/prospero/2015/01/johnson-accents

Fasold, R. W., & Shuy, R. W. (1970). *Teaching standard English in the inner city.* Washington, DC: Center for Applied Linguistics.

Fields-Carey, L., & Sweat, S. (2010). Using the *Voices of North Carolina* curriculum. In K. Denham & A. Lobeck (Eds.), *Linguistics at school: Language awareness in primary and secondary education* (pp. 272–276). Cambridge, UK: Cambridge University Press.

Getridge, C. M. (1997). Statement of Carolyn M. Getridge. U.S. Senate Committee on Appropriations: Subcommittee on Labor Health and Human Services of Education. Washington, DC: U.S. Senate.

Godley, A. J., Sweetland, J., Wheeler, R. S., Minnici, A., & Carpenter, B. D. (2006). Preparing teachers for dialectally diverse classrooms. *Educational Researcher, 35*(8), 30–37.

Hazen, K. (Forthcoming). Sociolinguistic outreach for the 21st century: Looking back to move ahead. In J. Reaser, E. Wilbanks, K. Wojcik, & W. Wolfram (Eds.), *Language variety in the New South: Change and variation.* Chapel Hill, NC: University of North Carolina Press.

Henderson, M. H. (2016). *Sociolinguistics for kids: A curriculum for bilingual students.* Unpublished doctoral dissertation, University of New Mexico.

Hutcheson, N. (2005). *Voices of North Carolina* [Video]. Raleigh, NC: Language and Life Project at NC State.

Lippi-Green, R. (2012). *English with an accent: Language, ideology, and discrimination in the United States* (2nd ed.). New York, NY: Routledge.

Lord, C., & Klein, S. (2010). Linguistics and educational standards: The California experience. In K. Denham & A. Lobeck (Eds.), *Linguistics at school: Language awareness in primary and secondary education* (pp. 76–90). Cambridge, UK: Cambridge University Press.

MacNeil/Lehrer Productions. (2005). *Do you speak American?* [Video]. Arlington, VA: Author.

Murphy, A. N. (2012). *Teaching dialect awareness in the college composition classroom: An evaluation.* Unpublished doctoral dissertation, Ball State University.

National Council of Teachers of English, & International Reading Association. (1996). *Standards for the English language arts.* Urbana, IL: National Council of Teachers of English.

Niedzielski, N. A., & Preston, D. R. (2000). *Folk linguistics.* New York, NY: Walter de Gruyter.

Pedersen, P. (1988). *A handbook for developing multicultural awareness.* Alexandria, VA: American Association for Counseling and Development.

Reaser, J. (2006). *The effect of dialect awareness on adolescent knowledge and attitudes.* Unpublished doctoral dissertation, Duke University.

Reaser, J. (2010a). Using media to teach about language. *Language and Linguistics Compass, 4*(9), 782–792.

Reaser, J. (2010b). Developing sociolinguistic curricula that help teachers meet standards. In K. Denham & A. Lobeck (Eds.), *Linguistics at school: Language awareness in primary and secondary education* (pp. 91–105). Cambridge, UK: Cambridge University Press.

Reaser, J. (2016). The effectiveness of webinars as a tool for sociolinguistic-based teacher professional development. *American Speech, 91*(2), 235–254.

Reaser, J., & Adger, C. (2007). Developing language awareness materials for nonlinguists: Lessons learned from the *Do you speak American?* curriculum development project. *Language and Linguistics Compass, 1*(3), 155–167.

Reaser, J., & Wolfram, W. (2007a). *Voices of North Carolina: From the Atlantic to Appalachia – Teacher's manual.* Raleigh, NC: Language and Life Project at NC State. Retrieved from http://linguistics.chass.ncsu.edu/documents/teacher_hi-res.pdf

Reaser, J., & Wolfram, W. (2007b). *Voices of North Carolina: From the Atlantic to Appalachia – Student workbook*. Raleigh, NC: Language and Life Project at NC State. Retrieved from http://linguistics.chass.ncsu.edu/documents/voncstudent.pdf

Rickford, J. R., & Rickford, R. J. (2002). *Spoken soul: The story of Black English*. New York, NY: John Wiley & Sons.

Rosenthal, M. S. (1977). *The magic boxes and Black English*. Washington, DC: ERIC Clearinghouse on Languages and Linguistics.

Sledd, J. (1969). Bi-dialectalism: The linguistics of white supremacy. *The English Journal, 58*(9), 1307–1329.

Sweetland, J. (2004). *Sociolinguistic sensitivity in language arts instruction: A literature and writing curriculum for the intermediate grades*. Unpublished manuscript, Stanford University.

Sweetland, J. (2006). *Teaching writing in the African American classroom: A sociolinguistic approach*. Unpublished doctoral dissertation, Stanford University.

Sweetland, J. (2010). Fostering teacher change: Effective professional development for sociolinguistic diversity. In K. Denham & A. Lobeck (Eds.), *Linguistics at school: Language awareness in primary and secondary education* (pp. 161–174). Cambridge, UK: Cambridge University Press.

Wheeler, R. S., & Swords, R. (2006). *Code-switching: Teaching Standard English in urban classrooms*. Urbana, IL: National Council of Teachers.

Wheeler, R. S., & Swords, R. (2010). *Code-switching lessons: Grammar strategies for linguistically diverse writers, grades 3–6*. Portsmouth, NH: Firsthand Heinemann.

Wolfram, W., & Reaser, J. (2014). *Talkin' Tar Heel: How our voices tell the story of North Carolina*. Chapel Hill, NC: University of North Carolina Press.

Wolfram, W., Reaser, J., & Vaughn, C. (2008). Operationalizing linguistic gratuity: From principle to practice. *Language and Linguistics Compass, 2*(6), 1109–1134.

Wolfram, W., Schilling-Estes, N., & Hazen, K. (1997). *Dialects and the Ocracoke Brogue*. Raleigh, NC: Language and Life Project at NC State.

Young, V. A., Barrett, R., Young-Rivera, Y., & Lovejoy, K. B. (2013). *Other people's English: Code-meshing, code-switching, and African American literacy*. New York, NY: Teachers College Press.

Appendix: An Inventory of Distinguishing Dialect Features

This appendix provides descriptions of many of the dialect features of American English mentioned in the text, as well as some features not covered. It is limited to phonological and grammatical features. For each of the features, there is a brief general comment about its linguistic patterning, as well as a statement about its social and/or regional distribution. We focus on items that are socially significant in terms of the standard–vernacular continuum, rather than those that are strictly regional, although many of the features are both socially and regionally meaningful. Our focus on vernacular patterns does not mean that there is not important linguistic variation in mainstream dialects; all dialects have distinctive linguistic features. Furthermore, it should be understood that variation exists within each named variety, so, for example, not all African American English speakers will have all of the features described for that variety.

As much as possible, we give straightforward descriptions of language features; however, for precision and efficiency, we do employ some technical language from linguistics, such as the distinction between voiced and voiceless consonants. For the purpose of accuracy, we maintain a distinction between phones (the sounds of the language) and phonemes (the contrastive units of sound). The former are enclosed in square brackets [ ] while the latter are in slanted brackets / /, according to the standard convention of the field. SIL International maintains an extensive glossary of linguistic terminology that explains this contrast: www-01.sil.org/linguistics/GlossaryOfLinguisticTerms/. To the extent possible, traditional orthography is used in representing forms, but this is not possible in all cases. As necessary, we employ both Wells' keyword system for vowels (see Table 0.1 on p. xiii) and the International Phonetic Alphabet for consonants and vowels. More information about these conventions can be found following the table of contents at the front of this volume and online at: https://en.wikipedia.org/wiki/Lexical_set and https://en.wikipedia.org/wiki/International_Phonetic_Alphabet.

Exhaustive descriptions of a full range of North American English dialects are found in Kortmann, Schneider, Burridge, Mesthrie, and Upton (2004); Schneider, Kortmann, Burridge, Mesthrie, and Upton (2004); and Wolfram and Schilling (2016). A thorough description of vowel variation in North American

English appears in Thomas (2001) and Labov, Ash, and Boberg (2006); and overviews of many American English dialects for general audiences are compiled in Wolfram and Ward (2006). More comprehensive descriptions of Southern American English vernaculars are found in works such as Bailey (2001), Cukor-Avila (2001), and Wolfram and Reaser (2014). More extensive descriptions of Appalachian English are found in Wolfram and Christian (1976) and Montgomery and Hall (2004). Descriptions of African American English structures are found in Rickford (1999) and Green (2002). Descriptions of Latino English appear in Bayley and Santa Ana (2004) and Santa Ana and Bayley (2004).

In describing dialect features, we often use the term *mainstream American English* to refer to varieties that do not include the dialect trait under discussion. Although this use is related to the term *Standard English*, it avoids some of the value judgments associated with the label *standard*.

Phonological Features

Consonants

Final Cluster Reduction. Word-final consonant clusters ending in a stop can be reduced when both members of the cluster are either voiced (e.g., *find*, *cold*) or voiceless (*act*, *test*). This process affects both clusters that are part of the base word (e.g., *find*, *act*) and clusters that are formed through the addition of an *-ed* suffix (e.g., *guessed*, *liked*). In mainstream American English, this reduction pattern may operate when the following word begins with a consonant (e.g., "bes' kind"), but in vernacular dialects and the speech of English language learners, it is extended to include following words that begin with a vowel as well (e.g., "bes' apple"). This pattern is quite prominent in African American English and English-based creoles; it is also common in dialects of English that retain influence from other languages, such as Latino English, Vietnamese English, Hmong English, and so forth. It is not particularly noticeable in other American English dialects.

Plurals Following Clusters. Words ending in *-sp* (e.g., *wasp*), *-sk* (e.g., *desk*), and *-st* (e.g., *test*) may take the "long plural" *-es* (phonetically [ɪz], made with the KIT vowel followed by a *z* sound) in many vernacular varieties, following the reduction of their final clusters to *-s*. Thus, items such as "tes'" for *test* and "des'" for *desk* are pluralized as "tesses" and "desses," respectively, just as words ending in *s* or other *s*-like sounds in mainstream American English (e.g., *bus*, *buzz*) are pluralized with an *-es* ending ("buses," "buzzes").

In some rural varieties of English, such as Appalachian and Southeastern coastal varieties, the *-es* plural may occur even without the reduction of the final cluster to *-s*, yielding plural forms such as "postes" and "deskes." Such forms are considerably rarer in African American English. They seem to be a function of hypercorrection, in which speakers who formerly produced "desses" for *desks* simply add the *k* while retaining the long plural *-es*, resulting in forms like "deskes."

Intrusive t. A small set of items, usually ending in *s* and *f* in mainstream varieties, may be produced with a final *t*. This results in a final consonant cluster. Typical items affected by this process are "oncet" [wʌnst], "twicet" [twaist], "clifft," and "acrosst." Intrusive *t* is primarily found in Appalachian varieties and other rural varieties characterized by the retention of older forms.

A quite different kind of intrusive *t* involves the "doubling" of an *-ed* form. In this instance, speakers add the "long past form" *-ed* (phonetically [ɪd], made with the KIT or COMMA vowel followed by a *d* sound) to verbs that are already marked with an *-ed* ending pronounced as *t* (e.g., [lʊkt] *looked*). This process yields forms such as "lookted" for *looked* and "attackted" for *attacked*. In effect, the speaker treats the verb as if its base form ends in a *t* so that it is eligible for the long past form that regularly is attached to verbs ending in *t* or *d*.

th *Sounds.* Despite being spelled with two letters, the "th" letter sequence represents one of two different consonant sounds in English. The "th" sequence can be a voiced fricative [ð], as in *bathe*, or a voiceless fricative [θ], as in *bath*. As a convenient shorthand, we refer to these two sounds collectively as "*th* sounds." A number of different processes affect *th* sounds. The phonetic production of *th* is sensitive to the position of *th* in the word and the sounds adjacent to it. At the beginning of a word, *th* tends to be produced as a corresponding stop, as in "dey" for *they* ([d] for [ð]), and "ting" for *thing* ([t] for [θ]). These productions are fairly typical of a wide range of vernaculars, although there are some differences in the distribution of stopped variants for voiced vs. voiceless *th* ([ð] vs. [θ]). The use of *t* in *thing* (voiceless *th*) tends to be most characteristic of selected European American and English language learner varieties, whereas the use of *d* for voiced *th* (as in "dey" for *they*) is spread across the full spectrum of vernacular varieties. Sometimes, English language learner varieties will also use the [s] sound for *th* as in "tees" for *teeth.*

Before nasals (*m, n, ng*, phonetically [m], [n], and [ŋ]), *th* participates in a process in which a range of fricatives, including *z, th,* and *v,* may also become stops. This results in forms such as "aritmetic" for *arithmetic* or "headn" for *heathen*, as well as "wadn't" for *wasn't*, "idn't" for *isn't*, and "sebm" for *seven*. This pattern is typically found in Southern-based vernacular varieties, including Southern-based European American dialects and vernacular African American English varieties.

In word-final position and between vowels within a word (i.e., in intervocalic position), *th* sounds may be produced as *f* or *v*, as in "efer" for *ether*, "toof" for *tooth*, "brover" for *brother*, and "smoov" for *smooth*. This production is typical of vernacular varieties of African American English, with the *v* for voiced *th* [ð] production more typical of Eastern vernacular varieties. Some Southern-based European American dialects, as well as some varieties influenced by other languages in the recent past, also have the *f* production in *tooth.*

Some restricted varieties use the stop *d* for intervocalic voiced *th,* as in "oder" for *other* or "broder" for *brother*, but this pattern is much less common than the use of a stop for *th* in word-initial position.

ch *and* sh *Sounds.* As with the *th* sounds described above, the letter sequences "ch" and "sh" typically represent single sounds rather than a sequence of sounds. As above, we use "*ch* sound" and "*sh* sound" to refer to the sounds represented by these spellings. Some Latino English speakers and English language learners may pronounce both of these sounds as "ch," leading to words like *cheap* and *sheep* both being pronounced as "cheap" (although they occasionally may both be pronounced as "sheep" by some speakers). This feature tends to fade in later generations.

r *and* l. There are a number of different linguistic contexts in which *r* and *l* may be lost or reduced to a vowel-like quality. After a vowel, as in *sister* or *steal*, the *r* and *l* may be reduced or lost. This feature is quite typical of traditional Southern speech and eastern New England speech. It is a receding feature of Southern-based European American dialects, especially in metropolitan areas.

Between vowels, *r* also may be lost, as in "Ca'ol" for *Carol* or "du'ing" for *during*. Intervocalic *r* loss is more socially stigmatized than postvocalic *r* loss. It is found in rural, Southern-based vernaculars, including vernacular African American English and vernacular Southern White English.

Following a consonant, the *r* may be lost if it precedes a rounded vowel such as *u* or *o* (GOOSE or GOAT vowels), resulting in pronunciations such as "thu" for *through* and "tho" for *throw*. Post-consonantal *r* loss may also be found if *r* occurs in an unstressed syllable, as in "p'ofessor" for *professor* or "sec'etary" for *secretary*. This type of *r*-lessness is found primarily in Southern-based varieties. Before a bilabial sound such as *p*, *l* may be lost completely, giving pronunciations like "woof" for *wolf* or "hep" for *help*. Again, this is characteristic only of Southern-based varieties. Other regional dialects (e.g., Pittsburgh, Philadelphia) sometimes vocalize *l* after a vowel to the point that it is almost indistinguishable from a vowel, thus making the words *vow* and *Val* sound the same.

Sometimes *r*-lessness causes one lexical item to converge with another. Thus, the use of *they* for *their,* as in "theyself" or "they book," apparently derives from the loss of *r* on *their*, although speakers who currently use *they* in such constructions may no longer associate it with *r*-less *their*.

An intrusive *r* may occur occasionally, so that items such as *wash* may be pronounced as "warsh" and *idea* as "idear." Certain instances of intrusive *r* are the result of a generalized pronunciation process, whereby *r* can be added onto the ends of vowel-final words (e.g., "idear"), particularly when these words precede vowel-initial words ("The idear of it" or "vanillar ice cream"). Other cases (e.g., "warsh") seem to be restricted to particular lexical items and are highly regionally restricted.

R and *l* variation is also typical with some English language learners. However, subtle differences in sound distribution and production exist among groups with different native languages.

Initial w Reduction. In unstressed positions within a phrase, an initial *w* may be lost in items such as *was* and *one*. This results in items such as "She's [ʃiz] here yesterday" for *She was here yesterday* and "young 'uns" for *young ones*. This appears to be an extension of the process affecting the initial *w* of the modals *will* and *would* in mainstream varieties of English (as in "he'll" for *he will* or "she'd" for *she would*). This process is found in Southern-based vernaculars.

Unstressed Initial Syllable Loss. Also called *ellipsis*, the general process of deleting unstressed initial syllables in informal speech styles of mainstream American English (e.g., "'cause" for *because*, "'round" for *around*) is extended in vernacular varieties so that a wider range of word classes is affected by this process—for example, verbs such as "'member" for *remember*, or nouns such as "'taters" for *potatoes*—and a wider range of initial syllable types (e.g., *re-* as in "'member" for *remember*, *su-* as in "'spect" for *suspect*).

Initial h Retention. The retention of *h* on the pronoun *it* ("hit" [hɪt]) and the auxiliary *ain't* ("hain't" [heɪnt]) is still found in vernacular varieties retaining some older English forms, such as Appalachian English and Outer Banks English. This form is more prominent in stressed positions within a sentence. The pronunciation is fading out among younger speakers.

Nasals. There are a number of processes that affect nasal sounds; there are also items that are influenced by the presence of nasals in the surrounding linguistic environment.

One widespread process in vernacular varieties is so-called *g-dropping*, in which the nasal sound represented as *ng* in spelling and pronounced as [ŋ] (as in the sound at the end of *sing*) in Standard English is pronounced as [n] (as in the sound at the end of *sin*). This process takes place when the *ng* occurs in an unstressed syllable, as in "swimmin'" for *swimming* or "buyin'" for *buying*. Linguists refer to this process as *nasal fronting*, or *velar fronting* because it involves fronting the velar nasal [ŋ], which is produced toward the back of the mouth. The nasal [n] is produced near the front of the mouth. Nasal fronting is found to some extent in all American English dialects though it occurs more frequently in the speech of vernacular dialect speakers than in mainstream English speech. It may be even more frequent in the English of some English language learners.

A less widespread phenomenon affecting nasals is deletion of the word-final nasal segment in items such as *man*, *beam*, and *ring*, particularly when the item is in a relatively unstressed position in a sentence. Although the nasal segment is deleted, the words still retain their final nasal character because the vowel preceding the *n* is nasalized. Thus, *man*, *beam*, and *ring* may be pronounced as "ma'" [mæ̃], "bea'" [bĩ], and "ri'" [rĩ], respectively, with the vowel carrying a nasal quality. Although this process affects the segment *n* most frequently, all final nasal segments may be affected to some extent. This process is typical of African American English. It can also be heard in the speech of some English language learners.

The phonetic quality of vowels may also be affected before nasal consonants, as in the well-known merger of the contrast between the KIT vowel [ɪ] and the DRESS vowel [ɛ] before nasals, as in *pen* and *pin*. Some Southern dialects restrict this merger to a following *n*, whereas others extend it to a following *m* (e.g., *Kim* and *chem* or *him* and *hem*) and [ŋ] in *bing* and *bengal*.

Devoicing. Consonant devoicing entails the phonetic change of voiced sounds to their voiceless counterparts, as in [d] to [t], or [z] to [s]. This pattern is quite prominent in dialects of English that retain influence from other languages, such as varieties like Pennsylvania German English, Wisconsin English, and Jewish English, so that words like *lose* sound like *loose*. It is especially common in Pennsylvania German English and Jewish English to devoice word-final voiced stops (e.g., *-b*, *-d*, *-g*), so that a word like *bad* sounds more like "bat." Word-final [d] devoicing is also common in African American English, although many times the final stop becomes glottalized, so that *wood* is pronounced more like [wʊʔ]. In Latino English, the *z* sound undergoes devoicing in all linguistic environments. A word like *easy* will be pronounced with an *s* sound [isi], as would *was* and *is*, both of which are pronounced with a *z* sound in other American English dialects. Latino English speakers may also devoice the *v* sound after vowels, as in "luf" and "haf" for *love* and *have*.

Other Consonants. A number of other consonantal patterns affect limited sets of items or single words. For example, speakers have used "aks" for *ask* for over 1,000 years and still use it in several vernacular varieties, including vernacular African American English. The form "chimley" or "chimbley" for *chimney* is also found in a number of Southern-based vernaculars. The use of *k* in initial *(s)tr* clusters as in "skreet" for *street* or "skring" for *string* is found in vernacular African American English, particularly rural Southern varieties. Such items are usually noticeable and tend to be socially stigmatized, but they occur with such limited sets of words that they are best considered on an item-by-item basis.

Vowels

There are many vowel patterns that differentiate the dialects of English, but the majority of these are more regionally than socially significant. The back THOUGHT vowel /ɔ/ of *bought* or *coffee* and the front TRAP vowel /æ/ of *cat* and *ran* are particularly sensitive to regional variation, as are many vowels before *r* (e.g., compare pronunciations of *merry, marry, Mary, Murray*) and *l* (compare *wheel, will, well, whale*, etc.). Although it is not possible here to indicate all the nuances of phonetic difference that are reflected in the vowels of American English, several major patterns of pronunciation may be identified.

Vowel Shifts. Several shifts in the phonetic values of vowels are currently taking place in American English. The important aspect of these shifts is the fact that the vowels are not shifting their phonetic values in isolation; rather, the systems of vowels are rotating in terms of where these vowels are articulated in the mouth. As noted in the text, one major rotation is the *Northern Cities Vowel Shift*. In this rotation, the THOUGHT vowel /ɔ/ moves toward the LOT vowel [ɑ], which then moves forward to the TRAP spot [æ], so that outsiders sometimes confuse *lock* with *lack*. The TRAP vowel [æ] raises into the area where DRESS [ɛ] is located. DRESS /ɛ/ moves backward in the mouth along with KIT /ɪ/ and STRUT /ʌ/. For example, the THOUGHT vowel /ɔ/, as in *coffee*, is moving forward toward the LOT vowel [ɑ] of *father*. Short and long vowels tend to rotate as different subsystems within the overall vowel system. See the diagram of this vowel shift at Figure 3.1 in Chapter 3.

Regionally, the pattern of vowel rotation started in western New England and proceeded westward into the northern tier of Pennsylvania; the extreme northern portions of Ohio, Indiana, and Illinois; Michigan; and Wisconsin. It is concentrated in the larger metropolitan areas. More advanced stages of this change can be found in younger speakers in the largest metropolitan areas in this Northern region, such as Buffalo, Albany, Cleveland, Detroit, and Chicago. Minority groups in these metropolitan areas tend not to participate in this phonetic shift.

The *Southern Vowel Shift* is quite different from the Northern Cities Vowel Shift. In this rotation pattern, the short front vowels (the vowels of words like *bed* and *bid*) are moving upward and taking on the gliding character of long vowels. In mainstream American English, the FACE vowel /e/ of *bait* actually consists of a vowel nucleus [e] and an upward glide to [i], whereas the DRESS vowel /ɛ/ as in *bet* does not have this gliding character, at least not in the idealized standard variety. In the Southern Vowel Shift, the DRESS vowel /ɛ/ of *bed* takes on a glide, becoming more like "beyd" [bɛɪd]. Meanwhile, the tense front FLEECE and FACE vowels, /i/ and /e/ respectively, as in *beet* and *bait*, are moving somewhat backward and downward. Simultaneously, the back GOOSE and BOAT vowels, /u/ and /o/ respectively, as in *boot* and *boat*, are moving forward. See the diagram of this vowel shift at Figure 3.2 in Chapter 3.

A third, more recent vowel shift is the *Northern California Vowel Shift*. Like the Southern Vowel Shift, the back vowels are moving forward, so the GOOSE vowel /u/ becomes more like "giws" and the GOAT vowel /o/ more like "gewt." But the front vowels are shifting in quite different directions. The KIT vowel /ɪ/ is rising towards the FLEECE vowel [i] before "ng" and lowering towards the DRESS vowel [ɛ] before other consonants. Meanwhile, the DRESS vowel /ɛ/ is lowering towards the TRAP vowel [æ], which in turn, is shifting in two directions. The TRAP vowel /æ/ becomes a diphthong like "stee-and" for *stand* before nasals, while it shifts towards the LOT vowel [ɑ] elsewhere, so that *hat* sounds closer to "hot."

Low Back Vowel Merger. One of the major regional pronunciation processes affecting vowels is the merger of the THOUGHT vowel /ɔ/ and the LOT vowel /ɑ/. This merger means that word pairs like *caught* and *cot* or *Dawn* and *Don* are pronounced the same. This merger radiates from several areas—one in Eastern New England, centered near the Boston area; one centered in Western Pennsylvania in the Ohio Valley; and one covering a large portion of the American West, excluding major metropolitan areas such as Los Angeles and San Francisco.

Other Vowel Mergers. There are a number of vowel mergers or "near mergers" that take place when vowels occur before certain kinds of consonants. The following mergers may occur before *r*, *l*, and the nasal segments (*m, n, ng*).

* THOUGHT /ɔ/ and LOT /ɑ/, as in *Dawn* and *Don* (Western Pennsylvania, Eastern New England, much of the Western United States, some Latino English speakers)
* FLEECE /i/ and KIT /ɪ/ before [l], as in *field* and *filled* (South; sporadically elsewhere)
* FACE /e/ and DRESS /ɛ/ before [l], as in *sale* and *sell* (South; sporadically elsewhere)
* GOOSE /u/ and FOOT /ʊ/ before [l], as in *pool* and *pull* (South; sporadically elsewhere)
* TRAP /æ/ and DRESS /ɛ/ before [l], as in *salary* and *celery* (Latino English)
* FACE /e/, DRESS /ɛ/, and TRAP /æ/ before [r], as in *Mary, merry, marry* (many areas of the United States, including the South)
* KIT /ɪ/ and DRESS /ɛ/ before nasals, as in *pin* and *pen* (South)

Different dialects may be distinguished by the kinds of mergers in which they participate. Thus, some varieties in the South and some other areas of the United States merge the vowels of *Mary*, *merry*, and *marry*, whereas the regional dialect of southeastern Pennsylvania and New Jersey that includes Philadelphia merges *merry* and *Murray* at the same time that it keeps these items distinct from *Mary* and *marry*.

Other dialects may be characterized by vowel shifts in which a vowel moves so close to another vowel that speakers from other dialect areas may think the two sounds have merged, but in reality, a subtle distinction between the two sounds is maintained. For example, the backed and raised PRICE vowel /ai/ of the Outer Banks of North Carolina in words like *bide* may seem quite similar to the CHOICE vowel [ɔi] (as in "boyd"), but it is maintained as distinct. Similarly, the KIT vowel /ɪ/ (as in *bit*) may be raised so that it sounds almost like the FLEECE vowel [i] (as in *beet*), particularly before palatals such as the sounds spelled "sh" and "ch," so that people may hear "feesh" for *fish* and "reach" for *rich*. Just as with the PRICE vowel /ai/ and the CHOICE vowel /ɔi/, however, a distinction between KIT /ɪ/ and FLEECE /i/ vowels is preserved. This near merger is also found in some mainland Southern varieties, including the Upper Southern variety of Appalachian English. Isolated varieties may also retain a lower vowel production of the TRAP vowel /æ/ before *r* so that *there* may sound like "thar."

TRAP /æ/ *Raising.* The TRAP vowel of words such as *back* or *bag* may be raised from its typical phonetic position so that it is produced closer to the DRESS vowel [ε] of *beg* or *bet*. The feature is found in a number of Northern areas and is an integral part of the Northern Cities Vowel Shift.

***Variants of* MOUTH /au/.** The vowel nucleus of words like *out, loud,* and *down* may be produced in a number of different ways. In one pronunciation, which is sometimes referred to as Canadian Raising because of its prominence in certain areas of Canada, the nucleus of the MOUTH vowel /au/ is pronounced as a mid-central rather than low vowel, so that a phrase such as *out and about* sounds like "oat and a boat" [əʊt n əbəʊt]. This pronunciation is found in coastal Maryland, Virginia, and North Carolina, as well as some scattered dialect regions in Northern areas. Other dialect areas (e.g., Philadelphia) pronounce the MOUTH vowel /au/ with a fronted nucleus, in the region of the TRAP vowel [æ], as in [dæʊn] for *down*; and there is at least one dialect area (Pittsburgh) where the MOUTH vowel /au/ may be produced with little or no glide as well, as in "dahntahn" [da:nta:n] for *downtown*.

In a somewhat different production, the glide of the MOUTH vowel /au/ may be fronted as well as the nucleus, so that *brown* [bræɪn] may actually be confused with *brain,* and *house* [hæɪs] may be confused with *highest*. This production is concentrated in the coastal dialects of the mid-Atlantic and Southeastern United States, such as those of Smith Island and Tangier Island in the Chesapeake Bay and the North Carolina Outer Banks.

***Variants of* PRICE /ai/.** Several different processes may affect the PRICE diphthong /ai/ in words such as *time, tide,* and *tight*. The [i] glide (FLEECE), which forms the second half of this diphthong (made up of [a] + [i]), may be lost, yielding pronunciations such as "tahm" [ta:m] for *time* and "tahd" [ta:d] for *tide*. This glide loss, or ungliding, is characteristic of practically all Southern-based vernaculars and is not particularly socially significant in the South. The absence of the glide is more frequent when the following segment is a voiced sound (e.g., *side, time*) than when it is a voiceless one (e.g., *sight, rice*), and only certain Southern European American varieties exhibit extensive ungliding of the PRICE vowel before voiceless sounds.

Another process affecting some varieties of American English involves the pronunciation of the nucleus of the PRICE diphthong /ai/ as a mid-central (STRUT vowel [ʌ]) rather than the low LOT vowel /ɑ/, so that *tide* and *tight* may be produced as [tʌid] and [tʌit]. This process often parallels the raising of the nucleus of the MOUTH diphthong /au/ and is also referred to as Canadian Raising because of its widespread presence in Canada. In the United States, this pronunciation is found in the Tidewater Virginia area and other Eastern coastal communities. It is especially common before voiceless sounds (e.g., [tʌit] "tight").

The nucleus of the PRICE diphthong /ai/ may also be backed and/or raised so that it sounds quite close to the /ɔi/ of *toy* or *boy* (i.e., /ai/ gets pronounced as something like the vowel in CHOICE). This backing and raising is associated with the Outer Banks of North Carolina, where speakers are referred to as "hoi toiders" for *high tiders*. A few other dialects of American English use a backed nucleus for the PRICE diphthong /ai/, including New York City English and some mainland Southern varieties.

Final Unstressed BOAT */o/.* In word-final position, mainstream American English *ow*, as in *hollow* or *yellow*, may become *r*, giving "holler" or "yeller," respectively. This "intrusive *r*" also occurs when suffixes are attached, as in "fellers" for *fellows* or "narrers" for *narrows*. This production is characteristic of Southern mountain varieties, such as those in Appalachia or the Ozarks, although it is found to some extent in rural varieties in the lowland South as well.

Final Unstressed COMMA */ə/ Raising.* Final unstressed COMMA vowels /ə/, as in *soda* or *extra*, may be raised to a high FLEECE vowel [i], resulting in productions such as "sody" [sodi] and "extry" [ɛkstri]. This production occurs in rural Southern vernaculars.

Other Variations of the COMMA *Vowel* /ə/. In most varieties of English, the vowel in unstressed syllables is reduced to a schwa-like quality (COMMA), so that, for example, *because* sounds like "buhcause" [bəkɔz] (vs. "bee-cause") and *today* like "tuhday" [tədei] (vs. "too-day"). However, speakers of Latino English are more likely to produce a non-reduced vowel closer to the FLEECE vowel or the GOOSE vowel, as in "bee-cause" [bikʌz] or "too-day" [tude].

ire/our *Collapse.* The sequence spelled "ire" is usually produced in mainstream American English as two syllables: The PRICE vowel /ai/ is followed by an "er" sound. Thus, *fire* sounds like "fi-er." In some dialects, this sequence can be collapsed into a one-syllable sequence where the vowel sounds similar to the LOT vowel /ɑ/ plus an *r*. This process yields pronunciations such as "far" for *fire* and "tar" for *tire*. It affects not only root words like *fire,* but also PRICE + *er* sequences formed by the addition of an *-er* suffix, as in *buyer,* that becomes "bar." A similar process affects *-our/ower* sequences, which phonetically consist of a two-syllable sequence involving the MOUTH diphthong [au] and *r,* as in *flower* or *hour.* These sequences may be reduced to a single syllable, so that *flower* sounds like "fla'r" [flɑr] and *hour* like "a'r" [ɑr].

Grammatical Features

Many of the socially significant grammatical structures in American English varieties involve aspects of the verb phrase. Some variation is due to the principles of readjustment discussed in Chapter 2, but some items have roots in the historical origins of different varieties.

Verbs

Irregular Verbs. There are five ways in which irregular verbs pattern differently in mainstream and vernacular dialects of English. For the most part, these different patterns are the result of analogy, but there are also some retentions of patterns that have become obsolete in mainstream varieties. These differences are as follows:

1. past as participle form
   "I <u>had went</u> down there."
   "He may <u>have took</u> the wagon."

2. participle as past form
   "He <u>seen</u> something out there."
   "She <u>done</u> her work."

3. bare root as past form
   "She <u>come</u> to my house yesterday."
   "She <u>give</u> him a nice present last year."

4. regularization
   "Everybody <u>knowed</u> he was late."
   "They <u>throwed</u> out the old food."

5. different irregular form
   "I <u>hearn</u> [heard] something shut the church house door."
   "Something just <u>riz</u> [rose] up right in front of me."

Dialects vary according to which of these patterns they exhibit. The majority of vernaculars in the North and South indicate Patterns 1, 2, and 3. Some rural vernaculars in the South may exhibit Pattern 5 in addition to the first three. Varieties subject to the influence of second language-learning strategies often reveal a higher incidence of regularization—Pattern 4—than other varieties.

Co-occurrence Relations and Meaning Changes. A number of different types of constructions can vary from dialect to dialect based on the types of structures that can co-occur with certain verbs. There are also meaning changes that affect particular verbs:

1. shifts in the transitive status of verbs (i.e., whether the verb must take an object)
   "If we <u>beat</u>, we'll be champs."

2. types of complement structures co-occurring with particular verbs
   "The kitchen <u>needs remodeled</u>."
   "The students <u>started to messing</u> around."
   "I'll <u>have</u> him <u>to do</u> it."
   "The dog <u>wanted out</u>."
   "Walt <u>calls himself dancing</u>."

3. verb plus verb particle formations
   "He <u>happened</u> in on the party."
   "The coach <u>blessed out</u> [swore at, yelled at] his players."

4. use of progressive with stative verbs
   "He <u>was liking</u> the new house."
   "She <u>was wanting</u> to get out."

5. verbs derived from other parts of speech (e.g., verbs derived from nouns)
   "Our dog <u>treed</u> a coon."
   "We <u>doctored</u> the sickness ourselves."

6. broadened, narrowed, or shifted semantic reference for particular verb forms
   "He <u>carried</u> her to the movies."
   "My kids <u>took</u> the chicken pox when they were young."
   "I been <u>aimin</u>'to [intending] go there."

For the most part, differences related to meaning changes and co-occurrence relations have to be dealt with on an item-by-item basis. All vernaculars, and many regional varieties, indicate meaning shifts and co-occurrence relations not found in mainstream American English to any great extent.

Special Auxiliary Verb Forms

A number of special uses of auxiliary forms set apart vernacular dialects of English from their mainstream counterparts. Many of these auxiliaries indicate subtle but significant meanings related to the duration or type of activity indicated by verbs or *verb aspect*.

Completive **done.** The form *done* when used with a past-tense verb may mark a completed action or event in a way somewhat different from a simple past-tense form, as in a sentence such as "There was one in there that done rotted away" or "I done forgot what you wanted." In this use, the emphasis is on the "completive" aspect or the fact that the action has been fully completed. The *done* form may also add intensification to the activity, as in "I done told you not to mess up." This form is typically found in Southern European American and African American vernaculars.

Habitual **be.** The form *be* in sentences such as "Sometimes my ears be itching" or "She usually be home in the evening" may signify an event or activity distributed intermittently over time or space. Habitual *be* is most often used in *be* + verb *-ing* constructions, as in *My ears be itching*. The unique aspectual meaning of *be* is typically associated with African American English, although isolated and restricted constructions with habitual *be* have been found in some rural European American varieties. It has also been adopted by some speakers of Latino English. In recent stylized uses often associated with hip hop culture, the form has been extended to refer to intensified stativity or super-real status, as in "I be the truth."

Be + s. In some restricted parts of the South (e.g., areas of the Carolinas where the historic influence of Highland Scots and Scots-Irish is evident), *be* may occur with an *-s* third-person suffix, as in "Sometimes it bes like that" or "I hope it bes a girl." However, *bes* is not restricted to contexts of habitual activity and thus is different from habitual *be* in African American English. *Bes* is also distinguished from *be* in contemporary African American English by the inflectional *-s*, but *bes* is a receding form, whereas *be* in African American English is quite robust and escalating.

Remote Time **béen.** When stressed, *béen* can serve to mark a special aspectual function, indicating that the event or activity took place in the "distant past," but is still relevant. In structures such as "I béen had it there for years" or "I béen known her," the reference is to an event that took place, literally or figuratively, in some distant time frame. This use, which is associated with vernacular African American English, is dying out in some varieties of this dialect.

Fixin' to. The use of *fixin' to* (also pronounced as "fixta," "fista," "finsta," and "finna") may occur with a verb with the meaning of *about to* or *plan to*. Thus, in a sentence such as "It's fixin' to rain," the occurrence of rain is imminent. In a construction such as "I was fixin' to come but I got held up," the speaker is indicating that he or she had intended to come. This special use of *fixin' to* is found only in the South, particularly in the South Atlantic and Gulf states. It has also been observed in Latino English speakers in the Southwestern and Southeastern United States.

Indignant **come.** The use of the form *come* as an auxiliary in sentences such as "She come acting like she was real mad" or "He come telling me I didn't know what I was talking about" may convey a special sense of speaker indignation. It is a *camouflaged form*, in the sense that it appears to be much like a comparable mainstream American English use of *come* with movement verbs (e.g., "She came running home"), but it does not function in the same way as its mainstream counterpart. It is found in African American English.

A- *Prefixing.* An *a-* prefix may occur on *-ing* forms functioning as verbs or as complements of verbs, as in "She was a-comin' home" or "He made money a-fishin'." This form cannot occur on *-ing* forms that function as nouns or adjectives. Thus, it cannot occur in sentences such as *"He likes a-sailin'" or *"The movie was a-charmin'." The *a-* is also restricted phonologically, in that it occurs only on forms whose first syllable is accented; thus, it may occur on "a-fóllowin'," but not usually on *"a-discóverin'." As currently used by some speakers, the *a-* prefix may be used to indicate intensity, but it does not appear to have any unique aspectual marking analogous to habitual *be* or completive *done*. It is associated with vernacular Southern mountain speech, but is found in many other rural varieties as well. To a lesser degree, an *a-* prefix also can be attached to other verb forms, such as participles in "She's a-worked there" or even to simple past forms as in "She a-wondered what happened."

Double Modals. Double modals are combinations of two modal verbs, or verbs expressing certain "moods," such as certainty, possibility, obligation, or permission. Possible combinations include *might could, useta could, might should, might oughta*, and so forth. Sentences such as "I might could go there" or "You might oughta take it" are typically Southern vernacular structures; in Northern varieties, modal clustering occurs only with the semi-modal *useta*, as in "He useta couldn't do it." Double modals tend to lessen the force of the attitude or obligation conveyed by single modals, so that "She might could do it" is less forceful than either "She might do it" or "She could do it." In some Southern regions, double modals are quite widespread and not particularly stigmatized.

Other Modals. Latino English in some regions includes a few distinctive uses of modals. In Los Angeles, some speakers might use a contracted form of *would* in *if* clauses (e.g., "If he'd be here right now, he'd make me laugh").

While all English dialects can contract *would* in the second case, the first contraction is unique to Latino English. Some speakers use *woulda* in these *if* clauses (e.g., "If I woulda been a gangster, I woulda been throwing up gang signs"). (Examples from Fought, 2003.)

Liketa *and* (Su)poseta. The forms *liketa* and *(su)poseta* may be used as special verb modifiers to mark the speaker's perceptions that a significant event was on the verge of happening. *Liketa* is an avertive, in that it is used to indicate an impending event that was narrowly avoided. It is often used in a figurative rather than a literal sense; for example, in a sentence such as "It was so cold, I liketa froze to death," the speaker may never have been in any real danger of freezing, but the use of *liketa* underscores the intensity of the condition. *(Su)poseta*, in sentences such as "You (su)poseta went there," parallels the mainstream American English construction *supposed to have*.

***Quotative* be like *and* go.** Over the past few decades, the use of *be like* and *go* to introduce a quote (e.g., "So she's like, 'Where are you going?' and I go, 'Where do you think?'") has shown phenomenal growth. Once associated with Valley Girl talk in California, it is now used throughout North America, as well as the British Isles, Australia, and New Zealand. It is also used in a wide variety of vernacular varieties, even some situated in relative cultural or regional isolation. Because of its relatively recent expansion, it is much more common among speakers born after the 1960s than those born earlier, although it is now even being adopted by some older speakers. Some speakers of African American English may still use *say* to introduce a quote, as in "I told him, say, 'Where you going?'" This use is rapidly receding. In fact, quotative *be like* is taking over in African American English as it is in other dialects. Quotative *be like* can also be used in a somewhat more figurative sense to introduce an imagined quote, or what the speaker was thinking rather than literally saying at the time, as in "I was like, 'What is wrong with you?'" A related form is quotative *be all,* as in a sentence such as "I was all, 'What's going on?'"

Absence of* be *Forms. Where contracted forms of *is* or *are* may occur in mainstream American English, these same forms may be absent in some vernacular varieties. Thus, we get structures such as "You ugly" or "She taking the dog out" corresponding to the mainstream American English structures "You're ugly" and "She's taking the dog out," respectively. It is important to note that this absence takes place only on contractible forms; thus, it does not affect *they are* in a construction such as "That's where they are" because *they are* cannot be contracted to *they're* in this instance. Furthermore, the absence of *be* does not usually apply to *am*, so that sentences such as *"I ugly" do not occur. The deletion of *are* is typical of both Southern European American and African American varieties, although the absence of *is* is not extensive in most

European American vernaculars. A more general version of *be* absence—that includes *am* and past tense—is sometimes found in the English of English language learners.

Subject–Verb Agreement. A number of different subject–verb agreement patterns enter into the social and regional differentiation of dialects. These include the following:

1. agreement with existential *there*
   "There was five people there."
   "There's two women in the lobby."

2. leveling to *was* for past-tense forms of *be*
   "The cars was out on the street."
   "Most of the kids was younger up there."

3. leveling to *were* with negative past-tense *be*
   "It weren't me that was there last night."
   "She weren't at the creek."

4. leveling to *is* for present-tense forms of *be*
   "The dogs is in the house."
   "We is doing it right now."

5. agreement with the form *don't*
   "She don't like the cat in the house."
   "It don't seem like a holiday."

6. agreement with *have*
   "My nerves has been on edge."
   "My children hasn't been there much."

7. *-s* suffix on verbs occurring with third-person plural noun phrase subjects
   "Some people likes to talk a lot."
   "Me and my brother gets in fights."

8. *-s* absence on third-person singular forms
   "The dog stay outside in the afternoon."
   "She usually like the evening news."

Different vernacular varieties exhibit different patterns in terms of this list. Virtually all vernacular varieties show Patterns 1, 2, and 5 (in fact, mainstream varieties are moving toward Pattern 1), but in different degrees. Patterns 6 and

7 are most characteristic of rural varieties in the South, and Pattern 8 is most typical of vernacular African American English. The leveling of past *be* to *weren't* in Pattern 3 appears to be regionally restricted to some coastal dialect areas of the Southeast, such as the Eastern Shore of Virginia and Maryland and the Outer Banks of North Carolina.

Past Tense Absence. Many cases of past-tense *-ed* absence on verbs (e.g., "Yesterday he mess up") can be accounted for by the phonological process of consonant cluster reduction described in the section on consonants above. However, in some instances, the use of unmarked past-tense forms represents a genuine grammatical difference. Such cases are particularly likely to be found in varieties influenced by other languages in their recent past. Thus, structures such as "He bring the food yesterday" or "He play a new song last night" may be the result of a grammatical process, rather than a phonological one. Grammatically-based tense unmarking tends to be more frequent on regular verbs than irregular ones, so that a structure such as "Yesterday he play a new song" is more likely than "Yesterday he is in a new store," although both may occur. In some cases, both phonological and grammatical processes operate in a convergent way.

Tense unmarking has been found to be prominent in the speech of English language learners and in American Indian English in the Southwest. In the latter case, unmarking is favored in habitual contexts (e.g., "In those days, we play a different kind of game") as opposed to simple past time (e.g., "Yesterday, we play at a friend's house").

Historical Present. In the dramatic recounting of past-time events, speakers may use present-tense verb forms rather than past-tense forms, as in "I go down there and this guy comes up to me . . ." In some cases, an *-s* suffix may be added to non-third-person forms, particularly with the first-person form of *say* (e.g., "So I says to him . . ."). This structure is more prominent in European American vernaculars than in African American English.

Perfective **be.** Some isolated varieties of American English may use forms of *be* rather than *have* in present-perfect constructions, as in "I'm been there before" for "I've been there before" or "You're taken the best medicine" for "You have taken the best medicine." This construction occurs most frequently in first-person singular contexts (e.g., "I'm forgot"), but can also occur in the first-person plural and in second-person contexts (e.g., "We're forgot"; "You're been there"). Occasionally, the perfect tense can even be formed with invariant *be*, as in "We be come here for nothing" or "I'll be went to the post office." Perfective *be* derives from the earlier English formation of the perfect with *be,* rather than *have* for certain verbs (e.g., "He is risen" vs. "He has risen"). In most cases, it is a retention of the older pattern.

Adverbs

Several different kinds of patterns affect adverbs. These involve differences in the placement of adverbs within the sentence, differences in the formation of adverbs, and differences in the use or meaning of particular adverbial forms.

Adverb Placement. There are several differences in the position of the adverb within the sentence, including the placement of certain "time adverbs" within the verb phrase, as in "We were all the time talking" or "We watched all the time the news on TV." These cases do not hold great social significance and are not particularly socially stigmatized. More socially marked is the change in order with various forms of *ever*, as in "everwhat," "everwho," or "everwhich" (e.g., "Everwho wanted to go could go"). These are remnants of older English patterns and are mostly dying out.

Comparatives and Superlatives. Most vernacular varieties of English exhibit some comparative and superlative adjective and adverb forms that are not found in mainstream varieties. Some forms involve the regularization of irregular forms, as in "badder" or "mostest," whereas others involve the use of *-er* and *-est* on adjectives of two or more syllables (e.g., "beautifulest," "awfulest"), where mainstream varieties use *more* and *most*. In some instances, comparatives and superlatives are doubly marked, as in "Most awfulest" or "More nicer." As we discuss in Chapter 2, both regularization and double-marking are highly natural language processes.

-ly Absence. In present-day American English, some adverbs that formerly ended in an *-ly* suffix no longer take *-ly*. Thus, in informal contexts, most mainstream American English speakers say "They answered wrong" instead of "They answered wrongly." The range of items affected by *-ly* absence can be extended in different vernacular dialects. These items may be relatively unobtrusive (e.g., "She enjoyed life awful well") or quite obtrusive (e.g., "I come from Virginia original"). The more stigmatized forms are associated with Southern-based vernacular varieties, particularly Southern mountain varieties such as Appalachian and Ozark English.

Intensifying Adverbs. In some Southern-based vernaculars, certain adverbs can be used to intensify particular attributes or activities. In mainstream American English, the adverb *right* is currently limited to contexts involving location or time (e.g., "He lives right around the corner"). However, in Southern-based vernaculars, *right* may be used to intensify the degree of other types of attributes, as in "She is right nice." Other adverbs, such as *plumb*, serve to indicate intensity to the point of totality, as in "The students fell plumb asleep." In some parts of the South, *slam* is used to indicate totality rather than *plumb*, as in "The students fell slam asleep"; *clean* may be used in a similar way in other areas, including some Northern dialects (e.g., "The hole went clean through the wall"). Additional intensifying adverbs found in these varieties include items such as *big old, little old, right smart,* and *right much,* among others. Dialects of younger speakers may incorporate innovative intensifiers. Some recent examples include *totally, hella,* stressed *so, sick, fucking, most,* and *dead* (as in "dead sexy"). Not all innovative intensifiers have the same longevity.

A special function of the adverb *steady* has been described for African American English. In this variety, *steady* may be used in constructions such as "They be steady messing with you" to refer to an intense, ongoing activity.

Other Adverbial Forms. There are a number of other cases in which the adverbial forms of vernacular varieties differ from their mainstream counterparts. Some of these involve word class changes, as in the use of *but* as an adverb meaning "only," as in "He ain't but thirteen years old," or the item *all* in "The corn got all" ("The corn is all gone/finished"). In many Midland dialects of American English, *anymore* may be used in positive constructions with a meaning of "nowadays," as in "She watches a lot of Netflix anymore."

Some vernacular dialects contain adverbial lexical items not found at all in mainstream varieties—for example, adverbs of location as in, "It's up yonder" or "It's thisaway, not thataway," and so forth. Other adverbial differences come from the phonological fusion of items, as in "t'all" from *at all* (e.g., "It's not coming up t'all"), "pert'near" (e.g., "She's pert' near seventy"), or "druther" (e.g., "Druther than lose the farm, he fought to keep it"). In parts of the South historically influenced by Scots-Irish, the adverb *whenever* may be used to indicate a one-time event (e.g., "Whenever he died, we were young"), rather than habitually occurring events (e.g., "Whenever we dance, he's my partner") as it does in most mainstream American varieties. Again, such differences must be considered on an item-by-item basis.

Negation

The two major vernacular negation features of American English are multiple negation, the marking of negative meaning at more than one point in a sentence (sometimes called "double negatives" or "multiple negatives"), and the use of the lexical item *ain't*. Other forms resulting directly from English language learning (e.g., "He no like the man") do not seem to be perpetuated as a continuing part of the vernacular English variety of such speakers once they have become proficient in English. An exception may be the negative tag *no* as found in some Latino English varieties, as in "They're going to the store, no?"

Multiple Negation. There are four different patterns of multiple negative marking in the vernacular varieties of English:

1. marking of the negative on the auxiliary verb and the indefinite(s) following the verb
   "The man <u>wasn't</u> saying <u>nothing</u>."
   "He <u>didn't</u> say <u>nothing</u> about <u>no</u> people bothering him or <u>nothing</u> like that."

2. negative marking of an indefinite before the verb phrase and of the auxiliary verb
   "<u>Nobody didn't</u> like the mess."
   "<u>Nothing can't</u> stop him from failing the course."

3. inversion of the negativized auxiliary verb and the preverbal indefinite
   "<u>Didn't nobody</u> like the mess." (meaning "Nobody liked the mess")
   "<u>Can't nothing</u> stop him from failing the course."

4. multiple negative marking across different clauses
   "There <u>wasn't</u> much that I <u>couldn't</u> do" (meaning "There wasn't much I could do")
   "I <u>wasn't</u> sure that <u>nothing wasn't</u> going to come up." (meaning "I wasn't sure that anything was going to come up")

Virtually all vernacular varieties of English participate in multiple negation of Type 1; restricted Northern and most Southern vernaculars participate in Type 2; most Southern vernaculars participate in Type 3; and restricted Southern and African American vernacular varieties participate in Type 4.

ain't. The item *ain't* may be used as a variant for certain mainstream American English forms, including the following:

1. forms of *be* + *not*
   "She <u>ain't</u> here now."
   "I <u>ain't</u> gonna do it."

2. forms of *have* + *not*
   "I <u>ain't</u> seen her in a long time."
   "She <u>ain't</u> gone to the movies in a long time."

3. forms of *did* + *not*
   "He <u>ain't</u> tell him he was sorry."
   "I <u>ain't</u> go to school yesterday."

The first two types are found in most vernacular varieties, but the third type, in which *ain't* corresponds with mainstream *didn't*, has only been found in African American English.

***Past-Tense* won't.** The form *won't*, pronounced much like the negative modal *won't*, may occur as a generalized form for past-tense negative *be*—that is, *wasn't* and *weren't*. Thus, we may find sentences such as "It won't me" and "My friends won't the ones who ate the food." Although the form probably arose through the application of phonological processes to forms of *wasn't* and *weren't*, *won't* now seems to serve as a past-tense analogue of *ain't* because both *ain't* and *won't* have a single form for use with all persons and numbers (as opposed to standard forms of *be + not*, which vary by person and number). Its use is restricted to rural Southern varieties, particularly those found in the South Atlantic region.

Nouns and Pronouns

Constructions involving nouns and pronouns are often subject to socially significant dialect variation. The major types of differences involve the attachment of various suffixes and the use of particular cases markings—that is, inflectional forms that indicate the role that nouns and pronouns play in particular sentences.

Plurals. Plurals may be formed in several different ways that differentiate them from plurals in mainstream American English. These include the following:

1. general absence of plural suffix
    "Lots of <u>boy</u> go to the school."
    "All the <u>girl</u> liked the movie."

2. restricted absence of plural suffix on measurement nouns with a quantifier
    "The station is four <u>mile</u> down the road."
    "They hauled in a lotta <u>bushel</u> of corn."

3. regularization of various irregular plural noun forms
    "They saw the <u>deers</u> running across the field."
    "The <u>firemans</u> liked the convention."

Plural absence of Type 1 is found only among varieties where another language was spoken in the recent past and, to a limited degree, in African American English. In Category 2, plural suffix absence is limited to nouns of weights (e.g., "four pound," "three ton") and measures (e.g., "two foot," "twenty mile") that occur with a quantifying word such as a number (e.g., "four") or plural modifier (e.g., "a lot of," "some"), including some temporal nouns (e.g., "two year," "five month"). This pattern is found in Southern-based rural vernaculars. Category 3 includes regularization of plurals that are not overtly marked in mainstream American English (e.g., "deers," "sheeps"), forms marked with irregular suffixes in mainstream varieties (e.g., "oxes"), and forms marked by vowel changes (e.g., "firemans," "snowmans"). In the last case, plurals may be double-marked, as in "mens" or "childrens." Some kinds of plurals in Category 3 are quite widespread among the vernacular varieties of English (e.g., regularizing non-marked plurals such as "deers"), whereas others (e.g., double-marking in "mens") are more limited.

Possessives. There are several patterns involving possessive nouns and pronouns, including the following:

1. absence of the possessive suffix
   "The <u>man hat</u> is on the chair."
   "<u>John coat</u> is here."

2. regularization of the possessive pronoun *mines*, by analogy with *yours*, *his*, *hers*, and so on
   "<u>Mines</u> is here."
   "It's <u>mines</u>."

3. use of possessive forms ending in -*n*, as in *hisn, ourn,* or *yourn.* Such forms can only be found in phrase- or sentence-final position (called absolute position), as in "It is hisn" or "It was yourn that I was talking about"; -*n* forms do not usually occur when followed by an object, as in *"It is hern book."
   "Is it <u>yourn</u>?"
   "I think it's <u>hisn</u>."

The first two types of possessives are typical of vernacular varieties of African American English, and the third type is found in vernacular Appalachian English and other rural varieties characterized by the retention of relic forms, although it is now restricted to older speakers in these varieties.

Pronouns. Pronoun differences typically involve regularization by analogy and rule extension. The categories of difference include the following:

1. regularization of reflexive forms by analogy with other possessive pronouns such as *myself, yourself, ourselves,* and so on
   "He hit <u>hisself</u> on the head."
   "They shaved <u>theirselves</u> with the new razor."

2. extension of object forms with coordinate subjects
   "<u>Me and him</u> will do it."
   "<u>John and them</u> will be home soon."

3. adoption of a second-person plural form to "fill out" the person–number paradigm (*I, you, he/she/it, we, you, they*)

   a. "Y'<u>all</u> won the game."
      "I'm going to leave <u>y'all</u> now."
   b. "<u>Youse</u> won the game."
      "I'm going to leave <u>youse</u> now."
   c. "<u>You'uns</u> won the game."
      "I'm going to leave <u>you'uns</u> now."

4. extension of object forms to demonstratives
   "<u>Them</u> books are on the shelf."
   "She didn't like <u>them</u> there boys."

5. a special personal dative use of the object pronoun form
   "I got <u>me</u> a new car."
   "We had <u>us</u> a little old dog."

The first four types of pronominal difference are well represented in most vernacular dialects of English. The particular form used for the second-person plural pronoun (Type 3) varies by region: 3a is the Southern form, 3b is the Northern form, and 3c is the form used in an area extending from Southern Appalachia to Pittsburgh. The so-called personal dative illustrated in Pattern 5 is a Southern feature that indicates that the subject of the sentence (e.g., *we*) benefitted in some way from the object (e.g., *little old dog*).

Other pronoun forms, such as the use of an object form with a non-coordinate subject (e.g., "her in the house") and the use of subject or object forms in possessive structures (e.g., "It is she book"; "It is he book"), are quite rare in most current vernaculars, except for those still closely related to a prior creole. The use of possessive *me*, as in "It's me cap," is occasionally found in historically isolated varieties that have some Scots-Irish influence.

Relative Pronouns. Differences affecting relative pronouns (e.g., *who* in "She's the one who gave me the present") include the use of certain relative pronoun forms in contexts where they would not be used in mainstream American English and the absence of relative pronouns under certain conditions. Differences in relative pronoun forms may range from the relatively socially insignificant use of *that* for human subjects (e.g., "The person that I was telling you about is here") to the quite stigmatized use of *what*, as in "The person what I was telling you about is here." One form that is becoming more common, and spreading into informal varieties of mainstream American English, is the use of the relative pronoun *which* as a coordinating conjunction (i.e., *and*), as in "They gave me this cigar, which they know I don't smoke cigars."

In mainstream American English, relative pronouns may be deleted if they are the object in the relative clause. For example, "Katie saw the dog that I bought" may alternately be produced as "Katie saw the dog I bought." In most cases where the relative pronoun is the subject, however, it must be retained, as in "Katie saw the dog that bit me." However, Southern-based varieties may sometimes delete relative pronouns in subject position, as in "Katie saw the dog bit me" or "The man come in here is my father." The absence of the relative pronoun is more common in existential constructions such as "There's a dog bit me" than in other constructions.

Existential it/they. As used in sentences such as "There are four people in school" and "There's a picture on TV," the American English form *there* is called an existential because it indicates the existence of something rather than a specific location (as in "There is where it should go"). Vernacular varieties may use "it" or "they" for *there* in existential constructions, as in "It's a dog in the yard" or "They's a good show on TV." "They" for *there* seems to be found only in Southern-based vernaculars; "it" is more general in vernacular varieties.

Other Grammatical Structures

There are a number of additional structures that occur in vernacular and regional dialects, including some that were once thought to be confined to vernacular varieties but have been shown to be quite common in informal mainstream varieties. An example is the structure known as *pronominal apposition*, in which a pronoun is used in addition to a noun in subject position, as in "My father, he made my breakfast." This feature is found in practically all social groups of American English speakers, although it is often considered to be vernacular. It is not particularly obtrusive in spoken language. It has also been found that the use of inverted word order in indirect questions such as "She asked could she go to the movies" is becoming just as much a part of informal spoken mainstream American English as indirect questions without inverted word order, as in "She asked if she could go to the movies." Other differences, such as those affecting prepositions, have to be treated on an item-by-item basis and really qualify more as lexical rather than grammatical differences. Examples are *of a evening/of the evening* ("in the evening"), *upside the head* ("on the side of the head"), *leave out of there* ("leave from there"), *the matter of him* ("the matter with him"), *sick at/in my stomach* ("sick to my stomach"), and *to for at* (e.g., "She's to the store right now"). Infinitive constructions such as *for to*, as in "I'd like for you to go" versus "I'd like you to go," or even "I'd like for to go," constitute a case of a restricted lexical difference. Similarly, cases of article use or nonuse, such as the use of articles with certain illnesses and diseases (e.g., "She has the colic"; "He had the earache"), affect only certain lexical items in particular dialects.

References

Bailey, G. (2001). The relationship between African American and White Vernaculars in the American South: A sociocultural history and some phonological evidence. In S. L. Lanehart (Ed.), *Sociocultural and historical contexts of African American English* (pp. 53–92). Philadelphia, PA: John Benjamins.

Bayley, R., & Santa Ana, O. (2004). Chicano English grammar. In B. Kortmann, E. W. Schneider, K. Burridge, R. Mesthrie, & C. Upton (Eds.), *A handbook of varieties of English, vol. 2: Morphology and syntax* (pp. 167–183). Berlin, Germany: Mouton de Gruyter.

Cukor-Avila, P. (2001). Co-existing grammars: The relationship between the evolution of African American and White Vernacular English in the South. In S. L. Lanehart (Ed.), *Sociocultural and historical contexts of African American English* (pp. 93–128). Philadelphia, PA: John Benjamins.

Fought, C. (2003). *Chicano English in context*. New York, NY: Palgrave.

Green, L. J. (2002). *African American English: A linguistic introduction*. Cambridge, UK: Cambridge University Press.

Kortmann, B., Schneider, E. W., Burridge, K., Mesthrie, R., & Upton, C. (Eds.). (2004). *A handbook of varieties of English, vol. 2: Morphology and syntax*. Berlin, Germany: Mouton de Gruyter.

Montgomery, M., & Hall, J. S. (2004). *Dictionary of Smoky Mountain English*. Knoxville, TN: University of Tennessee Press.

Labov, W., Ash, S., & Boberg, C. (2006). *Atlas of North American English: Phonology and phonetics*. Berlin, Germany: Mouton de Gruyter.

Rickford, J. R. (1999). *African American Vernacular English: Features, evolution, educational implications*. Malden, MA: Blackwell.

Santa Ana, O., & Bayley, R. (2004). Chicano English phonology. In E. W. Schneider, B. Kortmann, K. Burridge, R. Mesthrie, & C. Upton (Eds.), *A handbook of varieties of English, vol. 1: Phonology* (pp. 407–424). Berlin, Germany: Mouton de Gruyter.

Schneider, E. W., Kortmann, B., Burridge, K., Mesthrie, R., & Upton, C. (Eds.). (2004). *A handbook of varieties of English, vol. 1: Phonology*. Berlin, Germany: Mouton de Gruyter.

Thomas, E. R. (2001). *An acoustic analysis of vowel variation in New World English*. Durham, NC: Duke University Press.

Wolfram, W., & Christian, D. (1976). *Appalachian speech*. Washington, DC: Center for Applied Linguistics.

Wolfram, W., & Reaser, J. (2014). *Talkin' Tar Heel: How our voices tell the story of North Carolina*. Chapel Hill, NC: University of North Carolina Press.

Wolfram, W., & Schilling, N. (2016). *American English: Dialects and variation* (3rd ed.). Malden, MA: John Wiley & Sons.

Wolfram, W., & Ward, B. (Eds.). (2006). *American voices: How dialects differ from coast to coast*. Malden, MA: Blackwell.

Index

Abdul-Jabbar, K. 150, 156
Aboud, F. E. 23
Abrams, K. D. 155, 181, 193
academic English *see* Formal Standard
    English
Académie française 110
accent 9–10, 55, 242, 257
acronym 53, 120, 130
Adams, C. M. 61
Adams, M. 124
Adams, M. J. 210, 213
Adger, C. T. xv, 36, 102, 170, 237
adverbs 71–2, 285–6; adjective for
    adverb 191; adverb placement 285;
    comparatives and superlatives 71–2,
    285; intensifying adverbs 72, 285–6;
    -ly absence 72, 285
African American English (AAE) 83;
    absence of *be* verbs 65–6, 84, 87, 182,
    282–3; absence of modal auxiliaries
    182; *ain't* 18, 69, 287; final cluster
    reduction 57, 269; communicative
    strategies 90, 102, 181, 208;
    completive *done* 68, 280; creolization
    86, 88; and divergence from white
    dialects 88–9, 151; habitual *be* 66,
    68, 84, 243, 253–4, 280; indignant
    come 281; intrusive *r* 56; intrusive *t*
    56, 270; and language attitudes 233–4;
    multiple negation 18, 286–7; nasal
    fronting 58, 272; origins of 86–8; past
    tense *be* regularization 182; plural
    regularization 70; plural *-s* absence
    69–70, 87, 182, 185, 288; possessive
    regularization 289; possessive *-s*
    absence 70, 182, 289; quotatives 282;
    remote time *béen* 280; at school 7,
    89–90; slang 98; *str* clusters 59, 273;
    th sounds 270–1; third-person *-s*
    absence 66, 138, 182, 283; unstressed
    syllable loss 272; variation in 84;
    verbal play (sounding) 100, 209; word
    final devoicing 273; in writing 182,
    187; *see also* Ebonics
African American Language (AAL) 85
African Americans 87; cultural
    differences 7, 89–90
age grading 42
Alexander, C. 95
Algeo, J. 16
Alim, H. S. 90, 103, 154
Allen, H. B. 61
alphabetism *see* acronym
Alvarez, L. 224, 238
Amanti, C. 210
American Association for Applied
    Linguistics 159–60
American Dialect Society 124
American Indians 6–7, 24–5, 117–18,
    209, 220–1, 263; Cherokee 263;
    Lumbee Indians 24–5
American Speech-Language-Hearing
    Association 144–5, 147, 159
American Tongues 224, 238
American Tragedy, An (Theodore
    Dreiser) 110
analogy 37
Anderson, R. C. 209
Andrews, L. 172, 264
Ann Arbor court decision of 1979
    207
Appalachian English 182, 257;
    a-prefixing 250–2, 281; bare root
    verb forms 182; collective nouns 66,
    182; different irregular verb forms
    182; *-es* plural 269; existential *it* 182;
    final unstressed BOAT /o/ 277; final
    unstressed GOAT /o/ 60; initial *h*
    retention 55–6, 272; intrusive *t* 270; *-ly*
    absence 72, 285; nouns of measure 70,
    182, 288; past tense regularization
    182; plural *-s* absence 182; plurals

following clusters 269–70; possessive
-*n* ending 70, 289; in writing 182;
you'uns 70, 290
Appalachian Prison Book Project 228
Appalachian Writing Project 195
Applebee, A. N. 34
Argeton, E. 143
Arola, K. L. 191
Ash, S. 10, 34, 61, 269
Asian American English 95;
communicative strategies 99; dialect
variation 97–8; linguistic stereotypes
and parodies 97; *l* and *r* patterning 97;
at school 99; slang 98
Asian Americans 95–6; stereotypes of 96
Au, K. 221
Aud, S. 2, 145
Austen, Jane 117
Austen-Smith, D. 156

backronym 78
Bailey, G. 88, 269
Baker, B. 95, 211–12
Ball, A. F. 181, 198
Banaji, M. R. 25
Baratz, J. C. 262
Barham, I. H. 187
Baron, N. S. 121
Barrett, R. 153, 188, 194, 198, 233
Baugh, J. 3, 22, 28, 89, 238
Bayley, R. 269
Bean, J. 194
Bélanger, N. N. 206
Bell, A. 33
Beloved (Toni Morrison) 220
Benzing, L. 178
Beowulf 136
Bereiter, C. 113
Bereiter-Engelmann program 113
Bergman, Ingmar 119
Berlak, H. 144
Bernstein, B. 113
be verbs: absence of 44–6, 65, 84, 87,
182, 185, 282–3; habitual *be* 66, 68,
84, *243*, 250, 253–4, 280–1; leveling
of *is* 39, 283; leveling of *was* 40, 182,
243–4, 283; leveling of other past
tense forms 40, 243–4, 283
Biber, D. 180
bidialectalism 165
Bitterman, A. 35
Blake, R. 34, 114
blending 52–4

Boberg, C. 10, 34, 61, 269
Bolinger, D. 26
Borko, H. 207
borrowing 53, 79
Boser, U. 83, 89, 177
Bourdieu, P. 5
Bowie, D. 34
Bowyer, S. 119
Bracey, G. W. 130
*Bridge: A Cross-Culture Reading
Program* 218
Britt, E. 84
Britton, B. K. 225
van den Broek, P. 225
Brown, A. 120
Brown, A. L. 216
Brown, D. W. 35, 235, 237, 264
Brown, J. 95
Bucholtz, M. 95, 236–7
Bunch, G. C. 171
Buringh, E. 118
Burling, R. 164, 167
Burridge, K. 79, 268

Callahan-Price, E. 93–4
Canivez, G. L. 137
Canterbury Tales, The 16
Caramazza, A. 178
Carpenter, B. D. 34–5, 114, 237
Carroll, M. 196
Carter, P. M. 65, 91, 93–5
Carter, R. 180
Carver, C. M. 10–2
Cazden, C. B. 209
Chall, J. 210
Chambers, J. 33
Charity, A. H. *see* Charity Hudley, A. H.
Charity Hudley, A. H. 147, 202, 207,
237, 262, 265
Chaucer, Geoffrey 16, 79, 118–19
Cherokee language *see* American
Indians, Cherokee
Chestnutt, C. 220
Chicano English *see* Latino English
Christian, D. xv, 269
Chun, E. W. 97–98
Clark, A. D. 195
Clark, J. M. 134
classroom norms 100–2
Clay, M. M. 213
clipping 53, 58, 120
Clovis Crawfish (Mary Alice Fontenot)
214

code-meshing 151–4, 165, 188, 195, 197
code-switching 22, 151–3, 158, 202
coining 53–54
Cole, L. 145
Collins, J. 207
Comly, J. 116
Common Core State Standards (CCSS)
    35, 152, 161–3, 171, 187–8, 204, 211,
    234
compounding 52–4
Conference on College Composition and
    Communication 154
Conn, J. 34
Connors, R. J. 166, 193
consonants 269–73; ch and sh sounds
    271; consonant clusters 40; consonant
    cluster reduction 40, 57, 66, 183, 191,
    269, 284; consonant intrusion 56;
    consonant shifts 58–9; devoicing 273;
    initial *h* retention 55–6, 272; initial *w*
    reduction 57–8, 272; intrusive *t* 270;
    nasal fronting 272; nasals 272–73;
    plurals following clusters 269–70; *r*
    and *l* 57, 97, 271–2; *r*-lessness 56–7,
    79, 248–50, 271; *th* sounds 183,
    270–1
Contract with America 117
contrastive analysis 145, 152, 168–9,
    173, 187
conversion 54, 109
copula absence *see be* verbs, absence of
Craig, H. K. 140, 147, 167, 181–4, 202
Crandall, R. E. 257
creakiness *see* vocal fry
creole 29, 86–7; phonological features of
    269
creole languages: Berbice 86; Caribbean
    Creole English 104; grammatical
    features of 290; Gullah 86; Haitian
    Creole 86; Hawaii Creole English 104;
    Jamaican Patois 264; Krio 86;
    Louisiana Creole 86; Negerhollands
    86; Papiamento 86; Saramaccan 86;
    West African creoles 104
creolization 86
Crittenden, A. 225
Cronnell, B. 184
Cross, J. B. 34, 114, 237
Crystal, D. 103, 186, 198
Cucchiara, M. 194
Cukor-Avila, P. 88, 269
cultural norms 6, 99–102; *see also*
    classroom norms

Curzan, A. 39, 115, 117, 124
Cutler, C. 34, 114

Daniels, H. 185–8, 197–8
Dean, D. 35, 170, 198, 235
deficit position with respect to language
    1–6, 27, 158
DeJesus, J. M. 22–3
Delpit, L. 7, 34, 49, 89, 213, 220
Denham, K. 28, 162–4, 235, 237, 265
Denis, D. 120, 186
Denne-Bolton, S. 196
descriptivism 108
DeStefano, J. S. 184
DeVaney, T. 34, 114, 237
Devereaux, M. D. 265
*Diagnostic Evaluation of Language
    Variation – Norm Referenced
    (DELV-NR)* 140
dialect 7–9, 27; change 32–4; influence
    211; in literature 162–3, 187, 194,
    219–20, 235; interference 211; myths
    about 26, 34, 238, 254, 258, 260;
    patterning 245–54; regions 41
dialect awareness curricula: community
    based 257–8; components of 238–56;
    Educating the Educated 258, 260;
    in higher education 257–61;
    implementation of 256; in K–12
    232–7, 256; Pedersen's Multicultural
    Development Model 258; student
    ambassadors 260; student-led inquiry
    35, 43–7, 55, 69, 235–7
dialect differentiation: generational
    differences 41–2; grammatical
    differences 37, 65–72; pronunciation
    differences 36, 55–65; regional
    variation 41; sociohistorical factors
    41–3; vocabulary differences 36, 52–5
dialect diversity: training programs
    257–8; study of 234; *see also* dialect
    awareness curricula; dialect
    differentiation
dialect levels 10, 36–8, 43, 52, 179, 241;
    communicative strategies 37; grammar
    37, 242; pronunciation 36, 242;
    vocabulary 36, 241–2
dialect patterning 43–7, 245–54
dialect readers 217–8
*Dictionary of American Regional
    English, The* 48, 53, 103
difference position with respect to
    language 1–6, 27

difference versus deficit 141–3, 235–6
difference versus disorder assessment
  34–5, 139–40, 144–5
van Dijk, T. A. 225
Disney films: foreign accented English in
  22; gendered language in 28;
  vernacular dialect in 22
Dorr, R. E. 219
double negatives *see* multiple negation
Do You Speak American? 103, 109, 168,
  173, 238, 264
Drouin, M. A. 119, 185
Dumont, R. V. 209
Dunstan, S. B. 257, 260
Dyson, A. H. 34, 114, 173, 181

Eakle, A. J. 219
Eberhardt, M. 61
Ebonics 4–5, 25, 49, 84–5, 160; Oakland
  (CA) Unified School District 4–5, 49,
  151, 160
Echevarria, J. 164
Eckert, P. 34
Eddy, R. 194
edited American English *see* Standard
  English
edited English *see* Formal Standard
  English
editing 188–190; peer editing 190
educational aptitude 136–7
Eisenhart, M. 207
Eisenhauer, K. 22
Elbow, P. 153–4, 188, 194, 198
electronically mediated communication
  (EMC) 120
Elements of Style, The 110, 122
Elley, W. B. 187
Elsasser, N. 194
Emery, A. 120
Engelhard, Jr., G. 133
Engelmann, S. 113
English Accidence, The (Joshua Poole)
  116
*English Grammar; Made Easy to the
  Teacher and Pupil* 116
English Language Learners (ELLs) 93,
  98, 182–3, 196
English as a Second Language (ESL)
  94–5; placement tests 94
*English with an Accent: Language,
  Ideology, and Discrimination in the
  United States* 234
Erickson, F. 6, 172

Evangelou, E. 138
Evans, B. 34
Everson, M. G. 225

Fairbanks, C. M. 114
Farr, M. 185–8, 197–8
Fasold, R. 20, 22, 159, 218, 262
Feagin, C. 41
Fearless Jack (Paul Johnson) 215
Fecho, B. 147, 156–7
Fernald, A. 3
Fields-Carey, L. 261–3
figurative extension 54
figurative language 99–100
Fillmore, L. W. 209
Finegan, E. 65
Fischer-Baum, S. 178
Foorman, B. R. 206
Fordham, S. 89, 156
Formal Standard English 17, 19, 70,
  152
Foroutan, M. 196
Foster, M. 90
Foucault, M. 5
Fought, C. 22, 65, 93, 104, 282
founder effect 41
Fox, M. A. 2, 145
Franco, J. 143
Freedle, R. 135
Freppon, P. A. 221
Fridland, V. 34, 63
Fryer, R. G. 156
Fuchs, D. 143
Fuchs, L. 143

Gabrielson, S. 133
Gee, J. P. 90, 174
generational shift 41, 91–2
Genishi, C. 173
Getridge, C. M. 261
Giani, M. 95
Godley, A. J. 34–5, 114, 237
Goldring, R. 35
Goltz, H. H. 129
Gonzalez, N. 210
Goodenough, F. 2, 132
Gordon, B. 133
Graddol, D. 26
Grammar Girl 197
Gray, L. 35
Green, L. J. 65, 85, 103, 269
Greenwald, A. G. 25
greeting rituals 100

Grego, R. 194
Griffin, D. M. 202, 207
Grimm, J. 110
Grosjean, F. 91
Gülgöz, S. 225
Guo, J. 22
Gutierrez, K. D. 167

habitual *be see be* verbs
Hairston, M. 118, 166, 183, 193
Hall, J. S. 56, 65, 269
Hall, M. 219
Hall-Lew, L. 98
Hammer, C. S. 221
Hammond, B. 228
Hammond, C. 100
Hampton, S. 198
Hamzah, M. S. G. B. 196
Hansen, M. 177
Hansen-Krening, N. 196
Harmon, M. R. 192
Harris, J. 228
Harris-Wright, K. 90
Hart, B. 2–3
Harvard Dialect Survey 48, 79
Haswell, R. 194
Haviland, C. P. 134
Hazen, K. 48, 114, 237, 241, 244, 255
Heath, S. B. 3, 7, 173
Henderson, M. H. 26, 237, 262
Hendrick, R. 138
Hensel, S. L. 202
Herrnstein, R. J. 2–3
Hewitt, R. 174
hip hop: in African American English
    85; comparison to Shakespeare 120,
    124; culture of 280; language use
    in 120, 124; metaphoric language
    in 100
Hirshon, B. 100
Holt, G. 218
Hoover, M. E. R. 228
Hornberger, N. H. 28
House of Cards (Kevin Spacey) 13, 28
House on Mango Street, The (Sandra
    Cisneros) 220
Housing and Urban Development (HUD)
    28, 238–40
Hungry Giant of the Tundra, The (Teri
    Sloat) 203
Hutcheson, N. 238
Hymes, D. 38
hypercorrection 184–5

implicit attitudes 25, 152
inflection *see* intonation
informal standard English 17–18
institutionalized racism 144
International Literacy Association (ILA)
    see International Reading Association
International Phonetic Alphabet xiii, 268
International Reading Association (IRA)
    163, 198, 228, 234
intonation 36, 64, 73, 157, 179
Irvine, P. 194
*Is This English?: Race, Language, and
    Culture in the Classroom* 147, 156

Jackson, J. E. 140
Jackson, Michael 55
Jacobson, L. 3, 131
Jaeger, A. J. 257
Jamaican 87
jargon 122
Jasmine (Bharati Mukherjee) 220
Jencks, C. 136
John, V. P. 209
Johnson, S. 110
Johnstone, B. 179
Jonathan, A. 219
Jones, G. 34, 114, 237
Jordan, C. 221
Jordan, J. 157, 195
Joshi, P. 119, 186
Joy Luck Club, The (Amy Tan) 220

Kamhi, A. G. 228
Kemp, N. 119, 185
Kendall, T. 34
Kennedy, E. 194
Kewal-Ramani, A. 2, 145
Khazan, O. 64
Kim, J. 196
Kintsch, W. 225
Kinzler, K. D. 22–3
Klein, S. 256
de Kleine, C. 182
Kligman, D. 184
Klin, C. 123–4
Knobler, P. 150
Kohn, M. 93–4
Kolker, A. 224, 238
Kolker, C. 91
Kopp, W. 161
Kopriva, R. J. 138
Kortmann, B. 79, 268
Kozol, J. 131

Kubrick, Stanley 119
Kurath, H. 10
Kutz, E. 194
Kyto, M. 71

Labbo, L. D. 219
Labov, W. 10, 12, 34, 56, 61–3, 79, 88,
    95, 141, 146, 151, 158, 211–12, 218,
    221, 269
Lakoff, R. T. 124
Lamb, H. 187
language attitudes 22–3, 234, 236,
    238–9; in preschool 233
language change 32–4, 254–6;
    generational shift 42, 91–2;
    sociohistorical factors 41–3
language contact 83; African American
    English 83–90; Asian American
    English 95–9; and cultural norms
    99–102; generational shift 91–2; and
    language variation 57, 59; Latino
    English 90–5
language difference 8, 41
language discrimination 234; see also
    linguistic profiling
language disordered 36
language diversity see dialect diversity
language ideologies see language
    attitudes
Language and Life Project at NC State
    University, The 23, 28, 264–5
language prejudice see language
    discrimination
language variation see dialect
Lardner, T. 198
Lareau, A. 114
Latino English 90; bilingualism 91–2; ch
    and sh sounds 93, 271; communicative
    strategies 94; dialect variation 91, 93;
    final cluster reduction 269; fixin' to
    280–1; grammatical features of 183;
    labeling 90; language contact 57;
    modals 281–2; origins of 91;
    phonological features of 269, 271,
    273; regional variation 91, 93; at
    school 94; syllable stress patterns 65;
    in Texas 103; verb forms in 280–2;
    vowel mergers in 275; vowels of 277;
    in writing 183; z and v devoicing 92,
    273
Lee, H. 162
Lee, Stacey J. 96
Lehner, A. 194

Leki, I. 134
Lemov, D. 21, 161
leveling 39–40, 66, 206, 243–4, 283–4;
    see also be verbs
levels of dialect see dialect levels
Levin, D. 161
LeVine, E. 143
Linderholm, T. 225
Ling, R. 121
linguistic awareness/flexibility
    hypothesis 202
linguistic determinism 113
linguistic diversity 8
linguistic and environmental
    disadvantage 4
linguistic interference hypothesis 202
linguistic profiling 22, 28, 238–240; and
    housing discrimination 238–40
Linguistic Society of America 28, 159
Lippi-Green, R. 5–6, 15, 20, 22, 28, 234,
    257
literacy skills: and literacy rates 129;
    Yule–Simpson effect 129; see also
    National Assessment of Educational
    Progress (NAEP)
Lobeck, A. 28, 235, 237, 265
Loman, B. 64
Lopez, A. 237
Lord, C. 256
Lovejoy, K. B. 153, 188, 198, 233
Lumbee Indians see American Indians
Lunsford, A. A. 166, 193
Luntz, F. I. 117
Lynch, A. 91, 93

Mainstream American English 19, 269;
    see also Standard English
Mallinson, C. 147, 237, 262, 265
Marchman, V. A. 3
Mark Antony (Plutarch) 120
Martinez, A. Y. 153, 188, 194–5
Matsuda, P. K. 194
Maynor, N. 88
McCabe, A. 20, 99, 134
McCaig, R. A. 192
McCarthy, M. 180
McCrory, Pat 153
McCulloch, G. 121, 123–4
McDaniel, L. 61
McDavid, Jr., R. I. 61
Mchawala, C. 196
McIntyre, E. 221
McKay, S. L. 28

McNamara, D. S. 225
McPhail, I. P. 228
McWhorter, J. H. 218
Meachem, S. 119
meaning-based literacy instruction 213
Meaningful Differences in the Everyday Experience of Young American Children 2
Medieval English Dictionary, The 53
Medina, A. L. 216
medium of ethnic solidarity 87
Meier, D. 224–5
Meier, T. 228
Mendoza-Denton, N. 34
merger *see* vowel merger
Mesthrie, R. 79, 268
metaphorical extension *see* figurative extension
metaphoric language *see* figurative language
Michaels, S. 181, 208
Miciak, J. 95
Middle English Dictionary, The 79
Miller, J. 196
Millward, C. M. 39, 56, 59, 67, 70
Milton, John 118–19
Minami, M. 20, 99, 134
Minimal Competence Core 140
Minnici, A. 35, 237
Miozzo, M. 178
Miranda, Lin–Manuel 119
Mischinski, M. 225
Mitri, S. M. 202
Mizokawa, D. T. 196
Mohatt, G. 6
Mojarro, A. 237
Moll, L. C. 210
Montero, M. K. 219
Montgomery, M. 56, 65, 269
Moran, M. 143
Morkel, W. 34
Mountford, R. 135
Mufwene, S. S. 86
multiple modals *see* double modals
multiple negation 15–16, 18, 37, 286
Murnane, R. 201
Murphy, A. N. 257
Murray, C. 2–3
Myrick, C. 120

Napoli, D. J. 29
narrative structure 181
narrowing 54

Native Americans *see* American Indians
Native Son (Richard Wright) 220
National Assessment of Educational Progress (NAEP) 131–2, 135; *see also* literacy skills
National Council of Teachers of English (NCTE) 34, 121, 147, 154, 158–9, 173, 228, 234
National Council of Teachers of Mathematics (NCTM) 121
naturalness 40, 238
Neff, D. 210
negation 286–7; *ain't* 18, 69, 287; multiple negation 15–16, 18, 37, 286–7; negative tag *no* 286; past tense *won't* 288
Nero, S. J. 104
Newman, M. 98
Nguyen, T. 120
Niedzielski, N. A. 17, 55, 238
Nieto, S. 94
nonmainstream dialect 8–9
nonstandard dialect 8, 14
Noordin, N. 196
nouns 288–91; collective nouns 66, 182; plural *-s* absence 37, 39, 70, 288; possessives *-s* absence 289; plural regularization 288; possessive regularization 289

Oakland (CA) Unified School District 4–5, 151, 160
Obama, Barack 18, 153–4
O'Cain, R. K. 61
Ochs, E. 64
Ogbu, J. U. 156
ONPAR Project 138
Oral History (Lee Smith) 220
Orwell, G. 110
Outer Banks Brogue 19, 23–4, 272, 276–7, 284; consonantal features of 272; Hoi Toiders 60; Ocracoke Dialect 244–5; verb forms of 283–4; vowels of 276–7
Oxford English Dictionary, The 53, 79, 110, 116, 119

Palincsar, A. S. 216
Paradise Lost 118
Paris, G. 110–11
Parrish, B. 219
passive voice 109, 114, 116, 122–3
Patrick, P. L. 87

Pearson, B. Z. 140
Pedersen, P. 258
Pedersen's Multicultural Development
    Model 258
Pederson, L. 61
Penn Reading Initiative 212, 228
Perfetti, C. A. 206
Perry, T. 49
Pesetsky, D. 206
Peyton, J. K. 195–6
Philips, S. U. 6, 209
Phillips, M. 136
phonological features 269–77
pidgin 86–7, 264
Pidgin: The Voice of Hawai'i 238
Piestrup, A. M. 161, 169, 220
Pilonieta, P. 216
Pittsburghese 127–8, 277; variants of
    MOUTH /au/ 61, 276; *yinz* 37, 70;
    you'uns 70, 290; *y'uns* 37
Plaut, S. 211
Plester, B. 119, 186
plurals 288; collective nouns 66, 182;
    double–marking 289; -*es* plural 269;
    irregular plurals 37, 70; nouns of
    measure 70, 288; plural unmarking
    191; plurals following clusters 269–70;
    regularization 38–9, 288; -*s* absence
    37, 39, 87, 182, 185, 288
politically responsive prescriptivism 117,
    122
Pollock, K. E. 228
Pooley, R. C. 156
Poplack, S. 88
positive *anymore* 8, 72, 286
possessives: -*n* ending 70, 289;
    regularization 289; -*s* absence 87, 182,
    289
Prairie Home Companion, A (Garrison
    Keillor) 38
prepositions 291
Prescott, S. 6, 38
prescriptivism 79, 114
prescriptivists *see* prescriptivism
Preston, D. R. 17, 22, 55, 238
priming effects 32
principle of linguistic subordination 5,
    15, 23, 257
pronouns 70–1, 288–91; existential *it/
    they* 182, 291; extension of object
    forms 289–90; -*n* ending on
    possessives 289; personal dative 70,
    290; pronominal apposition 291;

reflexive pronouns 289; regularization
    70–1, 289; relative pronouns 290–1;
    second-person plural 37, 70, 93, 157,
    290; *un 70*; *y'all* 37, 70, 290; *yinz* 37,
    70; *you guys* 37; *youse* 37, 70, 290;
    you'uns 70, 290
proper names 54
Pullum, G. K. 122, 124
Purcell-Gates, V. 208, 221, 228
Putman, H. 177
Pyles, T. 16

Quinn, E. J. 202
Quintero, D. 177

Rapp, B. 178
Ravitich, Diane 147
Rayner, K. 206
Reaser, J. 26, 52, 80, 86, 88, 90, 118,
    153, 232–4, 237–9, 241–2, 245–6,
    251, 253, 256–7, 265, 269
reciprocal teaching 216
Reed, L. 195
regularization 38–9, 243–4, 254;
    comparatives and superlatives 71, 285;
    past tense regularization 38–40, 66–7,
    254–5, 283; plurals 38–9, 288;
    possessives 71, 289; pronouns 70–1,
    289; verbs 38–40, 66–7, 182, 254–5,
    278–9
restorative prescriptivism 116
retronym 78
Reyes, A. 96, 98
Reyes, P. 96
Reynolds, R. E. 209
Rickford, A. E. 218
Rickford, J. R. 29, 65, 86, 156, 218, 257,
    269
Rickford, R. J. 29, 156, 257
Risley, T. 2–3
r-lessness 56–7, 79, 248–50, 271
Roach, P. 64
Roberge, P. T. 87
Roeper, T. 140
Romaine, S. 71
Rosen, L. M. 193, 197
Rosenthal, M. S. 22, 233
Rosenthal, R. 3, 131
Rosner, J. 134–5
Routman, R. 210
Rubin, D. L. 20
Ruhl, D. M. 196
Rymer, R. 100

Samuels, J. 225
Santa Ana, A. 65
Santa Ana, O. 94, 269
SAT and SAT Subject Tests 129–30,
    134–6; *see also* standardized testing
Saunders, B. 153
de Saussure, F. 26
Sawhill, I. 201
Scarborough, H. S. 202, 207
Schatzman, L. 112, 181
Schilling, N. 36, 40–1, 49, 64, 80, 95,
    143, 153, 241, 244, 255, 268, 292
Schilling-Estes, N. *see* Schilling, N.
Schleppegrell, M. J. 167, 171
Schneider, E. W. 79, 268
Schneier, J. 120
Scholastic Aptitude Test (SAT)
    see SAT and SAT Subject Tests
Scholastic Assessment Test (SAT) *see*
    SAT and SAT Subject Tests
school English *see* Formal Standard
    English
school rituals *see* classroom norms
Schwartz, J. I. 202
Seidenberg, M. S. 206
Seymour, H. N. 1, 140
Shakespeare, William 53, 79, 117–20,
    124
Shaughnessy, M. P. 198
Shea, A. 125
*She Come Bringing Me that Little Baby
    Girl* (Eloise Greenfield) 201
Shirey, L. 209
Short, D. J. 164
Shuy, R. W. 22, 262
Simon, J. 109–11
Simpkins, C. 218
Simpkins, G. 218
Singler, J. V. 86
Skapoulli, E. 237
Slattery, T. J. 206
Sledd, J. 154, 158, 262
Smith, B. 92, 96, 99, 104, 182
Smith, M. L. 129
Smith, R. L. 138
Smitherman, G. 34, 87, 103, 114, 154,
    181, 188, 207
Snow, C. 201, 209
Songer, N. B. 225
Southern Vernacular English: absence of
    be forms 65, 84, 282–3; *ain't* 18, 287;
    a-prefixing 250–2, 281; *be* + *s* 280;
    be verbs *see main entry* for *be* verbs;

collective nouns 66; completive *done*
    68, 280; double modals 68, 281;
    existential *it/they* 291; final unstressed
    BOAT /o/ 277; final unstressed COMMA
    /ə/ raising 60, 277; final unstressed
    GOAT /o/ 243; *fixin' to* 280–1; initial *w*
    reduction 57–8; intensifying adverbs
    285–6; *-ly* absence 72, 285; multiple
    negation 37, 69, 286–7; *-n* ending on
    possessives 289; nouns of measure 70,
    288; past tense *won't* 288; personal
    dative 70, 290; *pin/pen* merger 60–1,
    247–8, 273; plural regularization 70;
    relative pronouns 291; *r* and *l* 271–2;
    r-lessness 56–7, 271; southern vowel
    changes 60–1; southern vowel mergers
    61–2, 189, 247, 273; Southern Vowel
    Shift 63–4, 274; th sounds 270–1;
    variants of PRICE /ai/ 60–1, 276–7;
    vowel mergers 189, 247, 273; *y'all* 37,
    70, 290; *yinz* 37; *y'uns* 37; *you'uns* 70,
    290
Spanish 90–3; Spanish as a threat 94–5,
    262–3
speech community 19, 23, 36–7, 46, 139,
    143
speech-language pathology 2, 59, 108,
    112, 118, 132, 158; African American
    English 85, 203, 206; oral language
    assessment 34–5, 132, 135, 140,
    143–5, 178,
spelling 183, 189
Squires, L. 186
standard 14
Standard American English 17–9
Standard English 17, 19; in text
    messaging 123, 185; written 163, 185,
    187–9
standard written English *see* Formal
    Standard English
standardized English *see* Formal
    Standard English
standardized language assessment 127–8,
    129, 140, 143–6
standardized testing: criterion–referenced
    tests 132–3; cultural and linguistic
    bias 133–8, 143, 145; and diversity
    131, 135; labeling bias 136; of
    language development 128–9; and
    language norms 128–9; norm-
    referenced tests 132–3, 135; ONPAR
    tests 138; SAT and SAT Subject Tests
    129–30, 134–6; test design 134–5;

question design 133–4; Yule–Simpson effect 129; *see also* test norming
standardized tests: ACT 134; *California Achievement Test* 137; ETS 134–5; GRE 134; LSAT 134; MCAT 134; New York State Regents 134, 143, 190–1; ONPAR tests 138; SAT and SAT Subject Tests 129–30, 134–6; *Virginia Standards of Learning Exam* 195; writing tests 187, 190–2
standardizing prescriptivism 115
Stanford–Binet test 132–3, 136–7
Starr, R. L. 98
Stauffer, R. G. 219
Steffensen, M. S. 113, 209
Stockman, I. J. 140
Strauss, A. 112, 181
Strauss, V. 134
Strunk, Jr., W. 110, 116, 122–3
Stuart-Smith, J. 33
Students' right to their own language statement 159, 173
stylistic prescriptivism 115–16
Swan, M. 92, 96, 99, 104, 182
Swann, J. 26
Sweat, S. 261–3
Sweetland, J. 35, 152, 187, 194, 202–3, 227, 233, 237, 256, 262
Swift, J. 110
Swords, R. 22, 152, 174, 233, 262
syllable loss 58

Tagliamonte, S. A. 120, 186
Talkin' Tar Heel: How our voices tell the story of North Carolina 80, 264
Tannen, D. 37–38, 79, 179
Tarczynski-Bowles, M. L. 119
Tarone, E. 64
Taylor, M. 209
Teach for America 161
Teach Like a Champion 161
Teaching Disadvantaged Children in the Preschool see Bereiter–Engelmann program
tense: past tense regularization 38–40, 66–7, 254–5, 283; past tense unmarking 185, 284
Terry, J. M. 138
Terry, N. P. 202
test norming 130, 132; bell curve 132–3; Stanford–Binet intelligence test 132
text messaging 107–8, 118–21, 123–4, 185–6

Thomas, E. R. 60–1, 63–5, 88, 269
Thompson, C. A. 182
Thurlow, C. 120–1
timing, language 64–5
Trampoline (Robert Gipe) 215
Tuan, M. 96

Upton, C. 79, 268

Valdés, G. 95
VanderStouwe, C. 237
Van Hofwegen, J. 42, 155, 167
Van Zanden, J. L. 118
Vaughn, C. 237
velar fronting *see* nasal fronting
verbs 278–84; absence of *be* forms 44–6, 65, 84, 87, 182, 185, 282–3; *a*-prefixing 250–2, 281; auxiliary verbs 66–9, 182, 272, 280–1, 287; avertive *liketa* and *(su)poseta* 16, 282; bare root forms 182, 278; *be + s* 280; completive *done* 68, 280; co-occurrence relations 279; different irregular forms 67, 182, 278; double modals 68, 281; *fixin' to* 280–1; habitual *be* 66, 68, 84, 250, 253–4, 280–1; historical present 284; indignant *come* 281; irregular verbs 38–9, 66–7, 254–5 182, 278; leveling of *is* 39, 283; leveling of *was* 40, 182, 243–4, 283; leveling of other past tense forms 40, 243–4, 283; meaning changes 278; modals 68, 182, 281–2; participle as past form 67, 278; past as participle form 67, 278; past tense regularization 38–40, 66–7, 254–5, 283; past tense unmarking 185, 284; perfective *be* 284; quotatives 69, 282; regularization 38–40, 66–7, 182, 254–5, 278–9; remote time *béen* 68, 280; subject–verb agreement patterns 65–6, 183, 191, 283; third-person -*s* absence 138, 185, 191, 283
vernacular 9
vernacular dialect 8; additivist position 152, 165, 170, 196; eradication position 152, 165, 196; linguistic pluralism position 152, 154; teacher bias 202
Villanueva, V. 191
de Villiers, J. G. 140
Vizetelly, F. H. 117
vocal fry 64, 79
Vogt, M. E. 164

Voices of North Carolina 238, 254
vowels 59–63, 274–8; Canadian raising
60, 79, 276–7; deletions 58; diphthong
60, 275–8; final unstressed BOAT /o/
277; final unstressed COMMA /ə/ raising
60, 277; final unstressed GOAT /o/ 60,
243; *ire/our* collapse 278; low back
vowel merger 275; monopthong 60–1;
Northern California Vowel Shift 275;
Northern Cities Vowel Shift 34, *63*, 79,
274; *pin/pen* merger 60–1, 247–8, 273;
southern vowel mergers 189, 247, 273;
Southern Vowel Shift 63–*4*, 274; TRAP
/æ/ raising 61, 276; variants of MOUTH /
au/ 60–1, 276; variants of PRICE /ai/
60–1, 276–7; vowel mergers 52, 59,
61–3, 247, 273, 275–6; vowel shifts
274; Wells' keyword system xiii,
59–60, 268

Wagner, S. E. 42
Walsh, B. 117
Walsh, K. 177
Wang, A. L. 196
Ward, B. 41, 49
Warner-Garcia, S. 237
Washington, J. A. 140, 147, 167,
181–4
Wassink, A. 34
Watson, J. S. 111
Wax, M. L. 209
Wax, R. 209
Weaver, C. 35, 192, 210
Weigel, H. 110
Weinberg, M. 132
Weisleder, A. 3
Weldon, T. L. 33, 84
Wells, J. C. xiii, 59–60, 268
Wells' keyword system xiii, 59–60,
268
Werner, C. A. 34, 114
Wheeler, R. S. 22, 35, 152, 174, 233,
237, 262

Where the Lilies Bloom (Bill Cleaver)
214
White, E. B. 110, 116, 122–3
White, J. W. 94
Wilkerson, C. 95
Williams, S. 134
Williams, V. 134
Woestehoff, J. 134
Wolcott, H. 209
Wolfram, W. xv, 33, 36, 40–2, 49, 57,
65, 80, 84, 86, 88, 90, 93–5, 118, 136,
143, 153, 155, 167, 218, 237, 239,
241–2, 244–6, 251, 253, 255, 257,
265, 268–9, 292
Wong, A. W. 98
Wood, C. 119, 186
Woodcock–Johnson test 136
writing: argument and narrative
structures 181; and cognition 178;
conventions 184; dialogue journals
195–6; differences from oral language
178–80; evaluation of 190–3; and
grammar 182–3; instruction and
curriculum 186–8; marking and
feedback on 193–4; mistakes 184; and
pronunciation 183–4; teaching 186–8;
in vernacular dialects 180–6, 194–5;
vernacular influences 181, 184
Wu, A. 98
Wu, F. 96
Wu, H. 140
Wyllie, M. 187

Yáñez-Bouza, N. 116
Yinz 238
Young, V. A. 153, 188, 194–5, 197, 198,
233
Youngman, S. 18, 153
Young-Rivera, Y. 153, 188, 198, 233
Yuasa, I. P. 64

Zentella, A. C. 3, 93
Zhang, L. 202

Since 1993, the **Language & Life Project** has been dedicated to research, graduate and undergraduate education, and outreach programs related to language variation focused on the American South. The work on language diversity has reached hundreds of thousands of curious minds through educational and cultural resources such as curricular materials, museum and outreach exhibits, public talks, trade books, and a host of media from documentary films to podcasts to oral history collections.

Videos

The Language and Life Project has produced 11 documentary films for public broadcast that explore language variation and cultural heritage. Learn about the history and development of African American English in **Talking Black in a America**, how Spanish speakers have enriched the linguistic landscape of the southeastern United States in **Spanish Voices**, or about the importance of speech on the heritage and identity in western North Carolina in **Mountain Talk**.

Books

Drawing on over two decades of research and 3,000 recorded interviews from every corner of the state, **Talkin' Tar Heel** introduces readers to the unique regional, social, and ethnic dialects of North Carolina, as well as its major languages, including American Indian languages and Spanish.

Based on extensive interviews with more than seventy Ocracoke residents of all ages **Hoi Toide on the Outer Banks** offers valuable insight on what makes Ocracoke special. By tracing the history of island speech, the authors open a window on the history of the islanders themselves.

Curricular materials

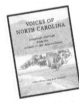

Endorsed by the North Carolina Department of Public Instruction, and designed to help teachers meet states standard course of study for 8th grade social studies, the 450-minute **Voices of North Carolina** curriculum requires no background in linguistics or specialized training to be taught successfully, and all the materials are offered free of charge.

Audio collections

These cultural resources preserve the reflections, songs, music and lore of communities at both ends of North Carolina. **Ocracoke Speaks** and **Ocracoke Still Speaks** celebrate the enduring identity of a unique Atlantic sea coast island, and **An Unclouded Day** and **The Queen Family** preserve the authentic language and life of Southern Appalachia.

 learn more and connect with us at **languageandlife.org**

youtube.com/user/NCLLP | facebook.com/NCLLP | twitter.com/ncstate_llp